J E HEFFERNAN

BRAZIL

1973

PRACTICAL NAVIGATION

PRACTICAL NAVIGATION

A Simplified Handbook of
Chart-and-Compass, Electronic,
and Celestial Navigation
for Boatmen

WITH 178 DIAGRAMS AND TABLES

W. S. KALS

ILLUSTRATED BY BARBARA PERRY

DOUBLEDAY & COMPANY, INC.
GARDEN CITY, NEW YORK
1972

ISBN: 0-385-00246-7
Library of Congress Catalog Card Number 72-76175
Copyright © 1968, 1969, 1972 by William S. Kals

Printed in the United States of America
First Edition

For Win

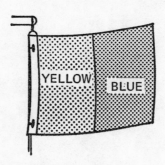

DESIRE TO COMMUNICATE

In this book I talk about *all* methods of navigation that are practical on small craft. That covers navigating by buoys and with chart and compass, electronic methods, and fixing your position by the sun, moon, and stars.

You may have been taught that there are waters for pilotage, and waters for celestial navigation. Wrong. You need chart-and-compass navigation in mid-ocean; celestial navigation can help you along the coast, even on a lake. (And you shouldn't wait for fog before you switch on your direction finder.)

To me, the pencil you use to plot direction and distance traveled, the electronic dials and beeps, and the sextant are just different tools for the same job. The job is getting position lines that tell you where you are at all times.

When you know that, it's easy to set a safe course to where you want to be, and to figure when you should get there. After a while you check your position again. If necessary, you correct your course or revise your estimated time of arrival.

That's about all there is to navigation. That's how you find Tahiti or the next marina.

W.S.K.

CONTENTS

ILLUSTRATIONS AND TABLES

PART ONE:
CHART-AND-COMPASS
NAVIGATION

1. Nautical Charts

Most of us first used navigation by eye. Rowing, you kept the dock squarely over the stern, occasionally glancing over your shoulder at your destination. Steering an outboard, you aimed the boat at that clump of trees on the far side of the lake.

A few bent propellers later you had acquired local knowledge. You knew where the rocks and sand bars were. You knew which buoys you could safely disregard, on which side to pass the others.

Navigation by eye and by local knowledge can let you down, even near home. Do you remember the first time you got caught in the dark? At first you worried about your reception at home. Soon you wondered how to *get* home. All the familiar landmarks were gone; lights popped up all over the place. "Is that a light ashore, a buoy, or another boat?" And then: "Where is that sunken rock I have to stay clear of?"

A few dozen miles from home we run out of local knowledge.

Then we need a different kind of navigation: pilotage. It's also called coastwise navigation, even when it's used on a lake or river. Nautical charts play such an important role in pilotage that you might call it chart navigation, although electronic and celestial navigation also use charts. You'll steer so often by compass, fix your position so many times by compass bearings, that you might also call it compass navigation.

Whatever you call it, you can learn its principles on dry land. After you've practiced it a few times on a boat, you'll never forget it.

It makes the whole country your cruising ground. You can trailer your boat anywhere, or fly to the coast and charter one. You may still run into seven kinds of trouble, but—in clear weather at least—navigation won't bother you. It's the same in Alaska, the Florida Keys, and anywhere in between. That includes rivers, waterways, and lakes.

You can even take your boat out of sight of land for a few hours and bring her back without guesswork.

Let's look at nautical charts first. Then I'll refresh your memory on reading depth, distance, and direction from a chart.

The first thing to learn about nautical charts is not to call them maps. That's not just a tradition like the one that changes a rope into a line when you bring it aboard. There's a basic difference between maps and charts.

Maps picture land areas and only incidentally do they show water. Road maps may show lakes, but you won't find many depth figures in the water, nor buoys, nor navigable channels. The motorist isn't interested in them.

Charts, on the other hand, show water areas, depths, aids to navigation, and shorelines. But they leave land areas practically blank, except for features that might help the navigator: mountain peaks, tall chimneys, radio masts . . .

Obviously these bodies of water are rendered in miniature. A chart the size of Lake Michigan would be awkward to handle.

Charts, though they might be based on aerial surveys, don't show objects as you'd see them from a plane. In an aerial photograph a buoy is a pinpoint. You couldn't tell it from a pail someone lost over the side. The chart shows the same buoy prominently, gives its color and even its sound—bell, whistle, or gong. If the buoy carries a light you can read its color and character—fixed or flashing—from the chart. In an aerial photograph the land isn't uniformly yellow, shallow water not necessarily light blue, deep water not likely to be white. Charts use this color scheme whenever the budget permits it.

Charts use other symbols; for instance, soundings, contour lines, and danger markings show depths.

For the moment, don't worry about all the chart symbols. You'll pick them up as we go along. Some symbols and abbreviations are so logical that you'll sight-read them the first time. Who wouldn't guess that an anchor or the letters "Anch" mean anchorage?

Other symbols are used so rarely, or give such specialized information, that you'd get along with just a vague acquaintance with them. The difference between a mosque and a minaret would hardly bother a navigator off New England.

And here's good news: All U.S. charts—ocean, lake, river, or Inland Waterway—use the same symbols. Better yet: The same symbols, with only minor variations, are used on nautical charts of all nations.

Charts are flat; the earth is spherical. It has taken geographers two thousand years to learn how best to draw large parts of the sphere on a flat sheet. How they solved the problem—more or less accurately—isn't your worry.

Almost all nautical charts are drawn on the Mercator projection. You'll recognize it by the straight-line, right-angle graticule. Graticule is the technical term for the grid formed by the lines of latitude and longitude, the reference circles on a globe. On a Mercator chart these lines form rectangles longer in the north-south direction. Near the equator the rectangles look square; the farther you move from the equator the more elongated they become.

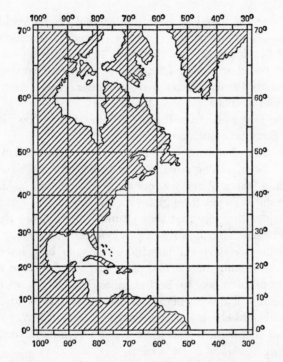

1. Mercator projection. The north-south running lines (meridians) are straight, parallel, and evenly spaced. The spacing between the lines that run east-west (parallels of latitude), which are also straight and parallel lines, increases toward the poles.

A polyconic projection is used on charts of some rivers and the Great Lakes. On charts that take in only a small area—a dozen miles of the Mississippi or the shore of Lake Michigan—the grid looks like a Mercator grid.

On a chart of the entire Lake Michigan you may notice that the meridians—the north-south lines—converge toward the pole as they do on a globe. The taper is only about 1 mile in 100. On the same chart the parallels of latitude—the east-west lines—are circles but you probably won't notice their curvature. You can safely treat the keystone-shaped elements of that chart as the rectangles of a Mercator chart. In the length of the lake you wouldn't be more than 1 mile off in distance, 1 degree in direction.

So you can use the same method for finding the direction of one point from another, and the distance between them, on all charts used in pilotage. Then you can steer in that direction, and when the distance is covered you'll be where you wanted to be. That's what makes charts useful in pilotage.

The usefulness is based on two fundamental properties built into the charts. One: Directions on the chart correspond to directions in nature. A point that lies due east of another point in nature is shown exactly east of it also on the chart. Two: Distances on the chart correspond to distances in nature. Points 2 miles apart in nature, on the chart show twice as far apart as points separated by 1 mile.

Before you buy a chart you'll have to know where you plan to cruise. Obviously. But that's not enough.

You have had a similar problem every time you took a trip in your car. You planned the trip using a map of the United States, or perhaps of the eastern United States. When you got to, say, Ohio, you picked up a road map of that state. To get through a city, say Toledo, you may have used an insert map of that city that showed much more detail than the main map. To find cousin Martha's street you looked on a city map.

On the water we have similar choices. If your only interest in Cape Cod is to avoid running into it, and using Cape Cod light as a landfall on your way from Bermuda to Boston, a *sailing* chart showing half the Atlantic Ocean will do. To plan a cruise from Norfolk to Nova Scotia, you'd use a *general* chart. For cruising in Cape Cod Bay, you'd pick the *coast* chart of that area. If you want to enter Plymouth, you'll be glad to have the proper *harbor* chart aboard.

The difference between all these maps and charts is scale, the amount of reduction of distances from nature to chart. That's simple enough.

For most people the trouble begins when they hear "small scale" and "large scale."

What exactly is scale? The figure 1:80,000, for example, indicates that 1 inch on the chart represents 80,000 inches in nature. One nautical mile —about 15 per cent longer than a statute mile—is about 6,076 feet, or about 73,000 inches. On a chart drawn on 1:80,000 scale 1 inch, then, is very roughly 1 nautical mile.

That's useful to remember because it's the scale used on the coast

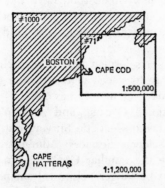 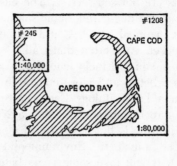

2. Choice of charts. The same area, Cape Cod Bay for example, will appear on many charts. It barely shows on this reproduction of chart ≭1000, which covers the area from Cape Hatteras to Cape Sable. On a sheet of about the same size, on chart ≭71 (Gulf of Maine and Georges Bank) Cape Cod Bay will be more than twice as large. On chart ≭1208 Cape Cod Bay, again enlarged, fills most of the sheet. Chart ≭245 zooms in on the harbors of Plymouth and its neighbors Kingston and Duxbury. (All these charts are published by the National Ocean Survey, the former U. S. Coast and Geodetic Survey.)

charts of the East and Gulf coasts of the United States, starting with ≭1201 at Quoddy Roads and ending with ≭1288 at the Rio Grande.

It also lets you estimate other scales quickly. On a 1:40,000 scale chart roughly half a nautical mile will be 1 inch. That is the scale of the Intracoastal Waterway charts and of many other inshore routes and bays used by small craft.

Harbor charts often—but not exclusively—use scales of 1:20,000 and 1:10,000. That makes 1 inch roughly one quarter or one eighth of a nautical mile.

With these figures in mind you should have the small-scale/large-scale confusion solved. The smaller the number that follows the 1, the smaller the area covered, the larger the scale, and the greater the amount of detailed information to be read from the chart.

Among all the different scales, which chart should you use in pilotage? In general, the one that shows the most detail, the largest-scale chart of the area. Obviously for an intricate channel or for finding a certain dock a 1:10,000-scale chart is better than one drawn on a scale of 1:40,000.

With this knowledge and having decided on the area you'll cruise, you could now go to your marine hardware store to buy the charts. If that store doesn't sell charts, someone there will know which of their competitors do.

Charts are not self-service. The customers would soon have them all mixed up and dog-eared. Some salesmen—experts in rope, paint, cocktail napkins, nautical jewelry, and a thousand other things—can find the chart locker. And often that's all.

Even if you are lucky enough to get a salesman who knows charts, there is a better and more enjoyable way to select charts. By the catalog. I should say catalogs. Each chart-producing agency has one.

NATIONAL OCEAN SURVEY of the National Oceanic and Atmospheric Administration is the new title of Coast and Geodetic Survey, until recently a branch of Environmental Science Services Administration (ESSA). It will take some years before the familiar C&GS designation will be replaced on all charts. It'll even be longer before salesmen and old-timers will get used to saying National Ocean Survey. This agency charts the United States coast and coastal rivers such as the Hudson (to Troy) or the Columbia (to Pasco).

The chart salesman will give you a catalog; it's free. Or you can write to Rockville, Maryland 20852. Catalog ⚓1 covers the Atlantic and Gulf coasts including Puerto Rico and the Virgin Islands. Catalog ⚓2 covers the Pacific coast including Hawaii, Guam, and the Samoa Islands. Catalog ⚓3 covers Alaska.

LAKE SURVEY CENTER of the National Ocean Survey, 630 Federal Building, Detroit, Michigan 48226 has taken over the Lake Survey from the Corps of Engineers. It issues charts for the Great Lakes and connecting waters from the New York State Barge Canal to Ontario's Lake of the Woods.

U. S. ARMY ENGINEER DIVISIONS chart the Mississippi and other rivers as follows:

Mississippi River above Cairo, and Illinois Waterway	536 South Clark Street Chicago, Illinois 60605
Mississippi River below Cairo	P. O. Box 80 Vicksburg, Mississippi 39180
Ohio River and tributaries	P. O. Box 1159 Cincinnati, Ohio 45201
Missouri River and tributaries	P. O. Box 103 Omaha, Nebraska 68101
Black Warrior, Alabama, Tombigbee, Apalachicola, and Pearl rivers	P. O. Box 1169 Mobile, Alabama 36601

TENNESSEE VALLEY AUTHORITY, Room 102-A, Union Building, Knoxville, Tennessee 37902 is the source for charts and information on the Tennessee River, its tributaries, and the TVA reservoirs.

CANADIAN HYDROGRAPHIC SERVICE, Chart Distribution Office, 615 Booth Street, Ottawa, Ontario, Canada, is the source for all Canadian charts. If you want the index and listing of nautical charts don't use the word "catalog." They issue—and sell—a catalog that includes waters and ice fields you probably won't care to visit. Instead ask for the free Information Bulletin describing the area you plan to cruise. For example: St. Lawrence River (#5), Nova Scotia, New Brunswick, and Prince Edward Island (#8), southern British Columbia, including Vancouver Island (#13), northern British Columbia, including the Queen Charlotte Islands (#14).

U. S. NAVAL OCEANOGRAPHIC OFFICE, Washington, D.C. 20390, issues charts for all other foreign waters. Until a few years ago this was called the Hydrographic Office, and these charts are still called HO charts, even officially. Their catalog, as you can imagine, is quite a tome. You can consult it at a chart agent's. There are only about forty HO chart agents in the fifty states. The catalog is broken down into an Introduction in three parts, and ten regional catalogs. Each regional catalog is sold for $.25, and so is Part II of the Introduction (the other two parts are free). The region most in demand by U.S. yachtsmen is Region #2 (Central and South America and Antarctica). It includes Bermuda, the Bahamas, the West Indies, and both coasts of Mexico.

All the catalogs—most of them charts themselves—let you visualize the area covered, give scale and price of the charts and lists of agents.

Chart agents sell at the published price, getting a small discount for their trouble. They are more likely to stock charts in constant demand. But this demand often creates a strange situation. Last summer in the Palm Beach area you couldn't get a chart to take you to Miami, inside or outside. I got them in a New York agency where they were out of the two Long Island Sound charts. You guessed it. I found those in Florida.

Some places have a storewide policy of paying postage on prepaid orders. I have sometimes beaten the long delay of special orders, at no extra cost, by ordering from one of them.

When ordering, make sure you specify the charting agency, or you may end up with a chart of Siberia, as I once did. You may want the upper Chesapeake C&GS #77. In Chicago you might get LS #77, which shows part of the eastern shore of Lake Michigan.

With the chart catalog of the proper area before you, what charts should you choose?

If you plan to deliver a boat, making the most miles in the least time, C&GS charts #77 and #78 (scale about 1:200,000) will get you down the Chesapeake from the Chesapeake-Delaware Canal to the Virginia Capes for $3 in charts. If you plan to enjoy the bay and poke into some of the rivers that run into it, you'll spend ten times that much for a couple of dozen charts with scales as large as 1:10,000. For a short cruise the five

1200 series charts, ✗1222–1226 (scale 1:80,000), will see you through for $7.50.

Most often your chart selection will be a mixture of large- and small-scale charts. Even when you plan a trip on the Intracoastal Waterway from New Jersey or Norfolk to Florida, you may want to carry more than just Inland Waterway charts. Sooner or later you'll get disgusted with traffic and bridges. With coast charts you can go outside in settled weather.

In a larger craft you may intend to go outside. When the weather sours, you can't use the coast charts to run the Intracoastal. They merely show its existence, give no details about buoys, depth, bridges, or stopping places.

One class of charts is designed for easy stowage and the special needs of the small-craft skipper. Logically enough, C&GS has named them small-craft charts, abbreviated SC following the chart number.

Unlike other charts, they are printed on both sides of the sheet and accordion-folded. They have been unexpectedly popular, and the series is being expanded from the Inland Waterway to rivers and strips of coastline.

Whenever there is still a choice—say between C&GS ✗518 and ✗518-SC—I'd get the small-craft edition. It gives tidal information for the current year, times of weather forecasts on local stations, and repair facilities and services available. The price, typically $1.50 or $2, is well worth it; especially where one SC chart—e.g., ✗114-SC-South Coast of Cape Cod and Buzzards Bay—replaces a half-dozen charts that would cost three times as much.

Since tide tables are useless the next year and facilities change rapidly, these charts are published every year.

Other charts are revised periodically. You'll find the date at the bottom of the chart. Edition date here means time of last major changes; revision means minor changes on the printing plates; corrected means brought up to date in print or by hand according to *Notice to Mariners*. These notices appear weekly, so "corrected to N.M. 25/72" means that no change after the twenty-fifth week of 1972—about the end of June—has been made.

Other chart agencies have adopted the small-craft chart idea. Some of these recreational charts are great bargains. One book of thirty-four charts (11×17¼ inches) sells for $2. More than eighty river charts of the Mississippi from Hannibal to the ocean, revised annually, paperbound, sell for $3.50. (These are the only charts, not for pleasure craft specially.)

Friendly oil companies, who hope you'll burn many gallons of their gas and oil, put out cruising charts. Like their land-bound cousins, the road maps, they are free.

I haven't heard many complaints about road maps. But I happen to know the man who claims the record for running aground in the Intra-coastal Waterway. He used oil company charts all the way. They are meant for planning; for cruising get regular charts.

For planning an ocean crossing or an around-the-world sail there is a type of chart that in spite of its name, pilot chart, has nothing to do with pilotage. It's the sort of chart Columbus' pilots—that is, navigators—would have liked to have. These charts are a delight for the bunkside navigator of the seven seas.

For $.50 you can buy the monthly pilot chart of the North Atlantic Ocean (HO ⚓1400) or the North Pacific (HO ⚓1401). For $3.50 you'll get an Atlas of Pilot Charts of the South Atlantic Ocean and Central American Waters (HO Publication 106), or an Atlas of Pilot Charts of the South Pacific and Indian Oceans (HO Publication 107).

The atlases are printed back to back, but the backs of the monthly charts are used for articles on navigational subjects. Some make fascinating reading in themselves; others, on ice limits for instance, may leave you cold.

You won't need pilot charts to plan a week's cruise, and you wouldn't sail to Greenland in February anyway. But apart from their dream-stimulating value, they make reading about long voyages—Captain Cook's or the latest singlehander's—more enjoyable.

Stowing charts can be a problem on pleasure craft.

Nautical tradition has it that charts must never, never be folded. But charts come in elephantine sizes such as 36×54 inches. Few pleasure craft, even large yachts, have room for chart drawers such as chart agents and ships use. Many skippers stow their charts rolled. That takes a lot of space, and the charts snarl at you when you try to unroll them.

I confess: For years I have flouted tradition, folded charts, and stowed them flat under my bunk mattress. Except for a little mildew, that worked well for me. I folded them printed side out; to protect them better you could fold them the other way, labeling the corners with a felt pen for quick identification.

You might buy a plastic chart case. I have seen them in several sizes, such as 20×26 and 25×40 inches. These chart cases have a plastic window that takes pencil well and can be wiped clean with a damp cloth. It's meant for doing your chartwork on, rather than on the surface of the chart directly.

An artist's portfolio, sold in any art store, will hold a lot of charts—folded. Perhaps you can find a hiding place for one of these in your hanging locker or under the cabin table.

When you have collected a mess of charts, some indexing system is needed. Without it you'll struggle into an anchorage on a coastal chart, forgetting that you have the harbor chart aboard. Or you find yourself buying the same chart twice. My personal system is to mark the chart catalog for every chart I bring aboard.

Having once lost my only pair of reading glasses over the side, I have never sailed without a chart glass since. Any good magnifying glass will do; I like a fairly large, square one. Eyeglasses can be kept aboard if you tie a string to them and wear them around your neck rather than in your breast pocket where they jump overboard when you bend down. Opticians sell such safety lines and also flotation devices.

2. Depth and Height

Unless you are an experienced chart user, you wouldn't believe how much you can read from a modern nautical chart. And even after you have navigated by chart for years, you'll discover still more details.

I promised to take you all over the chart. But I'll start with depth. If there isn't enough depth to let you go from here to there, you're not interested in direction, distance, aids to navigation, and all the rest.

I'll also talk a bit about height. After all, height and depth are closely related. There's another reason: They are sometimes hard to tell apart on a chart.

Here's a way to resolve most cases of such doubt. It's built into every nautical chart. Yet even some professional captains, after a lifetime of chart navigation, haven't heard of this simple code.

Charts use different type styles for things above the water, and in or under the water. Vertical type (roman) is used for features that are dry at high tide; *leaning type* (italic) is used for water, underwater, and floating features.

That's easily remembered. Buildings ashore are usually straight; on the water things often list. To the above rule there is but one exception: Soundings, the figures that indicate water depth, may be in vertical or slanting type. There's no mistaking them. They are always in the water.

Often the type style will be the only indication you'll have whether some charted feature is above or below the water. Say you see the words Fish Rocks on the chart.

Fish Rocks	*Fish Rocks*
In straight type it's above water: an islet.	In leaning type it's under water: a reef.

The symbols used on nautical charts of the United States National Ocean Survey (C&GS), Naval Oceanographic Office (HO), and Lake Survey (LS) are listed in a joint publication, called Chart No. 1. It isn't really a chart but a pamphlet of some twenty pages. Periodically updated, it sells for $.50 at chart agents. Get a copy when you lay in the next supply of charts. But you'll find it dull reading.

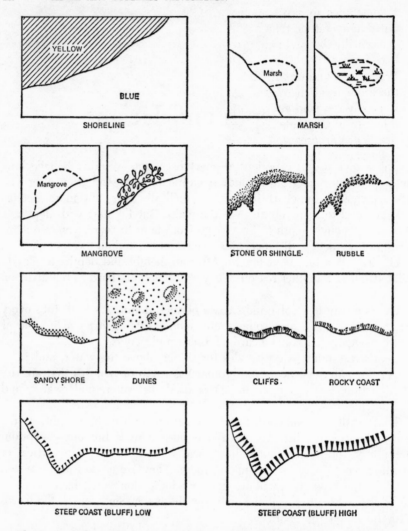

3. Chart symbols: coastlines. Solid line indicates high-water line. Shingle is similar to gravel, but coarser. Rubble means angular rock fragments, not worn smooth as stone, gravel, or shingle.

I'll try to make it easier for you to learn and retain.

You already know some important symbols; the first ones you'll notice when you unroll a chart are the colors. Unless—to keep cost down—the land is gray and the water white, you'll find this scheme:

> Yellow—for land
> Blue—for shallow water
> White—for deep water

Sometimes to save one color, especially on HO charts, the land is tinted gray rather than yellow.

Normally the land and water are separated on the chart by a solid black line, the coastline. If you had to make a chart, where would you put it? Where land and water meet. That's easier said than done. On most coasts the water level changes with the tides, so where do you draw that line? Logically the land ends at the high-water level of the sea. Since not all tides are of the same height a Mean High Water has to be chosen. For practical purposes you can call it an average high tide. The technical definition of the level actually chosen, Mean High Water all with capitals, is the average of all high waters during a complete tidal cycle, which takes about nineteen years.

The nature of the coast interests the boatman, who may want to land his dinghy, wreck his yacht, or fix his position. The chart shows it.

It would be most confusing to give the depths on charts from some high-water level. While you calculated how much the tide at the moment lacked from being high and subtracted that figure from the depth, you'd be aground.

So all coastal charts use some low water as a reference plane, called the datum of the chart. With this scheme you'll have more water under your keel most of the time than the chart shows. The datum is printed on the chart. For the Atlantic and Gulf coasts of the United States the datum is Mean Low Water. Mean again means a nineteen-year average. On charts for the Pacific coast, including Alaska, where two succeeding low waters are of very different level, the mean of all lower low waters is used.

In the Great Lakes there are no tides but rather marked seasonal changes in level. The reference plane there is called the low-water datum. In Lakes Michigan and Huron in a recent ten-year period the water level on an average was up to a foot higher (during the summer), never significantly lower. But extremes of 1 foot below the datum plane in summer and 1½ feet in winter have been recorded. (The 4 feet in winter and 5 in summer by which these lakes were higher would just add to the safety of your vessel.)

The important thing is to remember that water levels on the lakes can be below datum. Practically, that means that there'll be less water than the soundings on the chart indicate. When the lake is 1 foot below low-water datum, you'll find only 3 feet where the chart shows 4.

In coastal waters you'll encounter similar conditions when the actual tide of the moment is below the datum plane. You'll find more about that in the chapter on tides.

Between the coastline—high-water limit—and the datum plane—based on low water—there is the no man's land of the intertidal zone.

On charts that take in a large area, small-scale charts, the part of the beach that dries on the average tide will be too narrow to be shown. But on small-area, large-scale charts the drying line, the low-water mark, will be shown as a dotted line.

On charts that use the standard colors the area will be colored green. That's logical. Remember your kindergarten paintings? Yellow, for dry land, mixed with blue, for shallow water, gives green. Charts that use gray for the land will use a different shade of gray for the zone that uncovers at Mean Low Water or whatever datum plane is used. On Canadian charts you may find a yellowish rather than green tint.

Sometimes for clarity the word "uncovers" is added. The nature of the foreshore that dries is usually given.

Beyond the areas that uncover, or beyond the shoreline where the tidal zone is too narrow to be shown on the chart, begins the blue of the shallow water.

In that blue, and also in the white, you'll see a mass of figures that indicate the depth below datum at that spot. Before paying any attention to the actual figures glance at the title of the chart where it'll say *Soundings in Feet* or *Soundings in Fathoms.*

It makes a lot of difference. A fathom is 6 feet.

In Montreal I once conned the craft of a friend who had urgent business below. Avoiding the ship channel, I headed straight for our destination over soundings of 2, 3, and 4 fathoms. No problem; his schooner drew only 5 feet. The river must have been well above datum level or I would have run her hard aground. The soundings were in feet!

Even without looking at the title block of the chart I should have been warned by the absence of figures such as 3_2 (meaning 3 fathoms and 2 feet), which are customary for soundings of less than 10 fathoms.

Outside of soundings, you won't often run into fathoms. But 1 fathom is about the span of a man's outstretched arms, and so it lets you measure rope or line without a yardstick or tacks in the deck. Rope is still sold by the fathom.

On foreign charts you'll find soundings in meters. A meter is a little more than 39 inches, and so if you take a meter as 3 feet you'll be safe.

An absence of soundings on a chart usually is a warning to use a larger-scale chart. Duxbury Bay and Plymouth Harbor are uniformly light blue on chart ⚓1208, without a single sounding. The warning is also spelled out: Use chart ⚓245.

You may wonder at what depth shallow water ends. In other words, to what depth does the blue go? There is no universal rule. But you can always puzzle it out in a minute. On chart ⚓1208, for instance, you will find soundings to 17 feet in the blue part, no soundings of less than 19 feet in the white. The border, then, is at the 18-foot level on this chart. On an Intracoastal Waterway chart, say ⚓845-SC, you'll find no sound-

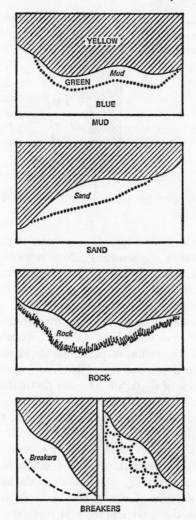

4. Chart symbols: foreshore. Dots follow low-water line. The area that un-covers—between low- and high-water marks—may be colored green. Nature of this intertidal zone may be shown by symbols, words, or both. Example: rock symbol with the word "Coral."

ings of less than 7 feet in the white. Here the cutoff between shallow and deep water is obviously 6 feet. These cutoffs at 1, or 3, or sometimes 6 fathoms are the most common.

Depth contours—lines connecting points of the same depth—are shown on many charts. There is a complicated set of codes printed in the pamphlet on chart symbols. Forget it. Use the same method you just

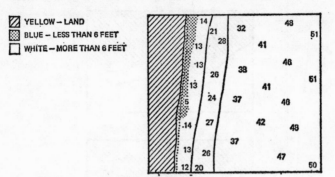

5. Chart symbols: depths, which are shown by soundings, contour lines, and blue color for shallow water.

used to find the depth at the blue-white border. If there are no soundings of less than 61 feet on the seaward side of a given line, it's obviously the 60-foot contour, the 10-fathom line. You don't have to memorize that it'll be a dash-dot-dash line.

You may wonder why they bother with all these soundings and the contour lines. But remember that charts are used by many different craft. A speedboat or a trimaran may draw only 18 inches of water, a tanker more than 40 feet. A submarine at periscope depth may draw 100 feet, submerged at cruising depth 250 feet. Charts let you figure whether you can get from your point of departure to your destination directly, or perhaps by some dogleg course, whether you need 3 feet of water or 300.

There's another reason. If you can measure depth, the depth information on the chart helps you in navigation.

The oldest method for measuring depth is undoubtedly the lead line (pronounced "ledd line"). Over the centuries sailors have evolved a code for marking the line to tell at a glance how deep the lead has gone down. By using different materials—leather, cotton, and wool—a sailor could feel the depth in the dark, something you can't do with plastic numbered markers. But the lead as navigational tool is just about dead now anyway. For exploration of creeks and anchorages most yachtsmen prefer a sounding pole, or even the boat hook suitably marked. For deeper water echo sounders are the choice of everyone who can afford one.

I'll talk much more about these depth finders later. Here I just want to show how known and charted depth can help you in navigation. Say you are off Chatham, planning on going north along the outer coast of Cape Cod, when you run into fog. Should you turn around and try your luck in Nantucket Sound?

A look at the chart will show you that you don't have to. The 30-foot contour runs practically parallel to the land. Even if the fog gets thicker and you can't see the land, as long as you stay in 30 feet of water you'll

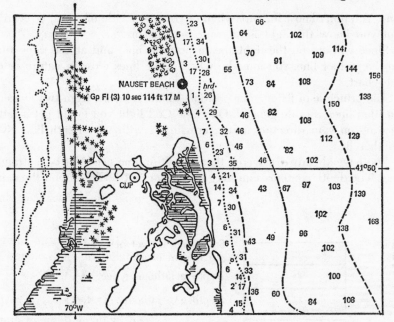

6. Depth contours as position lines. Measuring a depth of 123 feet while within the area of this chart, you'd know you'd be near the easternmost contour line shown, which connects points with the depths of 20 fathoms or 120 feet. Without additional information you would not know where along that line you are.

be all right. You can follow the 30-foot line right around the hook of the cape and into Provincetown Harbor.

In two minutes you can teach your helmsman to come right when the depth drops below 30, to come gently left when it gets deeper. If your helmsman follows orders—and that's easily checked—you can now relax, or worry about something else. You'll stay at or close to the 30-foot line on the chart.

You have just discovered the most useful concept of all forms of navigation—from pilotage to electronic and celestial navigation—the line of position, or position line.

It's typical of all position lines that you know you are on (or near) a certain line but not where on that line.

If it gets so foggy that you can't make out any landmarks, you won't know just where on the 30-foot depth line you are. If the fog clears enough for you to see Nauset Beach lighthouse abeam, you'll know exactly where you are: off the lighthouse on the 30-foot contour. You'll know your exact position; in navigator's language, you'll have a fix. You can think of the sighting of the lighthouse abeam as another position line. You don't know for sure whether you are 1 mile off, or 2, or even 3; but you know the light is on your port beam.

Since you are on the light-abeam position line, and at the same time on the 30-foot line, you must be where these lines cross in nature or on the chart.

The principle of fixing your position, obtaining a fix, from two crossing position lines is quite general. Off Cape Cod light you might get a radio bearing on your direction finder; crossing it with your depth line gives another fix.

You have already discovered that a position line need not be a straight line. The depth contour is an irregular curve that hooks around the cape.

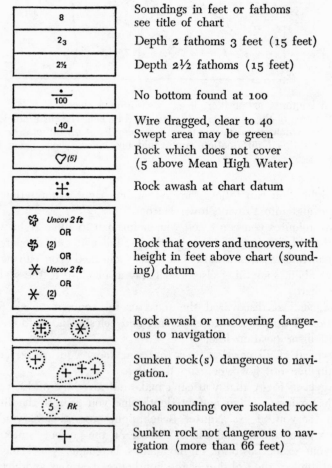

8	Soundings in feet or fathoms see title of chart
2₃	Depth 2 fathoms 3 feet (15 feet)
2½	Depth 2½ fathoms (15 feet)
100	No bottom found at 100
40	Wire dragged, clear to 40 Swept area may be green
♡(5)	Rock which does not cover (5 above Mean High Water)
⊹	Rock awash at chart datum
Uncov 2 ft OR (2) OR Uncov 2 ft OR (2)	Rock that covers and uncovers, with height in feet above chart (sounding) datum
⊕ ⊛	Rock awash or uncovering dangerous to navigation
⊕ (+ ++)	Sunken rock(s) dangerous to navigation.
(5) Rk	Shoal sounding over isolated rock
+	Sunken rock not dangerous to navigation (more than 66 feet)

7. Chart symbols: soundings and dangers.

Besides straight lines in visual bearings, we'll encounter circular ones and even hyperbolic ones.

A prudent skipper forgets all he may have learned in school about a line having no width. Position lines always have some width. Here your depth finder may be a little off; the tide level is probably not Mean Low Water; your helmsman may just have gone off to one side or the other. So you'll be most of the time *near*, not exactly on, the position line.

But if nothing goes wrong, you'll get to Provincetown, fog or no fog.

Not all coasts have been as neatly bulldozed by the ocean as the east coast of the Lower Cape. Most shores are strewn with little chart symbols, which sailors call "crap." If you hit one of them, you may crap out

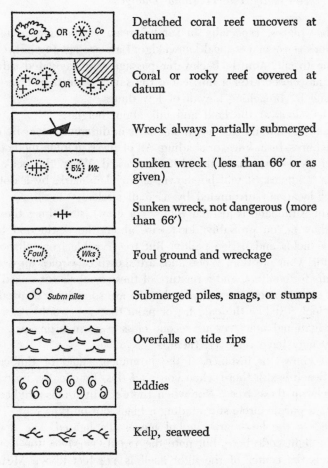

Detached coral reef uncovers at datum

Coral or rocky reef covered at datum

Wreck always partially submerged

Sunken wreck (less than 66' or as given)

Sunken wreck, not dangerous (more than 66')

Foul ground and wreckage

Submerged piles, snags, or stumps

Overfalls or tide rips

Eddies

Kelp, seaweed

8. Chart symbols: more dangers.

worse than throwing the wrong dice. In chart ※1 they are to be found under the heading Dangers.

Some of the dangers are not to your vessel but only to your anchors. You risk losing them in "foul" ground. If you anchor there or over a wreck because the fishing is good in such places, use an anchor and rode that you won't mind leaving behind.

You can see why charts can never be quite up to date. Someone may have planted a wreck somewhere since the last edition, revision, or even hand correction of the chart.

Shores and channels also change. Sometimes notes on the chart warn you. For example:

> NOTE: *Barnstable bar and harbor channels*
> *are subject to continual changes*

In other places, especially in sandy areas, you'll have to use your own sailor's sense or get local knowledge. Bars are apt to shift, channels are prone to silt. A little backwater passage you navigated safely last summer has closed after a hurricane; the same storm may have opened a new one by breaching a wall of low dunes.

Now let's look at the land and talk about heights.

Hills and mountains are shown on charts in different ways: by contour lines, hachures, form lines, or shading. All of these graphic methods show the relief. Peaks may have the altitude marked. When the peak is considered a landmark, it will be shown, as any landmark, by a dot giving the exact location, surrounded by a small circle.

Sometimes the land is just flat yellow (or gray), sometimes the vegetation is shown. You probably don't care about the distinction between cultivated fields and a rice paddy. But trees visible from offshore may help you fix your position. Woodlands are shown by circles for deciduous trees, stars for conifers, and a mixture of these symbols for mixed stands. Isolated trees that can serve as landmarks are sometimes charted. Their symbols look just like the oak, fir, or palm that you would draw.

As navigational aids trees are second class; a storm, a fire, or a logging company may have removed them.

I don't know, for instance, if the prominent stand of timber above Nauset Beach is still there when you read this. Practically, no navigator would rely on these trees. Not when there's a lighthouse right next to them. It's a purple circle surrounding a black dot on the chart. The purple added to the landmark symbol means it's lighted. We don't care about the light code here, but note the 114 ft. 17 M on the chart. The first means the center of the light itself is 114 feet above Mean High

Water. The height is given so you can calculate for yourself how far off you'll see the light.

We are all agreed, I hope, that the earth is round. From experience if not from geometry we realize that on a sphere you can only see a certain distance. You see farther from the masthead than from the deck; from a mountain you see even farther. It's simply a matter of height.

A light—if it's powerful enough—will be seen farther when it's higher. I could give you a table of visibility for powerful lights. But it's printed in every *Coast Pilot*. Also, the chart gives the range of visibility: for this particular light, 17 nautical miles. But the charted range is calculated for a lookout 15 feet above the water, Mean High Water, to be exact. If you are lower, the range will be less for you.

Here's an easy rule of thumb for calculating the limit of visibility of (powerful) lights aboard small craft: Deduct 2 miles from the charted range.

The navigator who has just crossed the Atlantic might draw a circle with a 15-mile radius around the light. The circle would show where he could first expect to see the light from the cockpit, in clear weather. As a position line—note that this one is circular—it's not very reliable. Under certain conditions he might "make" this light from 20 miles away or more. In a barely noticeable haze he may be within 7 miles before he'd see it.

The same caution is needed when making landfalls on a peak of a given height. Besides the possibility of having the wrong peak, or clouds hanging around it, temperature, pressure, and the layering of the atmosphere change the distance.

So my advice is not to pay too much attention to visibility tables and charted ranges of lights. Instead develop your own methods of estimating the distance from shore. When cruising in clear weather, knowing exactly where you are, study the windows ashore. At one distance you can count them, a little farther out you can't. Try that with and without binoculars. Then see at what distance buildings of a certain height, chimneys, water tanks, and similar objects fade from view. Since that depends on your eyesight, and your binoculars, you'll have to work it out for yourself. Also, you'll remember it better that way.

Here is good news: The chart symbols are now about half astern. When you get chart ✗1 you may want to glance at the abbreviations in "B" Coast Features and "S" Quality of Bottom. In this last concentrate on the first dozen entries where you'll find the bottoms you are most likely to need. You probably won't care about the difference between Foraminifera and Radiolaria. So don't make heavy weather of it.

3. Distance and Speed

Distance on a chart corresponds to distance in nature. The 2-mile stretch between buoys is just twice as long on the chart as the 1-mile distance between the bridges. What translates distances on the chart into distance in nature, or the other way around, is the scale of the chart.

If we used the metric system, the calculation would be easy. On the chart we'd measure in centimeters, in nature in kilometers. A kilometer equals exactly 100,000 centimeters. A nice round figure to work with.

But you are more likely to measure distances on the chart in inches, in nature in miles. You might use either of two different miles: nautical miles of about 6,076 feet, or statute miles of exactly 5,280 feet. Which you choose is up to you. On the Mississippi, where charts and markers give statute mile distances, you'd be wise to use those. In celestial navigation—even on the Great Lakes—nautical miles are the logical choice.

Some skippers decide on the miles they use according to the calibration of their speedometers. If it's marked in miles-per-hour they think they have to work in statute miles.

Not really. There's an easy way to convert statute miles into nautical miles or the other way around. A nautical mile is about 1.15 statute miles. Statute miles then are short miles. The s in "statute" and in "short" makes that easy to remember.

To get statute miles add 15 per cent to nautical miles. To get nautical miles subtract 15 per cent. For example: 10 nautical miles equal 11.5 statute miles. That's almost exactly right. Ten statute miles equal, close enough for practical pilotage, 8.5 nautical miles. Actually it's about 8.7 m.

A statute mile equals 5,280×12 or 63,360 inches. On a scale of 1:63,360, 1 inch on the chart would equal exactly 1 statute mile. Mississippi River charts are drawn on a scale of 1:62,500. On these charts 1 inch is, close enough, 1 statute mile.

On the 1200-series charts 1 inch is roughly 1 nautical mile. Actually, as we have seen, it's 72,913/80,000 or about nine tenths of 1 inch. Or, turning the fraction over, 1 inch on the chart equals about 1.1 nautical miles.

But you don't need any of this arithmetic, nor a ruler calibrated in inches. On whatever scale a chart is drawn, the latitude lines let you measure distance in nautical miles directly. That's made possible by this simple relationship: 1 minute of latitude equals 1 nautical mile.

That a nautical mile is 6,076.1 feet or exactly 1,852 meters matters little to you. What helps is that latitude, shown on all charts, is so simply related to the mariner's standard distance, the nautical mile. That works not only on charts, by the way, but on any map or globe. One degree of latitude, that is 60 minutes of latitude, equals 60 nautical miles (about 69 statute miles).

Everybody knows that the earth is not exactly spherical, but bulges at the equator and is flattened at the poles. That makes the length of a degree of latitude near the equator a little different from one near the poles. The internationally agreed value is a compromise, correct on the real earth about halfway between the equator and either pole. The difference at any other latitude is too small to bother the navigator.

Latitude lines, you will recall, run from east to west. So on charts that have north on top—the usual arrangement—they end on the left and right borders of the chart. From these vertical borders you can read distances very accurately in nautical miles. All you need is some means for transferring the distance to be measured to the border.

On big ships, dividers are used for this purpose. They are compasses with two steel points, rather like the drawing compass you used in school, which had one steel point and a pencil or lead. Dividers rust. On small craft they have a habit of going adrift. Sometimes they attack your toes right through your boat shoes. If you still want dividers, consider the one-hand model. You open it by pressing on top, close it by pressing nearer the points. That leaves you one hand to hang on with when the going gets rough.

You can also use regular dividers with one hand. I'd use a modified chopstick method: Hold one leg of the dividers with thumb, index, and middle fingers; the other leg rests between ring and little fingers.

For rough work, or after the dividers have fallen in the bilge, your fingers themselves make rustproof, nonpricking dividers. Your hand spans probably 9 inches, and does it more effectively than most dividers.

A dime-store rule will transfer distances nicely. Unless you're expert at reading eighths and sixteenths, I'd use the centimeter scale. There's nothing complicated about it. The numbers from one to thirty on a 12-inch ruler are the centimeters. Ten subdivisions divide each centimeter into millimeters. For our purpose you can forget all about these names. I'd read what measures 4⅞ inches as 123 or perhaps 12.3.

If you don't want any trade with centimeters and millimeters, even when they are nameless, you can get rules marked in tenths of inches in an engineering supply house. The divisions will be farther apart than on a millimeter scale (⅒ inch=2½ mm) but still close enough for everyday navigation.

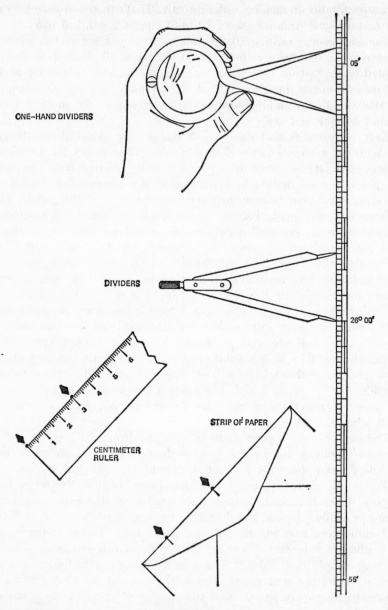

ONE-HAND DIVIDERS

DIVIDERS

CENTIMETER RULER

STRIP OF PAPER

05'

26° 00'

55'

9. Measuring distance from latitude scale of chart. One minute of latitude—left and right margins of chart—measures 1 nautical mile. Transfer distance with dividers, ruler, or a strip of paper. Distance between the buoys is 1.3 nautical miles.

You could also use a ruler and read nothing at all, using your thumbnail to mark the distance while you transfer it.

You don't even need a ruler. Any strip of paper will do. A business envelope or a strip from a letterhead will do nicely. Best perhaps is a strip of tracing paper, which lets you see the chart underneath. You'll find other uses for tracing paper in pilotage. With such strips you can use the left edge or an arbitrary zero mark as the left end of your ruler. Mark the right end with pencil, or score it with a fingernail. When there is already a fleet of marks on the strip I letter them as I measure. When things get too messy I throw the strip out and start a new one.

Primitive? Perhaps. But a paper strip gives the easiest solution for the distance when you have a lot of course changes. Say you're rounding some headland; what's the total distance? Start as usual at the left edge of the strip; mark the first leg of your course. Use that mark as starting point for the second leg, and so forth.

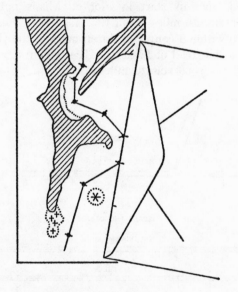

10. Paper strip is handy for adding distance after several course changes.

By whatever method you transfer your distances, use the latitude scale—along the left and right borders of a standard chart—never the longitude scale, which would be at top and bottom on such a chart. The grid lines on a Mercator chart form rectangles. So except near the equator, where the rectangles become square, the two scales are different. Prove it to yourself on any chart of your area. Or measure any illustration in this book that has a grid, e.g. fig. 1, p. 3. Near latitude

42 degrees the rectangles are only about three fourths as wide as they are high.

That brings up a fine point. Sailing charts and general charts cover a wide range of latitudes. You might use HO chart ✕1411 (Halifax to Hispaniola) for planning a cruise. How far is it from Long Island Sound to Miami? The rectangles are too square to be representative near Miami in latitude 26 degrees, too oblong off New York in latitude 41 degrees. An expert navigator would use the scale near 41 degrees for distances near New York, the scale near 26 degrees for distances near Miami. To get the distance between these points he would measure 1 degree halfway between these points, say between 33 and 34 degrees, and step this 60-mile distance off along the course line.

Many such distances have been worked out for you beforehand. The Intracoastal Waterway charts, for instance, show distances, in statute miles, measured from Norfolk. The westward-tending part of the waterway is measured from its start in Florida. Mississippi mileages are measured—also in statute miles—from the Head of Passes in the delta. So, unless you are within a couple of dozen miles of the Gulf of Mexico, you will be above the Head of Passes (AHP); where the Ohio joins the Mississippi you'll be 953.8 statute miles AHP.

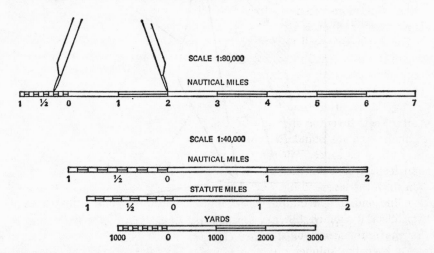

11. Graphic distance scales are printed on many charts. Top: 1200-series charts may give only scale in nautical miles (distance spanned by dividers is 2.3 n.m.). Bottom: On 800-series charts you will find, grouped together, scales in nautical miles, statute miles, and yards.

For good measure, quite literally, many charts show graphic scales in nautical or statute miles, and for large-scale charts also in yards. You transfer the distance to be measured just as you might have done to measure it from the latitude scale. Use dividers, ruler, or paper strip. But watch: Some charts have inserts on a larger scale than the main chart. Make sure you use the scale that belongs to the part of the chart you want to measure.

The yard scale ties in with nautical miles readily. A tenth of a nautical mile has a salty name, a cable or a cable's length. The last gives away its origin, the length of a ship's anchor cable. It's roughly 100 fathoms, 600 feet, or 200 yards. With the same degree of inaccuracy navigators often consider 1 nautical mile as 2,000 yards.

There is yet another way to get distances from the charts. Many plotters and course protractors, about which you'll read more in the next chapter, have scales printed on them. Typically they are both in nautical and statute miles and for charts on 1:80,000 and 1:40,000 scales. The trick here is to use the right measuring scale. The 1-inch-about-1-nautical-mile rule should wake you up to gross errors here.

Unless you are a type that forgets everything from one weekend to the next, you should have little trouble finding distances on charts.

Measuring distances on the water is another matter.

When you have run from Calamity Creek to Tousled Head, a distance of 10 nautical miles by the chart, you know you have covered 10 miles. But more often the problem is: How far have we come? and How much farther is it?

You can't very well tie a string to the dock you leave and let it pay out over the stern. But you could tow a log. That's a spinner—a small propeller—attached to a line, not unlike sash cord, that transmits the turns of the spinner to a counter. These logs are known as patent logs, taffrail logs (after their usual location at the stern), or Walker logs (after their inventor and one of the companies that still make them).

Such logs are standard equipment of the singlehanders who make long ocean passages. You can trim your sails, stream your log, go below, and let the boat sail herself. Sometimes you find an improbably small run since the last reading. The counter is barely turning. You haul in the log line and find a clump of sargassum wrapped around the spinner. You clear it, launch the log again, and fudge the record to make up for the unregistered miles.

To keep the spinner out of the water disturbed by your wake you might have to tow it 100 feet astern in a sailboat. On a cruiser moving at 15 knots, your log line should be 300 feet long, according to one manufacturer's instructions. Not very practical in pilotage waters. So hull-mounted, supposedly weed-free logs have been invented.

You can readily see that any distance-measuring device, such as the spinner, can give you your speed if you time a certain number of revolutions or count the revolutions in a given, rather short period.

Some instruments, though basically speed indicators, let you read

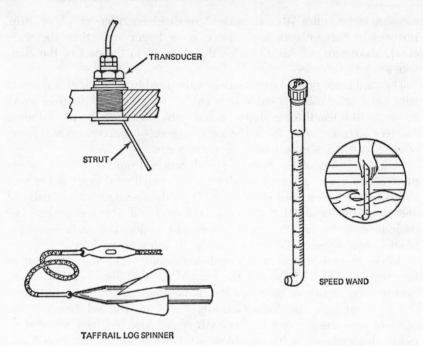

TRANSDUCER

STRUT

SPEED WAND

TAFFRAIL LOG SPINNER

12. Measuring speed and distance. Bottom: Spinner rotates when towed by boat. Line transmits revolutions to counter mechanism aboard. Top: The water pressure created by the motion of the boat acts on the strut, which projects through the hull. Transducer converts pressure into electricity; speed is read on a meter calibrated in knots or miles per hour. Right: Water level in tubes rises with increasing speed of the boat. You read the speed directly from graduations.

distance run directly, somewhat like the speedometer and odometer of your car.

But there's a difference. The road stands still, the water doesn't. Even if logs were absolutely accurate they'd measure your distance or speed through the water, not over the bottom or across the chart. Let me illustrate: Imagine a sailboat that moves at 5 miles per hour. Put her in a river that runs at 2 miles per hour. Downstream she'll cover 7 miles in one hour, against the current she'll cover 3. Clocked from shore she'd make 7 mph downstream, 3 upstream. The log, any type of log, will read 5 mph.

Let me bring in another sailboat, one that sails a little faster and covers 5 nautical, not statute, miles through the water in one hour. Such a boat would be said to be making 5 knots through the water. Knots means nautical miles *per hour* (so one doesn't say knots per hour). Against a 2-knot current she'll make 3 knots; with the current she'll make 7.

To convert knots into miles per hour, that is statute miles per hour, add again 15 per cent. To convert statute miles per hour into nautical miles per hour, that is knots, subtract 15 per cent (13 per cent would be more accurate, but 15 per cent seems easier).

Converting, then, is easy. If you have to do much of it you may work out a table for yourself. That'll be handy if your speedometer reads in knots but you find it convenient to work in statute miles or the other way around.

Much more useful than converting knots into mph or vice versa is the knack of estimating your present speed through the water but especially over the bottom.

On a powerboat, engine revolutions, the tuning of the engine, the condition of the propeller, the slickness or foulness of her hull, the number of people aboard, sea conditions—all change her speed. On a sailboat the strength of the wind—measured or estimated—its direction in relation to the boat's course, sails carried, weight distribution, the state of the sea—all influence her performance.

Is it then hopeless to try to estimate a boat's speed? Not at all. Proof: the clipper ships that, without chronometers and under overcast skies, got where they wanted. And today's skippers in predicted-log races where they have to pass control stations at predetermined times or lose points.

But you probably neither command clipper ships nor enter predicted-log races. How do you go about estimating your boat's speed? You time the run over a distance you can measure on the chart. That gives you your speed over the bottom. Then as long as conditions remain about the same, you assume that you are still making the same speed.

Suppose you navigate along the shore from Palm Beach to Miami. You have gone out through Lake Worth Inlet and noted the time when you turned south at the sea buoy. Exactly one hour later you are abeam of the sand sucker working on Boynton Inlet, which the chart calls S. Lake Worth Inlet. You measure the distance from the sea buoy: a little more than 13 nautical miles. So you have been cruising at somewhat more than 13 knots during the last hour. If the current doesn't change, the sea doesn't kick up, and you maintain the same number of engine revolutions, you'll make 13 knots again in the next hour.

Measure the distance to the Miami entrance, divide the miles by thirteen, and add the hours and quarter hours yet to go to the present time. You now have a fair idea of your time of arrival there.

Probably conditions will not remain exactly the same. But you can check your progress again at Hillsboro light, an unmistakable 136-foot-

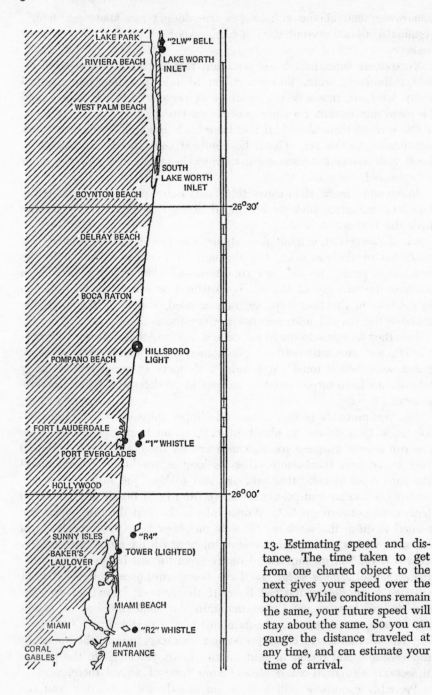

13. Estimating speed and distance. The time taken to get from one charted object to the next gives your speed over the bottom. While conditions remain the same, your future speed will stay about the same. So you can gauge the distance traveled at any time, and can estimate your time of arrival.

high tower, and at the entrance to Port Everglades, the harbor for Fort Lauderdale. I wouldn't try to count towns or water towers on this run any more than I would count small islands passed in the Keys. I'd concentrate on prominent land- and seamarks. Even a stranger will spot Baker's Haulover, where the sport fishermen are thick, and the buoy of Sunny Isles. At either of these places you're less than an hour's run from your destination. So you should be able to come up with an estimated time of arrival—ETA in navigator's shorthand—to the nearest five minutes. In this run of less than five hours you've had a chance to check your speed over the bottom at least five times.

If you have penciled times against each checkpoint, or kept some record of the run—if only in the margin of the chart—you have data to help you on the return trip, or any other trip along this shore. A few weeks later with the boat's bottom somewhat grassy, you'll drop some speed. If the water is choppier, you'll allow more time at the same number of revolutions. If conditions are better, you'll make better speed with the same RPMs, or the same speed with fewer revolutions.

You don't have to run several hours outside to get such data. The distance between two bridges on the Inland Waterway, where they grow like mushrooms after rain, would do as well. So would a run between any two markers, so far apart in so many minutes.

When you are interested in the speed of your boat at a certain setting, rather than today's speed over the bottom, you can eliminate the influences of current and wind. Time the same distance in opposite directions and add the runs. Say the southbound 1-mile run took five minutes forty-five seconds; the northbound run, six minutes fifteen seconds. The distance for the runs was 2 statute miles, the time exactly twelve minutes. Your speed was 10 mph.

For such speed trials many places have a "measured mile" shown on the chart. A set of two posts marks each end of the carefully measured distance. When the two posts are in line, whether you are 100 yards or 1 mile away doesn't matter, you are on the position line that marks one end of the mile. Here's a chance to enrich your nautical vocabulary. The two posts form a *range;* when they are in line, they are said to be *in transit,* you are *on* the range; anywhere except on that position line the range will appear *open.*

Again make runs in opposite directions. You don't count the time it takes to turn around and to get the markers again in transit.

As long as the minutes are multiples of two, three, and five (such as four, six, ten, twelve, fifteen), all of which divide nicely into sixty minutes, the speed is easy to calculate. Cruising, I sometimes cheat and for mental calculation call thirteen minutes twelve, or fourteen minutes

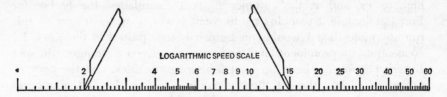

14. Logarithmic scale for speed-time-distance calculations is now printed on many charts. Each problem is solved in two steps using dividers or a strip of paper. In the examples that follow, arrow points to result. When the distance is in nautical miles, speed will be in knots; when the distance is in statute miles, speed will be in miles per hour.

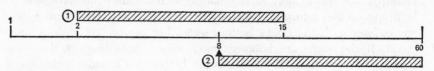

15. Finding speed. Step 1: Place one point of the dividers on miles run, the other on the minutes it has taken. Step 2: To get the speed (the distance to be covered in sixty minutes) place right point of dividers—without changing their span—on 60; read off speed at left point.
Example: 2 nautical (or statute) miles covered in fifteen minutes. Speed 8 knots (or mph).

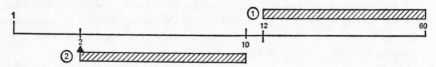

16. Finding distance traveled at a given speed. Step 1: Place right point of dividers on 60, left point on speed. Step 2: Without changing spread of dividers place their right point on minutes run; read off distance traveled at left point.
Example: Speed 12 mph, time traveled ten minutes. Distance covered 2 statute miles.

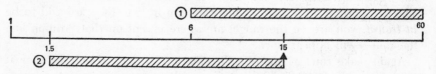

17. Finding time needed to cover a distance at a given speed. Step 1: Place right point of dividers on 60, left point on speed. Step 2: Without changing the setting of the dividers place left point on the distance to be covered, read off the time needed at right point.
Example: Speed 6 knots, distance to be covered 1.5 nautical miles. Time needed, fifteen minutes.

fifteen. For odd figures and distances you could use a slide rule or a circular gadget sold for these calculations.

But there is an elegant method using the logarithmic speed scale now printed on small-craft charts and their covers. Don't let the name scare you. They are easy to use once you catch on to the basic trick.

This scale helps you in making a chart of speeds that correspond to different engine revolutions, or throttle settings if you don't have an rpm meter installed. You make a few trial runs at various engine speeds. Then you plot on graph paper the calculated speed at each setting. Connect the points so plotted with a fair curve. Then you can read the speed for any intermediate setting; you can also read the setting for any desired intermediate speed.

Under sail, trial runs with carefully recorded wind speed and direction relative to your course have been made for some classes of boats. But so many variables enter into the problem that in the end the skipper has to develop a feel for his boat's speed.

The heel is a poor measure. To please a photographer you can make the boat heel while she's moving slowly to windward. Before the wind, moving much faster, she'll be practically upright.

The best indication of her speed, besides the feel on the tiller, is the fuss she makes in the water. You can also gauge her speed by the gurglings you hear in the forepeak. Every sailboat has her own repertoire of such sounds at different speeds.

But the helmsman can't very well run below to see if hardening a sheet, or freeing it a bit, has changed her chucklings. So for people who must really know, like racers, there are some speedometers specially designed for sailboat speeds.

The most sophisticated ones work about like this: An electromagnetic field is set up by a coil inside a streamlined, waterproof housing attached to the hull. Two buttons attached to the housing pick up the voltage generated as the boat moves through the electromagnetic field in the water, and transmit the voltage to a dial in the cockpit. It sounds like Baron Münchhausen pulling himself out of the swamp by his hair, but it works.

PRACTICE (3)

A boat gets clear of South Lake Worth Inlet (fig. 13) and starts on course for Miami at exactly 9 A.M. At 10:40 Hillsboro light is abeam.

1. What was her speed through the water on this leg? (If you want to work this with the logarithmic scale of fig. 14, divide both distance and time by two first.)

2. When will you expect to be abeam of the Port Everglades sea buoy (Whistle 1)?

3. You pass Baker's Haulover abeam at 12:37 P.M. What is your estimated time of arrival abeam Miami sea buoy?

4. What speed have you made *in miles per hour?*

5. What is the distance in *statute* miles between Hillsboro light and the Miami sea buoy?

ANSWERS (3)

1. 11 knots (it takes you five and a half minutes to cover 1 nautical mile).

2. At 11:35 A.M.

3. Between 10:40 A.M. and 12:37 P.M. you have covered about 21½ nautical miles. So your speed has remained the same. You'll expect to make the buoy at 1:24 P.M.

4. 12.6 mph.

5. 34½.

4. Direction

Charts, as we have seen, are so constructed that directions on every chart correspond to directions in nature. A point that's due east of another point in nature will appear exactly east of it also on the chart.

The grid lines on the chart are your first clue to direction. Meridians, the longitude lines, run north-south. Parallels of latitude run east-west. That's true whether the chart shows north on top—the usual arrangement —or is tilted to show more of a stretch of water on a given sheet of paper.

But these four directions are hardly enough. So every nautical chart also has a compass rose, or several roses, printed on it.

Right now we are interested in the outermost scale of these compass roses. You'll notice a five-pointed star above the zero mark. Star and zero both indicate true, geographic north. The scale reads clockwise through 360 degrees, making 360 degrees identical with zero degrees. Directly opposite north (zero or 360 degrees) you'll find south (180 degrees); east (90 degrees) is to the right; west (270 degrees) is left between north and south.

Memorize that and you have the basis for the whole direction business. (Professional navigators use three-figure notation for degrees, adding zeros before one- and two-place figures. Then the degree sign is not needed; three-place figures are automatically read as degrees. In this notation 9° becomes 009, 90° becomes 090, 190° becomes 190.)

All problems of direction in modern pilotage and navigation use the 360-degree system.

It wasn't always so. Not very long ago you would have called "north-by-east-one-quarter-east" what we now call 14 degrees. The point system is not only too clumsy for the modern navigator, it is also not accurate enough. The smallest unit, the quarter point, is about 2¾ degrees.

Be glad you don't have to learn to "box the compass," that is, recite the quarter points in proper order, forward and backward. Instead get familiar with the 360-degree system. The minutes spent memorizing a few figures will not only save time later, but will keep you from making gross errors in navigation. You won't steam west when you should be going east.

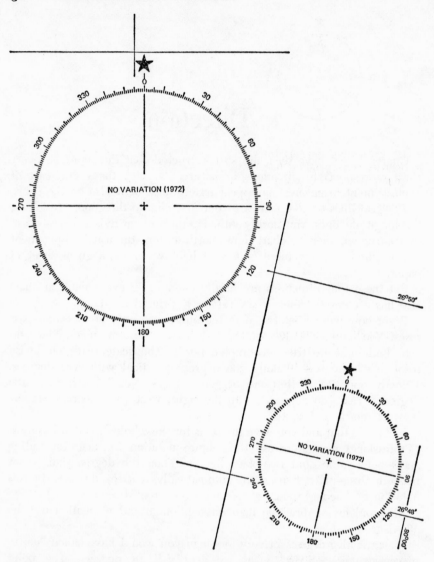

18. Compass roses on charts. Star and zero of outer scale indicate true north, so the outer compass rose is always aligned with the meridians of the chart. Most charts have north on top (upper figure). Charts of rivers and inland waterways are often tilted to conserve space (lower figure).

With only the four points N, E, S, and W—the cardinal points—well fixed in your memory you already know where, in which quadrant or quarter circle, to find any angle. For example, 130—between 090 and 180—must be between east and south.

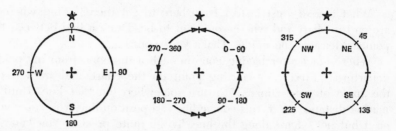

19. Estimating degrees from a few compass points. Having memorized the degrees corresponding to the cardinal points (left), you can tell in which quadrant (middle) to find any direction. Example: 300, between 270 and 360, must lie between west and north. Memorizing the values for intercardinal points (right) lets you narrow down directions. Example: 300, between 270 and 315, must lie between west and northwest.

The intercardinal points, NE, SE, SW, and NW, once memorized, will help you visualize angles even better. We still use these two-letter points, besides the one-letter cardinals, for vague directions such as winds and currents. You could get one step further in the point system, and use three-letter directions. NNE predictably lies halfway between N and NE, while ENE is to be found halfway between NE and E. But that's as far as I'd carry the point system.

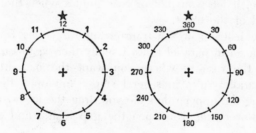

20. Estimating degrees from clockface. Every hour corresponds to 30 degrees. Example: 300 degrees is at ten o'clock.

Some people remember the degrees by using the face of a clock. You have known about clockfaces since third grade. To get degrees you just multiply the hours by thirty. Example: Where you'd find two o'clock you'll see 060 on a compass rose.

All problems in direction are really one. Since chart and nature agree in directions we can switch from chart to nature, or nature to chart.

"What course must I steer from here to get there?" Find where you are on the chart and where you want to be. Draw a line between these points. Measure the angle. That's your course.

"Where am I after having gone in such a direction from my point of departure?" Find your starting point on the chart, and from it draw the angle of your course. You are somewhere on that line. Until you mark a distance on it, this course line is a position line. You know you're on it but not where along the line. To be quite precise: You know you are on or *near* that line. Sloppy steering, compass error, wind, and current may have set you off course.

"There's a radio tower." If it's on the chart you can plot its direction from you on the chart. You know you are on that line, although you don't know your distance from the tower. Another position line.

We could go on and make the problem more complicated. But it'll always be a matter of measuring the direction of a line on the chart, or drawing a line on the chart in a given direction.

To do this drawing and measuring you need a pencil and some plotting tool. HB or 2B pencils, well sharpened, make neat, erasable lines. Hexagonal pencils or lead holders don't roll off your chart as easily as round ones. Art erasers are best for chartwork. So far most navigators agree.

But navigators have their pets among plotting tools. There is a wide choice. They could be grouped into two classes. One lets you transfer directions from the compass rose or to it. The other is independent of the chart rose; it lets you plot or read angles when the tool is aligned with the grid of the chart.

The classic instrument for transferring directions from the nearest chart rose is a set of parallel rules. Usually their span isn't wide enough to get from the rose to where you want the measurement. So you "walk" the parallel rules in several steps. You open them wide, then without letting the upper rule slide you drag the lower one to it. Then, holding the lower one, you open the gap again, and so forth.

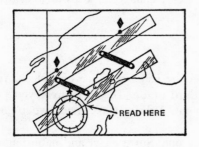

21. Parallel rules let you transfer directions on chart to the nearest compass rose. In this and following illustrations you measure course between two buoys. Arrowhead points to 60 degrees (060).

A cousin of the parallel rules is the sliding rule that rolls easily parallel to itself but not crosswise.

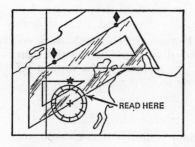

22. Two triangles, sliding one against the other, transfer course angle to nearby compass rose on the chart.

You can get the same result with a pair of draftsman's triangles.

All these tools, much used on big ships, often let you down. Just when you think you have the rule where you want it, you're off the edge. You can, of course, draw a line there and start from that. But I run out of patience quickly. You may like these tools on a proper chart table. Where small-craft navigators use them they work poorly.

So most small-craft skippers, who often must work in the corner of the galley or on their laps, prefer the other kinds of plotters, the ones that make their own angles anywhere on the chart, even when the chart is folded or on an uneven surface.

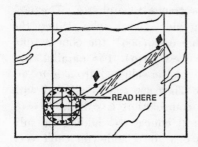

23. Movable-arm protractor, aligned with the grid lines on chart, lets you measure angles without referring to the chart rose.

One popular type, made in several models and sizes, combines a movable arm with a fixed plate that is to be aligned with any grid line, meridian or parallel.

A square or rectangular protractor, again aligned with the grid lines on the chart, is popular with many navigators.

Another type has a semicircular protractor attached to a straightedge. I'd prefer the protractor incorporated in the body of the straightedge. I'm in good company with this choice. U. S. Power Squadrons use it in

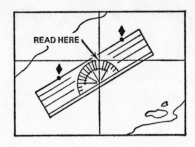

24. Protractor, aligned with course and centered on a grid line of the chart, lets you measure angles without reference to chart rose.

their courses. It's available with or without mileage scales.

All plotters work; none is ideal for all purposes. The movable-arm type is perhaps the simplest to learn to use. You only have to get its north mark in the direction of chart north, and align its edges with the chart grid. For good measure most of these plotters have additional lines printed on the plate; any of these lines can be aligned with any meridian or parallel, so you'll never run out of reference lines.

With a little practice you can do very good work with the Power Squadrons type. Perhaps you can borrow one and find out if you'd be happy with it.

Your feel for angles, or a quick look at a compass rose on the chart, will prevent gross errors with this and with any other protractor. Gross error usually means being exactly 180 or exactly 90 degrees off.

The 90-degree error is a specialty of protractor-type plotters. The 180-degree error is common to all plotting aids. Here's why. When the course from buoy #2 to buoy #4 is due east (090), the course from buoy #4 to buoy #2 is obviously due west (270). The parallel rule, the triangle, the movable arm, and the plotter—aligned from 2 to 4—don't know which way you want to go. They are just as aligned with the course from 4 to 2, the reciprocal course as it is called.

You can, of course, *calculate* reciprocal courses by adding or subtracting 180. If the original course was 090 you'd add—you can't very well subtract 180 from 90—and get 270. If the original course was 270 you'd subtract—if you added you'd get past 360—and get 090. To find the reciprocal course you then add 180 when the original course was less than 180; you subtract 180 when the original course was more than 180.

Practically, you won't need these calculations. You'll avoid errors of arithmetic by solving the problem graphically. The edge of the parallel rule or triangle that goes through the center of the compass rose and, say, 040, also goes through its reciprocal, 220. And protractors and plotters have a scale that lets you read the reciprocal course as easily as the other one. That's where the practice of gauging angles comes in. If you forget

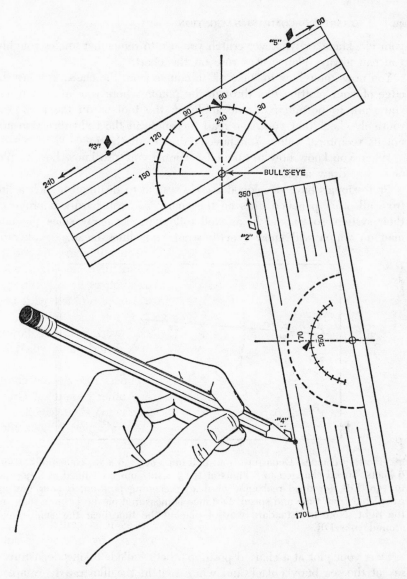

25. To find the course from buoy ⚹3 to buoy ⚹5 (upper figure) align top edge of protractor with the centers of the dots, which mark the location of the buoys. Slide the protractor so its bull's-eye lies over a meridian. Read the angle at the meridian on the outer scale. Here you'll get 60 and 240. From ⚹3 to ⚹5 the course is 060, from ⚹5 to ⚹3 it's 240.

Trying to find the course from buoy ⚹2 to ⚹4 (lower figure), you may not be able to reach a meridian with the bull's-eye. For such courses—nearly south or nearly north—center bull's-eye over a parallel of latitude and read the course on the inner scale. Here you'd get 170; 350 for the reverse course.

Placing a pencil at one of the given points and keeping the edge of the plotter against the point of the pencil makes your work easier regardless of course.

your clockface, or whatever crutch you use to remember angles roughly, you can always glance at a rose on the chart.

You now know how to "take off" a course from the chart. You lay the edge of your plotting tool through the points where you are and where you want to be and read the angle on the tool or on the rose. You routinely check that you have read the angle in the right direction and not its reciprocal value. You haven't drawn anything.

When you know how to take off a course you also know how to plot one: You draw a line.

Professionals have developed a code system to distinguish such a line from all other penciled lines on the chart. You can hardly improve on their system, so you might as well follow it, especially since the next man on watch will know exactly what your lines mean.

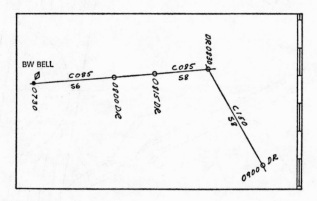

26. Plotting courses. Departure from bell buoy at 7:30 A.M., course 085, speed 6 knots. Speed changed to 8 knots at 8:15 A.M. Course changed at 8:30 A.M. to 150. DR, for dead reckoning or dead reckoning position, is your position calculated from time and speed. Distance is measured on the latitude scale, on the right. Note the standard way of placing the time near the small circles around your DR.

Start your plot at a charted position—that's called "taking departure"—say at the sea buoy (black and white bell in the illustrated example).

Mark the time of your departure. Times are always marked at an angle to the course line, if convenient at a right angle. Twenty-four-hour time is unmistakable and simpler to write than A.M. and P.M. If you are familiar with it, by all means use it. If you are hazy about it, there's a memory jogger starting on p. 90. You'll need it for reading tide and current tables. If you don't feel up to the job, forget it, use civil time. If you don't run at night, it'll usually be obvious whether it was seven-thirty in the morning or the evening.

Draw the course (085 in the example) starting at the point of departure. Glance at the compass rose if you like to make sure you have it right, not running almost west at 265.

Label the line writing C for course, followed by the course in three figures *above* the course line. You could add a T for true. In this chapter I deal only in true courses, that is, courses measured from geographic, true north. In the next chapter we'll work with magnetic courses. If you plot magnetic courses, you label them M. If you always write down true courses, or always magnetic courses, you don't need any label.

The course you have laid down is your intended course. Don't call it a heading. Heading is the direction in which the bow of your vessel points at a given moment. She could be heading 085 while at anchor or drifting. Yet while you are trying to steer a course of 085, most of the time she will be heading, say, between 080 and 090 in a moderate sea.

While talking about such fine points, let me introduce another term: "track." That's the course you've actually made good, your path over the bottom. You can see that a north wind or a south-going current will make your track come out to the south of your intended and steered course.

Below the course line write your speed (6) preceded by S. You could mark it kn or mph if there is any doubt. Since, practically, you'll always work in knots or always in miles per hour, you can leave off the label.

From time to time mark your position along the course line with a small circle and the time—at an angle. Label it DR for dead reckoning.

A navy ship in constricted waters would plot her position every three minutes at least. A singlehander in mid-ocean might put his down once a day, at noon. Your plot will be somewhere in between. Along shore or in a sound or lake I'd plot at least once an hour, on the hour. Often to give myself something to do I've plotted my DR every half hour. In a river or channel with a lot of markers it'd be silly to go to all this trouble. I'd simply mark the time of passing buoys and markers.

Dead reckoning, whatever its derivation—and there is some argument about that—means a calculated position. Don't call it "estimated position." That's another technical term with a specific meaning, which we'll encounter in the chapter on currents. And don't call it "assumed position." That's a term from celestial navigation, again with a fixed meaning.

How do you calculate your DR? From your speed and the time. Cruising at a given speed (6 knots) for a given time (from 0730 to 0800), you'll cover a certain distance (3 nautical miles). That's how we get our hourly position.

You will also have to mark your DR position whenever you change speed. If at 0815 you decide to rev her up from 6 to 8 knots, you draw the small circle 1½ nautical miles farther down the course line and label it. Your 8-knot dead reckoning begins here.

You also need a DR position whenever you change course (0830).

It is good navigational practice to change course (and perhaps speed) at well-fixed points. There isn't always a buoy where you want to turn. But as long as some charted landmark is in sight, you can locate the turning point better than by dead reckoning alone: You take a bearing.

The landmark could be a lighthouse, radio tower, a water tank, the charted cupola of a hotel, or a mountain peak. You can take a bearing of it and plot it on your chart.

A bearing is simply the course you would have to steer from your position—even if not known—to reach the lighthouse, radio tower, or whatever.

Obviously a battleship or ocean liner wouldn't turn her bow to the lighthouse to measure the angle. Neither need you. You might have some sighting device on your steering compass; perhaps you can sight over your compass. Unfortunately many of the most popular compasses don't let you do that.

So I highly recommend carrying a separate hand bearing compass for that purpose. This tool—about $50—illustrated at the beginning of the next chapter, lets you take very accurate bearings all around the horizon. It also lets you check and correct your main compass. And it serves as a spare when something goes wrong with your steering compass.

Even without a hand bearing compass and without turning your boat toward the landmark, you can take a beam bearing with any compass. As you know, an object is said to be abeam when it bears exactly 90 degrees—port or starboard—from the fore-and-aft line of your boat. You can squint along some athwartship line on your craft. When an object lines up with that line while your compass shows that you are right on course, you have a beam bearing.

A beam bearing is easily plotted. You just draw a line at right angles to your course through the charted landmark. Keeping your pencil at the mark while sliding your plotter in place makes that easy. Label the bearing with the time alongside and above the bearing line. That marks the line immediately as a bearing. The right angle marks it as a beam bearing. (Any other bearing would have the angle written below the line; three figures, followed by M or T if you wish.)

You'd be surprised how often sailing directions or the orders of the captain on a big ship call for a course change when a landmark is abeam. You could sail for 1,000 miles along any coast of the United States laying courses that always make a dogleg when abeam of a lighthouse or buoy. Make it easy for yourself; get in the habit of planning your own courses that way.

With a bearing compass you can take bearings of objects that aren't exactly abeam, or ahead, or astern. You are measuring the bearing of, say, a lighthouse *from your ship*. Not knowing the exact position of the

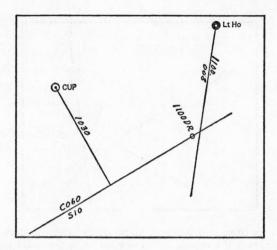

27. Plotting bearings. Cupola on your port beam (at right angles to your course) at 10:30 A.M. At 11 A.M. the lighthouse bears 008 True. That bearing does not quite check with your DR.

ship, but knowing the location of the lighthouse on the chart, you draw the bearing line *from the light*. Again I would not calculate the reciprocal. If the light bears 008 from you, you bear 188 from the lighthouse keeper. I'd ignore that, align my plotter for 008 with the pencil at the lighthouse, then draw a line toward the ship. Most of the time there won't be the slightest doubt on which side of the light the ship must be. Probably in the water, not on the land. When there can be doubt, your estimate of angles or a glance at the compass rose on the chart will check that the bearing *from* the ship to the light, or whatever, is correct.

You won't be surprised to hear that a bearing line is again a position line. You know you are at the time marked on that line but don't know just where. You can consider your planned course, the course line, as another position line. Until something better comes along to fix your position, you may consider yourself near the point where the bearing crosses the course. The closer the course over the bottom (the course made good) resembles the planned course, the closer to that position will you be.

You'll get a much better indication of your position if you can take bearings of two objects at—practically—the same time. The vessel at the time of taking the bearings must have been on the two position lines at once. There is only one point that is on both bearing lines, their crossing point. Mark that point with a small circle, label it "FIX," and start a new dead reckoning from this position. It's independent of wind, current, steering errors, and your estimate of the vessel's speed. That's

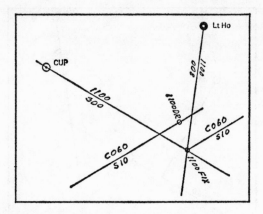

28. Plotting a fix from two bearings taken at the same time. At 11 A.M. the lighthouse bears 008, the cupola 300. You must be at (or near) the intersection of the two position lines. Label it "FIX" and start a new dead reckoning from that position.

why you abandon your former dead reckoning and start a new one with the fix as the new point of departure.

In pilotage waters charted landmarks are usually plentiful. So the navigator often has a choice of objects and a choice on when to take the bearings. Aim for objects so one bears about halfway between abeam and your bow, the other halfway between your beam and astern. That would make position lines that cross at near the ideal angle of 90 degrees. Avoid angles of less than 45 and more than 120 degrees.

If there's a third object, say on the other beam, take a bearing of that too and plot it. But don't be surprised if the three position lines don't meet in one point. More likely they'll form a small triangle, which sailors call a cocked hat.

The size of the triangle will give you an idea of the accuracy of your bearings and their plotting. These errors don't show graphically on a two-object plot. But they are there. Keep that in mind. Then you won't consider yourself exactly in the center of the small circle that indicates the fix, but in its vicinity.

Sometimes you'll have only a single prominent charted object in sight.

Then you can use a navigator's trick called a bow-and-beam bearing. Actually you take two bearings, the first when the object is well forward of the beam, the second when the object is about abeam. The most useful and easiest of combinations is the one where the first bearing makes an angle of 45 degrees with your course, the second exactly 90 degrees—a beam bearing. If you can make some sighting marks on your boat you won't even need a bearing compass for this job.

It's such a useful trick because in the 45-degree triangle of your plot two sides are the same length. From the time between the first and the second bearing and your known speed you can calculate the distance

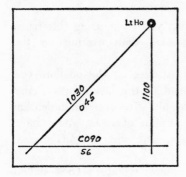

29. A four-point bearing lets you estimate the distance of an object abeam. Note the time when an object makes an angle of 45 degrees (four points) with your course, halfway between bow and beam. Note again the time when it is abeam. At that time the distance off equals the distance you've covered between bearings. Example: Elapsed time thirty minutes, speed 6 knots; the object abeam is (about) 3 nautical miles from you.

covered between taking these bearings. That's one side of the 45-degree triangle. It's the same length as the distance from the object to the vessel when she's abeam. Forty-five degrees is four points in the old-style compass notation, and so this double bearing is known as a four-point bearing.

While this bearing gives a good indication of your distance from the charted object when you are abeam of it, it doesn't deserve the name "fix." Your speed through the water is too much in doubt. Continue your dead reckoning.

There's another trick for finding the distance of an object abeam. This one is much less known than the four-point bearing and since it needs no plotting at all looks like magic.

Let me put it in a mathematical formula. Call S your speed in knots (or miles per hour). Call D the distance of an object in nautical (or statute) miles. When the object is about abeam its bearing from you will change S degrees in D minutes.

Example: Your speed is 8 knots. When a charted object, or an uncharted one for that matter, is about abeam, you time how long it takes for its bearing to change 8 degrees. If that takes *two* minutes the object is about 2 nautical miles from you. If it had taken one minute it would have been only 1 nautical mile away.

If your speed had been 8 miles per hour, rather than 8 knots, the distance would have been in statute, rather than nautical, miles.

The formula will only work when the object is about abeam, as I have said. Say your course is 360. Then an object is abeam when it bears 090. You could time how long it takes the bearing to change from 086 to 094, from 082 to 090, or even from 090 to 098. Don't ask at what bearing the calculated distance applies. As you can prove to yourself by plotting it, the distance barely changes between these bearings. The change in distance is less than the built-in inaccuracy of the formula, the uncertainty of your speed through the water, and the unavoidable error in taking the bearings.

Don't let a thought about inaccuracy keep you from using this trick. It's accurate enough for pilotage and quicker than waiting for the bearing to change four points.

You can see how you could use it, for instance, on the offshore run along the Florida coast imagined at the end of the last chapter. Any prominent object ashore, charted or not, would give you an indication of your distance from shore. Along this stretch of coast you'd have water towers, high-rise apartment buildings, and other targets abeam every few minutes.

In Chapter 10 I'll introduce you to another navigator's trick—called a running fix—useful where marks are far apart.

Let me say it just once more: Check directions—courses and bearings—against the compass rose you have memorized or one on the chart. Do that until it becomes second nature. Then you'll avoid the common mistakes of plotting 222 for 042 (wrong direction on the correct line) or 312 or 132 for 042 (parallel used in place of meridian, or wrong scale read). Plot these angles with the tool you plan to use and see how you could get them wrong.

Warning: Before you put your new-found knowledge to practical use, remember that in this chapter we have looked only at *true* courses and *true* bearings. In most areas the compass doesn't point to true, geographic north. You'll read about that in the next chapter. Also, a compass brought aboard a boat has to be adjusted for that boat. That's in the chapter after next.

PRACTICE (4)

1. Estimate the bearings of the land- and seamarks from the crossing point of the course lines in fig. 51.

2. Using whatever method you prefer, *estimate* the courses steered in fig. 10, starting at the north end of the chart.

3. *Measure* the courses steered in fig. 10, starting from the south end

of the chart. If you don't have a protractor at hand, draw the courses on tracing or tissue paper and measure them on the compass rose in fig. 18, top.

ANSWERS (4)

1. Clockwise you should have: about 075, 165, 255, and 345.
2. You should have approximately: 180, 215, 180, 110, 135, 190, 240, and 200.
3. You should have close to: 017, 061, 010, 319, 292, 002, 036, and 001.

5. The Magnetic Compass

To take a course from the chart you need only a simple tool. To steer that course you need a compass. On small vessels that will be a magnetic compass. Big ships use gyrocompasses, costly electrically driven devices. As backups even the biggest, latest ships still carry magnetic compasses driven by the never failing magnetic field of earth.

A compass will get you safely home when fog sets in, or when rain cuts visibility. It lets you steer the shortest route across a lake, and leads you back to a good fishing spot. It tells the sailing skipper how close he's sailing on the wind. All he has to do is tack once and compare the course before coming about with the one after; half the difference between the courses is his angle on the wind. Then he'll know just where to tack to fetch a mark. That's why you'll see a compass on a daysailer that never races out of sight of the clubhouse.

I carry a compass on a muscle-powered kayak in Florida's backwaters. Not because I'm a navigation nut, but all the saw grass and all mangroves look pretty much the same. And in the middle of the day, for several months of the summer, the sun is almost overhead—a very poor guide.

The mariner's compass works on the same principle as the simplest compass needle: One end of the needle points—more or less—north regardless of how you turn the compass housing. Instead of a needle moving over a card, a modern marine compass has a card that turns; magnets attached to the underside make it turn. You read the direction from graduations of the card against a line on the housing, the lubber's line. The lubber's line in the fore-and-aft direction of a craft indicates her heading. If she moves in the direction of her heading, it indicates her course.

A landsman's dry compass is useless on a boat. The needle would jiggle and hunt forever. A liquid dampens these motions.

A Boy Scout's liquid-filled compass has to be held horizontal to keep the needle from hanging up on the card or the glass cover. To keep the compass in operation on a rolling and pitching boat it has to be slung in gimbals. These concentric rings—one pivoted in the fore-and-aft, the other in the athwartships direction—are seen in flat-faced compasses such as the familiar box compass and Navy models. In recent spherical compasses they have disappeared into the innards; so these models are known as internally gimbaled. Sailboat models allow an extra wide angle of tilt to take care of roll after the boat is heeled almost rail down.

Many flat compasses can be fitted with sight vanes for bearing taking. With that type, if it's conveniently mounted, one can also squint at a landmark and come up with a fairly good bearing without vanes. That's difficult with some spherical compasses, impossible with others.

30. Hand bearing compass.

For that, the most convenient instrument is the already mentioned hand bearing compass. It'll also get you home when your steering compass has given out.

"Nothing ever goes wrong with a compass," you say. Oh no? Ann Davison on her solo voyage across the Atlantic was caught by a monster sea before even reaching Gibraltar. Everything in the cabin crashed from starboard to port. When she had picked her way through pans, books, navigation instruments, and detergent she found something had hit the compass and smashed it.

Hand bearing compasses have built-in lights. So you can take a bearing on a lighthouse or lighted buoy at night, then read the bearing by pressing a switch.

To read the steering compass in the dark you can have lights built on, or built in. Red light interferes less with your night vision than white and is preferred by many helmsmen. A dimmer that lets you regulate the brightness is great. All electrical gear is prone to seasickness. If you plan a night run, check the light in the afternoon. That'll give you time to tinker. (Most often it's the bulb contacts that have corroded and need some rubbing.)

To suit your steering position you can have the compass bulkhead- or shelf-mounted, or in brackets that adjust for either. Sailboats often have the compass mounted in a freestanding pedestal—binnacle—or sunk into the decksole in the cockpit. Some craft have it built into the column that carries the steering wheel.

All these models are made by a number of manufacturers and in different sizes. A 7½-inch job would look silly on a 16-footer. I'd choose the card first, on the basis of legibility. Most people find white markings on a black card easiest to read. On any but the smallest craft I'd choose a compass marked for every degree, or at least every other degree rather than every five. Personally I also like some points on my compass card. I don't use them as points but to help me in steering in degrees. On a course of 130, for instance, I can stay awake longer when I take my cue from the SE triangle than by watching the numerals, which all look alike when you stare at them long enough.

When you have found the right model, if you have a choice take it with built-in compensators. They make the compass easier to adjust to your boat.

Yes, your boat. The shiny, fresh-out-of-the-sealed-carton compass will point wrong on your boat. Almost any boat. But before we look into that, let's see where the compass points before you bring it aboard.

Only in a few places on earth does a magnetic compass point north.

Perhaps you remember Mrs. Schreivogel, your teacher in third grade. "A bar magnet inside the earth attracts the compass needle. Unfortunately that bar isn't where the earth's axis is. So instead of coming out with the brass shaft of the globe, at the poles, we have two magnetic poles some distance from the geographic poles. The magnetic North Pole is somewhere in the Canadian Arctic."

Fair enough for third grade. Actually the situation is much more complicated. Only in a few places does a compass point to the magnetic pole. Instead it aligns itself with the magnetic meridian of its location. That sounds like a quibble over words. But magnetic meridians—unlike geographic ones—are not neat great circles running from pole to pole. Instead they form very irregular curves that run all over the place on a chart of the world.

So magnetic north, the direction where a compass indicates north, can't be predicted from your location. You have to get it from your chart.

On the charts used in pilotage it's shown by two compass roses, one inside the other.

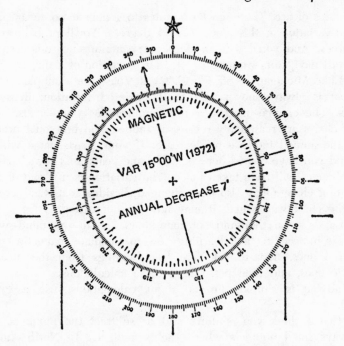

31. Compass rose on chart. The outer scale, aligned with the grid of the chart, shows true direction. Star marks its zero point.

The inner scale shows magnetic direction in degrees. Arrow marks its zero point (magnetic north). (The innermost, unlabeled scale gives magnetic direction in points and quarter points.)

The outer scale, the one we used to find and plot courses in the last chapter, gives true directions, based on geographic north. The inner scale gives magnetic directions; its north shows where an undisturbed compass would point north. In fact, you may consider the inner rose as the card of a corrected compass at your location. (Like some compass cards it shows both degrees and points, although the points and quarter points here are not labeled.)

Except on a line that now runs, for instance, from northern Canada, through Lake Michigan, and to the east coast of Florida, the inner rose will be tilted against the outer. The angle of tilt is the *variation* of the compass. (To confuse you, land people call it declination.) It is called west when the compass points west of true north, east when the compass points east of true north.

On every compass rose on the chart the variation is given in degrees and minutes of arc. There are 60 minutes to 1 degree; so 14°45′ means that the variation at this place is 14¾ degrees. You'll probably call it 15 degrees. And you'd call 14 degrees 15 minutes 14 degrees. Most small-craft navigators would disregard any variation of 1 degree or less. As on Lake Michigan or off Florida's east coast, for example.

A year is always shown next to the printed variation. Reason: It changes. The change—usually a few minutes per year—is also given. If your charts are reasonably recent, as they should be, you'll probably ignore the annual increase or decrease. If your charts came with the boat, and you have owned her yourself some years, toss the charts out. Many changes will have taken place. The variation is just one of them. The rate of change may also have changed; besides, if it was increasing when the chart was issued, it may now be decreasing.

Thousands upon thousands of man-hours are—to my mind—wasted each year in teaching and learning how to calculate magnetic courses from true ones, how to calculate true bearings from the measured magnetic ones, and then performing these calculations.

My advice is simple: Forget about calculations; use a graphic method.

Not that I think you couldn't add or subtract the numbers. They are always small numbers where yachts navigate. In North America, for instance, they range from west 25 degrees off Nova Scotia to east 25 degrees off British Columbia.

You probably could also learn when to add, when to subtract, and where it's west and where east. (You'll notice it's west on the East Coast, east on the West Coast of the United States and Canada.)

In the graphic method you don't have to remember any of that. No rules or code words to learn. A single line drawn—or imagined drawn—on your chart converts from true to magnetic, from magnetic to true; you use the same technique whether the variation is west or east. Doesn't that sound simple?

You use the compass roses on your chart. You may remember that the outer rose is true, the inner magnetic. You don't even have to remember that. The alignment of the outer rose with the grid of the chart marks it as the true one. If that weren't enough, the inner one is labeled "magnetic."

To convert from true to magnetic, or the other way around, you draw a line from the center common to both roses through the known course or bearing, and read the unknown on the other rose.

You don't even have to draw the line.

If you use parallel rules or triangles to transfer directions directly from the chart rose, you simply align these tools with the proper rose—inner for magnetic, outer for true.

Graphic method for converting true direction to magnetic, or magnetic to true. On a compass rose of the chart draw a line from the center through the known course or bearing; read the unknown course or bearing on the other scale of the compass rose.

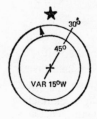

32. Variation 15° West. Given true course 030. Draw line from center to 30 degrees on the outer, true scale. Read magnetic course, 045 on the inner, magnetic scale.

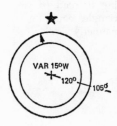

33. Variation 15° West. Given bearing 120 magnetic. Draw line from center through 120 degrees on inner, magnetic scale. Read true bearing 105 on outer, true scale.

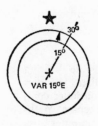

34. Variation 15° East. Given true course 030. Draw line from center to 30 degrees on outer, true scale. Read magnetic course, 015, on inner, magnetic scale.

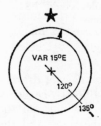

35. Variation 15° East. Given bearing 120 magnetic. Draw line from center through 120 degrees on inner, magnetic scale. Read true bearing, 135, on outer, true scale.

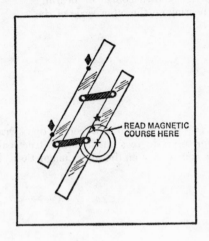

36. To take off magnetic course between buoys align parallel rules. Read magnetic course (045) on inner compass rose without bothering to read true course. (Two triangles could be used in same manner.)

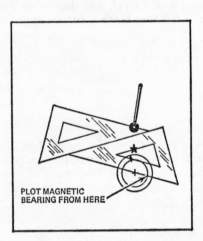

37. To plot magnetic bearing (120) of light align triangles with 120 degrees on inner compass rose and its center. Without bothering about outer rose draw parallel line through the light. (Parallel rules could be used in same manner.)

With plotters that generate their own angles—by protractor scale or movable arm—you still don't have to draw the conversion line on the chart rose. Just lay the plotter across the center of the roses and the known number of degrees on the proper rose. Then read the converted degrees on the other rose without drawing the line.

At this point you may wonder if all these conversions are really necessary. Couldn't we always operate on true directions? You could

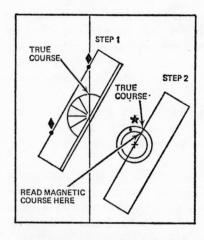

38. To take off magnetic course between buoys align plotter with buoys and chart grid; read off true course (030). Then align plotter with center of compass rose and 30 degrees on the outer scale. Without drawing the line read the magnetic course (045) on the inner scale. (A movable-arm protractor could be used in same manner.)

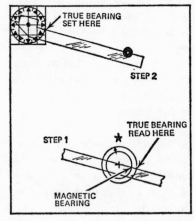

39. To plot magnetic bearing (120) of light align plotter with center of compass rose and 120 degrees on inner scale. Without drawing the line read true bearing (105) on outer scale. Move protractor arm to 105 degrees; align it with light when fixed part is aligned with chart grid, and draw the bearing line. (A protractor could be used in similar manner.)

most of the time on big ships, where gyrocompasses show true courses, and where bearings are taken with repeater gyros giving true bearings.

On pleasure craft and other small vessels we might be tempted to work always in magnetic directions. The steering compass is magnetic, and bearings are taken with magnetic compasses. The hitch is that chart grids are drawn in true direction and many references the navigator uses also give true directions, for example *Coast Pilots*, Current Tables, and Light Lists.

So occasionally, even on your own boat and without wanting to pass exams, you will have to convert. But most of the time you can forget instructors and textbooks and work your pilotage in magnetic directions only.

But the compass rose conversion method becomes automatic after a few days anyway, especially since you are not likely to use westerly variation one day and easterly the next. You may even find that without any effort you'll learn when to subtract and when to add. If it comes easy, use the arithmetic. But there's nothing wrong with working all problems of pilotage graphically. Navigators make fewer mistakes with the graphic method; that's why they print double roses on every chart used for pilotage.

On charts that cover large areas, the variation may change from one area of the chart to the next. To take care of that, roses are scattered over the entire chart. You should always use the one nearest to where you are working the chart.

On charts that cover an entire ocean there's not space enough for all needed roses. So only true roses are shown. On a voyage from the English Channel to Panama, for instance, you'd start with a variation of about 10 W, run up to 23 W, then down to zero, and finally to about 3 E. (You'll get all these figures from lines printed on the chart.) On such a voyage you'd better learn to add and subtract. But you'll have plenty of time to puzzle out the addition or subtraction business. Your plotter may have the rules printed right on it.

When in doubt, as a last resort, use your head. Imagine what an inner rose would look like, or even sketch it. Westerly variation places the zero of the inner rose west of true north, somewhere in the three hundreds. Easterly variation places the zero of the inner rose east of true north, somewhere in the low numbers.

How accurate do you have to be in actual navigation? Much will depend on where you are. In a channel an error of 50 feet sideways will have you aground on a spoil bank. Along shore or on a large lake you could be a mile or two off and still "make" the next buoy. How that translates into angles is easily remembered:

> An error of *1 degree* will
> set you off *100 feet*
> in a run of *1 nautical mile.*

And since 1 nautical mile is roughly 6,000 feet,

> An error of 1 *degree* will
> set you off *1 nautical mile*
> in a run of *60 nautical miles.*

Without much error you can read statute miles for nautical miles. You can also use the formula for *any* small angle. Example: A 3-degree error will set you off 300 feet in 1 mile; so will a 1-degree error in 3 miles. In a run of 30 miles a 2-degree error will set you off 1 mile.

Taking off or converting courses accurately, and steering carefully, will only get you there if your compass is compensated, that is, adjusted for your boat. And that's our next subject.

PRACTICE (5)

Using the compass rose shown in fig. 31, work the following problems graphically:

1. Find the magnetic courses when true courses are:
(a) 355   (b) 320   (c) 293   (d) 255   (e) 105

2. What is your true direction *from* the objects that give these magnetic bearings:
(a) 058   (b) 152   (c) 175   (d) 192   (e) 097

ANSWERS (5)

1. (a) 010   (b) 335   (c) 308   (d) 270   (e) 120
2. (a) 223   (b) 317   (c) 340   (d) 357   (e) 262

6. Compass Adjusting

To steer a course or to take a bearing you use a magnetic compass. Only in a few places does such a compass point to true north. Everywhere else you have to correct that error—the variation—by adding and subtracting, literally or graphically.

That's fairly simple. But the result will be accurate only if the compass on your boat really points to magnetic north.

And that's very unlikely. It may happen on a plastic or wooden rowboat, or a Bahamian sloop with rocks for ballast and rope for rigging. On most vessels structural parts, hardware, the engine, electrical circuits, and electronic gear will cause another compass error: deviation.

You can look at it this way: Acted upon only by the magnetic field of our planet, all compasses at a given locality will point in the same direction—magnetic north. The difference between true north and magnetic north is the variation. In the same place on-board influences will make the compasses on different boats point in different directions. The difference between the readings of your compass and an undisturbed one, which would point to magnetic north, is your deviation. In short: Variation goes with the place, deviation with the vessel. You can remember that by the *a* in variation and place, the *e* in deviation and vessel.

How do you allow for the magnetic influences that disturb your compass? Get rid of them. I don't mean throw your engine overboard, or replace your iron keel with rock ballast. No, adjust the compass to cancel the deviation-causing magnetic field aboard.

Here's why. Unlike variation, deviation changes on every heading of your craft. You can't just add 5 degrees or subtract 5 degrees. You may have to add 5 degrees on one heading, 10 on another, subtract 4 on yet another, and so on all around the compass.

It gets even more complicated when you take a bearing. The correction doesn't depend on the measured bearing, but on the heading on which you have taken the bearing.

It isn't obvious why the deviation should change on every heading. But think of all the magnetic influences aboard as concentrated in one spot. Your engine here, your gas tank there, the radio in the corner all add to one single magnet. Then as the vessel changes heading all around in a circle, the disturbing magnet will circle the compass, pulling or pushing the card this way or that.

On most craft this imaginary magnet will be near the fore-and-aft line. Reasons: Boats are longer than wide, and most of the disturbing gear is near the keel line. So usually the error will be least when the boat heads about north or south, magnetic. Then the disturbing magnet and the earth's magnetic field are more or less in line. The error will be greatest on headings of near east or west, magnetic.

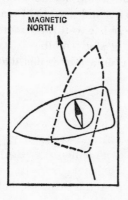

40. The needle of a compass will point to magnetic north however you turn the housing of the compass. In the same way, on a magnetically neutral vessel the needle will point to magnetic north (arrow) regardless of the heading of the boat.

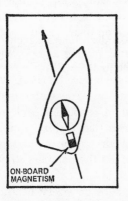

41. A single bar magnet here represents the sum of all magnetic disturbances aboard. When the vessel's heading brings that magnet in line with the compass needle, the compass reading is not disturbed. The magnet only weakens (or strengthens) the magnetic field of earth. On this heading the deviation is zero.

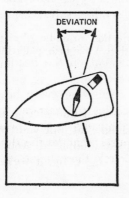

42. On this heading the on-board magnetism, represented by the bar magnet, pulls the compass needle to the right of its undisturbed position. The compass needle will point to the east of north, about 30 degrees in the sketch. On this heading you will have 30 degrees easterly deviation.

All the disturbing magnets aboard imagined as one magnet gives a clue to how we can get rid of the disturbances. Place a magnet of the same strength in such a position that it opposes the disturbing magnet. Practically, two magnets are used to this end. One is placed parallel to the fore-and-aft line, the other at right angles to it.

With this scheme any skipper can adjust his own compass on a wooden or plastic hull. On steel hulls, and that would include ferro-cement craft, more correctors—two soft iron spheres and a vertical magnet—have to be placed properly. That work is best left to a professional compass adjuster unless you are willing to make a study of it.

You may be tempted to call in an adjuster even on a nonferrous craft.

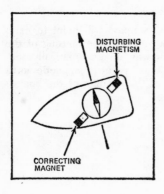

43. Theoretically, the disturbing magnetism could be corrected by placing an opposing magnet at the right spot.

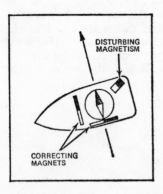

44. Practically, correction for on-board magnetism is easier with two magnets, placed as shown.

He'll go through the same steps you can take yourself and charge you several times the price of this book. You can stand that, but your professionally compensated compass is not going to stay adjusted. Another radio aboard, a new gas tank, a nearby stroke of lightning, a welding job—all will make a new adjustment necessary.

So you might as well learn the art of compass adjusting. Especially since you may need it on a cruise, far from the nearest adjuster.

Reading about it and doing it for the first time, it may seem complicated. It isn't really, if you follow a system. You place two magnets if your compass does not have built-in compensators. If it has,

Basis of compass adjustment with two magnets.

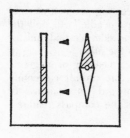

45. Magnet parallel to compass needle attracts both ends equally, has no turning effect.

46. Magnet parallel to compass needle repels both ends equally, has no turning effect.

47. Magnet at right angles to compass needle—one end attracts, the other repels the needle, makes it turn.

you turn two screws. But don't fiddle. The chance of hitting the right combination is no greater than the chance of tuning a piano if you are tone-deaf.

Whether your compass has built-in compensators, or external magnets, start with a survey of the compass and its surroundings.

The compass has to be solidly mounted on the boat. You can't compensate a compass that'll sit here today and 1 foot over tomorrow. The center line of the compass must be exactly parallel to the keel line of

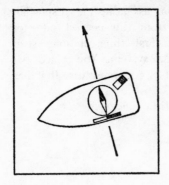

48. Practical compass adjusting. Step 1: Since on most vessels deviation on west and east headings is greatest, it is dealt with first.

The vessel is put on an exact magnetic west (or east) heading. The needle of an undisturbed compass would now point athwartships. An athwartship correcting magnet, being parallel to the needle, will have no effect.

A fore-and-aft correcting magnet, at right angles to the compass needle, will pull the compass needle to one side. Turned end for end, it will pull it to the other.

With the vessel on a heading of magnetic west (or east), the fore-and-aft correcting magnet is moved—toward the compass or away—until it makes the compass read exactly 270 (or 090).

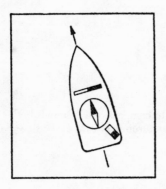

49. Practical compass adjusting. Step 2: After compensating the compass error on magnetic west (or east) heading, the north/south errors are dealt with.

The vessel is put on an exact magnetic north (or south) heading. The needle of an undisturbed compass would now point fore and aft. The fore-and-aft correcting magnet already in place, being parallel to the compass needle, has minimal effect.

An athwartship correcting magnet, at right angles to the compass needle, will pull it to one side. Turned end for end, it will pull it to the other.

With the vessel on a heading of magnetic north (or south), the athwartship correcting magnet is moved—toward the compass or away—until it makes the compass read exactly 360 (or 180).

your boat. If the compass is mounted on the center line, you may be able to sight it on the bow staff or stern staff, or on a sailboat forestay or permanent backstay. If you mount the compass with the lubber's line off, all courses will be off. If the compass is mounted to one side of the center line of the boat, the lubber's line and the pivot of the card must be exactly parallel to the fore-and-aft line.

Don't trust right angles of shelves or bulkheads. For eye appeal they are often slightly curved. Use string, tape measure, and carpenter's square in combination to get the lubber's line straight.

For fastening the compass use brass, not steel, screws and washers.

An externally gimbaled compass should be centered in the gimbal rings, and they should have no play.

Radio, direction finder, echo sounder should be in their permanent mountings. Nothing that can affect the compass should be near it; tools, pocket radios, camera equipment all have to be kept away from the compass. If the compass is mounted on a bulkhead, don't overlook such gear on the far side.

An aircraft "swings" for compass correction by having its tail hauled around. On the water it's usually easier to run predetermined courses to "swing ship."

So you will have to find an area out of traffic and free of current where you can run half-mile courses in an east-west and north-south direction. The wind should be calm when you make the runs. The absence of wind, current, and seas makes your courses coincide with your headings. You adjust your compass on different headings. To get these headings you steer the courses.

To get these courses while actually working on the compass you have a choice of several methods. My favorite is a helper with a hand bearing compass. The helper doesn't have to become a compass adjuster.

First you'll have to find a good observation spot for your helper. The bearing compass has to be held or fastened exactly on the center line of the boat. If you can find a spot near the stern where the bow staff or forestay is clearly visible, fine. Otherwise station the observer in the forepart and have him sight the stern staff or backstay. Some midship object, perhaps on the deckhouse, will serve as a backsight and keep the compass on the center line of the boat. Or you may drive a tack on the center line as a guide for holding the bearing compass.

Your helper's job is to direct you on the desired course and keep you on it. When the helper sights over the stern, you are, of course, steaming the reciprocal course from the one shown on the bearing compass. That shouldn't be difficult. The courses will always be the same: 000, 090, 180, and 270 magnetic. Magnetic means as shown by an undisturbed compass. Is your bearing compass in an undisturbed area? Except next to a wire stay, or directly above an anchor winch, the compass usually isn't disturbed. You can quickly make sure. Sight on a point, at least half a mile away, that bears 000 or 180. Move the hand bearing compass a foot to the left and right. The reading should stay the same. Move it a foot fore and aft. Then sight a distant object that bears 090 or 270 and repeat the moving of the compass. If the bearings don't change, you have found a magnetically neutral spot.

All that remains by way of preparation is a code of signals. Bearing compasses are easily read to 1 degree; with a little understanding between bearing taker and helmsman it's an easy matter to steady on these courses. When on course, you may discover a landmark of opportunity dead ahead and steer for that.

Another good method for getting courses for compass adjustment on inland waters is from the chart. Get out a large-scale chart of the area. Draw mental courses parallel and at right angles to magnetic north (from the inner compass rose on the chart). You'll find several that end at a conspicuous, charted object. The most useful symbols are shown in the illustration. The one you'll see the most often is the circled dot of the landmark. The nature of the mark is always given, in plain language or abbreviated. For example: mast, spire, tower (TR), monument (MON), cupola (CUP), tank, chimney (CHY), flagstaff or flagpole (FS, FP), radio tower (R TR), television tower (TV TR).

Having found some possibly useful landmarks, step on deck and locate the actual objects. That, by the way, is a great exercise in chart reading. For starting points buoys—leaning diamond above a dot on the chart—docks, and centers of bridge spans will do nicely. If you are very lucky you'll find two ranges. There might be a buoy in front of a distant landmark exactly on the course you intend to steer—a range ahead. On the reverse course you can still keep them in line—a range astern.

Often you won't find such ready-made ranges on the chart. But as soon as you start steering the course for a mark you'll find it lines up with some object in the background (or foreground) to give you a range. It might be a tree lining up with a tank, or a flagpole lining up with a gable.

If you are working in an area away from other boats, you may even plant your own range. A plastic bottle, a string and rock for anchor, will make a temporary buoy. But pick it up when you're through. The string could wrap itself around somebody's propeller.

Professional adjusters use a number of other references. One is the bearing of the sun calculated for the exact date and time of observation. It looks very scientific but ranges will serve you as well with less trouble.

Now let's proceed with the actual adjustment of a compass with built-in compensators. You'll need a nonmagnetic screw driver for the adjusting screws. Look for them. On some models they may be hidden by a housing that has to come off for adjusting. There will be a screw on the fore or aft end of the compass (or both) which may be marked E&W, and a screw or two on the side of the compass, possibly marked N&S.

A dime will fit some of the adjusting screws. For others it's not hard to whittle a wooden screw driver from a piece of hardwood. That's the only tool you'll need.

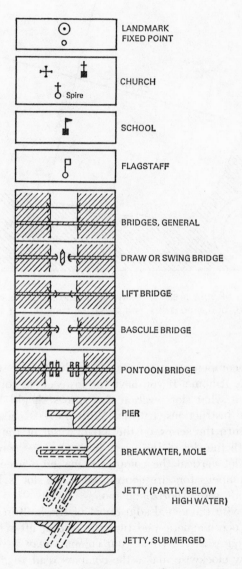

50. Chart symbols: man-made structures.

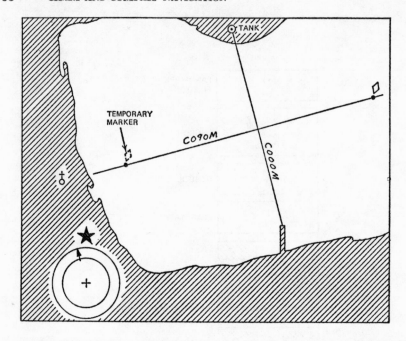

51. Detailed chart of your area will show land- and seamarks on the magnetic courses (090, 270, 000, and 180) you need for runs during compass adjustment.

Next set the compensators to zero. You don't have to unship the compass and take it home. If you have the instructions for this compass, they'll tell you in what slot position the screws should be set. If you have not got the instructions, try this. With the boat headed magnetic north or south, turn the screw on the left or right of the compass. Say you find that with the slot of the screw horizontal the compass is about right; with the slot vertical the compass seems 20 degrees or more off. Obviously the compensators are neutral when the slot is horizontal. Set the forward or aft screw horizontal too.

Now proceed with the actual adjustment of the built-in compensators.

Step 1: Head 090 magnetic and turn the fore or aft screw until your compass reads 090 exactly. At first your compass may have read 100. If turning the screw clockwise makes the compass read 105, you are going the wrong way. Turn it counterclockwise.

Take your time. If you use the bearing compass method, have your helper confirm that you are right on course. Otherwise check your range.

If it's more convenient to make the first run on 270 magnetic, do so; but don't start with a north or south run.

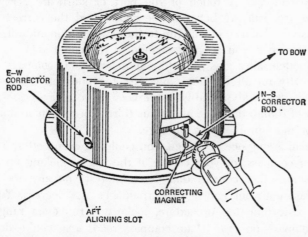

52. Compass with built-in compensating magnets. In this popular Ritchie compass the compensating magnets are in neutral position when the adjusting slots are horizontal. As in all compensating systems, the magnets that remove deviation on east and west headings are forward and aft of the compass card; the magnets that remove deviation on north and south headings are on the sides of the compass, port and starboard. (Internal compensating magnets change angle, rather than distance from the compass; the effect is the same.)

Step 2: Head 180 magnetic. Turn the adjusting screw at the *side* of the compass clockwise or counterclockwise until the compass reads 180 exactly.

If it's more practical to make this run to the north, head 000.

In theory the two adjustments are totally independent and your compass should now be adjusted. With practical magnets—in the compensators and the compass card—we have to do a little more work.

Step 3: Head 270 magnetic. (If your first course was 270, head now 090.) Turn the fore or aft screw to remove *one half* the error on this course. Example: At first when you steadied on this heading your compass may have read 272. Make it read 271, halfway between the shown and the correct heading.

During this run you will have much time left over. Use it to turn switches on and off. The compass should not change when electric windshield wipers, compass light, cabin lights, radio, etc. are on. If you find a change, move the offender, say the radio. The wires to the compass light should be twisted, not running parallel to one another and thereby creating a magnetic field when direct current flows through them.

Step 4: Head 000 magnetic. (If your second course was 000, head 180.) Turn the screw at the side of the compass to remove *one half* the error on this heading. Example: At first on this leg the compass may have read 358. A touch of the port or starboard screw should bring it to 359, halfway between the shown and the correct heading.

Again use the balance of this run to turn switches on and off, and take corrective action if you see any change in the compass.

On a wooden, fiber glass, or aluminum boat your compass will now point correctly on all headings, not just the ones on which you adjusted. The error will probably not exceed 1 or 2 degrees. According to our rule of thumb that'll be about one third of a mile in 10 miles. Good enough for most problems in pilotage.

If you plan a long ocean voyage, you could do even better. You could adjust your compass for your course at the risk of picking up a degree more on some other courses that don't interest you anyway. Say you have worked out your course to Bermuda as 134 degrees. You could, after the basic four-step procedure, make one run on a range—or by bearing compass—on 134. If the compass reads 134, you're done. If it doesn't, you could fiddle until it does. Personally, I'd leave it alone and remember the compass reading, say 136. That's the course I'd steer, 136, by compass. And I wouldn't rely on the compass alone to get me there, but use all the electronic help and celestial sights I could get.

When your compass lacks built-in compensators you can still adjust it yourself. Instead of twiddling two screws, you place two bar magnets where they'll do the job.

You can buy ready-made correcting magnets for about $5 a pair in marine hardware stores. You might also find magnetic rods, wires about the thickness of a pencil lead. In either, the length of the magnets should match the diameter of the compass card. Four-inch magnets for a 4-inch card. If you can't find the rods in a store, try to talk a compass adjuster out of them. They may come painted red on one end. All the red ends in a bundle must face the same way. Even without paint you can align them quickly by their effect on the compass. They should all attract or repel the compass.

Compass adjusters often prefer the rods. They let you make the magnet as weak or as strong as fits the available space. Ready-made bars may have to be placed inconveniently far from the compass to get the proper adjustment.

The rods, in my experience, rust rather badly. So I pack them in grease and place them in a copper tube.

The preparation for the adjustment is the same as that described for a compass with built-in compensators. Everything in its permanent place, tools etc. removed, axis of compass parallel to keel, compass solidly mounted with brass screws. You arrange for a helper with bearing compass at a magnetically clean spot, or find landmarks and ranges to give you exact headings in magnetic N, S, E, and W.

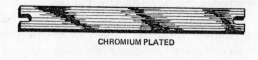

CHROMIUM PLATED

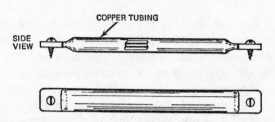

COPPER TUBING

SIDE
VIEW

53. Compensating magnets for a compass that lacks built-in correctors. Top: ready-made bar. Bottom: magnetic rods in copper tube with flattened ends.

You will need some tape for temporary fastening of the magnets, and four brass screws—and the necessary tools—for their permanent mounting.

Here is the tested method of placing external magnets to compensate your compass.

Step 1: Head 090 magnetic. (If it's more convenient from your starting point to run west, head 270 magnetic, but don't start adjustment on a north or south course.) Keep one correcting magnet at least 6 feet away from the compass. Place the other bar magnet either left or right of the compass, about level with the card, exactly in the fore-and-aft line and so that the center of the magnet is in line with the center of the card. Now move the bar magnet toward or away from the compass to make it read exactly 090. If at first the compass read 100 and now reads 105, turn the magnet end for end.

Measure all the distances and angles to make sure your geometry is true. Check that you are exactly on the wanted heading. Then tape the magnet in place.

Step 2: Head 180 magnetic. (If it's more practical to make this run north, head 000 magnetic.) When on course, slide the second magnet—fore or aft of the compass—about level with the card, exactly in the athwartship line (at right angles to the fore-and-aft line and the first-placed magnet) and so that the center of the magnet is in line with the center of the card. Now move the magnet toward or away from the compass to make it read exactly 180. Reverse the magnet if it makes the reading worse.

You can see that moving the magnets toward or away from the compass has taken the place of turning adjusting screws in a compass with built-in compensators. Reversing the bar magnets takes the place of turning the screws in the opposite direction. With built-in compensators—and the compass properly aligned in the fore-and-aft line—you don't have to worry about centering the magnets and getting them exactly in the fore-and-aft line or at right angles to that line. It's all done for you.

But it's still fore-and-aft magnets, or their adjustment screws, that control the adjustment on E/W headings; athwartship magnets, or their adjustment screws, control the adjustment on N/S headings.

You minimize the remaining small errors as follows:

Step 3: Head 270 magnetic. (If your first course was 270, head 090 magnetic.) Slide the fore-and-aft-placed magnet parallel to itself, moving it left or right a bit to remove *one half* of the error on this heading. Example: When you first steadied on this heading the compass read 268. Slide the magnet until it makes the compass read 269, halfway between the shown and the correct heading. Screw this magnet in place.

During the rest of this run work the switches to make sure the circuits they control don't affect the compass.

Step 4: Head 000 magnetic. (If your second course was north, head 180 magnetic.) Slide the athwartship magnet parallel to itself, fore or aft, to remove *one half* of the error on this heading. Example: At first on this leg the compass may read 003. A slight movement will make it read between 001 and 002, halfway between the first shown and the correct heading. Screw this magnet in place. Again work the switches.

Your compass is now compensated.

On sailboats you may have one more problem. When the boat heels, the compass in its gimbals remains horizontal while the magnetic field of all the disturbing influences aboard lists to one side or the other. So a sailboat on a given heading may show a different compass reading on the port tack and on the starboard tack. When she rolls, perhaps sailing before the wind, her card may swing back and forth.

If the condition is serious, it can be taken care of after the other adjustments have been made.

Try this: Place a bar magnet vertically under the middle of her compass. In the northern magnetic hemisphere the end that attracts the north end of your compass card should be uppermost. Make a north or south run when conditions make her roll, and raise the magnet until the card becomes steady. Secure this magnet well; should it tilt or flop it would upset your compass.

Occasionally a compass will resist your best efforts at compensation. I'd first look for something really strange, such as a steering wheel of the automobile variety. The steel reinforcements under the plastic covering may be magnetic.

Then I'd make another survey of the vicinity of the compass. Before I'd take out some wiring or replace steel parts with brass or bronze ones, I'd explore the compass area with my hand bearing compass. When you get it near something magnetic its card turns.

Then, still before going to much trouble, I'd unship the compass to find out if perhaps a foot to one side or the other it doesn't behave perfectly normally.

A radio or television repair shop will demagnetize any parts you bring in. It's the work of three minutes and shouldn't cost very much.

If cost doesn't matter too much, there is another solution—a master compass, installed somewhere far away from the usual magnetic influence of electronic gear and instrument panels, with repeaters that are not moved by nearby magnetism. You can have a repeater at the steering station, one on the flying bridge, and one—upside down—above your bunk to watch your helmsman's performance. After installation of the master which includes compensation you have nothing to worry about until something magnetic gets stored near the master compass. Then it and all its slaves will go off.

So even with these clever compasses, and much more with the regular ones, you have to check all the time.

You don't have to mount any great production for that. All you do is read the compass when you need it least, when you are perfectly sure of your course. Running from one buoy to the nearby next one, steering on a range, or in a channel so narrow you couldn't be wrong, read your compass and compare it with the magnetic course on the chart.

Returning between the same buoys, on the same range, or the same narrow channel, read the course again. The compass should read the exact reverse course. If the buoyed channel from the yacht club to the first official buoy tends 175 magnetic, on your return trip your compass should show 355. If it doesn't, there's something wrong with the compensation of your compass.

A Nova Scotia lobsterman told me his secret of compass correction. "Keep a wet glove under the compass at all times."

"Fresh water or salt?" I asked practically.

"Salt. Fished out of this place for forty years. Never a speck of trouble with my compass. To the sea buoy it's south-one-half-east. Coming in, fog or sleet, I steer north-by-east-one-half-east."

One doesn't have to be expert in the point system to see that $N \times E\frac{1}{2}E$ is not the reciprocal of $S\frac{1}{2}E$. It's about 017 against 174 degrees. The salt-water-soaked glove missed by about 23 degrees.

In pilotage waters you'll have frequent chances to check your compass. You may wonder what you'd do on an ocean crossing.

You could use sunrise and sunset for twice daily compass checks. My

Practical Boating gives a table for every day of every year for latitudes from Cape Horn to Londonderry. You would also use celestial navigation on such a voyage. As you'll see in the last part of this book, every sextant sight gives a bearing. So you can check your compass whenever you can take a sight of the sun, the moon, planets, or stars.

7. Buoys, Beacons, and Lights

Anyone who has traveled on a commonly used waterway has seen buoys—lighted and unlighted—beacons, and lights erected to help the navigator. He probably has heard bells, gongs, whistles, and stationary foghorns.

On any nautical chart you'll see diamonds, triangles, purple circles, and other symbols that stand for these aids.

It all seems terribly complicated and takes up one third of the booklet of symbols, Chart No. 1.

Even if you don't know port from starboard, you can with a little effort get a sound working knowledge of aids to navigation you are likely to find in your cruising waters.

You have to know left from right. The more nautical port and starboard is easily remembered. A vessel's running light is red on her left side; port wine is red. Hence the jingle "There's red port left." A vessel's running light is green on her right, starboard side. So other people remember "A bright [for right] green star."

Then you have to remember four chart symbols and what they stand for.

54. Basic chart symbols for buoys, beacons, and lights.

BUOY — *Floating* aid to navigation is shown on the chart by sloping diamond above a dot. The dot marks the location of the buoy. The diamond may slope to right or left.

BEACON — *Fixed* aid to navigation, a board or arrow on a pole for example, is shown on the chart by a triangle. Its center marks the location. Contrary to everyday use, beacon means an *unlighted* aid, a daymark.

LIGHT — *Lighted* aid to navigation is shown on the chart by black dot inside larger purple dot or under a purple torch. The black dot marks the location of the light. A fixed beaconlike structure that carries a light is shown as a light. A lighted buoy adds the purple dot or torch to its black dot.

But what about colors and shapes of these aids? The general rule for waters of the United States and Canada is simple. You will find red aids on the right (starboard) side of the channel when you return from seaward. Memory aid: Red, Right, Returning.

This rule applies in coastal waters, on navigable rivers including the so-called Western Rivers, streams marked by the Uniform State Waterway Marking System, the Intracoastal Waterway, the Great Lakes, and the Tennessee Valley waterways.

The universal rule needs a definition on what returning means. When you enter a harbor from seaward, that's obviously returning. Going upstream in any river that eventually runs into the sea is obviously also returning. That's still true of Western Rivers. But tradition there names the banks left or right as you would have them going down the river. On the Mississippi, for instance, going from New Orleans toward St. Louis, upriver, you'd be returning. So you'll have red aids on your right hand. But they'd be on what by river convention is the *left* side of the channel.

State waterways consider going upstream returning even if the water runs into a lake that has no obvious outlet to the sea. At times an arbitrary decision has to be made as to what's upstream. Don't worry— it'll be clear enough. Red buoys and black buoys will be used in pairs and you run between them (keeping to your right).

The Intracoastal Waterway with its many connections to the sea needs some artificial definition of what returning means. Going to Key West, Florida, or to Brownsville, Texas, is considered returning.

The same convention will see you through passages, say between the shore and an off-lying island, along the coast. In such passages on the Atlantic coast, consider going generally south as returning. On the Gulf Coast, going generally north and west is returning. On the Pacific coast, going north is returning. So add Alaska to Key West and Brownsville, and you'll have that rule down too. Or, if you prefer, think of coasting in a clockwise direction as returning.

The Great Lakes follow the general rule. Proceeding from the outlet of any one lake is to return from seaward; so is entering port.

That one rule Red, Right, Returning—with a few conventions added— tells you on which side to expect red navigational aids. More important: it tells you on which side to leave an isolated buoy or marker. If it's red and you are returning, you leave it on your right (starboard) side.

Obviously, black aids will be on your left (port) hand when you are returning. You'll leave black buoys on your left.

Equally obviously, going toward the sea, downriver, red aids will be on your left.

At times colors are hard to distinguish at a distance. So daymarks and unlighted buoys of different colors may have different shapes. Red aids will have pointed tops: Daymarks may be triangles, never squares; unlighted buoys will have cone-shaped tops. Such a buoy is called a nun, abbreviated N. Numbers on red aids will always be even.

Black aids will have flat tops: Daymarks may be square, never triangular; unlighted buoys will have flat tops. Such a buoy is called a can, abbreviated C. Numbers on black aids will always be odd.

At night red aids will show red (or white) lights. Lighted black aids will show green (or white) lights. Don't worry about white lights being used on both red and black aids. With a chart you'll always be able to tell whether the buoy is red or black.

(On the Western Rivers red buoys that flash white will always flash two flashes, black buoys single flashes.)

Here then is the basic scheme:

RETURNING FROM SEA (entering harbor, going upstream, coasting, or following Intracoastal Waterway clockwise)

	LEFT (port)	RIGHT (starboard)
Color of aid:	Black (Trim: green)	Red
Number:	odd	even
Unlighted buoy:	can	nun
Daymark:	square	triangle
Light:	green (or white)	red (or white)
On chart:	black	red (or white)

Perhaps you could use "odd, square green-black can" as a memory aid. On charts that for economy don't use the full range of colors, red buoys are left white. On other charts their red is the purple of lights.

Channels are often marked by strings of aids—lighted and unlighted buoys, daymarks, finger markers pointing toward the channel, etc.— on both sides of the channel and forming unmistakable gates. At other places the aids are staggered, marking now the port, now the starboard limit of the channel. Where the danger to navigation is on one side of the channel only, you may find only that side buoyed.

Yet another way is to mark the middle of the channel. That can't be done with black and red buoys—the black buoy for upriver traffic would at the same time have to be red for downriver navigation. So black and white vertically striped navigational aids are used (abbreviation BWVS). You might also find only BW next to a symbol that shows the vertical stripe. Cans or nuns may be used interchangeably, but daymarks are characteristic octagons, never triangles or squares.

Since these aids would have to be both odd and even, numbers are never used. Letters are optional. Only white lights are used on mid-

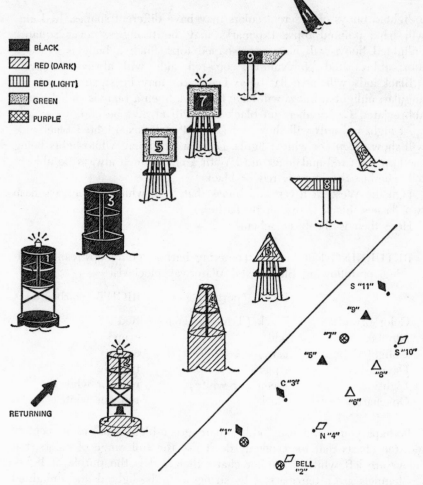

BLACK
RED (DARK)
RED (LIGHT)
GREEN
PURPLE

RETURNING

S "11"

"9"

"7"

"5"

S "10"

"8"

C "3"

"6"

"1"

N "4"

BELL
"2"

55. Basic United States aids to navigation. How they look on the chart (right) and on the water (left).

On your right hand, "returning," you'll have red, even-numbered, pointed aids with red (or white) lights.

At the channel entrance 2 is a lighted bell buoy; 4 a cone-topped buoy, a nun (N); 6 a beacon or daymark, fixed and unlighted, triangular—i.e. pointed; 8, a finger marker, painted in two shades of red, points to the channel, another beacon or daymark; 10, a spar buoy, painted red, may taper but—an exception to the rule—is not specially pointed. Spar buoys (S) are being phased out.

On your left hand, "returning," you'll have black, odd-numbered, flat-topped aids with green (or white) lights.

At the channel entrance 1 is a lighted buoy; 3 is a cylindrical buoy, a can (C); 5 is a square, i.e. flat-topped beacon—the number may be green on white, white on black, whatever makes it stand out best against the landscape; 7 carries a light, and so on the chart it is a light, not a beacon; 9, a green and black finger marker, points to the channel; 11 is a black spar buoy of the same shape as the red one.

channel markers. Regardless of the letter on the buoy, the light will flash letter *A* in Morse Code (abbreviated MoA), that is, short-long.

There is just one more basic situation: junction of two channels. The solution is clever: standard aids with red and black horizontal bands. The top band indicates the preferred channel. If it's red and you want the main channel, read it as a red buoy. If it's black and you want the main channel, consider it as a black buoy. Cans or nuns, square or triangular daymarks will be used to conform with the top band.

Again the buoy would have to be both odd and even, so numbers are out; letters are optional. The color of lights on junction buoys will conform to the top band—green or white for black, red or white for red—

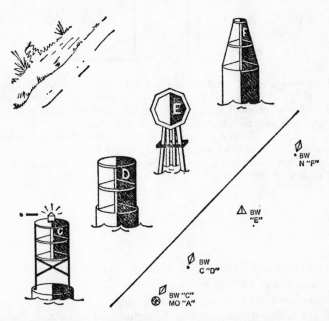

56. Mid-channel aids to navigation. How they look on the chart (right) and on the water (left). All these aids are black and white, vertically striped. Only white lights are used on them, always in a dot-dash sequence (Morse letter A). They carry letters rather than numbers. Cans and nuns may be used interchangeably; daymarks are octagonal.

and the light will always be interrupted quick-flashing. It will flash rapidly for four seconds, then be dark for about four seconds, and so on.

If you are a born sea lawyer, you may already have thought of one more situation. What buoys will they use where the Intracoastal Water-

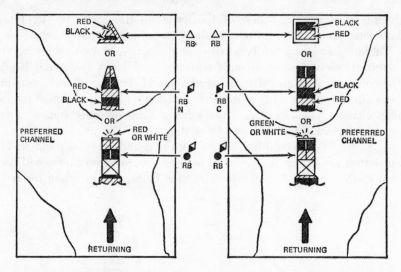

57. Aids to navigation at junctions are red and black, horizontally banded. The top color, shape, and color of light (if any) indicate the preferred channel.

LEFT: Preferred channel makes off to the left: Red top color, nun or triangular daymark tell you to leave these aids to the right.

RIGHT: Preferred channel makes off to the right: Black top color, can or square daymark tell you to leave these aids to the left.

CENTER: Chart symbols for junction buoys are the same whether preferred channel makes off left or right.

way with its artificial convention about returning runs into, or crosses, waters buoyed the natural way?

That has been taken care of very simply.

1. All Intracoastal Waterway aids, lighted or unlighted, have yellow trim. It might be just a yellow band on a buoy or pointer, or a yellow frame around the square or triangular daymarks.

2. Where the Intracoastal Waterway coincides with another waterway, shapes and colors are based on the primary waterway. But these aids carry yellow squares or triangles like the daymarks of the Intracoastal.

So you can have nuns with yellow squares or triangles, and cans with yellow squares or triangles.

When you enter the Muddy River from seaward you proceed by the Red, Right, Returning rule, ignoring the yellow markings.

Southbound on the Intracoastal, which in Georgia crosses the Muddy River, you ignore the color and shape of the river buoys. You navigate by their yellow squares and triangles only. You leave triangles on the right, squares on the left, as you have done before you came to the river crossing.

Edge-of-channel, mid-channel, and junction buoys take care of the vast majority of lights, buoys, and daymarks you'll see in the navigable waters around and in the United States.

But you should also recognize the handful of special buoys in use.

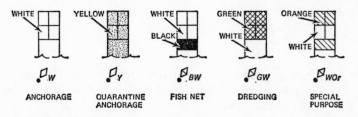

58. Special buoys mark areas for anchorage, warn of fish nets, dredging operations, etc.

Don't be too concerned about the multitude of possible light codes on aids to navigation. Here's a quick rundown.

Fixed (F) lights are rarely used; they don't stand out as navigational aids.

Flashing (Fl) lights—less than thirty flashes per minute—are by far the most common. Currently most lights flash every six, four, or two and a half seconds (ten, fifteen, or twenty-four times a minute). You don't need a stopwatch to tell them apart.

Quick-flashing (Qk Fl) lights—at least sixty flashes per minute—are used where special caution is needed, at turns in the channel, constrictions, wrecks.

Occulting (Occ) lights are eclipsed at regular intervals. Unlike a flashing light, an occulting one is on longer than off.

Interrupted quick-flashing (I Qk Fl or Int Qk Fl) lights—four seconds of quick flashing, then four seconds of darkness—as we have seen, light, red-and-black-horizontally-banded buoys at junctions. They also mark obstructions that can be passed on either side.

Morse A (MoA) lights—flashing short-long about eight times a minute—mark mid-channel black-and-white-vertically-striped buoys.

You need to recognize just two more terms.

Group (Gp) in combination with flashing or occulting means some repetition. GpFl (2) means flashes in sets of two. GpFl (1+2) means single flashes followed by double flashes, etc.

Alternating (Alt) always refers to a change in color. Alt Fl W G translates into alternate white and green flashes.

LIGHT   BELL   CAN   NUN   SPAR   BEACONS

59. Symbols used on Canadian charts are easy to interpret when you are famil-iar with the United States symbols for lights, buoys, and beacons. Lighted buoys add the purple torch to the chart symbol.

Cruising in Canadian waters will not present you with problems of buoyage. The buoys look a bit different both in nature and on the chart, but the system is the same.

The system of buoyage and the appearance of the buoys may be totally different in other countries. You may even have a Black, Right, Returning rule.

You don't have to go foreign to run into different buoyage. Waters not under Coast Guard control are buoyed by the Uniform State Water-way Marking System.

The regulatory markers, not unlike those used on highways, are clear enough. So are the red and black stream buoys. You'll find cans on both sides of the channel, but on the right side they are red, and the num-bers are still even on that side, odd on the left. Lights and reflectors are red and green, lights flashing.

So far so good. The difference of the system is in three buoys de-signed for waters that have no definite channels and to mark obstruc-tions that you might approach from more than one direction. Think of a lake without definite flow and scatter some islands in it. Then how would you apply a definition of returning to all the possible courses you could steer?

A *red-striped* white buoy simply means: Don't pass between buoy and nearest shore.

A *black-topped* white buoy means: Pass to the north or east of this buoy. You could remember that by thinking of the sooty-black north-east.

A *red-topped* white buoy means: Pass to the south or west of this buoy. You could remember that by thinking of the red-hot southwest.

All three buoys mark dangers, and so logically enough their lights, if used, would be quick-flashing (white). Reflectors are white.

In whatever waters you cruise, the best way to learn buoyage prac-tically is to compare the buoys you see—the more the better—with the ones on the chart.

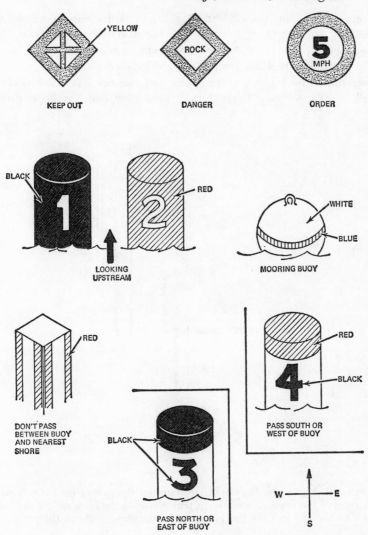

60. Uniform State Waterway Marking System.

When you are familiar with the different aids, try this postgraduate course. Figure out why this buoy, beacon, or light and not some other was used here. And why here and not some other place down the line. You'll discover why a pair of aids forming a range is used to mark a critical channel, especially where a crosscurrent can be expected. And that will make you a better helmsman. When you see a range on the chart, you'll be prepared for the current.

Your practice in mentally placing buoys will come in handy when something isn't right. Daymarks get knocked down, buoys do break loose or get dragged out of place. Sometimes a buoy isn't visible because some clown has tied his boat to it. (Strictly prohibited!)

Sometimes the buoys on the chart and the ones you see don't jibe at all. A channel may have shifted, or a new one has been dredged.

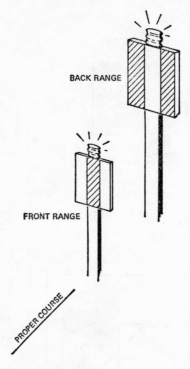

61. Principle of ranges. Only when you are on the proper course will you see the stripes of the front range line up with those on the back range; only on the proper course will you see the range lights one directly above the other.

I was in a minor distress off Guilford when my schooner started to leak rather badly. I needed a harbor and ran for the West River, clearly buoyed on my chart. There were some buoys around but none matched the chart. I spent a cold night at anchor pumping. Explanation: The buoys had been shifted to show the entrance to a new dock by the East River. The chart, although recent, did not yet show the change.

Sometimes you'll find the wrong aid. That happened to me off Nova Scotia. I was looking for Lurcher Shoal lightship to use as a departure

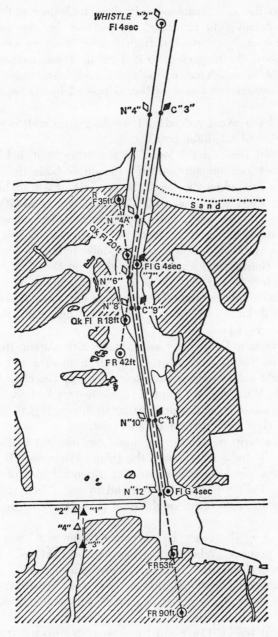

62. Buoyage at an inlet shows use of buoys, beacons, lights, and ranges (two fixed lights in line).

for a hop to the U.S. mainland. My dead reckoning put me within 2 miles of it. A sun sight confirmed my position. No sign of a lightship, an object not easily overlooked from 2 miles away or even 4. Then I spotted a buoy. Running close to it, I found it was temporarily replacing the light vessel. That undoubtedly had been announced in the *Notice to Mariners,* but like most lazy skippers I hadn't kept up with the latest.

You may have wondered when I would get around to talking about the best lights of all, lighthouses.

On the chart they usually look like any other light, a black dot that gives the exact location, surrounded by a purple blob; the letters Lt Ho are optional. But when the height is 114 feet, it's probably not just a lantern on a stick. If it's followed by a notation 17 M, it's a powerful light visible 17 miles on a clear night from 15 feet above the water. Remember to deduct 2 miles from the range for cockpit observation. For most pleasure craft it will be a 15-mile light.

The light characteristics are always given on the chart; for example, Nauset Beach light Gp Fl (3) 10 sec. No two lights in the same area will have the same characteristics. If you see three flashes every ten seconds you'll know it's Nauset, and not Cape Cod Fl 5 sec, nor Chatham Gp Fl (4) 30 sec.

Even in daytime lighthouses are valuable aids. Again, they will differ from one another in a wide area. Jupiter light is a red brick tower, Hillsboro light a black and white skeleton affair. The chart doesn't show that, though. We'll see in Chapter 11 where you find that information.

Here are some general rules for using buoys, lights, beacons, and other aids. They may save you some grief.

1. Plan your trip as a series of runs from one aid to the next. That may sound silly for a run on, say, the Inland Waterway. But even there a few minutes' planning is in order. Get a general idea of the direction of the route. Follow it quickly from end to end. Then you won't have to search for the next chart, or the inset that shows an area on a larger scale.

Running along the coast, laying courses from sea buoy to sea buoy is accepted practice. Where you can't see the next aid, work out the course to steer (and the distance) before you cast off.

2. Don't think navigational aids are only for deep-draft vessels. Disregarding channel markers, I have managed to paddle a canoe aground on a spoil bank along the Intracoastal Waterway.

3. Don't cut buoys. Don't run from buoy #2 to #6. Buoy #4 may mark a sunken rock ledge waiting for your keel.

4. Don't hesitate to make dogleg courses from one aid to the next. The fuel and time saved aren't worth the risk. Doglegs add very little to the straight-line distance. A 15-degree course change and return

to base course, for instance, adds only 4 per cent to the total distance.

5. Go close enough to buoys to identify them positively by their color, shape, sound apparatus, and numbers or letters. Many vessels have come to grief after a navigator had seen a buoy just where he expected it; but it was another buoy.

6. Lay courses *away from danger*. Rather than aiming for the next mark, keep to its safe side. Then poor steering, a small compass error, wind, or current won't have you in danger before you make that mark.

PRACTICE (7)

Refer to fig. 62 for the following questions.

1. How many lighted ranges do you see on this chart? Why are they used?

2. Why is buoy ✗2, besides being lighted, equipped with sound?

3. What's the purpose of N 4 and C 3?

4. Why is the 18-foot red light, south of buoy ✗8, quick-flashing?

5. Why is the light on buoy ✗7 green rather than white?

6. What sort of aid will you expect at buoy 1 and 3 at the left bottom part of the chart?

ANSWERS (7)

1. Three. All are to keep you in the narrow dredged channel. Entering, you'll first be guided by Qk Fl R 18 ft (front) and F R 42 ft (rear), then by F R 53 ft (front) and F R 90 ft (rear). Leaving, you'll be guided on the first leg by Qk Fl 20 ft (front) and F R 35 ft (rear); the fixed 53- and 90-foot lights serve as a range astern. On the second leg you'll have the entering range as a range astern and the whistle buoy ahead.

2. It's the outermost buoy for entering this inlet, the sea buoy. In poor visibility you should hear it even if you can't see it yet.

3. This pair of buoys funnels traffic into the channel.

4. As all quick-flashing buoys and lights do, it warns of imminent change in course.

5. White here could be confusing.

6. A black-white-green *square* daymark or a black and green pointer.

8. Tides

If your boating is restricted to man-made reservoirs, inland lakes, even the Great Lakes, much in this chapter won't concern you.

On the coast the skipper has to know about tides. "Coast" here is a stretchable word. In Troy, N.Y., well over 100 miles up the Hudson River, he'll still get 5-foot tides. In Quebec City, several hundred nautical miles from the open ocean, he'll still find 14-foot tides.

Tides are, strictly speaking, the regular up and down movements of the sea. Often the same word is used to mean the currents caused by these movements, ebb and flow. I'll talk about those in the next chapter.

The up and down movement is caused by the pull of moon and sun on the oceans of the rotating earth. The small but near moon exerts more than twice the tide-raising force of the large but distant sun.

At the times of new and full moon the two forces pull in the same direction; near those dates—usually a couple of days later—we get the highest tides of the month, spring tides. When the moon is at first or last quarter the two forces work against each other; near those dates we get the smallest tides of the month, neap tides.

There are other factors. The changing distance of the moon is one. When the moon is closest to earth—in perigee—the moon's attraction is greater than when it's at its farthest point—in apogee. When spring tides fall near the time of perigee, you can expect an extra large tide range. The range of a tide is the difference between low water and the next high water, or high water and the next low water.

Besides the many astronomical factors—"moon rides high" and "moon runs low" is another one—the shape and depth of ocean basins influence the tides. That explains the 30-foot ranges in the Bay of Fundy and the 2-foot ranges in the Gulf of Mexico.

The practical boatman in tidal waters wants to know how much water is supposed to be at such a spot at such a time.

He can find that out for charted tidal waters anywhere in the world. The tedious work has been done for him. When the survey for the chart was made, a tide gauge in the area recorded the state of the tide, the height of the sea level at the time, twenty-four hours a day.

All the raw soundings taken during the survey were brought to a common reference plane, the chart datum. Then the graphic record of the tide gauge was analyzed. The varying positions of moon and sun are known for any given time, so they can be correlated with the tides shown by the record.

Long before computers kept charge accounts and guided spacecraft to the moon, two tide-predicting machines—one in Washington, the other in Liverpool—could take the result of this analysis and give tide predictions for any day of any year at the location of the original tide gauge.

In the United States machine prediction started in 1885. In 1912 Tide Predicting Machine №2 was put into service and kept working until 1965. Since 1966 an electronic computer calculates the tide and sets the type for the tide tables.

In the United States, National Ocean Survey of the National Oceanic & Atmospheric Administration publishes these tables. They are sold by what you probably still call U. S. C&GS chart agents; current price per volume $2. Two volumes will interest the North American boatman: East Coast of North and South America (including Greenland), and West Coast of North and South America (including Hawaiian Islands). Two other volumes cover the rest of the world.

It wouldn't be practical to give daily tide predictions for every harbor up and down the coast. And it isn't necessary. Tide patterns hold over large areas. For example, all the places along the east coasts of the two Americas from the Arctic Archipelago to the islands at the edge of Antarctica, and including Greenland, Bermuda, the Bahamas, and the West Indies, can be found from the tides at only forty-eight reference stations. You'll find the tides for these stations in the East Coast tide tables.

In the same volume you get corrections that let you calculate the tides at about two thousand subordinate stations in the area. I'll show you also how to find tides at unlisted points, say your own dock.

Small-craft charts give similar tidal information for the area the chart covers and for the year of issue. An SC chart issued in September 1972 would show tides to September 1973, for example.

Tide tables show the times and heights of high and low waters. I'll show you a simple way to get the approximate water level between these extremes.

Don't object to the word "approximate" in the last sentence. All tide predictions, however accurate they may look in print, are approximate. They are based on average conditions. Wind, barometric pressure, and—where they apply—abnormal river levels will influence the actual tides.

You can readily see how a wind blowing into a bay will pile up the water and hamper its outflow during the ebb. So both high and low waters are likely to be higher. And their times will be later. An offshore wind will have the opposite effects.

Less obvious is the influence of the atmospheric pressure. But it's there. High pressure literally weighs on the water, depresses its level, and pushes it up in an area of low pressure. Here is a rule of thumb: A drop of 1 inch in barometric pressure will raise the tide about 1 foot. And a rise above normal will depress the tide by the same amount. Most of the time you won't notice the change or will fail to connect it with the barometric pressure.

It becomes very noticeable during hurricanes, when the low pressure adds to the height of the storm-whipped, shoreward-driven seas. On the Gulf of Mexico, where the tidal range is small, the barometric effect may dominate the tide pattern in some places. Spring and neap tides are masked by it; high waters may become lower than normal low waters; at low tide offshore sand bars unexpectedly dry when a high glass combines with a strong offshore breeze.

In estuaries the tide tables take seasonal changes of river level into account. But droughts and freshets will upset the predictions not only of the levels of high and low waters, but also their times.

Even away from rivers, with normal weather, you'll often think the predictions grossly off. The tide table may tell you to expect high water at 11 A.M. At 2 P.M. the current is still coming in where you are. Are the tables wrong? Probably not. The current, strange as it may seem, can come from seaward after high water. Long after. Or it can run out after low water. Long after.

On the outer coast, the flood will begin at about the time of low water, end at about the time of high water. Then the ebb will begin; it will end at about the time of low water. In bays, channels, and rivers, "slack"—the time of change of current from flood to ebb, or ebb to flood—can't be predicted from the times of high and low water by any general formula.

The times of the "stand" of the tide—when the level stops rising or falling—are what's predicted in the tide tables.

Each page covers three months, so four pages per station are needed for the daily prediction for every reference point. Each month is divided into two columns; the days of the week are given in unmistakable abbreviations. Times are in local standard time—for Miami, for instance, the time at the 75° W meridian, Eastern Standard Time.

That means daylight-saving time is not used. When you are on fast time, summer time, Eastern Daylight Time, the predictions will be slow one hour. Add one hour to conform with your watch.

The tide tables use the four-figure, twenty-four-hour system, just as

MIAMI HARBOR ENTRANCE, FLA.

TIMES AND HEIGHTS OF HIGH AND LOW WATERS

	JANUARY					FEBRUARY					MARCH				
DAY	TIME H.M.	HT. FT.	DAY	TIME H.M.	HT. FT.	DAY	TIME H.M.	HT. FT.	DAY	TIME H.M.	HT. FT.	DAY	TIME H.M.	HT. FT.	DAY	TIME H.M.	HT. FT.
1 F	0442 1100 1718 2324	-0.4 2.7 -0.3 2.6	16 SA	0454 1106 1724 2336	0.0 2.1 0.0 2.0	1 M	0006 0618 1224 1842	2.4 -0.3 2.3 -0.6	16 TU	0542 1142 1800	0.1 1.9 -0.2	1 M	0500 1106 1724 2348	-0.5 2.5 -0.8 2.5	16 TU	0430 1024 1642 2306	0.1 2.5 -0.3 2.2
2 SA	0536 1154 1812	-0.3 2.6 -0.3	17 SU	0536 1148 1806	0.1 2.0 0.0	2 TU	0106 0718 1318 1942	2.3 -0.1 2.1 -0.5	17 W	0024 0624 1224 1848	1.9 0.3 1.8 -0.2	2 TU	0554 1154 1818	-0.2 2.3 -0.6	17 W	0506 1100 1724 2354	0.2 2.0 -0.2 2.1
3 SU	0030 0636 1248 1906	2.5 -0.1 2.5 -0.3	18 M	0018 0624 1224 1848	1.9 0.2 1.9 0.0	3 W	0218 0818 1418 2048	2.1 0.1 2.0 -0.4	18 TH	0118 0718 1312 1948	1.8 0.3 1.7 -0.1	3 W	0042 0648 1254 1918	2.3 0.0 2.1 -0.4	18 TH	0554 1148 1812	0.3 1.9 -0.1
4 M	0130 0742 1348 2012	2.4 0.1 2.3 -0.3	19 TU	0112 0712 1312 1936	1.9 0.3 1.9 0.0	4 TH	0324 0930 1530 2154	2.1 0.2 1.9 -0.3	19 F	0224 0824 1418 2054	1.8 0.4 1.7 -0.2	4 TH	0148 0754 1400 2024	2.1 0.2 1.9 -0.2	19 F	0042 0648 1242 1912	2.0 0.4 1.9 0.0
	0242	2.4					0330	1.9			2.0	20 SA	0148	2.0 0.3			

	JANUARY					FEBRUARY					MARCH				
				1518 2124	2.7		1606 2218	2.1									
14 TH	0342 0954 1606 2212	-0.3 2.3 -0.1 2.1	29 F	0336 0954 1606 2218	-0.8 2.7 -0.8 2.7	14 SU	0424 1030 1642 2300	-0.1 2.1 -0.3 2.0				14 SU	0318 0918 1536 2148	-0.1 2.2 -0.3 2.3	29 M	0348 0948 1606 2230	-0.5 2.7 -0.8 2.8
15 F	0418 1030 1648 2254	-0.1 2.3 -0.1 2.1	30 SA	0430 1036 1654 2312	-0.7 2.6 -0.7 2.6	15 M	0500 1100 1718 2342	0.0 2.0 -0.2 2.0				15 M	0354 0954 1606 2224	0.0 2.2 -0.3 2.2	30 TU	0436 1036 1700 2324	-0.3 2.5 -0.6 2.6
			31 SU	0518 1130 1748	-0.5 2.5 -0.7										31 W	0530 1130 1754	0.0 2.3 -0.6

TIME MERIDIAN 75° W. 0000 IS MIDNIGHT. 1200 IS NOON.
HEIGHTS ARE RECKONED FROM THE DATUM OF SOUNDINGS ON CHARTS OF THE LOCALITY WHICH IS MEAN LOW WATER.

63. Tide tables published by National Ocean Survey. Daily predictions for a reference station, called table 1.

the armed forces do. The first two figures mean hours, the second two figures minutes. So 0000 is midnight, 0001 is one minute later. To the hours from one to nine add a zero to make up four figures—0915 is 9:15 (A.M.).

Noon is 1200; 12:59 P.M. becomes 1259. One minute later, civilian and military usage begin to differ sharply. One o'clock becomes 1300 in military usage; two o'clock becomes 1400. Twelve is added to all afternoon and evening (P.M.) hours. One minute before midnight is 2359.

If you feel rusty in this way of writing time, check yourself on the following examples. Watch especially for the common mistakes of reading 1800 for 8 (instead of 6) P.M., and of subtracting an hour for daylight-saving time when you should add it.

The tide table gives:

16	0454	0.0
SA	1106	2.1
	1724	0.0
	2336	2.0

How would you put the times in a) Eastern Standard Time, b) Eastern Daylight Time?

You should get: a) 4:54 A.M., 11:06 A.M., 5:24 P.M., 11:36 P.M. and b) 5:54 A.M., 12:06 P.M., 6:24 P.M., 12:36 A.M. (Sunday). The last one was tricky. One hour after Saturday 11:36 P.M. is Sunday morning. Right?

This carry-over into the next day sometimes gives only three entries for one day in the tide tables in place of four. The tides get—very roughly—one hour later each day. You can see that the last tide of Sunday, January 17, would fall on Monday, January 18. Sunday would have only three entries in the tide tables.

The heights are given in feet and tenths in the tide tables. If you prefer you wouldn't be far off if you read the tenths for inches. You'd read 0.5 for 5 inches instead of 6. At worst you'd read 9 inches for 0.9, which is 10.8 or almost 11 inches.

The heights are given above the datum of the chart, which here is Mean Low Water. Practically, you add the height of the tide to the sounding on the chart to get the depth there at a given time. If the chart at a given spot shows 4 feet, while the tide level is 2.0, you will have 6 feet of water there.

You will notice from our example and the illustration that the tide tables don't specify whether a given time is the time of high or low water. You get that from the figures for heights. In our example, 0.0 must be low water, 2.1 and 2.0 must be high waters.

Occasionally you will find a minus sign before a low-water height. It means that this low water is *below* the level of the chart datum. You'll have less water than the soundings indicate. Example: Charted depth 4 feet, low water —0.5; you can expect 3.5 feet of water.

The range of a given tide is easily found. For example:

4	0130	2.4
M	0742	0.1
	1348	2.3
	2012	—0.3

Between 1:30 and 7:42 A.M. the water level drops from 2.4 to 0.1; the range is 2.3 feet. From 7:42 A.M. to 1:48 P.M. the tide rises from 0.1 to 2.3; the range is 2.2 feet. From 1:48 to 8:12 P.M. the level drops from 2.3 to zero and then some more to —0.3; range of this tide, 2.6 feet.

By the way, this pattern of tides is typical of tides on the Atlantic coasts of the United States and Canada and of coasts in many other parts of the world. Two high waters of approximately the same height are followed by two low waters of approximately the same height about equally spaced through the day, that is, about six hours between changes.

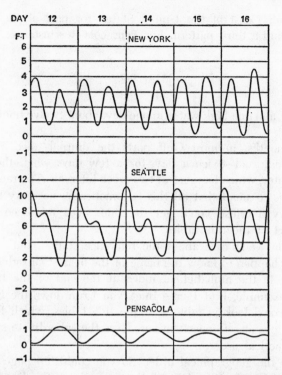

64. Tide patterns. Top: In about twenty-five hours two high waters of about the same height are followed by two low waters also of about equal height. Example: East Coast of North America.

MIDDLE: In about twenty-five hours two high waters of very different height are followed by low waters also of very different height. Example: West Coast of North America.

BOTTOM: In about twenty-five hours a single high water is followed by a single low water. Example: Gulf of Mexico coasts (at least during part of each month).

There are other patterns.

On the Pacific coasts of the United States and Canada, for example, a day's tides may be listed like this (for Seattle):

0212   8.7
0848   0.9
1554   11.1
2142   4.9

There are still two high and two low waters about equally divided into the day, but the high waters are of quite different height and so are the two low waters—0.9 as compared to 4.9. That last is the reason for the chart datum on this coast being Mean *Lower* Low Water.

On the Gulf Coast of the United States—for part of the month at least—you'll find a third pattern. For Pensacola, for instance, you might find:

0512   0.0
1742   0.9

Only one low and one high water in one day, about twelve hours between changes.

In most months, in most Gulf ports the diurnal—once a day—tide becomes semidiurnal—twice a day—for a few days when the moon is near the equator, which happens at two-week intervals. The range of tides in this area is so small that all this is, practically, not very significant.

Wherever you cruise you'll get the tides at a reference station in the front part of the tide tables.

Usually you won't care about the reference station, but some other place. If you happen to know the name of the nearest subsidiary station, you'll find it in the alphabetical index at the end of the tide tables. To find, for example, Fort Pierce Inlet, you'd run down the F's and get 2895. Then you'd look in table 2 of the tide tables, which follows the daily predictions at reference stations. Here the subordinate stations are listed in numerical order.

That's also the geographical order. So you could flip pages until you come to "FLORIDA, East Coast," then run down the lines until you land on 2895 Fort Pierce Inlet (breakwater).

Next to that you'll find the position (latitude and longitude), which sometimes helps you find an unknown station in a known area.

Bold type refers you to the reference station to use, here Miami Harbor Entrance. The next four columns, headed Differences, give the corrections to apply to Miami's daily predictions to get the data for Fort Pierce Inlet. Plus signs mean add; minus signs, subtract. Here you'll find that you should subtract fourteen minutes from time of high water, eighteen minutes from time of low water. You are supposed to add 0.1 foot—quite negligible—to the height of high water; low-water height is the same as in Miami.

Occasionally you'll find an asterisk in front of the height correction in place of a plus or minus sign. That means multiply. At Jupiter Inlet (2903), for instance, the ratio is 0.80. The tides, both high and low, are 80 per cent the height of Miami tides. When Miami lists 3.0 feet, it's supposed to be a 2.4-foot tide at Jupiter Inlet.

Small-craft charts show a great many stations in the facilities chart. Besides the approach depth and depth alongside, they list a simplified correction (to the nearest quarter hour) for every dock and marina. They also give the mean range of tides at these points. By comparing

TABLE 2.—TIDAL DIFFERENCES AND OTHER CONSTANTS

No.	PLACE	POSITION		DIFFERENCES				RANGES.		Mean Tide Level
		Lat.	Long.	Time		Height		Mean	Spring	
				High water	Low water	High water	Low water			
		° ' N.	° ' W.	h. m.	h. m.	feet	feet	feet	feet	feet
	FLORIDA, East Coast			on MIAMI HBR. ENT., p.118						
2891	Ponce de Leon Inlet------------------	29 04	80 55	+0 06	+0 20	-0.2	0.0	2.3	2.7	1.2
2893	Cape Kennedy-----------------------	28 26	80 34	-0 41	-0 41	+1.0	0.0	3.5	4.1	1.8
2894	Sebastian Inlet--------------------	27 52	80 27	-0 23	-0 31	-0.3	0.0	2.2	2.6	1.1
2895	Fort Pierce Inlet (breakwater)------	27 28	80 17	-0 14	-0 18	+0.1	0.0	2.6	3.0	1.3
2897	Fort Pierce (City Dock)-------------	27 27	80 19	+1 51	+2 11	*0.28	*0.28	0.7	0.8	0.3
2899	St. Lucie Inlet (Jetty)------------	27 10	80 09	-0 20	-0 21	+0.1	0.0	2.6	3.0	1.3
2901	Sewall Point, St. Lucie River-------	27 11	80 12	+1 34	+2 33	*0.40	*0.40	1.0	1.2	0.5
2903	Jupiter Inlet (near lighthouse)-----	26 57	80 05	+0 51	+1 09	*0.80	*0.80	2.0	2.4	1.0
2905	Port of Palm Beach, Lake Worth------	26 46	80 03	0 00	+0 12	+0.1	0.0	2.6	3.1	1.3
2907	Palm Beach (ocean)-----------------	26 43	80 02	-0 21	-0 18	+0.3	0.0	2.8	3.3	1.4
2909	Hillsboro Inlet--------------------	26 15	80 05	+0 13	+0 36	-0.2	0.0	2.3	2.7	1.2
	Fort Lauderdale									
2911	Bahia Mar Yacht Club-------------	26 07	80 06	+0 28	+0 32	-0.2	0.0	2.3	2.8	1.1
2913	Andrews Ave. bridge, New River-	26 07	80 09	+1 06	+1 28	-0.7	0.0	1.8	2.2	0.9

*Ratio.

65. **Tide tables.** Tidal constants for subordinate stations, printed in table 2, let you find times and heights of high and low water at places along thousands of miles of coast. The constants are to be applied to the daily predictions at the few dozen reference stations of table 1.

the range at any one dock with the mean range at the reference station, you can get a fair idea of the range of any specific tide. The mean range at Miami Harbor Entrance is 2.5 feet. If today's morning tide has a range of 3.7 feet, it's obviously a good spring tide. If the mean range at your dock is listed as 2.0 feet, you can expect around 3 feet there on this tide.

If your dock happens to be at or near one of the facilities listed on an SC chart or very close to one of the subsidiary stations in the official tide tables, fine. If not, you can get your own local corrections by observing a few tides. Several observations are needed to eliminate, as much as possible, the influence of barometric pressure and wind.

Find a sea wall or piling for your observation and attach a yardstick. The kind paint and hardware stores give away for advertising will do nicely. Then around the times of predicted high and low waters, at quarter-hour intervals or so, watch the water level.

Pay no attention whatever to the current.

At the times of high and low waters the change in level is very small. It may be totally obscured by the tiniest ripples. But the rise and fall before and after these extremes is the same. So if the level at eleven o'clock (falling) is the same as it was at nine o'clock (rising), then high water was halfway in between at ten o'clock.

A few general rules may help you find your own corrections. If you are farther from the source of tides than the nearest known station, your range is likely to be less, and both high and low waters will be later. Most of the difference in level is likely to be at high water. It's easier for most people to add and subtract than to work in ratios. That should make you favor a plus or minus correction over a ratio.

It's often useful to have a rough table in your head.

One simple trick is to add one hour to yesterday's high and low times. The average daily delay is closer to fifty minutes. But it's useless to worry about ten minutes here. The actual delay varies from about half an hour to one and one quarter hours. So just add an hour and you won't be far off.

There's another even more impressive and useful trick of mental tide calculation. It's based on this simple fact: At any one place, on the same phase of the moon high water will occur always at about the same time.

Say in your area on a full moon day the tide is high at eight in the morning. It will again be high at about eight in the evening on the same day. It will also be high at the same times on the next full moon, and on all full moons to come. Better yet, it will also be high at the same times on days of *new* moon.

In most places low water will be about six hours after high; that makes low water around two in the afternoon and two in the morning when the moon is new or full.

You can predict the tides for the day after full moon by adding one hour, or fifty minutes if you prefer. The next day it'll be again that much later. After about a week the tides will have switched. They now will be *low* at eight in the morning and evening, high at two in the morning and afternoon. The reason? Seven times the average delay of about fifty minutes is about six hours, the usual interval between high and low waters.

Seven days after full moon, the moon is at last quarter; seven days after new moon it's at first quarter. On these days you may want to start a new count, adding again an hour—or fifty minutes—per day. A week later you'll be back to new or full moon. Then you start the calculation all over.

For your location the basic tide table will look like this:

Day of	High Water		Low Water	
	A.M.	P.M.	A.M.	P.M.
Full Moon	8	8	2	2
Last Quarter	2	2	8	8
New Moon	8	8	2	2
First Quarter	2	2	8	8

In between these days add fifty minutes
or one hour for each day elapsed.

So all you have to remember is the time of high and low water on a full-moon day. Figures as simple as seven and one, or nine and three.

Any wall calendar will give you the phases of the moon. How close will you be on your times? You can check it yourself. You'll probably find that your maximum error will not exceed one hour, your average error is probably no more than one half hour.

How far will you be off in your estimate of the height of a tide by this crude formula? That'll depend on the range of the tide. If the range is 3 feet, and you're off a whole hour, your estimate will be 3 inches off. If the range is 4 feet, you'll be 4 inches off. If it's 8 feet, you'll be 8 inches off.

If you're only one half hour off in time, the error will be less than half that.

You've probably noticed that tide levels don't rise or fall uniformly. On a rising tide, for instance, very little happens in the first hour. Then the level rises at an increasing rate until half tide. At half time between low and high water the level will be halfway between low and high. Then the rise slows; in the last hour the level again changes little.

On a falling tide the change in rate is the same.

Set up a tide gauge where the range is 3 feet and the time of rise six hours. You'll get the following readings:

Hours:	LW	1	2	3	4	5	6
Inches:	0	3	9	18	27	33	36

On a similar falling tide you'll get the following readings:

Hours:	HW	1	2	3	4	5	6
Inches:	36	33	27	18	9	3	0

Looking closer at these figures, you'll notice a change in level of 3 inches, followed by one of 6, which increases to 9 in the hour before mid-tide. After mid-tide the 9-inch rate drops again to 6, and finally to 3 inches per hour.

On this 3-foot tide, all the rates were multiples of 3 inches. That leads to a general rule which lets you predict the water level at any time between low and high water, wherever their interval is about six hours, say between five and a half and six and a half hours.

TIDE RISING		TIDE FALLING	
Height of next HW minus		*Height of last HW minus*	
Height of last LW=H feet		*Height of next LW=H feet*	
TIME	LEVEL	TIME	LEVEL
Since LW	*Above LW*	*Since HW*	*Below HW*
Hours	*Inches*	*Hours*	*Inches*
LW	0×H	HW	0×H
1	1×H	1	1×H
2	3×H	2	3×H
3	6×H	3	6×H
4	9×H	4	9×H
5	11×H	5	11×H
6	12×H	6	12×H

Example: Range 3.0 feet; 4 hours after LW the level will be 9×3 inches above LW. 4 hours after high water the level will be 9×3 inches below HW; compare this with tide gauge that showed 9 inches above LW.

The formula is the same for rising and falling tides; all you have to remember are the figures. The zero and 12 are obvious. The 6 is easily remembered—half time, half level. I remember the 1 and 11, as practically nothing changes in the first and last hour. That leaves only the 3 and 9.

Perhaps the easiest way to remember is not by the numbers themselves, but by their differences, the rate of change in fall or rise:

Numbers: 0 1 3 6 9 11 12
Difference: 1 2 3 3 2 1

If you don't care to weigh down your brain with this, you don't have to. Table 3, Height of Tide at Any Time, in the tide tables gives the same information for intervals from four to more than ten hours, not just for about six hours.

You now know how to read tide tables, how to find tides at unlisted places, even how to estimate the times of high and low from a calendar. And you know how to estimate or calculate the water level at any time between high and low water.

What good is all that?

If you operate in shallow tidal waters, you'll be living tides. By shallow I mean shallow compared to the draft of your boat. An 8-foot channel is deep when you draw only 3 feet; the skipper of a ketch that draws 6 feet will worry; but the captain of a monster that draws 8 feet can still use it safely for perhaps eight hours out of every twelve. He'll just have to wait a couple of hours after low water. Then the tide will supply the margin of safety until perhaps two hours before the next low water, when the water gets again a bit thin.

If he has a choice, that captain is going to use this channel on a rising rather than a falling tide. If he runs aground on a shoal spot, the tide will soon float him free again. On a falling tide he would have to work himself off quickly—before the tide drops even more—or wait several hours for the return of the tide.

Do you like gunkholing, sticking your bow into bays and creeks where it has no business? Often the chart leaves such places without soundings. It's unlikely that you'll find tidal differences for such waters in the tide tables. Must you keep out? No, just make it a rule to explore only on a rising tide; and quit well before high water.

If there's enough water to float her, a masted vessel may slip under a fixed bridge at low tide where she might not go through at high.

These tricks are known as playing the tides.

A local skipper may advise you, "Just watch the tides." Perhaps he means the "watch" literally, in the sense of keeping your eyes open. On any shore—sandy, pebbly, cliffy—you'll find natural high-water marks. A terrace in the sand, wrack on the shingle, a black line on rocks, mussels on pilings—all are tide gauges to the savvy skipper.

You can play a game similar to playing the tides far inland where there are no tides. Wouldn't you feel silly having just gone the long way around an island in the Mississippi to meet a tug and barges coming out of the short cut? How did the tugboat skipper know it was safe? Local knowledge? Perhaps. More likely he looked at the last gauge he passed that showed him the stage of the river.

Anchoring in a strange place, or picking up somebody's mooring, a careful skipper will sound all around the boat. Say you find 5 feet; you draw only 3. Isn't that all right? It may be, if it's low tide right now. But if now the level is 2 feet or more above the next low tide, you'll be aground before long.

Depth at a dock is of the same importance. Dockmasters will assign you a space where you are supposed to be afloat at all times. But unattended docks and town wharves will have you sitting in the mud, or worse, unless you check. In some harbors all vessels take the ground at low tide. The secret there is to be in a spot where yours will enjoy her sitz bath. If in such a place you are lying to a dock, make sure she'll lean against the dock and not outboard. Giving her a list toward the dock by shifting weight or with a stout line ashore may do it. If possible, stay aboard until she gets ready to flop and help her make up her mind. And then stay a little longer, until the wake of a passing boat won't make her change her mind.

If you have cruised in areas of great tidal ranges, you'll know all about the use of spring lines to keep your vessel in place. And everyone has heard of clowns who tied a dinghy up in some place to come back and find her hanging straight down.

I too had heard the tale, and when I first docked in the notorious

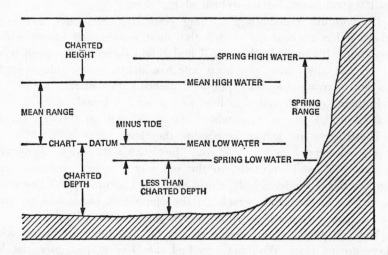

66. Tide levels. Depths on charts are measured from a low-water level, heights (and clearances under bridges, etc.) from a high-water level. The tide tables use the same reference plans as the chart.

To get the depth at any given time add the height of tide at the moment to the charted depth.

Mean range is the difference in level between Mean Low and Mean High Water. Spring range is greater than mean range, the tides rising higher and dropping lower.

Bay of Fundy I was all prepared. I don't mean I knew how to tie up in that monstrous rise and fall of water level. I used a dodge. I asked for permission to tie up to a local boat. The other boat would tend her lines and my schooner would ride up and down with her, both hulls protected by fenders between them.

That was a wise move. When I went ashore I had walked over the other vessel and down a plank. It must have been high tide. When I came back a few hours later the tops of my masts were below the level of the dock!

I'm not always that smart. Since 1962 I have calculated the tide tables for the *Yachtsman's Guide to the Bahamas*. Then one day in the Exumas

I rowed myself ashore. The tide was falling—no question about it—so I just hauled the dinghy up on the beach.

I had more fun ashore than I had expected. The tide came back, as predicted. The dinghy floated off. Embarrassing!

PRACTICE (8)

Using the tables shown in figs. 63 and 65 answer the following questions:

1. Near Miami Harbor Entrance, on Tuesday, March 30, at 9:30 P.M. Eastern Standard time
   (a) is the tide rising or falling?
   (b) when is the next high water predicted?
   (c) what depth should you expect where the chart shows 5 feet?

2. For Sunday, February 14, give times (in everyday manner) and predicted height for high and low water, A.M. and P.M., at
   (a) Fort Lauderdale, Bahia Mar Yacht Club
   (b) Sewall Point, St. Lucie River

3. On Monday, February 15, what depth will you expect at 9 A.M. at Miami Harbor Entrance where the chart shows 4 feet?

4. On Saturday, January 30, at a dock where Miami data need no corrections your boat has grounded at 12:30 P.M. When can you expect her to come afloat again?

ANSWERS (8)

1. (a) Rising (LW was at 5 P.M.). (b) 11:24 P.M. (c) 7.6 feet (5+2.6).
2. (a)   4:56 A.M. —0.1   (b)   6:57 A.M. 0.0
       10:58 A.M.   1.9   12:04 P.M. 0.8
        5:14 P.M.   —0.3   7:15 P.M. —0.1
      11:28 P.M.   1.8   —*   —*
(*Next HW 12:34 A.M. 0.7 on Monday, February 15)
3. Depth 5.5 feet. (Range of this tide 2 feet, time between tides six hours; at the time given it is 18 inches above low-water level; 4+1½=5.5.)
4. At about nine in the evening. (She grounded about two hours after high water; the level here on that day will be the same again two hours before the next high water predicted for 11:12 P.M.)

9. Currents

The dictionary definition that best fits my use of "current" here is: mainly horizontal movement of water or other fluids. Most of us don't cruise in submarines, and so we are mainly interested in surface currents. The navigator meets them everywhere, not just in the ocean, but in rivers, canals, and lakes.

And not just water currents. When you jockey a houseboat in absolutely still water, you won't arrive at the point steered for except on a windless day. Any breeze will set you off downwind, to leeward; you'll make leeway.

That's obvious, you say. But there's yet another current. When your carefully worked dead reckoning position doesn't agree with a fix, whom will you blame? Yourself for estimating the speed wrong? A moody compass? The helmsman for sloppy steering? No. The expert navigator blames it on current. That'll be a highly personal current. Another vessel on the same run will find a different current. So will you the next time you make that trip.

All these things—river flow, tidal streams, ocean currents, leeway, and errors in speed or direction—will put your craft at a spot other than the one you expected. The navigator, then, defines as current anything that messes up his dead reckoning.

Don't get me wrong. That doesn't mean the navigator most of the time doesn't know where he is. No. He corrects for known currents, and even for unknown ones. That's what this chapter is about.

You don't need a book to tell you about some of these corrections. You already know, for example, what'll happen when you power at 8 miles per hour on a river that flows at 2 miles per hour. When you go downstream the river current will add to your speed; you'll make 10 miles per hour. When you go upstream the river current opposes your progress; you'll cover only 6 miles in one hour.

"That's obvious," you say. "But where do I find the speed of the current?" Most of the time you won't find it on a chart or in some book. You have to work it out yourself. If you covered 5 miles in one half hour, and maintain the same speed and the river doesn't change in character, you won't be far off by estimating your position 10 miles down after one hour, or even 20 miles after two hours. By then you have probably passed a bridge or other recognizable landmark to give you a navigational fix.

Most currents won't be so obliging. They won't set exactly in the direction you are going, or exactly in the opposite direction.

The direction of a current, by the way, is called its *set*. It's measured in degrees from true north like a course. It is the direction *toward* which the current moves. A set of 045 means the current moves *toward* the northeast, unlike a northeast wind, which blows *from* that quarter.

The speed of a current is called its *drift*. It's measured in knots or in statute miles per hour. You'll find it convenient to use the same units of measurement for the speed of the current and your boat, both in knots or both in mph.

You can solve all current problems by imagining your boat having two motions at once. Through the water she makes her course and speed to arrive after a certain time at her dead reckoning position. At the same time the water through which she sails moves over the bottom with the set and drift of the current. The moving water takes the boat along. That's her second motion.

To allow for that second motion is easy when the set and drift of the current are known. You simply move her dead reckoning position as if it had steamed itself for the given time with the course (set) and speed (drift) of the current. The point where the boat then arrives is called her estimated position.

On the chart you'll abbreviate it EP. Standard practice uses a small square to mark the estimated position. That distinguishes it from dead reckoning and other positions, which are marked by circles.

It makes no difference how often you apply the current correction. You could move the DR with the current every half hour, and start a new dead reckoning from that EP. You could allow for the current every hour. Or you could allow for it at the end of your run, say after four hours. The estimated position after four hours would be the same.

It doesn't even matter how you change course or speed or both. If you have been under way for four hours in a 1-knot current setting 045, your estimated position will be 4 nautical miles NE of your dead reckoning position, however you got to the DR position. You could have reached that position fast or slow, in a straight line or on a zigzag course.

That certainly isn't obvious. But think of yourself again as sailing through a slab of water while that slab moves over the bottom. It won't matter at what point on the surface of the slab you are, after a given time the moving slab will have carried you the same distance in the same direction, even if you reached that point by absolutely nothing, just drifting. You could have reached the same point by making a full

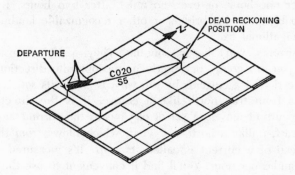

67. Sailing without current; at a given course and speed. The boat's dead reckoning position after one hour will be her true position over the bottom.

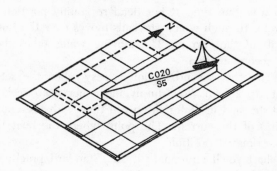

68. Sailing in a current of 2 knots setting northeast. The mass of water through which the boat sails moves. (Think of a toy boat in a pan of water sailing while someone moves the pan over the bathroom floor.) After one hour her dead reckoning position will not be her true position over the bottom. (In the same corner of the pan the toy boat will be over a different tile on the floor.)

circle or sailing three sides of a triangle course. You could have gone twice as fast and circled twice. None of that makes any difference to the displacement of the estimated position from the dead reckoning position.

That makes applying current correction simple. It's done with pencil and plotter right on the chart. Textbooks show three current problems, but they are solved in the same manner.

You already know how to solve the first problem, allowing for a known current. You plot your DR position and move it as if it had sailed

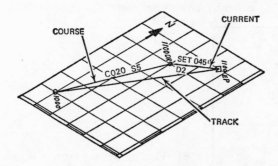

69. Geometry of sailing in a current. To plot the true position of the vessel, first plot her dead reckoning; then move the DR position as if it had sailed for the same length of time with the set and drift of the current. In a known current the point so plotted is her estimated position (EP).

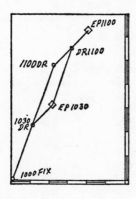

70. Timing of correction for current makes no difference. Allowing for current after one hour or every half hour leads to the same estimated position.

with the current for the time the current has acted. That gives your estimated position.

Here's the second problem: You get a fix—by cross bearings, electronically, by celestial navigation—at some distance from your dead reckoning. You now consider the displacement of your dead reckoning to the fix as the current. It doesn't matter whether the current is real or imaginary. As long as conditions remain the same, and until you get another fix, you can apply it as a current to any future dead reckoning position to get an estimated position. (You have started a new dead reckoning at the fix, as is the custom.)

Suppose the "current" was caused by wind pressure on your boat, leeway. By applying the current to the next dead reckoning position

All current problems are really the same problem.

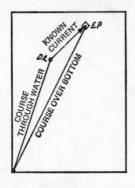

71. Plotting known current—Apply known current to dead reckoning position to get the estimated position.

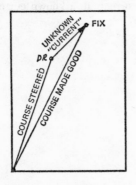

72. Finding unknown current (real or fictitious)—Measure difference between dead reckoning position and a fix.

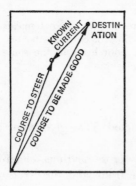

73. Laying course to allow for current—Apply known current *from* destination to get point to steer for.

you have allowed for that leeway. Your next estimated position will probably be a better indication of her position than simple dead reckoning.

You can also use the current—a known one—to correct your *course*. That's the third common current problem. Here the question is: What course must I steer in the presence of this current to get directly to my destination?

In the solution, the destination becomes your estimated position. You work backward toward a dead reckoning position from which the current, in the time you're under way, will set your craft to the destination.

Practically, you plot the set of the current in reverse from the destination. You'd plot a NE (045) current toward the SW (225). Before you can lay off the distance, you have to estimate your sailing time. If it'll take you three hours, lay off three times the speed of the current; if it'll take you two hours, twice the drift of the current. These times are for reaching the intended DR position. Since the distance from where you are now to that position will vary with the current correction, you may have to do a bit of trial-and-error work.

Often it is simplest to assume a reasonable round running time—say two hours, or two and one half hours—plot the current, and adjust the running speed to make the distance in the assumed time.

Extreme precision in this, or any current calculation, is a waste of time. The current isn't ever exactly known; your speed won't be exactly what you think, and your steering is bound to be a little off, even when your compass is not.

In working out a course that'll take a slow boat across a strong current, you may make a discovery: You can't get there from here. Perhaps already as a youngster you found you couldn't row to a point directly across a swift river. If you were smart, you also discovered the solution to the problem: Row upstream out of the current, before crossing. The same reasoning prompts sailing yachts to cross the Gulf Stream taking their departure from Fort Lauderdale or Miami rather than from Palm Beach.

Currents, such as the Gulf Stream in that area, have been carefully measured for many years. You can get figures for every month of the year and for almost any point in the stream. They are, of course, averages. A strong south wind will add to the current. A strong north wind may diminish it somewhat; it will also kick up fierce seas that'll upset your speed, your dishes, and perhaps your insides.

Just as in a river, the current in the Gulf Stream is not the same from one shore to the other. Average speed allowance figures have been calculated for every month. But a sailboat becalmed in the swiftest part of the stream will be set north at a faster rate.

The Gulf Stream, as you probably know, is part of a giant current system that covers most of the North Atlantic. The trade winds push water from the African side toward the Gulf of Mexico in the North Equatorial Current. The Gulf Stream and its successor, the North Atlantic Drift, bring it back toward Europe and down along the west coasts of Spain and North Africa.

Similar carrousels go around the South Atlantic, the Indian, and the North and South Pacific oceans. You'll meet the cool southward flow—offspring of the Japan Stream—off the West Coast as the California Current. You can get the allowance to be made for these currents from the pilot charts and atlases already mentioned.

The winds certainly are partly responsible for these oceanwide currents. But most sailors grossly overestimate the influence of *local* winds on the surface motion of the sea. Lightships on station on the Atlantic and Pacific coasts of the United States have measured winds and currents for years. Their findings: At eighteen out of twenty lightships it took a 40-knot gale to get a half-knot current going.

Much lesser winds will create a private current for you: leeway. The more surface your craft presents to the wind, and the stronger the wind, the more leeway you'll have to allow for.

Nathaniel Bowditch in his *New American Practical Navigator* gave a table for leeway of a full-rigged ship. Under close-reefed topsails the navigator should have allowed two points, for example.

Now you won't find such tables. You'll have to work the allowance for yourself. Even for the same surface and wind strength you'll have to make very different allowances for power cruisers, sailboats, and houseboats. Also, as every wind sailor knows and you can readily see, a sailboat will make very little leeway when the wind is astern, a lot when the wind is on the beam.

With much experience you may someday have the leeway of your own craft all figured out. By that time she'll be so old, you'll trade her in. Or you yourself may be ready to swallow the anchor.

Frequent fixes are the best way to estimate leeway or any other current. We are lucky we don't have to rely solely on visual bearings, but have several electronic methods, described in the second part of this book, besides celestial sights, discussed in the third part.

Even without these fixes you are not as helpless as you might think. You could try an old sailor's trick, the range astern, to get your current and to compensate for it. Plot your point of departure and your intended course. Run the course line ashore. Perhaps you're lucky and it hits some prominent landmark. The greater the distance between your departure and the object, the better. All you have to do when you reach your point of departure, say the sea buoy, is to steer the course that keeps the range closed, the two objects in line—in transit—astern. Then you'll be on a position line that runs through your departure and your destination. If you continue on the course that follows that position line after you have lost sight of your marks astern, you'll get to your destination—if conditions remain the same.

Often the course line carried ashore will not hit some charted landmark. You can still use a variation of this method. After taking your departure and putting the boat on course, look back. Isn't there some building in transit with your sea buoy? The gable on the Miller house, the flagpole at the high school, the peak of Sugar Hill all may be on the chart, you just didn't recognize them as landmarks.

If there's no range, charted or otherwise, you can use a single mark astern to correct your course for current, leeway, and what have you. Steer your intended course, say 045, for about a mile from the sea buoy. The distance isn't critical but shouldn't be more than a third of the distance where you'll lose the mark. Now take a bearing.

If you had made good a course of 045 magnetic, the sea buoy should now bear 225 magnetic from you, the exact reverse of your course. Probably it won't. Say your bearing compass reads 205. Come right until the bearing becomes 225. Try a new course. On the 045 course your course error was 20 degrees, you had made good 025. Now try 20 degrees to the other side of your course, 065. After a while take another bearing on the sea buoy. If it doesn't bear exactly 225, correct again. This correction will probably be very much smaller than the first, perhaps only a couple of degrees. The course that'll keep the buoy bearing 225 will get you to the destination that would bear 045 magnetic if you could see it.

If instead of a sea buoy you are lucky enough to have a lighthouse, or a radio tower, or a chimney as a mark astern, you can carry the course correction many miles to sea or into the lake.

It won't do where you encounter changing currents. It won't help, for instance, in crossing the Gulf Stream from southern Florida. Near shore you'll be outside the edge of the stream; there might even be a current that runs south near shore. That'd be a poor indicator for the soon-to-be-encountered 3.5-knot northerly current.

If you operate in tidal waters, you'll meet *tidal* currents. They are created by the changes in level—high and low water—but their relationships are complicated.

You may be able to check a few of the following generalities in your own area.

In the open ocean tidal currents are negligible.

Near shore flood and ebb are more likely to run parallel with the shore than toward and away from shore. Not so near the mouths of bays and rivers.

Along shores without bays and river mouths the current will slack and turn at about the times of high and low water.

In a small bay with a large entrance to the ocean the water levels inside and on the beach are likely to be about the same. At the entrance the current will be strongest when the tide rises and falls most rapidly, that is, halfway between high and low waters.

In a large bay with a narrow entrance the greatest difference in levels is likely to be when it's high or low water outside the entrance. So contrary to most people's expectation, the strongest current at the entrance will be near the time of high or low water. The current will be slack at about mid-tide. On the usual six-hour tide, slack water would be approximately three hours after high and after low water.

You can't guess the strength of tidal current from the tidal range of a place. (Boston has twice the tidal range of San Francisco; yet the current is considerably stronger in San Francisco.) But at the same place the current will be stronger when the tidal range becomes greater during spring tides.

In a tidal river the tidal current, like the normal flow, will be strongest near the outside of a bend. In straight stretches the strongest current is likely to be in the middle; along the banks expect to find little current or even a countercurrent.

Expect strong currents, and somewhat erratic ones, where a waterway connects two bays. Example: the East River, which connects Long Island Sound and New York Bay. Only accidentally will the level be the same in both bodies of water. So you get a flume effect. That was called "hydraulic" current, but the word is being phased out; all currents are really hydraulic.

Over shallow or broken ground expect tidal currents to create tide rips, overfalls, anything up to a minor local disaster area for small boats.

Such conditions are often marked on nautical charts. So also sometimes are the speed and direction of tidal currents.

74. Chart symbols: currents.

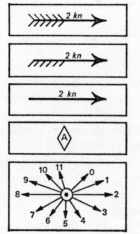

Current (arrow indicates set, figure the drift)

Flood (tidal current moving toward land or up tideway)

Ebb (tidal current moving away from land or down tideway)

Reference mark (spot for which current data are tabulated elsewhere on the chart)

Rotary current (in some basins, e.g. Gulf of Maine, Gulf of St. Lawrence, tidal currents change direction in a twelve-hour cycle; length of arrow indicates strength of current)

At times you may want to, or have to, avoid adverse current. In some passes on the inland route to Alaska, for instance, the current may run faster than your boat. Then the strategy will be to get through at slack water. The faster a tidal current, the shorter will be the period of weak current, say a current of less than one half knot. Here is a useful guide:

Maximum Current Velocity (knots)	Weak Current lasts minutes
1	72
2	36
4	18
8	9

Example: For a current that will reach a maximum strength of 4 knots, you will have 18 minutes (9 before and 9 after slack) during which the current will not exceed ½ knot.

After the time of weak current the velocity increases rapidly. A useful figure to remember is this: At half time between slack and maximum current, typically one and a half hours before and after slack water, the current will reach three fourths of its maximum velocity.

To find the times of slack water you'll use the tidal current tables published by the National Ocean Survey (formerly Coast and Geodetic Survey). Their format is similar to the same agency's tide tables. For the Atlantic coast of North America twenty reference stations serve as a basis for subsidiary ports, rivers, and bays from the Bay of Fundy to the Texas coast. For the Pacific coast of North America (and some places in the Philippines, China, and Japan) the same system lets you predict tidal currents from Baja California to Alaska.

One of my most frustrating sails was working my way up to Delaware Bay. Scared of fish traps, I stayed in the main channel or near it. In the light breeze I should have made between 3 and 4 knots under sail. Under power I could have made 5 knots. Either way I got nowhere. Reason: On the 50-mile run to Reedy Island during the ebb, which here as in many places lasts longer than the flood, I was stemming a current of about 2 knots. So over the bottom I'd make 1½ to 2 knots; under power I could have made a glorious 3 knots.

What can you do about such conditions? Study the current diagrams given in the current tables. They look complicated. But the time it takes you to puzzle over them is worth it.

The instructions are all there. You'll find proof of what you may have expected: You'd be best off starting at the beginning of the flood.

You'll also find that, had I only taken time to study the problem, I could have had a helping current for most of the way. A 6-knot vessel could carry the flood all the way from Brandywine Shoal to Reedy Island, getting a 1½-knot boost all the way.

Such current diagrams are printed in the annual tables for Boston Harbor, Vineyard and Nantucket sounds, New York (East River and Ambrose Channel), Delaware Bay and River, and Chesapeake Bay.

Tidal current charts, priced at $1, giving direction and velocity of tidal currents for every hour of the tidal cycle, are also available for the following areas: Boston Harbor, Narragansett Bay, Long Island and Block Island sounds, New York Harbor, Delaware Bay and River, Upper Chesapeake Bay, Charleston Harbor, San Francisco Bay, and Puget Sound. If you navigate in any of these areas, get them at your NOS (C&GS) chart agent. The fuel saved the first time you don't fight the current will pay you back. It'll even pay for the annual current tables you need with these charts. (Except for the charts of New York Harbor and Narragansett Bay, which tie in with the annual tide tables.)

For close-in boat handling, tables, diagrams, and charts don't give enough information about currents. For anchoring and getting under way, docking and leaving docks, you need a current meter.

Where do you get that? You've already got one under your cap: two sensors—your eyes—under the visor, a computer ready to be calibrated inside your skull.

The calibration takes a lifetime.

Watch seaweed if you can see any: Does it lean? In what direction? Does it yaw from side to side? Watch piles: Do they show little eddies? A vortex? A pile-up of water on the upstream side? Watch things float past the dock: Which way and how fast? Watch boats anchored nearby: How do they lie? Do they yaw much? How taut are their mooring or anchor lines? Watch buoys: Are they upright, leaning, bobbing? Eddies? Upstream pile-ups?

Current, I know, is only one factor. Wind and how it combines with the current makes maneuvers into problems.

The smart skipper takes his time to study the situation and to work on the problem. Sometimes there is no safe approach. In tidal currents there's still an out: Can you anchor off or pick up a mooring until the current slacks? Then you'll only have the wind to reckon with.

PRACTICE (9)

1. From the sea buoy off Lake Worth Inlet to West End (Grand Bahama Island) is a distance of 55 nautical miles, the course is 095 True. Allow 2½ knots northerly set for the Gulf Stream averaged over the whole crossing. Find the course to steer for a boat cruising at 10

knots. (Plot the problem on any convenient scale and measure the course to steer.)

2. Look at fig. 134 and note the 0800 DR, the 1200 DR, and the 1200 fix. What current seems to have acted on this vessel during these four hours? Give set and drift.

ANSWERS (9)

1. Course to steer 109 T. (The crossing will take five and a half hours; in that time the current will carry the vessel 13¾ nautical miles to the north. So you must steer for a point that much south of West End.)

2. The fix is almost due south of the 1200 dead reckoning position, hence a south-going current. The fix is about 4½ nautical miles from the dead reckoning position, so the velocity of the current appears to be 1.1 knots.

10. Practical Pilotage

In earlier chapters we have looked at different elements of pilotage. Charts, depths and heights, distance and speed, directions of courses and bearings, the magnetic compass, navigational aids, tides and currents have passed in review.

As you went along you picked up an acquaintance with chart symbols. You now know all the important ones, and some of the most useful abbreviations.

Again and again you came across the concept of position lines.

Now we are ready to pull all the bits and pieces together, and to add a few finishing touches.

The navigator thinks of pilotage as an ongoing task from departure to arrival.

Suppose you have done your homework and worked out a compass course from your point of departure to your destination. You know your boat's speed. Your compass is compensated. Is that enough?

Let's see. Take waters without any current, a day without any wind. You're cruising at 10 knots, making your intended course within 2 degrees. That's very good steering. Your speed is probably not so certain. Give it a latitude of 10 per cent and you'd make 9 knots, or 11.

At the end of three hours you'd be 3 miles ahead or astern of your dead reckoning position and a mile either side of your course. That doesn't sound bad. Now imagine you've hit a submerged log and are leaking badly. The Coast Guard will have to search 12 square miles to help you.

That was under better than average conditions. With a bit of current and some wind, the area of search would be much larger. The average helmsman wouldn't keep your boat that close to her course. That error could easily double the search area.

Perhaps you don't travel 30 miles now. But someday you will; that's not the time to learn the system. Also, most of the time you'll be in currents, set off course by winds, with a helmsman who overcompensates, holding her upwind all the time. Then a much shorter run could endanger your vessel and crew.

Even on inland passages a lot of skippers run into navigational troubles. One of the hazards of the Intracoastal Waterway is the crossing of Albemarle Sound. It's only about 15 miles wide, but beset by currents, and often nasty. The last time I saw it, the entrance to the waterway was hard to spot when you approached it from the north.

In such a place a wise skipper would lay a course definitely to one side of the entrance, perhaps 3 miles west of it. When he approaches the shore and can't see the entrance, he'd be fairly confident that the entrance must be to the east. On the direct course he'd have to toss a coin to decide which way to search for it first.

Until you can handle confidently such a problem, or a three-hour run, you are not really a pilot, however many hours you have driven a boat.

Here's what happened to a friend, a shrimp boat captain from Georgia. Shrimping was poor on his home grounds, while good catches were reported off the Dry Tortugas in the Gulf of Mexico. In company of four other shrimp boats, he took off for Key West. No problems in navigation.

There, being the loudest talker, he was elected to lead the flotilla. He chose to run at night, having little faith in his ability to find the place in daylight. At night on this run of about 60 miles he'd only have to keep clear of the land. If he came within 17 miles of his destination, the 151-foot-high light on Loggerhead Key would get him there.

A night run to make your landfall on a powerful light is a good idea. If possible, time your departure to arrive at the destination at daybreak. Then you have the light to get you there, daylight to enter the harbor.

The other shrimpers followed his wake . . . and got lost with him.

What was his mistake? Almost certainly that he did not make good the course or courses he had planned. He should have planned his entire trip as a series of short legs: from the Key West sea buoy to a point abeam of Sand Key light, to a point abeam of Cosgrove Shoal light, to a point abeam of the quick-flashing bell buoy. On a course from that point to his destination he would soon pick up Rebecca Shoal light; before bringing that light abeam, he probably would already have seen the loom of the Tortugas light on Loggerhead Key.

At no time would he have been out of sight of navigational aids that could have fixed his position. In a pleasure boat, being lower, your visibility would be 2 miles less than the charted range of the lights. But you'd be without light in view for only a couple of miles or so.

The trick is to take bearings and plot position lines besides keeping a dead reckoning. At first this continuing plotting sounds like a lot of work. Believe me, it isn't. After a few well-plotted trips, it becomes almost automatic. And it pays off when poor visibility or some other hazard makes things hairy.

You'll recall that a single bearing gives you only one position line,

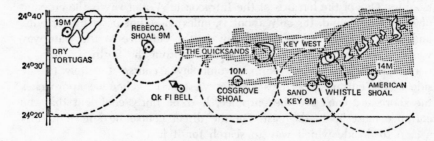

75. Planning courses to take advantage of aids to navigation. Dashed circles indicate range of lights for a lookout 15 feet above the water. On a night crossing an observer at that level would never be out of sight of some navigational light. Even in the cockpit a pleasure boat you would not be without lighted aids for long.

A westerly course from a point 2 miles south of the Key West whistle buoy until you sight the bell buoy south of the Quicksands will keep you out of shallow water (shaded area). Then you could safely alter course to WNW until within range of the light at your destination, the Dry Tortugas.

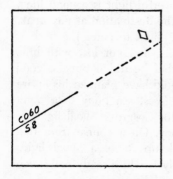

76. A bearing of an object ahead (or astern) checks direction of your course.

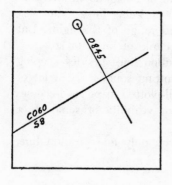

77. A bearing of an object abeam (port or starboard) checks distance made good.

not a fix. Don't turn up your nose at such single position lines. They can tell a lot.

A bearing on an object ahead or astern shows whether you are making good your course. A bearing on either beam tells how far you have come along your track.

After the shrimp boat skipper raised Loggerhead Key light, all he had to do was follow the position line toward its source. When he brought Cosgrove Shoal light abeam, he knew exactly how far he'd come since the sea buoy.

The special usefulness of position lines ahead and astern, or on either beam, is not restricted to visual bearings. We'll encounter them again in electronic and celestial navigation.

At times a bearing on a single object can keep you off a hidden danger, a rock ledge, shoal, or sunken rocks. I like to think of such so-called *danger bearings* as if I were important enough that someone had erected a lighthouse just for me. If he really knew his job, he would

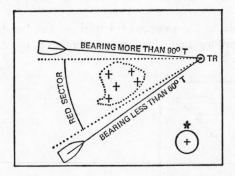

78. Danger bearings. Think of the tower as a lighthouse with a red sector to warn you of the dangerous rocks, and stay out of the red sector.

Whatever your course, you'll be clear (north of the rocks) if you stay out of the area where the bearing of the tower becomes less than 090 T. You'll be clear (south of the rocks) if you stay out of the area where its bearing becomes more than 060 T.

have put up a light with a white and a red sector, the red sector to warn me away from danger; the white sector to wave me on.

I can hear you objecting, "Bearings ahead, astern, and abeam, and danger bearings are unusual." Admitted.

But you already know how a beam bearing can be combined with an earlier bearing in a four-point bearing.

You'll also recall the trick of estimating the distance of an object abeam. The captain of the shrimp boat could have timed the change in bearing of Sand Key light. If he cruised at 7 knots, he would have timed the change of 7 degrees, say from 353 to 000, the course being almost due west. If he got two minutes fifteen seconds, he would have known his distance off—2¼ nautical miles. Just right for a safe passage without adding much to the distance.

This quick calculation and the four-point bearing are really special cases of a most useful navigator's trick, the *running fix*. That's a graphic method of getting a fix from *one* object. You take two bearings of the same object. By advancing the first position line as if it had traveled at the speed and on the course of your vessel for the time between bearings, you can cross it with the second position line. The crossing point of the two position lines gives a fix. It isn't as accurate a fix as you'd get from taking—at practically the same time—bearings on two objects. Any error in course or speed will show in the running fix.

Even so, most navigators begin a new dead reckoning at a running fix. You can modify that. Start a new reckoning when the running fix places the ship nearer danger than your dead reckoning. If it gives you more offing from the shore, continue the reckoning. That way you'll have a margin of safety.

The running fix is the most useful trick of the coastwise navigator. Study the illustrations that show its plotting step by step. Then work

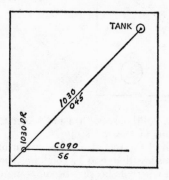

79. Running fix (1). First bearing of tank at 1030 gives usual position line, labeled in the customary fashion.

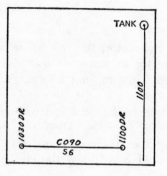

80. Running fix (2). Second bearing at 1100 on the same tank does not agree with 1100 dead reckoning.

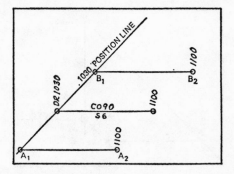

81. Running fix (3). At the time of the first bearing, instead of at the 1030 DR position you could have been anywhere on the 1030 position line, say at A_1 or B_1. That would change your 1100 DR to A_2 and B_2.

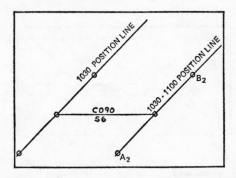

82. Running fix (4). A line through A_2, the 1100 DR, and B_2 allows for any 1100 DR position whether you started from A_1, B_1, or anywhere in between. You'll notice that this line is parallel to the position line from the first bearing, and goes through the 1100 DR position. Being the 1030 position line moved forward—at the speed and in the direction of your craft—it is called an "advanced" position line and labeled 1030–1100.

an example of your own. Ideally the two position lines should cross at about 90 degrees. Forty-five degrees is still fair. A lesser angle makes the crossing point subject to too much error for a small change in the plot of the position lines.

You may wonder about the error of a two-object fix. Most navigators neglect the few seconds between taking the two sights. At 10 knots, or at 10 miles per hour, a boat moves roughly 1,000 feet in one minute. If you took the two bearings half a minute apart, the second one was taken about 500 feet farther along the track. For an object 10 miles away, that'll make very little difference. The bearing will have changed

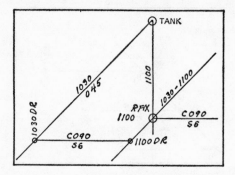

83. Running fix (5). The intersection of the advanced position line and the position line from the second bearing is the only point that agrees with the two bearings and the direction and speed of your vessel. It gives a running fix, labeled R FIX. This position is more probable than a mere dead reckoning position, so you start a new reckoning from it.

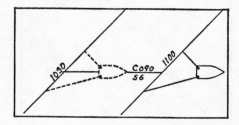

84. Running fix (6). Memory aid: Imagine your vessel towing the earlier position line at her speed and course for the time of advance. Here in one half hour the vessel towed the 1030 bearing line 3 nautical miles due east.

less than one half degree. For an object only 2 miles off, the bearing could have changed 2½ degrees. How much it really changes will depend on its position from you. Abeam the bearing will change rapidly; nearly ahead or astern the change will be unnoticeable.

Before you get too upset about such inaccuracies, remember the experiment of three bearings taken at the same time. To eliminate the error of motion, try that at anchor or when still in the water. The three position lines will form a little triangle, the cocked hat (fig. 86).

Geometrically, two lines—and so any two angled position lines—must cross at a point. Don't let that fool you. These position lines are subject to the same errors as the three lines. Think of them as narrow triangles, their crossing forming an area rather than a point. Give all position lines mentally some width, for safety's sake (fig. 87).

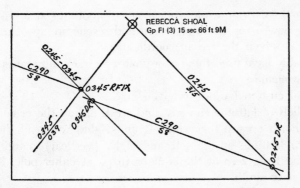

85. Running fix—example: During passage from Key West to the Dry Tortugas (fig. 75) Rebecca Shoal light bore 315 at 0245. One hour later, on course 290 at 8 knots, the navigator has not yet sighted Dry Tortugas light. Rebecca Shoal light now bears 039. He crosses the new bearing line with the 0245 position line moved parallel to itself, 8 nautical miles, in the 290 direction, that is, through his 0345 DR position. The crossing point of the advanced position line and the 0345 position line gives the 0345 running fix, from which he starts a new dead reckoning. Dry Tortuga light, according to his plot, should appear very soon, dead ahead. (A lookout in the rigging or on the flying bridge would already see it.)

But don't plot these bands. Just show position lines, bearings, and courses on the chart, preferably in the standard notation. And teach the rudiments of plotting to your family and crew. Then if you fall overboard, they'll find their way home or to some other place. With a running plot, knowing at all times where you are, you'll be prepared when rain or fog make visual pilotage practically impossible. If you should need help for one reason or another, you can give your location precisely.

You can give that location in several unmistakable ways.

The simplest, perhaps, is "on the way from — to —, so many miles out." The Coast Guard plane won't have any trouble finding a yacht reported "20 miles out on the way from Government Cut to Bimini."

When there's a charted object near you, there is a better way—by direction and distance. "One mile west of Cable-and-Anchor Reef buoy" is better than "4 miles out from Rowayton bound for Huntington."

There is a third way, usually neglected in pilotage, but well worth knowing—by latitude and longitude. The friendly lobsterman who'd come to help you off ⚓10 buoy won't come out if you give your latitude and longitude. The Coast Guard would find you. Sometimes, when there are several buoys or harbors that sound alike on a static-ridden Mayday, that's the best way.

Don't use latitude and longitude unless you are certain you'll get it right, every time, even while your boat is about to sink under you. It's amazing how many hours of search and rescue are spent on finding people who've given the wrong coordinates.

You probably have used these coordinates to track hurricanes. Let me refresh your memory.

By general custom latitude is given first.

The parallels of latitude run east and west. So, on the usual nautical chart with north on top they run left and right. You read the figures that indicate latitude at the left and right (vertical) margins. They are numbered from zero at the equator to 90 at either pole. They are labeled north or south.

The meridians of longitude run north and south. So, on the usual nautical chart with north on top they run up and down. You read the figures that indicate longitude at the top and bottom (horizontal) margins. They are numbered from zero at Greenwich to 180 near the international date line. They are labeled west or east.

As a memory aid you could try:

lAtitude lines run Across the chart
lOngitude lines run dOwn the chart

Or you could remember the place where it all started, the Mediterranean Sea. It's much longer (from east to west) than it's wide (from north to south).

Or think of a globe: The longitude circles, being all great circles, are longer than the latitude circles, which get smaller and smaller toward the poles. (Only the equator is a great circle; the poles are the smallest possible circles, mere points.)

Or think of a Mercator chart: The meridians of longitude are the longer sides of the rectangles that form that chart grid.

Eventually almost everyone remembers which is latitude, which longitude. The numbering is another matter. Every day, navigators all over the world make mistakes in numbering.

Here's the easiest way I know to remember that:

In the *Northern* Hemisphere the numbers (of degrees of latitude) *increase toward the north.*

In the *Western* Hemisphere the numbers (of degrees of longitude) *increase toward the west.*

In North America—in the Northern and Western hemispheres—the numbers increase toward north and west. That's against the way we write and read—toward the top and toward the left.

The rule, of course, works in reverse. If on a chart 41 degrees is below 42 degrees on the right and left margins, it's a chart of some part of the Northern Hemisphere, although the label N is not printed. In the same

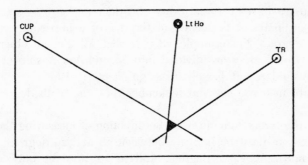

86. Cocked hat is the name of the small triangle formed by three position lines, such as bearings taken at the same time on three different landmarks.

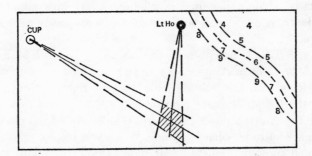

87. Areas of uncertainty border all position lines. Left: Errors in taking and plotting bearings make position lines into narrow triangles. Right: Other position lines become bands. Here a navigator who measures water depth as 36 feet is not necessarily on the 6-fathom line but likely within the 5–7 fathom band shown. Bands also surround limits of visibility of lights, calculated distance off, etc.

way, when 71 degrees is left (west) of 70 degrees on the top and bottom margins of a chart, it shows some part of the Western Hemisphere, although the label W is not printed. (Cape Cod Bay would be on that chart.)

In practice you are not often going to cross the meridian of Greenwich, the 180th meridian, and the equator. So the labels will remain the same for you for long stretches. For most of my readers it'll be N after latitude, W after longitude. So monotonously that, except on an exam, it wouldn't matter if you left the labels off. The Coast Guard isn't going to go looking for you in south latitude or east longitude.

You'll remember that 1 degree of latitude is 60 nautical miles. To give a position we have to break down the degrees to some smaller units.

The coordinates of the center of the eye of a hurricane are given in tenths of degrees. For example, 28.5° N 78.3° W. For all other purposes both kinds of degrees are divided into 60 minutes. A ship at the same position would report herself in 28°30′ N, 78°18′ W.

No problem here once you remember that one tenth degree must be 6 minutes.

Where the errors come in is in the direction of measuring the minutes. Clearly, 28°30′ must be halfway between 28 and 29 degrees; so 28°30′ must be north, above 28 degrees. And 78°18′ must be between 78 and 79 degrees, but nearer 78, and to the west, to the left, of it.

Yet every day thousands of navigators will plot it to the right at 77°42′ W longitude, or below at 27°30′ N latitude. It'll pay you to double-check until picking off or plotting coordinates becomes second nature.

On charts of the scales used in pilotage, every fifth minute, or even every minute, is numbered, so these mistakes are easily avoided with a little care.

You'll recall that, except near the equator, the grid of a Mercator chart is formed by rectangles, not squares. So you must measure minutes of latitude on the latitude scale (left or right), minutes of longitude on the longitude scale (top or bottom).

Where the grid is slanted, the figures usually are all the clue you need to see what's latitude, what longitude. When you see 80°14′ on a Florida chart, you'll know that must be longitude (west). It couldn't possibly be latitude; that would be less than 600 miles from the North Pole.

You won't be far off if you treat the polyconic charts you'll use in pilotage as though they were drawn on the Mercator projection. The difference will be negligible on river and harbor charts. On a chart that takes in a whole Great Lake you'll minimize the error by using the upper longitude scale for the upper part of the chart, the lower for the lower part.

(A bar-side expert may drop into his conversation yet another type of nautical charts: gnomonic charts. You will never use them in pilotage.

(On charts drawn on the gnomonic projection, a straight line between any two points represents the shortest distance between them on the spherical earth, the so-called great-circle distance.

(Over distances up to a few hundred miles, the difference between a great circle and a straight line on a Mercator chart—a rhumb line—is negligible.

(Only when you cross entire oceans will you be concerned with great circles. Distances are awkward to measure on these charts, and a great-circle course requires—theoretically—constant course changes. For these two reasons most ocean voyagers use great-circle charts only for planning.

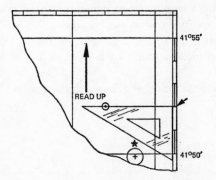

88. Latitude is measured on right or left margins of chart. Note that in the Northern Hemisphere the figures increase upward. Triangle lets you plot (or measure) latitude, here 41°52′ N. You could also use dividers, or strip of paper, to measure distance from nearest horizontal line.

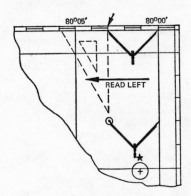

89. Longitude is measured on top and bottom margins of chart. Note that in the Western Hemisphere the figures increase toward the left. Dividers let you plot (or measure) longitude, here 80°03′ W. You could also use a strip of paper to transfer the distance from the nearest vertical line, or use a triangle against upper or lower margin of chart.

They then transfer a few convenient points of the great-circle course to a Mercator chart, and steer straight courses between these points.

Now back to common problems. Harbor charts split the minutes. There are 60 seconds to 1 minute of latitude or longitude. Again watch the direction. Seconds—like minutes and degrees—increase in number in North America up and to the left, north and west.

You may want no truck with latitude and longitude. I agree that in pilotage you can get along without them, except for hurricane tracking, tide tables, light lists, and chart correcting (something you may also want to avoid).

You may need them in electronic navigation, and you can't do without these coordinates in celestial navigation.

You may also hear a distress call giving position in latitude and longitude. You might be close enough to help if only you knew where the distress was.

Become a full-fledged pilot and learn that extra bit of magic.

11. Publications

Do you now know all there is to be known about small-craft pilotage? Of course not. I don't mean you need practice. Nor do I mean you still have to find out how to shape a course to avoid crashing into another vessel. I'll talk about that in the next chapter.

I mean you still lack facts. You know how to read charts. You know how to plot courses, bearings, and positions on your chart. You even know how to make your compass agree with directions on the chart. Charts, charts, charts.

But charts don't tell the pilot everything he needs to know. You've already seen that, in some areas, you'll need tide tables and current tables. Even the small-craft charts don't tell everything, although they list such unchartables as depths at docks, repair facilities, and available comforts and supplies.

For more local information you look in pilot books. For the waters around the United States you'll use the *Coast Pilot*, published by the National Ocean Survey, the former Coast and Geodetic Survey. Here is their coverage:

East Coast	Volume
Eastport to Cape Cod	1
Cape Cod to Sandy Hook	2
Sandy Hook to Cape Henry	3
Cape Henry to Key West	4
Gulf of Mexico, Puerto Rico and Virgin Islands	5
West Coast	
California, Oregon, Washington and Hawaii	7
Alaska: Dixon Entrance to Cape Spencer	8
Cape Spencer to Beaufort Sea	9

These books—there is now no volume 6—sell for $2.50 in hard covers, real bargains crammed full with information.

Typically a volume starts with an index of the charts needed to navigate in the area, navigation regulations, and local conditions of wind, weather, and tides, before taking up the detailed description of each section of coast or waterway. The introductory chapters answer such questions as when drawbridges will open, times and dial settings for radio weather forecasts, and routes complete with true courses and distances.

In the appendix you'll find distance tables (in nautical and statute miles), climatological tables for key points in the area, even addresses of local government offices and the phone number of the weather bureau.

The advice in the main portion of *Coast Pilot* can't be found anywhere else. Sample: "Small craft should not try to make Dry Tortugas from Key West, due to the rough nature of the sea around Rebecca Shoal."

Or you may be tempted to use Jupiter Inlet, which looks straightforward on the chart. The *Pilot* says, "Breakers extend across the bar. Small boats of the fishing fleet use the inlet. It is never used by strangers."

The chart shows Jupiter light Gp Fl (2) 30 sec 146 ft 18 M. That's fine at night, you won't have any trouble telling it from its neighbors. But suppose you sight a lighthouse after a crossing of the the the Gulf Stream. It would be nice to be able to identify it positively. The *Pilot* says, ". . . shown from a 105-foot red brick tower on the north side of the inlet . . . A radiobeacon is about 100 yards eastward of the light."

Hillsboro light, which the lighthouse you see could be, is described as follows: ". . . shown from an octagonal pyramidal skeleton tower with central stair cylinder, lower third of structure white, upper two-thirds black, on the beach on the north side of the inlet. A radiobeacon is at the light."

Often the *Pilot* will lead you to a delightful anchorage or a place of refuge from weather:

> Manatee Pocket is a protected body of water about a mile in length and 0.2 mile in width. It had a controlling depth of 4½ feet in 1971. The entrance is 0.6 mile west of the intersection of the St. Lucie River and the Intracoastal Waterway. The channel at the entrance is marked by daybeacons. Gasoline, diesel fuel, and fresh water can be obtained at any of several marine service stations. Small boats can obtain protection from tropical storms in Manatee Pocket. The holding bottom is good. Yachts can anchor anywhere for overnight stops.

Towns are described with special emphasis on repair facilities for boats. Often from the general description of a place you can infer whether it'll solve your personal emergency, from Tanqueray gin to the Sunday *Times*.

The *Pilots* aren't written specially for yachts. Sometimes that can help you. You can get the steamer lanes of coastwise travel and so avoid them.

The *Coast Pilots* are revised every few years. Between revisions annual supplements are issued. You get the latest supplement when you buy the book. The supplements are cumulative, that means you only have to worry about the last one. Postcards bound into the book will get you the supplements on publication, free.

The corrections are in order of page number and identified by lines. Some will be of no interest to you, others may be vitally important.

To save the work of making all the corrections that might interest you, there are two safe methods. The first is to make it a habit *always* to scan the latest supplement for possible corrections of the page you have just consulted. The other method, which I use, probably saves time in the long run and seems safer yet. I circle the page number in the book on any page that has a correction that might possibly concern me. It might take a quarter hour to mark a three-hundred-page *Pilot*.

In 1970 volume 4, Cape Henry to Key West, was revised. It does away with supplements. The *Pilot* is in soft covers, the price dropped $.50, no supplements will be issued. Instead a new edition will replace it every year. This disposable system is going to spread to the other volumes as they become due for revision.

For foreign waters the United States Naval Oceanographic Office publishes similar books, called *Sailing Directions*. They are loose-leaf books kept up by inserting *Changes*. Price per volume, including *Changes* to time of sale, and ring binder, is $4.50; the charge for later *Changes* is $.35.

The volumes most likely to interest readers of this book are:

British Columbia, Southern Portion	HO Pub. №10
British Columbia, Northern Portion	11
Nova Scotia, Bay of Fundy and Cape Breton Island	12
The Gulf and River St. Lawrence	13
East Coast of Central America and Mexico	20
The West Indies I, Bermuda, Bahamas and Greater Antilles	21
The West Indies II, Lesser Antilles and Venezuela	22
West Coast of Mexico and Central America	26

For the Great Lakes the National Ocean Survey, succeeding the Corps of Engineers (Lake Survey), publishes annually, at the beginning of the shipping season, the *Great Lakes Pilot*. The price of the *Pilot*, $3.25, includes supplements issued monthly from May to October.

The Canadian Hydrographic Service issues a *Great Lakes Pilot*, revised every few years, at $5 per volume as follows:

> Volume I: Lake Ontario, Lake Erie and Lake St. Clair including
>   Lake Simcoe, the Trent-Severn, and Rideau Waterways
> Volume II: Lake Huron and Georgian Bay, and Canadian Shores of
>   Lake Superior

Its *St. Lawrence River Pilot* covers the river from Cap des Rosiers (on the South Shore) and Rivière St. Jean (on the North Shore) to Kingston, and includes the Saguenay, Richelieu, and Ottawa rivers.

All these pilot books are available through the chart agents that handle publications of these agencies. Addresses for mail orders were given in Chapter 1.

There is one book of sailing directions that you will not need for pilotage. But if you enjoy books about sailing voyages, or plan to sail across the Pacific or around the world, or just like to dream bent over pilot charts, this book is for you. *Sailing Directions for the World,* published by the British Admiralty, is based on the logs of sailing masters and written for sailing vessels (and "low-powered steamers").

Several of the agents for U. S. Naval Oceanographic Office charts also sell British Admiralty publications—you'll find them listed in the Navy chart catalog—any one of them should be able to order this book for you if he hasn't got it in stock.

For many recreational boating areas local cruise guides are published by some state agency, development commission, fish and game department, conservation department, or whatever it may be called.

Other guidebooks are commercially published. They range from indispensable—like the *Yachtsman's Guide to the Bahamas*—through highly literate descriptions of personal cruises, to advertising interrupted by chamber of commerce information.

The best way to find out how useful such guides are is to study them in the book corner of your marine hardware store. Boating people who have cruised the area may also recommend books they have found helpful, and warn you about the shortcomings of others.

The list of useful pilotage publications would not be complete without mention of light lists. The Coast Guard publishes the Light List for the United States in five volumes, as follows:

	Volume
Atlantic Coast (from St. Croix River, Maine, to Little River, South Carolina)	1
Atlantic and Gulf Coast (from Little River, S.C., to Rio Grande, Texas)	2

	Volume
Pacific Coast and Islands	3
Great Lakes	4
Mississippi River System	5

Prices vary, currently between $2 and $4.75. Available from Superintendent of Documents, U. S. Government Printing Office, Washington, D.C. 20402. You can also get them from those National Ocean Survey chart agents that handle Coast Guard publications. They are listed in the NOS chart catalog.

I would not rush to get any of these light lists myself. They tell more than you may want to know. I believe that all the information you are likely to need in normal pilotage can be found in the *Coast Pilots* and on the charts. It isn't the cost of the lists, nor the space they take up aboard. I can't be bothered to keep them up to date, as one should.

And that brings me to *Notice to Mariners.*

This is published weekly by the U. S. Naval Oceanographic Office and prepared jointly with National Ocean Survey and the U. S. Coast Guard. The *Notices* cover the world. No casual boatman can keep up with the information they spew out, typically seventy-five pages a week. They correct charts, light lists, radio-aid lists, and other publications. Broken down into areas from A—Canada (except British Columbia), Greenland, Iceland—to Q—Antarctica—and cleverly indexed, they are models of efficiency.

But do you need to know that a buoy on the north coast of Madagascar—Majunga approach—has been changed? Or when surface-to-air missile exercises will be held off Kauai?

You'd do better with the *Local Notices to Mariners* issued by each Coast Guard district. There are a dozen districts but one or two will probably cover your cruising area. A letter to the district commander will get you on the free mailing list. If you just want to see what these notices contain, your chart agent should have a copy.

The U. S. Coast Guard has published a *Recreational Boating Guide,* publication CG-340, which in less than one hundred pages gives a mass of useful and authentic information. The price of this pamphlet is $.45. If you can't find it locally, and don't want to wait for shipment from the Superintendent of Documents, you can order it as a paperback reprint from Paperback Library, 315 Park Avenue South, New York, N.Y. 10010, for $.75 plus $.10 for postage. Title number 64-118.

If you want to read more about pilotage here are some suggestions.

The classic, Bowditch, first published in 1801 by Nathaniel Bowditch and more than one hundred years ago taken over by the U. S. Navy, has been revised many times as Publication ⚓9, *American Practical Navigator.* The last edition has more than fifteen hundred pages, sells for $7.

It's intended for the professional worldwide navigator rather than the small-craft skipper. About 200 pages deal with pilotage. If you like that sort of thing, you'll find some mathematical tables useful in pilotage among the more than 270 pages of tables. As an argument settler Bowditch is unsurpassed.

For prestige if not for actual use, many yachts carry Dutton's *Navigation and Piloting,* published by the United States Naval Institute, Annapolis, Maryland. About 250 of the more than 700 pages deal with pilotage. Price, $15. Designed as a text for the study of Bowditch, it isn't easier reading than Bowditch itself. Having been revised since Bowditch, it is now more up to date on electronic navigation.

Meant for the pleasure boatman is Chapman's *Piloting, Seamanship and Small Boat Handling,* published by *Motor Boating.* In fifty years it has grown from two hundred to seven hundred pages. But you won't find a page 700. To help students of U. S. Power Squadron and Coast Guard Auxiliary courses who may not have the latest edition, new pages are lettered rather than numbered. After page 334 comes 334(a), 334(b), for example. It covers pilotage very thoroughly, electronic navigation sketchily, celestial navigation not at all. As the title states, it covers much more than pilotage, including subjects not promised in the title, such as weather and flag etiquette. It's a source of most information a small-craft skipper may want. Before you have read through it—if you ever do—the next edition will be out (about $10, depending on binding).

There are many other books for the boatman. Some are specialized—about sail handling, racing, or maintenance. Where they are general, most of them cover the same ground that Chapman covers.

One book is different. It was written to include much of what other boating books left out: distress, falling overboard, wrecking, dinghy management, navigation without instruments, comfort aboard, hints for boat living . . . I should know, I wrote it. It's much easier reading and more fun than this book. If you plan a southern cruise, it will prepare you for that in its chapters on weather in the palm belt, pilotage in coral waters, skin diving for boat work . . . It's Kals, *Practical Boating* (Doubleday, $7.95).

12. Rules of the Road

You can't work out a course and let an orangutan or automatic pilot steer it. You're not alone on the water. Rules to regulate the traffic are needed.

You expected that. But did you expect that in and around the United States four separate, complete sets of rules are in force at this time? Someday these rules may get unified. Until then we have to live with four sets of rules depending on the waters we sail.

The confusion isn't quite as bad as it sounds. It's not unlike the highway code muddle. The laws vary from state to state. Yet once you have learned to drive an automobile you can operate it fairly successfully in all states without knowing the fine points. And you can get along in Canada and Mexico too.

Let's first roughly define the four areas.

Rules	Area of Application	Pamphlet
International	High seas and coastal waters seaward of line marked on chart where Inland Rules take over	CG-169
Inland	Coastal waters landward of line marked on chart where International Rules take over; harbors, rivers, and other navigable waters of the United States except as stated below	CG-169
Great Lakes	The Great Lakes and their connecting waters and tributaries as far east as Montreal	CG-172
Western Rivers	(a) The Mississippi River between its source and the Huey P. Long Bridge in New Orleans, its tributaries and their tributaries (b) Part of the Atchafalaya River (c) The Red River of the North	CG-184

The pamphlets covering these various sets of rules are obtainable, free, from any Coast Guard inspection office or chart agent, or from the Commandant, U. S. Coast Guard, Washington, D.C. 20226.

If you went from, say, Milwaukee by way of Chicago to the Illinois River, down the Mississippi to the Gulf of Mexico, you would have to use all four sets of rules. Most of us will stay within the area of one or two sets. And you'll seldom be in doubt what rules apply.

The Inland-International boundary is always shown on the chart. The description of that boundary line takes eight pages in print. In general it follows the trend of the coastline, and connects the outermost buoys. That takes in quite a sweep at times. For Massachusetts Bay, for example, the line runs from Cape Ann lighted whistle buoy ⚡2 to Boston lightship, and from there to Cape Cod light.

Let me show you that for the pleasure boatman things aren't as bad as the four sets of rules suggest.

All four sets require certain lights. Most readers will probably navigate "inboards, outboards and auxiliaries—that is sailboats with engines—not over 65 feet in length." (That leaves—besides commercial vessels—sailboats without engines, and boats propelled by oars.) Under Inland, Great Lakes, and Western Rivers rules they all carry the lights prescribed in the Motorboat Act of 1940. That's simple enough, isn't it?

But that leaves out International Rules. It sounds as if you needed one set of lights for all United States waters, a different one for International waters. You don't. The Motorboat Act specifically lets you carry the lights of the International Rules.

That leaves out sailboats that have no engines. Up to 40 feet in length they wear the same lights in all waters. The main difference between an auxiliary's lights and a sailboat's lights is that the sidelight must be visible 1 mile for auxiliaries, 2 miles for sailboats. A matter of bulbs in most lights. Sailboats over 40 feet in length require 3-foot screens on sidelights in International waters.

Rowboats and canoes under all three U.S. rules carry a lighted lantern ready to exhibit to prevent collision. In international waters—a poor place for rowboats—the same craft carry an electric torch or lighted lantern ready to exhibit to prevent collision.

Even if I have convinced you that the four jurisdictions can be served by one set of lights on any given craft, you may say, "That concerns the boatbuilder, not me. The business of lights is much too complicated, and I never run at night anyway." Or perhaps, "I run a powerboat, what lights sailboats carry doesn't concern me."

You'd be totally wrong. The lighting scheme does concern you vitally: The steering rules—even in daylight—are based on the sectors the lights cover. The system of sectors is really simple. And you must at night be able to tell a sailboat from a power-driven one.

Remember that sailors used to divide a circle into 32 points, which makes a quarter circle 8 points.

The sidelights are green on the right, starboard side (right-green-star) and red on the left, port side (red-port-left). Each covers 10 points. So each shows over an arc from right ahead to 2 points abaft its beam.

A powerboat shows a white light in the forepart of the vessel. That light covers the arcs of both sidelights together, 20 points.

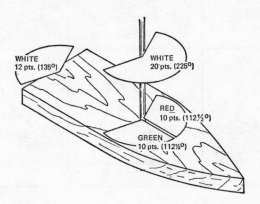

90. Basic lights. Red and green sidelights each covering from dead ahead to two points (22½ degrees) aft of beam. On power-driven craft also a white light that covers the same arc as the two colored lights together. Stern light, also white, covers the remaining arc.

The remaining 12 points are covered by a white stern light.

That's all there is to the basic scheme. Minor variations, by jurisdiction and by size of boat, permit combining the stern light with the light in the forepart. Or make you carry the white forward light at a certain height, or at the bow.

Only power-driven craft carry the white forward light. An auxiliary under power—sails up or not—wears it. Under sail alone a boat doesn't show a white forward light.

Minor points regulate separate or combination sidelights and their screens. Sidelights of a small vessel are easily obscured by waves. So to make herself more visible a sailboat under International Rules is permitted to carry also a 20-point red light over a 20-point green light on her foremasthead.

But these are, as you can readily see, details. What I want you to keep in mind is the basic light scheme: 10-point sidelights, 12-point stern light, 20-point white forward light. The last is for power-driven vessels only.

MOTORBOAT ACT

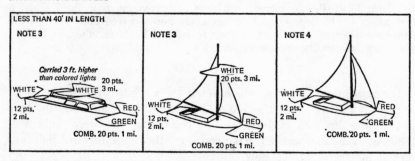

INTERNATIONAL RULES

NOTES: 1. Stern light not required on Great Lakes.
2. Sailboats without engine: separate sidelights, visible 2 miles.
3. Or separate sidelights. Craft 40 to 65 feet carry white 20-point light at least 9 feet above gunwales.
4. Or separate sidelights. Vessels over 40 feet in length carry separate sidelights with 3-foot screens.

91. Lights required between sunset and sunrise, under the Motorboat Act (U. S. Inland, Western Rivers and Great Lakes Rules) and International Rules (Mandatory Outside U. S. Inland Rules Boundaries, and on the High Seas; Optional Under Motorboat Act).

Memory aid: With minor exceptions, a craft driven by sail *and* power carries the same lights as one driven by power; a craft driven by sail alone carries the same lights as one driven by power except for the forward white light.

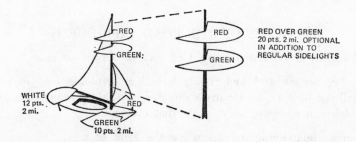

92. A sailing vessel may, under International Rules, carry on the top of her foremast, clearly separated, a red light above a green light, both visible at a distance of at least 2 miles. This is in addition to the regular sidelights.

From this basic lighting scheme we can derive the basic steering rules. When you see both sidelights of another boat at night—the other vessel also would see both your sidelights—you are meeting her end on. By night and by day when two vessels meet end on, both turn to the right, pass port to port.

In narrow channels you are in a permanent meeting situation, so you keep to the right side of the channel. In such channels vessels of less than 65 feet in length shall not hamper the passage of a vessel that can navigate only inside the channel.

A vessel approaching you so that at night she would see *one* of your sidelights is "crossing." You yield to vessels in your right, green, sector.

A vessel approaching from a direction where at night she would see your stern light is "overtaking." She has to look out for you.

Vessels driven by sails only—no white forward light at night—and boats under oars—lantern—have the right of way over power-driven craft.

The basic rules could be summarized as follows:

1. Meeting: Turn right.
2. In narrow channels: Keep right and keep out of way of deep-draft vessels.
3. Crossing: Yield to the craft on your right.
4. Overtaking: Keep out of way of overtaken craft.
5. Yield to vessels under sails and oars.

I would have hesitated to paraphrase the Rules of the Road, or any other legal document. In leaving out exceptions, one is likely to mislead the reader. But the job had already been done officially. On small-craft charts you'll find the following simplified rules:

RULES OF THE ROAD (ABRIDGED)

Motorless craft have the right of way in almost all cases.

Sailing vessels and motorboats less than sixty-five feet in length shall not hamper, in a narrow channel, the safe passage of a vessel which can navigate only inside that channel.

A motorboat being overtaken has the right of way.

Motorboats approaching head to head or nearly so should pass port to port.

When motorboats approach each other at right angles or obliquely, the boat on the right has the right of way.

Motorboats must keep to the right in narrow channels, when safe and practicable.

Mariners are urged to become familiar with the full text of the rules for the area of operation.

You'll find them in the pamphlets mentioned above. International and Inland rules are printed side by side in pamphlet CG-169 to bring

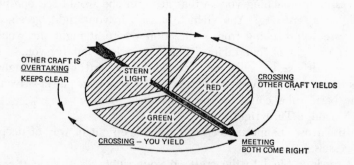

93. Steering rules based on light sectors. *Meeting* head on or nearly so, each vessel could see both sidelights of the other. Both vessels alter course to starboard. *Crossing:* A vessel which could see either of your sidelights is crossing. Yield to vessels in your green sector; maintain course and speed when other vessel is in your red sector. *Overtaking:* Vessel in your stern light sector, seeing neither of your sidelights, is overtaking you. She has to stay clear, you maintain course and speed.

out their—often word by word—similarities and their differences. As laws go, they are models of clarity.

Knowing that many readers will not study the pamphlets, I'll give you the most important Inland steering rules for powerboats in a little more detail.

MEETING—Two vessels, each in sight of both sidelights of the other, head to head, or nearly so, pass port to port. Both vessels alter course to starboard, to the right, so they will pass left side to left side.

Either vessel signals one short blast of her whistle. The other answers one short blast. Translation: I am directing my course to starboard for a port-to-port meeting. Answer: Understood, so will I alter.

When two vessels, nearly head on, meet on such courses that they will pass clear of one another, they may pass starboard to starboard.

The first vessel to signal blows two shorts. The other vessel replies promptly with two shorts, meaning starboard-to-starboard passing understood.

You must never answer one blast with two or the other way around. When in doubt give four short blasts: Danger! Wake up!

Meeting a large vessel, you can gauge the risk of collision by looking at her masts. When they are in line, or nearly so, she's headed right for you. At night she will have two white lights, range lights, in line. In a collision you have more to lose than the ocean liner. Also, her wash is a hazard to you, yours isn't to her. So under the rules of common sense, get out of the way, fast.

Here as in all other situations of changing course, change radically. Don't inch the wheel over, turn it smartly. Don't alter 5 degrees; the pilot on the other vessel might miss your alteration or put it down to sloppy steering. A 20-degree change will not be overlooked.

What will that do to your dead reckoning? Nothing if you use an old pilot's trick. Time how long you have been on the new course. Then run for exactly the same time 20 degrees to the other side of your base course. Say your base course was 090. You have turned right 20 degrees to a course of 110. After five minutes you come left to a course of 070. Hold that course for five minutes and you'll be back on the base course line. Resume your original course of 090. You don't have to worry about the added distance. It'll be considerably less than a tenth of a mile for every mile of detour.

CROSSING—A vessel is considered to be crossing another's course when she approaches her anywhere from not quite head on to 2 points abaft either beam.

When two vessels are crossing so as to involve risk of collision, the vessel which has the other on her own starboard side shall keep out of the way of the other.

In other words, you yield to a vessel in the sector covered by your green sidelight, a vessel that approaches from your right. The other skipper has you in his left, red, sidelight sector and so has the right of way over you.

How can you tell whether risk of collision is involved? Take a bearing on the other vessel. If it doesn't appreciably change during her approach, that risk exists.

The right-of-way vessel, the privileged vessel, keeps her course and speed.

The yielding vessel, the burdened vessel, shall slacken speed, stop or even reverse to pass astern of the other craft. Under some conditions you may want to turn radically to port to parallel her course. Don't pass ahead of a vessel crossing in your danger sector.

An optional whistle signal of one short blast may be given by the privileged vessel. It means: I have the right of way and shall continue on my course and speed.

OVERTAKING—A vessel is considered overtaking when she approaches another vessel anywhere from 2 points abaft the starboard beam to 2 points abaft the port beam. That is, she approaches in the sector covered by the stern light.

When you cannot be certain whether you are overtaking or crossing—close to 2 points abaft either beam—the rules decide it: You are overtaking.

The overtaking vessel shall keep out of the way of the overtaken vessel. And once you have been the overtaking vessel, no later course change can make you into a crossing one. You can't start by overtaking and then demand the right of a vessel crossing.

Unlike the driver of an automobile, you have a choice on which side to overtake. You let the other vessel know which side you have chosen by blasts on your whistle. One blast means: I'm directing my course to starboard, shall pass you on your starboard side. Two blasts mean: I'm directing my course to port, shall pass you on your port side. The overtaken vessel, if she thinks the maneuver safe, will answer with the same number of blasts. If she believes the maneuver unsafe, she will answer with the danger signal, four or more short blasts. You are not allowed to pass until you have reached agreement by whistle signals, and the vessels have reached a point where it is safe to pass

While the passing vessel must keep clear until she has passed, the overtaken vessel must not crowd upon the course of the overtaking vessel or cross her bow.

A sailboat that overtakes a powered craft has to keep clear.

Sailboats—and all other craft—also yield to vessels that can't readily get out of their way, for instance vessels fishing with nets or trawls.

SAILBOATS approaching one another so as to involve risk of collision

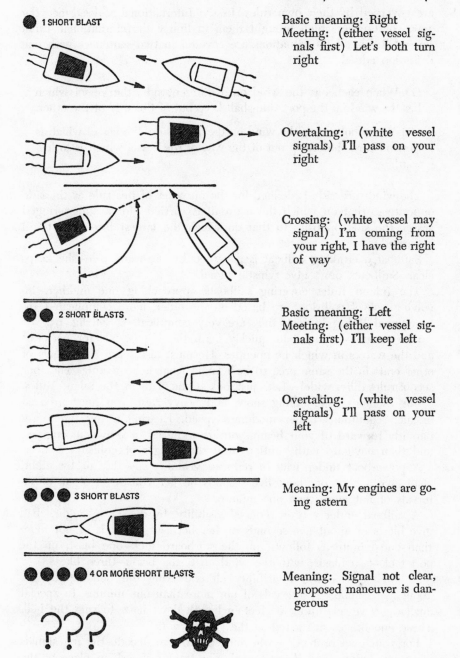

1 SHORT BLAST

Basic meaning: Right
Meeting: (either vessel signals first) Let's both turn right

Overtaking: (white vessel signals) I'll pass on your right

Crossing: (white vessel may signal) I'm coming from your right, I have the right of way

2 SHORT BLASTS

Basic meaning: Left
Meeting: (either vessel signals first) I'll keep left

Overtaking: (white vessel signals) I'll pass on your left

3 SHORT BLASTS

Meaning: My engines are going astern

4 OR MORE SHORT BLASTS

Meaning: Signal not clear, proposed maneuver is dangerous

94. Whistle signals (powerboats only).

are governed by their own rules. In the International Rules, since the 1960 conference which brought them in line with International Yacht Racing Rules, all the situations are covered in two sentences with one definition added.

(i) When each has the wind on a different side, the vessel which has the wind on the port side shall keep out of the way of the other.

(ii) When both have the wind on the same side, the vessel which is to windward shall keep out of the way of the vessel which is to leeward.

The windward side is defined for the purposes of this rule as the side opposite to that on which the mainsail is carried (for a square-rigged vessel, the side opposite to that on which the largest fore-and-aft sail is carried).

Sailboat overtaking sailboat is governed by the usual rule—she keeps clear. Sailboats don't give whistle signals.

The Inland Rules covering sailboats approaching one another, involving risk of collision, are based on the older, more complicated International Rules. In fact, they are very complicated. See fig. 95.

FOG SIGNALS—Anyone can quickly learn the fog signals for his craft and the waters in which he operates. He must also learn the signals of other craft in the same area so he'll know what he's meeting. The four sets of rules differ widely. Let's just look at one of them, the Inland Rules.

Fog includes mist, falling snow, and heavy rain. You must proceed in such conditions under moderate speed. Hearing a fog signal apparently forward of your beam, you are required to stop your engines, and then navigate with caution until the danger of collision is over.

A powerboat under way in reduced visibility, by day or by night, shall give a blast of about five seconds on her whistle or siren, at intervals of not more than one minute.

A sailboat under way in reduced visibility, by day or by night, shall give blasts of about five seconds on her horn, at intervals of not more than one minute as follows: on the starboard tack—one blast; on the port tack—two blasts; with the wind abaft the beam—three blasts.

At anchor in reduced visibility all craft ring the bell rapidly for about five seconds at intervals of not more than one minute. In special anchorages vessels under 60 feet in length don't have to ring the bell. These anchorages are listed in the Coast Pilot.

For your own protection you must be able to decode the fog signals of vessels towing and being towed. The towing vessel, in place of the one long blast, gives three blasts on her whistle or siren: one long, two shorts. The towed vessel may give the same signal on her foghorn (but not on whistle or siren).

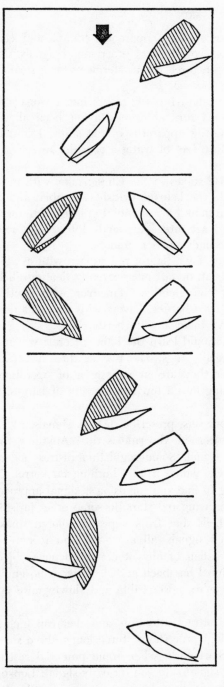

The vessel running free keeps out of the way of a vessel which is close-hauled.

The vessel close-hauled on the port tack (with the wind coming from her left) keeps out of the way of a vessel close-hauled on the starboard tack.

The vessel running free on the port tack keeps out of the way of a vessel running free on the starboard tack.

The windward vessel running free keeps out of the way of a downwind vessel running free on the same tack.

The vessel with the wind aft keeps out of the way of the other vessel.

95. Inland Rules of the Road for sailing vessels. In all sketches the wind comes from the top of the page. The black boat is to keep out of the way of the white vessel.

That's easy enough to memorize. The apparently complicated code for sailboats is really simple when you think of other sound signals. One always means starboard; two, port; three means sternway for a steamer, here it means wind over stern, more or less.

Even I can remember the fog rules. But fog scares me. I won't start out in it, and when I'm caught I turn chicken. Having been all but blasted out of the water by the fog apparatus of big ships, I lose no time getting out of their way. In 6 feet of water I consider myself safe from run-downs by supertankers.

I've taken my chances with fish stakes in the Chesapeake, with moss-covered rocks in Nova Scotia, in the kelp of British Columbia, and on the far side of spoil banks on the Inland Waterway. I got out of the way, anchored, and sat it out. Once I sat three days and—don't report me—didn't ring my bell for five seconds once a minute.

You should recognize the diver-down flag, a red square with a white slash, displayed from a vessel, boat, or raft or apparently floating all by itself. It means skin divers in the vicinity. Maneuver with caution. Snorkels are hard to see, heads even harder. Divers with air tanks don't show on the surface at all. Give them a wide berth.

For your own protection you should learn the lights of craft you may encounter in your waters, especially tugs. The two or three white-all-around-the-horizon—or whatever they are in your area of operation—lights will keep you from crashing into a towline, a string of barges, or a raft of logs.

The Rules of the Road, all four sets, prescribe distress signals. As far as the small-craft skipper is concerned, the rule is this: Anything that brings help is a good distress signal. Some regulation distress signals aren't too practical on a yacht, e.g. flames from a burning tar barrel. On the other hand, nobody is going to fine you for using a signal approved for the high seas, say rockets throwing red stars, in some other jurisdiction. Hand-held flares, signal shells shot from a pistol, colored smoke, continuous whistle, horn, or bell signals—all are good and recognized attention-getters. So is waving a flag or any other conspicuous object. Recently a special small-craft signal has been added. It needs no equipment at all. Just stand where you're most visible and slowly raise and lower your arms.

Whatever method you use to attract attention—and that can include blinking with a mirror, or sending three shorts, three longs, three shorts with a flashlight—keep it up. Start early when some potential rescuer comes in sight and keep making signals. Reason for early signal: Lookout is inclined to concentrate on the forward horizon. Reason for the late signal: Someone loafing near the stern may spot you.

Better yet: Stay out of trouble.

PART TWO:
ELECTRONIC NAVIGATION

13. Echo Sounding

Pilotage, chart-and-compass navigation, is a refinement of navigation by eye. It lets you navigate by buoys and other aids in strange waters. You can find courses, steer them by compass, and fix your position in any area for which you have a detailed chart. It also lets you estimate tides and currents in unfamiliar places.

But that traditional system of navigation has its limitations: It's still navigation by eye.

Electronic systems—the subject of the next chapters—extend the vision of the navigator. One system lets you see into the depth of murky water; another lets you take bearings on objects you can't see—objects below the horizon, or obscured by darkness, rain, and fog. One system lets you measure the distance to an unseen object; other systems let you fix your position hundreds, even thousands of miles from land.

Big ships, and planes, use several systems of electronic navigation. Some are so bulky you couldn't stow them on a yacht; some would drain your batteries in five minutes; others would only bankrupt you. But some fit neatly in every way on small craft.

Many boats carry a radiotelephone. But asking a friendly skipper, or the Coast Guard, "Can you tell me where I am?" isn't electronic navigation.

Even more boats carry electronic depth finders, echo sounders. They have virtually replaced the lead line as a navigational tool. Except in very shallow water the lead has to be heavy to sink to the bottom quickly enough. Then "swinging" the lead and retrieving it becomes hard work. And you may have to slow down to give the lead time to reach the bottom before you ride over it. With all that effort and inconvenience, several minutes may elapse between soundings.

An echo sounder gives soundings continuously, without effort.

Sounding has little to do with sounds we hear. It comes from an obsolete verb that meant to go deep—as a whale sounds—or to probe deeply—as a doctor does with a sound. Here "to sound" is to plumb the depth—as with a plumb (or lead) line. The depth figures on the chart are soundings. When you are in water so deep you can't conveniently measure its depth, you are "off soundings."

Someone may quibble that an echo sounder isn't an electronic device but uses sound signals and their echoes. Take the batteries out of that man's set. He'll realize that without electronics we couldn't amplify the echoes. Moreover, the signal used in modern echo sounders can hardly be called sound. You and I can't hear them. They are too high in pitch; higher even than ultrasonic dog whistles.

Navigation by sound is still useful. A lookout still listens for the sound of breakers, or vague noises from shore. In the often foggy and rain-swept inland passage to Alaska, the navigator still blows the whistle and counts the seconds until he hears the echo returned by the shore.

Sound in air travels a nautical mile in about five and a half seconds. You may have measured the distance of a stroke of lightning that way. If the sound of thunder reached you eleven seconds after you'd seen the flash, it was 2 miles away.

When you hear an echo the sound has traveled to the shore and back. So an eleven-second delay between whistle blast and echo means the shore is 1 nautical mile away. In round figures, each second of delay means a distance from shore of a tenth of a mile, 1 cable.

In the steep-walled inlets of British Columbia, tugs used a similar trick to keep their log tows in mid-channel. The skipper would give a short blast on the whistle. If the echo from the right came back before the one from the left, he'd ease to port. If the left echo came first, he'd ease to starboard.

An electronic depth finder sends inaudible sound waves downward, then listens for their return from the bottom. Translating the delay between ping and echo it indicates the depth.

So the name "echo sounder" describes it well. You could call it an electronic depth finder. Since "sounder" means depth probe, we shouldn't call it a depth sounder. You may call it a fathom meter, but Fathometer is the trademark of one particular brand. You may think sonar is a very scientific way to describe this method of measuring depth. But the sonar of World War II (sound navigation and ranging) sent its beam almost horizontally, hoping to detect an echo from a distant submarine or surface ship. To confuse matters, Sonar is the trademark of another make of echo sounder. When you are more interested in its use for fishing than for navigation, you may call it a fish finder.

The forerunner of the modern echo sounder used a hammer banging on the forepart of the hull with a microphone picking up the echo in the afterpart.

Modern depth finders use a more elegant system. A device called a transducer, outside the hull, replaces both hammer and microphone. Acting as an ultrasonic loudspeaker, it sends out a ping, and then, acting as a microphone, it receives the echo. The signal is fed to a black box that amplifies it and passes it on to the display unit.

Perhaps the simplest such display would be a neon light bulb on a revolving arm. The signal is sent when the bulb is on top. The bulb flashes when the echo arrives. The speed of sound in water is about 4,800 feet per second. If the arm that carries the bulb makes twenty-four revolutions per second, the bulb will be at the bottom position of its first trip around when a signal has traveled 100 feet. That breaks down to 50 feet down and 50 feet back. The depth indicated by that flash would be 50 feet.

Supplying current to a revolving light bulb creates a contact problem. So many depth finders have the bulb stand still while a slit in front of it rotates. The effect is the same: You'll see the flash when the echo arrives. Many echo sounders let you connect more than one indicator. You could have one near the wheel, one by the chart table; or one in the cockpit and one on the flying bridge.

Echo sounders manufactured in the United States are calibrated for a speed of sound—or ultrasound—of 4,800 feet per second. Actually that speed varies a little with temperature, pressure, and especially salinity. Even in fresh water sound travels a bit faster than the speed assumed in calibration; so the error is always on the side of safety. There'll be more water than indicated by your instrument.

The soundings on modern charts were taken with echo sounders calibrated to the same speed as yours. Since salinity and the other factors remain virtually constant at any one place, your soundings and the ones printed on the chart are directly comparable.

Sometimes they'll disagree wildly. You may read, as in the example above, 50 feet where the chart shows 150 feet. What has gone wrong? Nothing. On the scale of the example—once around equals 100 feet—the 150-foot echo will show on the 50-foot mark on the *second* turn of the indicator. If your instrument has different ranges, switch to greater depth. That slows down the rate of rotation. If you drop to twelve revolutions per second, the flash will come at the three-quarter point of the first revolution of the bulb or slit.

This second-round echo business seems like a serious shortcoming of depth finders. In practical navigation it seldom is. Even when you've outrun the deepest range, you'll seldom be in doubt which is correct. And you don't often get suddenly from 50-foot depths into 150-foot depths. The intermediate sixties, seventies, etc. will warn you when you've outrun your 100-foot scale.

Also, the deeper echo will be weaker than one from less depth. If you turn down the amplifier gain—a knob comparable to the volume control on a radio, and usually marked "Sensitivity"—weaker echoes will disappear, stronger echoes, from nearer bottom, will remain.

The same knob also eliminates double echoes in very shallow water. These echoes are bounced off your hull, back to the bottom, and are picked up again on their second or third round trip. You'll spot them easily: If the first flash is at 10 feet, the second will be at 20, a third one at 30. Deluxe models may have an automatic volume control.

You can simply ignore multiple echoes by following the general rule: *Read the least depth.* That applies also to the flashes themselves, which have some width. The least depth, the trailing edge of the flash, the first return is what matters.

The width of the flash is easily explained. The sound waves spread out as they go deeper, just as the beam of a flashlight spreads with distance. The first echo to come back is from the nearest point of the bottom. That's not necessarily directly below the transducer, but nearest

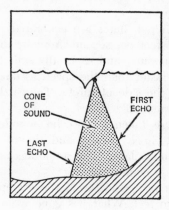

96. Principle of echo sounding. Transducer mounted on hull sends out a burst of sound or ultrasound waves. Reflected from the bottom, the signal is picked up by the same transducer. Time elapsed between sending and receiving the signal gives indication of depth.

Under water the signal spreads into a cone of sound, so the echo will last longer than the original burst of sound. A range of depths will be indicated. The first echo measures the least depth within the cone, not necessarily directly below the transducer.

to it. Other points within the beam of the signal report back later. Early models had cones of coverage as wide as 60 degrees. Now narrower beams are used, down to a few degrees for surveying and for spotting individual fish.

It depends mainly on your transducer. They come in a variety of mountings. One type is simply dunked overboard; another is permanently mounted low on the transom. Some are mounted alongside the keel. The most popular installation is somewhere low on the hull, in a through-hull tube, or on an externally mounted fairing block. A sailboat may need two transducers; one would be in the acoustical shadow of the keel when she heels.

Regardless of the type of transducer, you'll sometimes get two depth readings.

A school of fish, large or small, may cause the first reading, the true bottom the second. Fishermen claim they can often identify the species of fish from the echoes displayed on a strip chart.

You may have heard of the deep scattering layer, a phantom bottom probably caused by small sea creatures. It's below the range of most small-craft echo sounders, near 200 fathoms by day, closer to the surface by night.

A layer of fresh over salt water, and sudden temperature changes with depth will give you trouble if you look for enemy submarines. You probably won't.

But you'll get true double bottoms. A layer of mud sends the first echo, the underlying rock the second. That shows beautifully on depth recorder charts. It won't confuse you if you read the least depth on your flasher model. Before long you may even get good at guessing the bottom material.

Depth finders for small craft use very little current. They are available for common boat voltages, or run on their own dry cell batteries.

Some units combine amplifier and indicator unit, others have them separate. The two-unit models let you keep the amplifier's disturbance far from the compass. But check the display unit—on and off—when compensating your compass.

Your echo sounder also needs adjustment. The transducer, though below the water line, is not at the lowest point of your boat. That saves transducers and leaks when you touch bottom. (By the way: It must never be mounted flush with the hull. It has to protrude through the curtain of disturbed water and air bubbles pulled along by the skin of your craft.)

The unadjusted reading of the echo sounder is neither the actual depth of water nor the clearance under your hull. Many depth finders have a screw that lets you adjust the zero setting.

Some skippers adjust for "water under the keel." In 10 feet of water with a 4-foot draft such a skipper would adjust the zero setting until the instrument read 6 feet. That's fine if you use the echo sounder only for keeping water under her keel.

When you use it also for navigation—I'll come to that in a minute— setting the zero to conform with the water level makes matters easier, I think. In 10 feet of water, regardless of your boat's draft, you'd adjust the zero screw until the instrument reads 10 feet.

With an echo sounder that has no zero adjustment you'll have to re-member your corrections. With the transducer 3 feet below the water line the instrument will read 7 feet in 10 feet of water. You then have to subtract 1 foot to get depth under the keel; add 3 feet to get the actual depth of water at that spot.

It becomes quite automatic. Some depth finders are even more automatic: They ring an alarm when you get to a pre-set depth. Give yourself plenty of warning. No skipper in his right mind would set the alarm to his draft. That'd make it into a you-have-run-aground alarm. You don't need that.

With its accurate, effortless, continuous soundings a depth finder is a great safety device for the small-craft skipper. Can it get him into trouble? Indeed it can, when he forgets its principle: The search beam is directed downward and bounces up; it does not look ahead of your vessel. On a rocky shore you may be in 30 feet of water one minute, run head on into a rock the next.

The accuracy of echo sounders makes them great tools for navigation in some areas. Typically your depth finder will be accurate to less than 1 foot at minimum depth, within a few per cent of true depth at maximum range. This accuracy and the even greater accuracy of nautical charts often give the pilot position lines, and sometimes a fix. Navigating by comparing measured with charted depths has an impressive name: bathymetric navigation.

To make your measured depths comparable with the charted soundings, you must refer them to the datum of the chart. When the tide has raised your craft 8 feet above the datum plane—Mean Low Water—you must deduct 8 feet from your readings before you compare them with the figures on the chart.

The tide tables use the same reference plane as the charts. Where it's necessary to allow for tides—including minus tides—you can use table 3 in the tide book to get the height at any time. Where the tidal interval is about six hours you can use the simpler method I discussed on p. 98.

In the open ocean, as opposed to sounds and bays, the change in tide level will probably be too small to matter.

In lakes the correction for water level will not change from hour to hour, but may change from week to week. When the lake is below charted level, you'll have to subtract from the printed figures.

This is written during a drought in Florida. Lake Okeechobee is 3 feet below its charted level. If my depth finder, set to read from the water line, showed 8 feet, I'd expect the chart to show 11 feet at that spot.

It doesn't help much here that the soundings on the chart agree with my measurement. There are many, many places in this lake that show 11 feet. But when my measured depth disagrees with the depth shown on the chart for my dead reckoning position, I'd know that I'm not where I thought I was.

You may say that's rather negative navigation. True. But how many ships would still be afloat if their navigators hadn't trusted their reckoning?

Sometimes a single sounding can fix your position. Say the deepest spot in your lake is 40 feet. If your depth finder shows 40 feet, or perhaps 39 or 41, that's where you are. You've got a fix.

On a large lake there may be two or three spots with 40-foot soundings. But often the vaguest knowledge of your whereabouts will positively identify the one spot where you measure the same depth. Such deep spots in shallower surroundings—blue holes—will often locate your exact position in coastal waters.

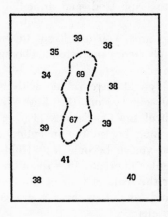

97. A deep spot amid shallower soundings may give a navigational fix.

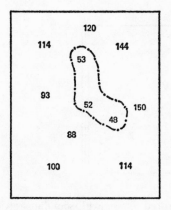

98. A shallow spot amid deeper soundings may also give a navigational fix.

The opposite, shallow soundings surrounded by deeper water, will do the same. I'm not just talking about sunken islands or seamounts, but such everyday spots as reefs and wrecks. Here, any echo sounder will also often act as a fish finder. Providing shelter for the fish, these are often the productive spots. That's the reason for dumping car bodies to make artificial reefs.

You've discovered in pilotage what useful position lines depth contours make. You don't have to remember the code that distinguishes the various depth lines. If you find soundings up to 59 feet landward of a dash-dot-dash line, and soundings of 61 feet or more to seaward, you'll know that's the 60-foot contour, the 10-fathom line.

Along gently sloping flat shores these lines often give a fair indication of your distance from land. Such shores are common. One reaches from Sandy Hook, New Jersey, all the way to southern Florida.

You have seen (pp. 16–17) how in thick weather a skipper could follow the 30-foot contour line from Chatham to Cape Cod, and around the Cape right into Provincetown.

If you'll study a chart of your cruising area, you are likely to find such a contour line that you could ride safely into a protected anchorage or harbor.

My lost shrimp boat skipper (p. 115) could have ridden with his echo sounder just outside the 20-fathom curve from the Key West whistle buoy right to the bell buoy south of the Quicksands (fig. 75).

Here's a method, recommended since long before the invention of echo sounders, for locating yourself when you've become lost. Hold a straight course and take soundings at regular intervals. Plot them on a piece of tracing paper properly spaced for the scale of your chart. Then shift the tracing of your course line and soundings over the chart until your soundings match those on the chart.

99. Tracing paper method of matching measured depths with soundings given on nautical chart. Plot soundings taken at regular intervals (here every five minutes) to the scale of the chart (at 6 knots one half mile apart). Lay tracing oriented for your course (300 T) over the chart; slide it about to get best match with charted soundings.

Where my shrimper friend got lost the method wouldn't have worked. The chart there shows too many soundings between 11 and 15 fathoms arranged in what seems random order. In fact, I've tested the method on several charts by making tracings one day, trying to fit them the next. I'd still be lost.

Sometimes you can fix your position off a river mouth or opening to a bay. You follow a contour line and watch your compass at the same time. The contour line in many places will parallel the shore until material of the bar forces it away from shore. Such bars often give a depth contour, say the 10-fathom curve, a distinct "nose." For many miles you have been on the 10-fathom curve, steering due north by your compass. When you come to the beginning of the nose you have to

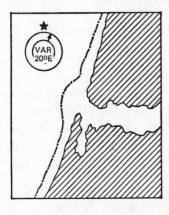

100. Decreasing depths on steady course locates vessel—here on offshore bar at mouth of bay.

steer west of north to stay in 10 fathoms of water. When you get into deeper water on that new course and have to turn east of north to continue on the 10-fathom line, you're on the tip of the nose.

The reverse of a build-up at the mouth of a river or bay will make the contour lines approach the shore. Where an ancient glacier has bulldozed a submarine furrow you'll fall into deeper water when you maintain a course parallel to the shore. At such a canyon your echo

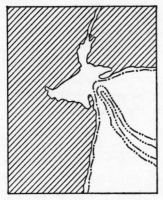

101. Increasing depths on steady course locates vessel—here approaching edge of submarine valley.

sounder, though set to maximum sensitivity and range, may fail to show bottom. In Navy language, you've lost tracking.

You then have two crossing position lines: the continuation of the contour line you've been following, and the depth beyond reach of your echo sounder, the first wall of the submarine valley.

Lost tracking—make certain it isn't just a malfunction—will also locate your vessel over a deep pool, or blue hole, if it's the only one in the vicinity.

Impressed with the usefulness of your echo sounder for navigation, don't overlook its basic limitation for safety. To repeat: It does not look ahead.

In Nassau a yachtsman, just returned from the Exumas, asked, "What's all the fuss about coral heads? Going and coming, my depth finder never showed less than 8 feet." He had come over the Yellow Bank, which on the chart is measled with little crosses. If he'd been just a little to the north of his course, he'd have brushed Middle Ground, which besides the crosses carries the note "forest of shallow coral." Yet his echo sounder had shown 8- to 12-foot soundings. Of course; it won't show a coral head until you are over it. Too late. (A chapter in my *Practical Boating* shows how you *can* spot them in time.)

Even in northern waters, where there are no coral heads, a depth finder can let you down. Have you read James Dugan's delightful *The Great Iron Ship?* It's the story of the *Great Eastern,* 693 feet long and designed to carry almost twice as many passengers as the *Queen Mary.* At the entrance to Long Island Sound she discovered a rock still named after her. The pilot had just taken over. Soundings were about 40 feet when the men on the bridge heard a dull rumble. The ship heeled a few degrees to port. The passengers slept.

A diver later inspected the damage: a hole 9 feet wide and 83 feet long. An echo sounder, if it had been invented in 1862, would not have given warning of this rock needle, which rises to within 24 feet of the surface.

Navigation by echo sounder is habit-forming. When his machine quits, a skipper may forget that the deep-sea lead and some work also give soundings.

He may also get so wrapped up in his newly discovered bathymetry that he forgets to tie in soundings with other position lines, say visual bearings. When visual bearings are lacking he could use position lines from a radio direction finder. That's what the next chapter is about.

14. Radio Direction Finding

If you've ever carried a portable radio, you probably have discovered that turning the set changes the reception. Facing the transmitter, the set brings in a station well; turn it about 90 degrees and the reception fades.

The built-in aerial—usually a coil wrapped around a ferrite rod—explains this effect. When the radio waves from the station hit the rod broadside, reception is best; when they hit it endways, reception is poorest.

Many years ago, when we still used loop antennas, it became obvious that this effect could be used to get navigational position lines and fixes.

If you try your radio as a direction finder, you'll be disappointed. You have to turn it through a wide arc before the volume changes. An automatic volume control circuit (AVC) is built into every receiver to keep the sound level approximately constant. When the signal weakens the set amplifies it more; when the signal gets stronger it amplifies it less.

Even with the automatic volume control made inoperative, you'd find it difficult to find the direction of *best* reception. The volume will remain about the same as you turn the set through 20 or 30 degrees. The direction of least volume is much easier to gauge. Turn the set a few degrees and you'll hear the signal clearly, then barely, then clearly again.

In the middle of the near-silent zone, the *null*, the ferrite rod points in the direction of the radio waves.

You don't have to rely on your sense of hearing. You can show the strength of the signal on a meter. You turn the set and watch the needle. When it points to the lowest reading, you've got your null.

Practically, it's simpler—and more accurate—to have the aerial outside the set, perhaps mounted on top. Then the set remains in place and you rotate only the aerial. A 360-degree scale lets you read the exact direction of the aerial.

Combine the reading on that scale with the heading of your craft —both taken at the time of nulling—and you've the direction of travel of the radio waves. If you know where they are coming from, you can plot a position line on your chart.

There might be a doubt whether you measured the direction of the radio waves coming or going. Either end of the rod—often still called *loop*—may be facing the transmitter. That'll seldom bother you. Off the east coast of Florida a bearing of 090 is clearly impossible. You'd be on dry land. A shore station has to be west of you, bearing 270.

When doubt is possible, you can eliminate it electronically by connecting a second aerial to your set. The second aerial—a whip, for example—is nondirectional. Hitching it up with the directional antenna mysteriously makes one of the two possible nulls disappear. For the final measurement you disconnect the second antenna. It's used only to get the sense of the bearing; that's why it's called *sense* antenna.

If you converted a radio—null meter, rotating aerial, bearing scale, sense antenna, no automatic volume control—and tried it for getting bearings from broadcasting stations, you'd still be disappointed in the results.

First, there's the problem of identification. Broadcasting stations are closely bunched on the dial, especially near the high-frequency end. In home waters you may recognize an announcer's voice, but on a network program you may have to wait half an hour before the station identifies itself.

Then, the radio waves don't come from the studio in the downtown hotel, but from the transmitter aerial that might be in a cabbage patch miles from the studio. How do you draw a position line from the transmitter when you don't know where it is?

Worse, over land the waves from the broadcasting transmitter don't travel exactly in straight lines. Hills may deflect them. Also, crossing from land to water, radio waves bend. This coastal refraction, or land effect, has to do with different reflecting and conducting properties of land and water. It's least when the waves cross the coast at right angles, greatest when they travel more or less along the shore.

Transmitters close to shore may give fairly reliable radio bearings. Their towers are shown on nautical charts, giving call letters (e.g. WQXT) and frequency (e.g. 1340 kHz) next to the R TR, which identifies the landmark symbol. The dot inside the circle is the exact location. (The abbreviation kHz stands for kilohertz, a unit we called until recently kilocycles, one thousand cycles per second; in the same way mHz, for megahertz, has replaced megacycles—one million cycles per second.)

Most navigators use broadcast stations on the AM band, which operate on frequencies between 535 and 1650 kHz, only when they can't find anything better for radio direction finding. They usually can: Marine radio beacons. You'll find them not only on the coasts of North America and the Great Lakes, but along most seacoasts of the world.

Radio direction finders are built primarily for reception of these beacons and typically cover a band of 190–420 kHz. Most also cover the AM band, many the marine band (2–4 mHz), some also parts of the VHF or UHF bands, useful for weather forecasts twenty-four hours a day.

Direction finders differ in sensitivity—the ability of bringing in weak signals—and selectivity—the ability of separating a strong signal from a weaker one near it on the dial. Depending on quality, number of bands covered, and refinements and conveniences, direction finders typically cost between $100 and $200. Refinements may include noise-limiting circuits that squelch interference, lights for scale and null meter, battery tester, etc.

Most sets now have a beat frequency oscillator, put in operation by a switch marked BFO. While not essential for direction finding, BFO helps with reception of Consolan signals, discussed in the next chapter. It also lets you receive single side band (SSB) in the marine band, soon to be the only sanctioned transmission on these frequencies.

Radio direction finders often operate on their own dry batteries. You can also run them, and other gear such as depth finders, off a hot-shot battery. It's cheaper, lasts longer, and you don't risk a messy leak inside your set. Or you can run them with little drain off your ship's batteries.

The marine radio beacons are marked on nautical charts. Look for a purple circle around a landmark or light symbol. Purple circles are used around other electronic aids (but not for entertainment radio towers); marine radio beacons are identified by the letters R Bn.

Off Savannah, for example, you'll find such a symbol with the notation 317 . . — — & — added. If you tune to 317 kHz you'll hear two dots and two dashes repeated for fifty seconds and followed by a long dash. That ten-second dash—now standard on marine beacons in the United States—is the best time to null your set by ear. Then the cycle repeats.

You don't have to learn Morse code. The dashes are three times as long as the dots, the repetition helps in identification.

The Savannah beacon has a nominal range of 20 nautical miles; other beacons carry much farther. So there aren't enough frequencies to keep them all separated. As a remedy, in many areas several beacons—usually six—transmit in turn on the same frequency. Example: On the southern Atlantic coast of the United States the following share 294 kHz:

Name	Characteristic	Sequence	Range
Frying Pan Shoals	— —	I	70
Georgetown	. . — .	II	30
Charleston	.	III	70
Tybee	. — . — .	IV	70
Jupiter	. — — —	V	125
Cape Kennedy	— — . .	VI	55

Frying Pan Shoals light station starts the cycle of transmissions on the hour. It'll sound its two dashes for fifty seconds, then sign off with a ten-second dash. Georgetown transmits next for one minute, and so on down the line until after Cape Kennedy's long dash Frying Pan Shoals comes on the air again, six minutes after the hour.

In many areas this multiple use of one frequency not only allows more beacons, it also helps the navigator. He gets several radio bearings without retuning his receiver.

The charts don't show the group sequence of the beacons. Perhaps a card giving the beacons in your area came with your set. Make sure it's up to date. You can compare it with the light list published by the U. S. Coast Guard.

The Naval Oceanographic Office lists radio beacons in *Radio Navigational Aids* (publication 117A covers the Atlantic—including the Great Lakes—and Mediterranean; 117B covers the Pacific and Indian oceans). Charts of small areas guide you to a detailed description of every beacon. Both volumes come in ring binders ($5), but you can buy the contents without binder ($3.50) and keep the pages that interest you in your own folder.

In the lists you'll find some beacons described as "low power, for local use only." Such beacons, often placed at the entrance to some bay or harbor, don't carry far enough to need an identifying signal. In the United States they all use the same characteristic: a series of half-second dashes for 13.5 seconds; then 1.5 seconds of silence; then the dashes again.

Besides these beacons meant to guide you to a harbor, and the ones for landfall and coastal navigation—often at lighthouses, lightships, and the structures that have replaced lightships—you can use beacons intended mainly for air navigation.

The ones useful for marine navigation are shown on nautical charts. The symbol is the same as for marine radio beacons, with the word "aero" added.

The one on Bimini (396 — — . . — . . . — . . .) helps you in crossing the Gulf Stream. Its range is 75 miles, and you'll hear it before you leave Florida. On the Florida side you'll probably ignore Miami aero beacon, well inland, using rather the marine beacons on Fowey Rocks and at Hillsboro light.

The basic technique for using a radio direction finder is simple. Switch on the set. Switch the band selector to beacon band, probably marked LF for low frequency, then tune to the given frequency. Identify the beacon by its code signal and turn the loop aerial to get the null.

If at the time of your finding the null the bearing scale (also called *azimuth ring*) is set so that its zero faces forward, exactly in the fore-and-aft line of your craft, the indicator gives a *relative* bearing. That's a

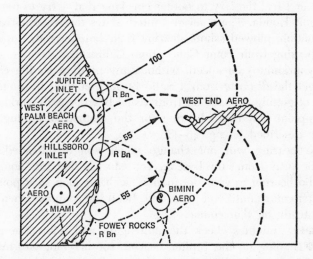

102. Overlapping radio beacons provide navigational fixes. Light list gives normal range for marine beacons—shown as dashed circles—but not for most aero beacons. However, Bimini's range (75 miles) is listed.

bearing relative to your craft. Straight ahead is 000, astern is 180; 090 is on the starboard beam, 270 on the port beam.

To get the proper zero setting quickly, the direction finder should be secured more or less permanently to the boat. A low fence of quarter-round molding, or two battens and two straps of shock cord, will do that nicely. There's another reason for keeping your direction finder always in the same spot: your compass. If you moved it about, its magnetism—mainly in the loudspeaker—would upset your carefully adjusted compass. The farther you can get it from the compass, the better. Three feet is the accepted minimum.

I'll come to yet another reason for permanent installation a bit later.

With the 000–180-degree line of the direction finder parallel with the fore-and-aft line of your vessel, zero toward the bow, you can check —even without using the sense antenna—that you're reading the correct bearing and not its exact opposite.

The rule is simple: The bearing of a land station will continuously pull aft as you steam along.

If at one time a beacon was broad on the starboard bow (relative bearing 045), later it will be abeam (090) and keep moving aft. If the first bearing was broad on the port bow (relative bearing 315), it will move aft, reading 270 when on the beam.

Whenever I feel too lazy to bother checking that, I try to remind myself of Point Honda. There seven United States destroyers, steaming in tight formation, plowed ashore, tearing their bottoms out. Cause: a reciprocal bearing from Point Conception, California.

When you know your speed, without any plotting on the chart you can also get the *distance* from a radio by its changing bearing. Any of the tricks of getting distance off from visual bearings will work. You can use the 4-point and beam bearing, or the method of timing a mark abeam, as described on pp. 46–48.

A radio bearing will *not* change when you are headed directly toward (or away from) the beacon. You can use that for "homing." To ride a radio bearing to your destination, set your loop so it points dead ahead. Alter course until you get a null. Read the compass when you get it. Then steady on that course.

After a few minutes check the null again and refine the course if necessary. Homing on the Jupiter beacon, southbound, you might first get a course of 173 M. Five minutes later, when you hear its dot-dash-dash-dash again, you may correct that to 175 M. You'll get a fresh check every six minutes.

This method is so accurate that lightships have been rammed by vessels homing on their radio beacons in thick weather. So now some of the few lightships still on duty send out a warbling note over their identifying signal. When you hear the warble it means: Change course, you're too darn close.

I know of no good name for it, but you can also home in reverse, run away from home using a radio beacon at your point of departure. As with a visual bearing, that lets you check on the accuracy of your course made good, leeway, and current. The radio beacon will help you long after you would have lost a visual bearing astern.

Crossing a known current such as the Gulf Stream, most navigators would not use a radio beacon ahead or astern for homing or running away. Of course, you'd get to Bimini from Miami if you were to home the Bimini aero beacon, but you'd have to change course all the time. To allow for the stream, most navigators would set a course to a point south of Bimini, then check their progress with radio bearings and fixes plotted on the chart.

They would combine the relative bearings of the direction finder with the boat's heading to get magnetic bearings of the beacons. You can plot such a magnetic bearing exactly as you would plot a visual bearing taken with a bearing compass.

You can combine the reading of the direction finder with the heading by compass mathematically or graphically.

Say the direction finder gives 280 degrees relative, the heading is 045 M; the beacon then is 325 M from you. You'd plot it, in the opposite direction from the beacon, using the inner compass rose on the chart. The line you've drawn is your position line. Label it with the time as you label any bearing line. You may add the letter *R*, to show that it's a radio, not a visual, bearing.

You could also draw a line near your approximate position to indicate your heading, 045 M, and draw a second line at the relative bearing, 280, toward the radio beacon. (Holding the pencil point on the beacon helps with the mechanics of drawing that line.) If your course was 045 M, your course line will serve as the first line in this method. But often you'll be a few degrees off course when you get your null; then you'd have to draw the heading line.

On many direction finders you can set the bearing scale to any desired degree mark. That lets you combine radio bearings and magnetic headings with a minimum of thought. It doesn't matter whether your compass has the lubber's line at the far side or near you. As long as the azimuth scale and your compass can be aligned to read the same figure, the scale will do the figure work.

To be able to align the two, you must be able to read the compass squarely—not from the side—at the moment of nulling. Yet the direction finder should not be too near the compass. That's sometimes not easy to arrange.

You may wonder why they don't build a compass directly into a direction finder. Before you rush off to the patent office with that idea, let me assure you that it has been done. In several models. One simply attaches the aerial to a regulation hand bearing compass. You read the radio bearing as you would a visual bearing. To get away from the magnetism in the loudspeaker, many such devices use earphones instead.

To make the direction finder's compass read correctly, you'll have to get away from on-board magnetic disturbances. You'll always have to use the direction finder in the same spot. You can check it for magnetic cleanliness as you did for compass adjustment with a hand bearing compass (page 65).

Models with built-in compasses do away with the bother of allowing for the boat's compass heading. But you may not like to have to pop out of the cabin when homing or running away from home. Before you buy such a direction finder, or any other, try one of the same kind borrowed from a friend, or on approval from a store.

You'll soon find out that you can use all radio position lines like visual bearings. You can cross a position line from a radio beacon with any other—a depth contour for instance—to get a fix. If nothing better is available, you could plot a *running* radio fix by plotting a first line of position, moving it forward as though you had dragged it through the water at the speed and on the course of your vessel, and crossing it with a later position line from the same radio beacon.

More often you'll cross one radio bearing with that from another radio beacon. Navigators label the intersection of such position lines RDF FIX. (You can use R to mark radio position lines, but R FIX would mean *running* fix to most navigators.)

If you can cross three position lines at the same time, so much the better. Three radio bearings will probably not make a neat little triangle as you'd get from three visual bearing lines. Reason: Radio bearings, however carefully taken, with the best equipment, are less accurate than visual bearings. Under good conditions, on the beacon band, your error will likely be of the order of plus or minus 2 degrees.

In the hour before and after sunrise and sunset a single bearing may have a much larger error. Repeat the bearing a couple of times to see if it changes. At these times of day the null, which normally is easily found, may be smeared over as much as 10 degrees.

Even with this "night effect," it sounds as if a radio direction finder would make an expert navigator out of anyone who can afford one. It's a great tool.

But it's only a tool; so is a saw. You wouldn't expect to build a dining room chair the first time you laid hands on a saw. A square box for the ship's cat would be a challenge. Don't then follow the example of many owners of RDF sets and wait for the first fog to see if it'll get you home. On the contrary, use it in clear weather, in familiar waters, where you know your position anyway.

The instruction book that comes with the set will get you started, even if it has been written by an engineer, who knew too much, or a sales executive, who knew too little.

Good-weather practice will make you familiar with the tricks of homing, getting position lines, and plotting radio fixes. It will also introduce you to the beacons—marine and aero—in your cruising area. Then you won't have to count dots and dashes, but will recognize beacons as you recognize a skipper's voice on the ship-to-shore before he identifies himself.

You'll become familiar with the oddities of your radio direction finder. Regardless of make or model, it probably won't point true on *your* boat, just as a perfect compass brought aboard won't show true direction. With direction finders it's not magnetism aboard that upsets them, but electric conductors—masts, aerials, rigging, stanchions, railings, and such. We can't counteract radio deviation with magnets as we do with magnetic deviation. We can only find the errors and allow for them.

On a Bahamian smack with its wooden mast, rope rigging, and without aerial and cockpit awning hoops, you wouldn't have any radio deviation. On a more typical sailboat with wire rigging and perhaps an aluminum mast, you'll have errors of several degrees on some relative bearings.

It's the *relative* bearing that matters here, the direction of the arrival of the radio waves with respect to your boat; her heading at the time doesn't matter. When your bow faces the transmitter—relative bearing 000—your direction finder may null at 005. It'll show the same 5-degree error whether you approach the transmitter beacon from the east or the west, or any course in between.

You are likely to find the greatest errors when the radio waves arrive halfway between bow and beams, or on the quarters. That's on or near relative bearings of 045, 135, 225, and 315.

A steel or aluminum craft may have unpredictable errors all around the card. A fiber glass or wood cruiser may be comparatively free of radio deviation except on a couple of relative bearings.

You'll want to know how good or how bad RDF is on your boat. You may be tempted to test it dockside. No good. Wires, lampposts, and other boats will spoil the test. You've got to get away from shore. Also away from overhead power lines and bridges. (San Francisco Bay charts carry a warning not to rely on any radio bearing within one half mile of Golden Gate Bridge.)

You'll avoid making the test when night effect is probable.

You're interested mainly in the beacon band, so you'll have to test your set on a beacon. It'll probably have different—very likely larger—errors on the entertainment band. You'll choose, if possible, a beacon that operates continuously, not as part of a group. (You'd waste five minutes out of six waiting for it to come back on the air.) A marker beacon will do nicely.

In sight of such a beacon you can check a hand-held direction finder with built-in compass easily. You compare the radio bearings it gives directly with visual bearings. For that purpose such a direction finder has sight vanes, similar to gunsights, that let you use it for visual bearings.

You have already checked some spot on deck and found it magnetically undisturbed. Now in an area out of traffic, a mile or two from the beacon, you put the boat in a series of relative bearings. That sounds complicated but is easy. Head straight for the beacon; the beacon over the bow is relative bearing 000. If you made a slow circle, say to the left, you'd soon have the beacon on the starboard beam—relative bearing—relative to your bow, that is—090. When the beacon is astern, the relative bearing will be 180, and so on.

Have someone steer the boat while you concentrate on taking bearings. Have him head for the beacon and hold a steady course. You null the radio signal, then quickly take a visual bearing. If the two agree within 2 degrees, say radio bearing 045, visual bearing between 043 and 047, tell the helmsman to come left 15 degrees and steady on that course. You again take a radio and a visual bearing, and have him come left again 15 degrees. You repeat this routine clear around the compass.

Since you're moving about, the bearings will differ during this set of observations. That doesn't matter as long as the radio bearing and the visual one at the same spot agree tolerably well.

If all the bearings agree more or less, say within 2 degrees, you'll probably want to forget the whole business. Perhaps on one or two sets of bearings you'll be several degrees off. Often you can see the trouble-maker. The ship-to-shore aerial when in line with the beacon may throw the direction finder off. If it's just in one or two directions, I'd make a mental note never to use it in that direction. In the future I'd change course a few degrees whenever a beacon was "behind" such a trouble-maker. To avoid a course change you could find another spot on deck for the few disturbed directions. While still in sight of the beacon you could check them out on the relative bearings on which you plan to use them.

Unfortunately—especially on a sailboat with its many stays—you may find disturbed directions all around the compass. Some experts recommend insulating the stays at their lower fittings. That may work. But it'll deprive you of the lightning rod protection of your grounded mast.

If you use a hand-held direction finder with its own compass, don't listen to experts who'd have you make a radio deviation card for all the various errors. You'd lose the advantage of the built-in compass. The correction depends on the relative bearing, not the direction finder reading. So you'd have to consult the ship's compass to calculate the relative bearing. Just what you had tried to avoid.

With many and sizable deviations you'd be better off with a set that uses the ship's compass in the first place. These sets too have sight vanes on the rotating aerial. That lets you compare radio bearings of a beacon in plain sight if you have a very open deckhouse with just a few posts. On many boats even a contortionist couldn't take visual bearings with the direction finder. (No use carrying it on deck; you want to know its errors where you'll use it.)

Perhaps you could have a helper take visual bearings with a hand bearing compass on deck, while you work the radio bearings below. For a quick check that's a good method.

If you find many deviations or several large ones, you can make a deviation card by another method. Work with a continuously operating beacon 20 or more miles away, and at a location you can pinpoint on the chart. The idea here is that moving about in calibrating your set will not change the bearing of the beacon. When the beacon is 20 miles away you only have to stay within a 2,000-foot circle to keep the magnetic bearing of the beacon constant within one half degree.

Put the azimuth circle of the direction finder on zero, straight ahead. It'll stay that way for the rest of the calibration.

Next put the loop aerial also on zero, dead ahead.

Now head for the beacon and steady on the course that gives a null. If by the chart the radio beacon bears 045 M, the compass should read 045 when you get the null. If it does, you've no error on relative bearing 000.

Next set the loop to 015 and come left until you get a null again. Without radio deviation the compass should now read 030. If it does, you've no radio deviation on relative bearing 015.

You can see the pattern: The setting of the loop—the relative bearing—added to the compass reading should equal the magnetic bearing of the radio beacon.

If on the next test, loop at 030, the compass reads 013, the sum is 043 instead of 045. On all future readings on relative bearing 030 you'll have to add 2 degrees to compensate for the radio deviation.

A clipboard will keep all these figures straight. It'll also help when you get past 360 degrees, as you will on the next course. The loop is set to 045; the compass should read 360. Sum 405. Just subtract 360 from these readings to bring them back to the familiar scale. (For 405 write 045.)

You can continue the calibration swing—backing and filling if necessary to stay in the 2,000-foot circle.

On some headings the sum of relative bearing and compass reading will be greater than the correct bearing. Then your correction for radio deviation will be minus. You'll have to deduct the deviation found from radio direction finder readings at these relative bearings.

Here's how your clipboard may look:

Bearing of radio beacon per chart 045M

RDF Loop (relative bearing)	COMPASS (heading of boat)	RDF (magnetic bearing)	CORRECTION to relative RDF bearing
000	045	045	0
015	030	045	0
030	013	043	+2
045	357	402=042	+3
060	...	...=...	..
...	...	...=...	..
345	061	406=46	−1

If the error gets no worse than 3 degrees all around the compass, I'd be more than satisfied. After all, that error also includes the magnetic deviation left on your compass after compensation. And that deviation depends on the heading of the boat. So calibrating at a different spot you'd get different corrections.

If you find homing and its reverse useful in your area, try a few courses with the loop exactly in the fore-and-aft line. I'd like to have them close to accurate. I wouldn't give up boating and spend the season in preparing deviation cards for direction finder and compass.

You may find RDF errors tolerable on most loop positions, badly off on a few others. On some sets you could mark these positions by sticking

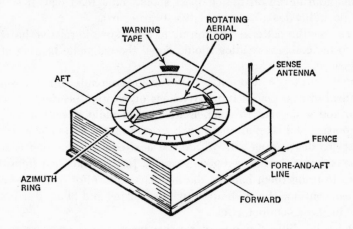

103. Radio direction finder. Tape warns of area of relative bearings with large radio deviation.

colored tape to the housing of the set. Whenever the loop points to a colored patch, you'd disregard it. To get a reliable radio bearing you could change course to bring the loop into an area where there's no tape.

On such sets you could tape the corrections directly to the top of the direction finder. Regardless of the heading of the boat and the setting of the azimuth ring, the loop aerial of a permanently mounted direction finder points to the same spot on the set when its on the same relative bearing. And—once more—it's the relative position of the aerial to the fore-and-aft line of your craft that counts in radio deviation.

Until you get the feel for the accuracy or inaccuracy of radio bearings, the formula for angular error in pilotage will help you. You'll recall that an error of 1 degree sets you off roughly 1 mile in 60.

A 3-degree error, 20 miles from the radio beacon, also causes a 1-mile error. Ten miles from a beacon the same 3-degree error will cause a half-mile error in your position. So will a 6-degree error 5 miles from the beacon.

An automatic direction finder (ADF) saves you the trouble of fiddling to find the null. It either automatically rotates an antenna, which may be outside, or works by some internal electronic magic. The sensing also is taken care of automatically. A dial shows the relative bearing of a beacon when the azimuth dial is set to zero; it shows magnetic bearing when you set it to the compass reading of the moment.

Automatic direction finders are usually more accurate—and always more expensive—than sets you null manually. But they don't know what errors your compass has on various headings. They are also subject to radio deviation caused by on-board metallic conductors. The expert who installs the ADF may swing ship with you and supply you with a radio deviation chart.

Some radio beacons at lighthouses and lightships are synchronized with their fog signals. A long blast of the foghorn may coincide, for example, with the beginning of the long dash on the radio signal, according to the Coast Guard light list. If the sound reaches you five and a half seconds after you hear the start of the dash on your direction finder, you're 1 mile from their common source. If it takes eleven seconds, you're 2 miles away. Just count the seconds, divide by five, and you get the distance in nautical miles accurately enough.

You probably know that radio waves, supposed to travel in a straight line, on the spherical earth take the great circle route. On the usual nautical chart, drawn on the Mercator projection, a straight line is not a great circle. In the latitudes in which we operate, and at the distances at which we use radio direction finders, the difference between the great circle track and the position line plotted as a straight line will not exceed 1 degree in bearing. Forget it.

If you don't expect too much, your radio direction finder will serve you well. With it, every radio beacon becomes a lighthouse easily identifiable in daylight, often guiding you when a lighthouse would still be below the horizon. In poor visibility, marker beacons lead you to the harbor entrance. Running along shore, you can measure your progress and your approximate distance from land by the beacons you pass abeam.

Don't rely on a beacon 50 miles away to pinpoint your position. A prudent skipper would trust it to get him within perhaps 5 miles of the plotted position line. That's close enough to make a visual landfall, say in the Bahamas.

Don't get too dependent on navigation by radio direction finding. Like any other piece of electronic gear on the water, your RDF may give up. In the era of transistors, battery failure is the most common complaint. Luckily it's also the easiest to remedy.

15. Consolan (Consol) and Omnirange

Most direction finders, as a bonus, let you get position lines from Consolan and Consol stations.

Radio beacons, the prime targets of direction finders, are for near-the-coast navigation. Harbor beacons have a range of a few miles, and landfall beacons carry past 100 miles. Consolan and its European cousin, Consol, reach out more than 1,000 miles from the transmitter.

For these stations you don't use the direction-finding ability of the set; it just acts as a receiver without automatic volume control and perhaps with a built-in beat frequency oscillator. The American stations transmit just below the beacon band, the European ones right in the beacon band.

You may use the direction finder's rotating aerial turned for maximum signal. A simple outside aerial, preferably vertical, will work even better.

Since you don't measure from what direction the signal comes, you don't have to worry about radio deviation. And you get a position line without referring to your compass.

The transmitter tells you on what position line you are. It's a sophisticated system originated by the Germans in World War II. Three antennas, about a mile apart, radiate a pattern of dots and dashes. In a keying cycle—typically lasting thirty seconds—the aerials generate sixty dots in one direction, sixty dashes in another. Halfway between you'd receive thirty dots followed by thirty dashes. You don't even need a stopwatch. The beginning and end of each keying cycle is clearly marked by a silent period, typically lasting 2.5 seconds. So you start your count when you first hear dots or dashes. All you have to do is count to sixty at the most.

Such a simple code can only identify 120 different directions: 60 directions starting with a dot, 60 starting with a dash. If you divided that code over the 360 degrees of the compass, the lines of position they indicate would spread out beyond any usefulness. One thousand miles from the transmitter the lines would be 50 miles apart.

So the code is used in a narrow sector, perhaps 12 degrees wide. It's repeated in the next sector. Now 1,000 miles from the transmitter the position lines will be only a few miles apart. In offshore navigation, for which the system was designed, a few miles don't matter.

Your dead reckoning will identify the sector you're in. If there's any doubt, you can check it by using your direction finder as a direction finder.

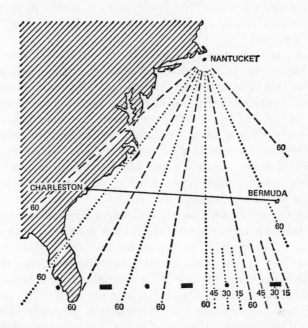

104. Consolan chart (simplified) shows sixty-dot and sixty-dash position lines from Nantucket. The dots and dashes near the bottom identify sectors. In the right-hand corner, position lines are shown fifteen counts apart as they are on the nautical chart.

On a trip from Charleston to Bermuda you'd start out in a dash sector of Nantucket Consolan; you'd hear dashes (thirty-five of them) before dots (twenty-five). As you sail east, the number of dashes will diminish and the count of dots will increase. Ninety miles out, you'll be down to zero dashes and sixty dots; you're entering a dot sector.

Now the number of dots will diminish and the count of dashes increase as you sail on. About 100 miles after entering the dot sector you'll get out of it, and into another dash sector. And so on. In all, you will have passed four position lines where the count was sixty dots, the first 90 miles from Charleston, the last 30 miles from Bermuda. On this trip—between 500 and 600 miles from the transmitter—position lines with the same count are on an average 180 nautical miles apart. Surely you can keep your dead reckoning that accurate.

Actually near Charleston you won't hear thirty-five dashes and twenty-five dots. Tuned to 194 kHz, the frequency of Nantucket, with BFO on, AVC off, you may first hear the call letters TUK in Morse (— . . — — . —) followed by a two-and-a-half-second pause. Then the keying cycle begins and you start your count. You'll hear a string of dashes each three eighths of a second long. Then comes a short period of a continuous tone signal—the equisignal—followed by a series of dots each one eighth of a second long.

Think of the equisignal as a mixture of dashes and dots. Say you counted thirty-three dashes before the equisignal, twenty-three dots after it. There should have been sixty dashes and dots in all, but you only got fifty-six. Four units were lost in the equisignal. To unscramble that mixture, you call half of the lost units dashes, the other half dots. Your corrected count then is thirty-five dashes and twenty-five dots.

Farther east your count may be twenty-six dots, the equisignal, then twenty-eight dashes. You've counted fifty-four units in place of sixty. Dividing the missing units again equally, you correct your count to twenty-nine dots and thirty-one dashes.

But what do you do with an odd difference? Say you counted twenty-five dots and thirty dashes, a total of fifty-five units. You can't divide the missing five units evenly. Give two to the first signal, three to the one you heard last. (Corrected count: twenty-seven dots, thirty-three dashes.) The reason for this rule: Your ear follows the signal better into the twilight zone than it judges the emergence of the first new signal.

When you're not sure that you counted right, you only have to wait two and a half seconds. Then the keying cycle repeats, and you can count again. If you miss it again, it'll repeat again after a few seconds for station identification.

Except when static is bad or someone or something aboard interrupts, counting is a fairly simple operation. Earphones may help sometimes, but with a loudspeaker you can have someone else count as a check on your own tally.

Correcting the count becomes a bit complicated near a sector border, where the dashes at the beginning of the cycle are about to be replaced by dots, or the other way around. You may want to forget the whole business and wait until you're clearly in the next sector.

Or you may puzzle it out yourself. Perhaps I can help you with that.

When you were eastbound out of Charleston, the number of dashes at the beginning of the cycle kept diminishing. Say now you're down to one dash, equisignal, fifty-five dots. That's still easy. Corrected count: three dashes, fifty-seven dots.

A few miles farther east you'll hear no dash at all at the beginning of the cycle. It starts with the equisignal, continues with fifty-six dots.

~~~~~~ 56 DOTS   2 DASH

~~~~~ 56 DOTS ~~ 1 DASH

~~~ 56 DOTS ~~~ 60 DOTS

~~ 56 DOTS ~~~~ 59 DOTS

56 DOTS ~~~~~ 58 DOTS

105. Corrected Consolan count near sector border, passing from dash into dot sector. Left, the signal; right, the count. Example: Equisignal followed by fifty-six dots (top line) gives a two-dash count. Passing from dot into dash sector, read dash for dot, and dot for dash.

By the rule, you divide the missing units equally. You'll count that as two dashes, fifty-eight dots.

Now it gets even trickier: You hear the equisignal, fifty-six dots, and a little more equisignal. That's to be counted as one dash, fifty-nine dots.

Then you'll hear equisignal, fifty-six dots, more equisignal. When the twilights at the beginning and the end of the count are of equal length, you're exactly on the sector border, where the count is zero dashes, that is, sixty dots.

Then, as you continue to make easting, the equisignal will get shorter at the beginning of the cycle, longer at the end. Corrected count fifty-nine dots. When all the equisignal is at the end, after fifty-six dots, you split the missing units and call it fifty-eight dots. When finally you hear a dash after the equisignal that followed fifty-five dots, you're back to the standard format. Corrected count: fifty-seven dots, three dashes.

Granted, near the sector border the corrections are confusing. But it isn't as bad as it sounds. If you misjudged the length of the two equisignals at the beginning and end of the cycle, you'd get sixty in place of fifty-nine dots or the other way around. In our example that would put you only three miles off.

In all Consolan and Consol bearings you are only interested in the corrected count of the signal you heard *first*, say twenty dashes.

How do you use that count; in navigator's terms, how do you plot that as a position line?

By far the easiest way is to use a chart that includes Consolan (or Consol) lines. For our example you could use HO 1411 (Halifax to Hispaniola), which shows the entire route from Charleston to Bermuda on a scale of 1:3,063,000. Another chart to use with Nantucket Consolan is HO 16510 (Newport to Cape Romain including Bermuda). Cape Romain is near Charleston. The chart is on a scale of 1:2,128,500; on its back is HO 16510A (Plotting Chart Newport to Bermuda), scale 1:1,058,-000.

For San Francisco Consolan (192 kHz) you'd use HO 527 (North Pacific, Eastern Part), scale 1:5,990,000. Or, if it covers your area, the larger-scale HO 16377S (Plotting Chart Pacific Yacht Races—San Pedro to Honolulu including Acapulco and Mazatlán), scale 1:4,790,000.

Don't expect any of these charts to show every dot and dash count. That would mess up the chart too much. Only every fifteenth or twentieth position line may be printed. The lines are close enough to being straight that you can draw your position line with a straightedge. A twenty-dash position line will obviously lie between the thirty-dash and the fifteen-dash lines printed on the chart. And it'll be closer to the fif-teen-dash line.

But the printed lines fan out, so the twenty-dash line will be parallel with neither of the charted lines. Instead it will everywhere divide their distance—fifteen units—in the ratio of five units to ten units.

That lets you plot your position line. You can suit yourself how you divide the distance mechanically. The principle is always the same: You divide the distance between two neighboring lines. You can use a dime-store ruler's millimeter scale, an engineer's scale, or dividers and the diagram that's printed on many charts.

I like tracing paper best. Copied from an interpolating diagram or constructed from scratch, the tracing only takes a few minutes to make. Use fifteen or twenty radiating lines to match the separation of counts on your chart. Then slide and turn the tracing in place between the printed lines near your dead reckoning position. Mark the division point by pricking through the tracing paper with dividers, or simply emboss the chart with the point of your pencil. Repeat the operation on the other side of your dead reckoning position. Connect the two marks, and you've drawn the position line for your Consolan count.

There's another way to plot these position lines. *Radio Navigational Aids*, HO 117A (Atlantic) and HO 117B (Pacific), gives the true bearing from the Consolan transmitters for every dot and dash count.

But you can't plot these bearings directly on a Mercator chart even when it includes the point of transmission. Reason: Consolan position lines, being great circles, become curved on a Mercator chart. To get around this difficulty the same publications list corrections, which depend on your latitude and longitude at the time of getting the Consolan count. En route from Charleston to Bermuda the corrections would vary from −3.1 to +1.5 degrees. It's easy to get the sign wrong, and impossible to draw the lines as accurately as the charts do. So I'd forget that method except when caught without the Consolan chart.

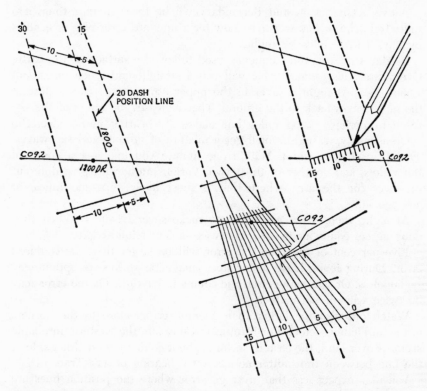

106. Plotting Consolan position lines. Left: the principle. Right: use of a scale to divide the distance between printed lines. Middle: transparent interpolator used to divide that distance. Point of dividers pricks chart.

How accurate are Consolan position lines? Between Charleston and Bermuda, a distance of 765 nautical miles, about halfway between the transmitter and its normal range, we get more than four hundred different dot and dash counts. That averages to about 2 miles for a change of one dot or one dash. On a parallel course in the latitude of the southernmost Bahamas you'd get a change of one unit on an average every 4 miles. On other courses you'd get different change rates.

Also, the sectors of repeating patterns vary in width. A few sectors aren't used at all. They are clearly marked "Unreliable" on Consolan charts, and left blank in the tables. Within about 50 miles from the transmitter the system is not usable.

Elsewhere the signal when it travels over water is considered accurate 95 per cent of the time to within 1 mile for every 170 miles' distance from the transmitter by day, within 2 miles by night.

Between Charleston and Bermuda you'll be three to four times 170 miles from Nantucket, so you'll allow for a standard error of 3 or 4 miles by day, 6 to 8 miles by night.

By day waves of the frequency used follow the surface of the earth. Over water this *ground wave* will travel straight and reach out about 1,000 miles. At night a layer in the upper atmosphere reflects part of the same waves back to the ground. That increases the range of the *sky wave* to perhaps 1,400 miles but makes its bearing more uncertain.

Occasionally, at night, you'll get a mixture of ground and sky waves. That'll upset your count. Within one minute you may get a count of thirty dots, and another of thirty-two. Various authorities give different distances for the area where that is most likely: 250–400 miles, or 300–700 miles.

At night, then, it's a good idea to make several counts. When they don't agree, count again—at least twice—a few minutes later.

Five per cent of the time the error will be larger than the standard error. During ionospheric disturbance—magnetic storms—reception may be hopeless. Or you may get erratic counts in daytime. Or the error may be twice what it normally is.

Watch out also for larger than average errors close to the borders of the unreliable sectors. For Nantucket Consolan, the western unreliable sector is over land; the eastern sector is about 20 degrees on either side of the line between transmitter aerials, on a bearing of 115 True.

You may expect less than average error where the position lines are spaced closest, at right angles to the line of towers near bearings 025 and 205 T.

No prudent skipper will navigate close to shore in poor visibility relying on Consolan position lines only. In open waters, say on a sail from New England to Nova Scotia, he may give them more weight than position lines from radio bearings from distant beacons.

To get a fix you can cross Consolan position lines with others, such as depth curves and radio bearings.

I wish I could say you can cross one Consolan position line with another to get a fix. You can't. Only one Consolan station operates on the Atlantic coast, one on the Pacific.

In European waters a string of Consol stations from the Arctic to Spain gives the navigator fixes hundreds of miles from shore. Consol differs from Consolan only in technical details. You've nothing new to learn. With a direction finder, a chart that shows Consol lines, and perhaps HO 117 for station details, you are ready for Consol fixes.

In North American waters you'll have to make do with single Consolan position lines. In the example, Consolan provides a good check on your progress since the position lines come in more or less abeam. But once you've lost the Charleston radio beacon (range 70 miles), you have no check on your course. About 100 miles out, your depth finder will find no bottom. You will have made some allowance for the current of the Gulf Stream, but with the tools so far discussed you have no way of checking on the course actually made good.

By dead reckoning, with a compensated compass, you'd probably make it within the 120-mile range of Bermuda's Gibb's Hill radio beacon. Then you could home on that until you make a visual landfall. If you come within 50 miles you'd also have the aero beacon at Kindley Field.

Now suppose for a moment that Bermuda had no radio beacons. You could find it by Consolan alone. From the beginning you'd lay a course clearly to one side or the other of Bermuda. Say you aimed for a point 50 miles northwest of Bermuda, tried to make good a course of 088 instead of the direct 092. You'd run down your easting by Consolan until you come to the fifty-dot line that passes just west of Bermuda.

Plotting that position line on the chart, you'd find it runs 157 to 337 T. Having aimed that far northwest of your destination, you'd be confident that Bermuda lies toward the southeast. So you'd set the course 157 T. You'd even have a check on the course made good here. You'd be following a Consolan line of position, so the count should remain constant at fifty dots.

That example illustrates two points: One, steering on purpose to one side of your destination saves searching in the wrong direction. Two, you can home on a Consolan count just as on any other position line.

The last can be very useful at times. Sailing, for example, from Wilmington, North Carolina, to St. Augustine, Florida, you'll notice on chart HO 1411 that Cape Fear and your course happen to lie on a fifteen-dash Consolan line. If you count—corrected—sixteen or more dashes before the equisignal, you are west of your course; if you count fourteen or fewer dashes, you are east of it.

Sometimes a Consolan position line can serve as a danger bearing. Because it isn't as clear-cut as the red sector of a lighthouse, give yourself a margin of safety of a couple of dots or dashes. Cape Hatteras is an example. As long as your count of dots doesn't get higher than thirty, you'll clear all outlying hazards.

Don't count too much on Consolan. The ionosphere may foul you up or your set may give up at sea. I would not, for instance, plan to find Bermuda by Consolan and radio beacons alone. Especially not since one receiver serves for both Consolan and direction finding.

I'd use celestial navigation, which—weather permitting—gives position lines at least as accurate as Consolan and lets you get a fix every few hours. But that has nothing to do with electronic navigation, so I leave it for the third and last part of this book.

Anyone who has sat in the cockpit of a plane wonders why sailors don't use *omnirange,* called *omni* by pilots, and officially known as VOR for Visual Omnidirectional Range.

It's a short-range navigational system. The very high frequency (VHF) waves used—between 108 and 117 mHz—don't follow the curvature of earth. So the range of VOR is theoretically "line of sight." Practically, sailboats with tall masts will get the signal 30 miles from the transmitter, powerboats to about 25 miles.

If your cruising area has one or more airports nearby, omni may be useful to you. But you'll need a special receiver. Several manufacturers now build models for marine use, operating off standard batteries, with very low power drain. They also supply the simple dipole aerial you'll need.

Never mind the theory. The operation of these sets is very simple. You turn on the power, select the channel, and listen for the station identification (in code, voice, or both). You then twirl a dial until the needle on a meter lines up with its index mark. Say the dial now reads 180. That means you are on the 180-degree radial. Three hundred and sixty radials fan out from every VOR station; each marks a magnetic degree. In our example you're 180 degrees magnetic from the station.

No aerial to turn, no compass to read, no corrections to make.

You could plot the position line—180 degrees magnetic—from the omni transmitter using the inner compass rose. Then you can use that position line as you would any other.

If you wanted to "run away" from the location of the station, you'd steer a course of 180 M. If you wanted to home on that radial, you'd steer the reverse course, 360 M. Your set may save you even that calculation. When the word "from" appears in a window the bearing is from the transmitter; when the word "to" appears, the bearing is toward the station.

The bearings will be accurate to 1 degree. The VHF band is little disturbed by static and interference. As a bonus, omnirange stations report the weather including wind direction and strength and any advisories for your area every half hour.

You won't find VOR stations on nautical charts. The suppliers of your set will have a map that shows the ranges operating in your area. Or you can get their latitude and longitude from a pilot friend, and plot the ones that you may plan to use.

On aeronautical charts look for the center of a compass rose near an airport. The word VORTAC next to it indicates the VOR you're interested in. The TAC part of the installation gives the aviator the distance from the station.

In many areas you may find omni more useful than radio direction finding. And it's free of radio deviation, and independent of your compass. If enough boatmen get interested in omni, we may yet see *marine* omni transmitters making navigation on the water simpler and safer.

16. Radar

If you're old enough, you may recall England's secret defensive weapon at the outbreak of World War II: radar. It let her defenders, even at night and through clouds, spot and track intruding planes. Hence the acronym, formed from *radio* *detection* *and* *ranging*.

Perhaps your television weatherman shows showers in your area as they appear on the radarscope at the weather bureau. When you follow hurricane advisories you become aware that the National Weather Service tracks these storms by radar even when they are still hundreds of miles from its stations at San Juan and Miami.

You may have seen naval ships steaming along with bedspring-sized aerials whirling. Knowing that big ships routinely use radar to avoid collision, you may have wondered in your armchair about the *Andrea Doria/Stockholm* and similar disasters.

But why bring radar into a book on small-craft navigation?

Two reasons. One: You should know how your craft shows up on a ship's radar screen. (It probably doesn't, unless you do something about it.) Two: Radar is not just an anticollision device but a great navigational tool. In recent years radar sets have gone down in space required, weight, power needed, and price. Now larger yachts can use radar. How does it work? You don't have to be an electronics expert to grasp the principle of radar. Think of it as an echo. The time it takes a whistle signal to bounce back from a cliff gives a measure of its distance from the ship. Your sense of hearing gives a rough indication of the cliff's direction.

In radar we send a short radio signal instead of a whistle blast. The transmitting antenna rotates, spraying the horizon with a narrowly focused beam. If the beam encounters no reflecting surface, there's no echo. If it does, the radio waves bounce back.

Traveling at the speed of light—about 162,000 nautical miles per second—the signal comes back before the antenna has moved more than a small fraction of 1 degree; the same antenna, then, can be used for both sending and receiving.

From the angle of the antenna you get the bearing of the reflecting object. From the time it takes for the round trip of the signal you get its distance.

At the speed of light we can't use a stopwatch as we do for timing sound signals. A mechanical gadget, such as depth finders use, is still much too slow. Instead the returning signals are displayed on a cathode ray tube, a sister of the picture tube in a television set.

Synchronized with the rotating aerial, a radial line sweeps around the circular screen of the "scope." When the aerial faces directly ahead, the line on the scope points straight up, to twelve o'clock. When the aerial has moved through 30 degrees, so has the sweeping line. If in that position the aerial receives an echo, a blip appears on the two o'clock radius. The quick return from a nearby object will show as a blip near the center of the scope; a return that took longer, from a more distant object, will be farther out.

A phosphor coating on the inside face of the tube keeps the blip glowing until it is repainted at the next sweep when the aerial faces in that direction again.

That gives the illusion of a still picture. The position of the ship is at the center of the scope. Every radar-reflecting object shows in its true place from the ship, both in direction and in distance. Even in the dark and through fog.

Now you feel safe. You know ships use radar. So they can see you, and won't run you down. Wrong! Your wood or fiber glass craft is not a radar-reflecting object.

I once had a vivid demonstration of that. I was on the bridge of a freighter southbound along the coast of Mexico. Visibility was good, but under a heavy overcast the night was inky. In the moderate sea the helmsman, having little to do but stay awake, looked ahead into the night most of the time. The lookout, on monkey island directly above the bridge, was an alert, sharp-eyed fellow.

I too looked ahead much of the time. Every few minutes I'd glance at the radarscope: empty except for the distant shoreline.

Suddenly, less than a mile ahead, lights appeared like fireflies. It looked as if all of Mexico's fishing boats were working in one spot, each saving her lights until the last moment.

And not a single blip on radar.

These, of course, were wood boats. Only conducting surfaces reflect radar waves. A steel or aluminum hull, however small, should show up on radar. It will unless it gets lost in the reflections from the tops of waves. In rain, the echoes from the drops may hide a yacht from a ship's radar.

To make yourself more visible on radar, hoist a radio reflector as high as you can. Reflectors—most fold flat for stowing—made of metallic sheet or wire mesh, sell for a few dollars. High in the rigging, such a reflector may be visible on radar from 10 miles away. It is designed as a nest of mutually perpendicular planes, and a few square

107. Radar reflector, placed as high as possible on your craft, makes her more visible on ships' radar screens.

feet show as brightly as 100 square feet of metal broadside on. Your reflector may be as visible as a small steel freighter.

The United States Coast Guard advises all coastal fishing boats, yachts, and other small craft to have efficient radar reflectors permanently installed. At the very least, hoist one in fog and when operating in shipping lanes, or crossing them, at night.

In distress, or adrift in a boat or rubber raft, hoping to be searched for, hoist a metallic object as high aloft as you can. A galvanized pail or a few feet of aluminum foil on an oar may do it. Coast Guard cutters and planes with their radars may be searching for you during the night and in poor visibility.

If your only interest in radar is how you look to others, that's about all you need to know. But what about the use of radar on your own craft?

Let's go back to the example. You had a blip at 30 degrees. You'd measure that on a degree scale that surrounds the radarscope. The set also displays range rings electronically. The first ring may indicate a distance of ½ mile; the second, 1 mile; the third, 1½ miles. For objects farther away you could switch to the next range, on which the rings might indicate 2, 4, and 6 miles.

Suppose you are on the low range and the blip of a buoy shows on the third ring; it is 1½ miles away. (The tops of the buoys now in use are designed as radar reflectors.) You now not only have a position line but a fix. The distance gives you one position line, a circle with a radius of 1½ miles centered on the buoy; the bearing—030 relative—gives you the second position line. The two position lines thus fix your position in relation to the buoy.

It's the ability to measure *distance* that makes radar such a useful navigational tool.

And it's probably for navigation that a small-craft skipper will install radar. Avoiding collision is likely to be secondary on a maneuverable craft, but on big ships that's the main purpose of radar. And for good

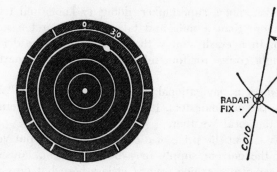

108. Radar as navigational tool. Left: A known buoy appears on your radar screen at 030 relative, on the third half-mile range ring. Right: plotting radar fix. Your course and the relative bearing give one position line, the distance from the buoy the second (circular) one.

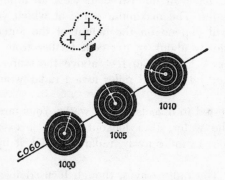

109. A fixed object on radar. On either side of your vessel, a fixed object will constantly pull aft, first at diminishing range, then after you've passed it abeam, at increasing range.

110. Danger line on radar. To pass a radar-reflecting object at a safe distance on your port hand, draw a mental line straight down the screen at that distance. Whatever your course, as long as the object doesn't get nearer the center than the line indicates, you'll pass safely.

reason. A large tanker, not a supertanker, doing 17 knots and trying a crash stop, skids more than a mile and takes more than ten minutes to come to a stop. In a crash stop with full emergency rudder she'd continue on a *straight* course for four minutes and for three quarters of a mile.

A radar installed as a navigational aid lets the small-craft skipper get out of the way of such monsters. It delivers a bonus: Sometimes it lets you outguess the local weather.

The cost of radar—about the price of a compact car—may put you off. On a sailing craft the current supply may be a problem. Power consumption may be 200 watts, which sounds little ashore but on 24 volts means a current drain of about 8 amps. Space isn't likely to be a problem. The display unit—the size of a truly portable television set—can be mounted on a shelf, bulkhead, or overhead. The transmitter-receiver unit has shrunk in size until now it can be incorporated, with the drive motor, in the base of the aerial. That leaves only the stowage of the power unit, which is about the size of a 5-gallon can.

The aerial must have an unobstructed view all around the horizon; the higher, the better. The maximum range at which you can spot an object by radar will depend on the height of the antenna. The radar horizon is theoretically about 15 per cent farther from the aerial than the visual horizon. A lookout 40 feet above the water could spot an object on the water 7.2 nautical miles away; radar would spot it from 8.3 miles.

You aren't interested in objects *on* the water. Your targets will always stick up *above* the water. If a lookout at the level of the antenna could spot an object 10 miles away, radar will pick it up when it's still 11.5 miles away.

There's a limit. The radio waves, though focused in a narrow beam, spread out. And only a very small fraction of the energy sent out gets back to your aerial. Eventually the echo gets too weak to register on your screen. With an input of 200 watts that limit may be at about 15 miles.

It isn't obvious, but every radar set also has a minimum range. While your aerial transmits, the receiver circuits are disconnected. If an echo arrives before the transmission has ended, you'll receive nothing. The transmitted pulses are very brief, and so the minimum range may be of the order of 50 or 100 feet.

The beam the aerial sends out, by the way, is narrow only in the horizontal plane. It's perhaps 30 degrees high to keep the target in view when your vessel pitches or rolls.

Radar sets for small craft vary greatly in details. But most operate in the 3-centimeter band, that is, on a wavelength of about 3 centimeters, a frequency of about 10,000 megahertz. The X-band (5,200–11,000 mHz) includes not only the 3cm band (9,320–9,500 mHz) but also the 5cm band (5,400–5,825 mHz) used on some radar sets. The S-band (1,550–5,200 mHz), which includes the 10cm band, is not used on small-craft radars.

Your set may include an anti-clutter-sea switch that suppresses some of the echoes from the waves. An anti-clutter-rain switch reduces echoes from raindrops.

Big-ship radars are hooked up with the gyrocompass system. At the flick of a switch you can turn the picture to show true north on top.

But there's nothing wrong with the display having the ship's head on top. In fact, you may find it easier to visualize. An object dead ahead is on top, an object astern at the bottom; objects abeam are left or right on the center line.

You'll plot bearings as you'd plot position lines from radio direction finding as relative bearings, relative to your heading by compass. It's best to measure the radar bearing when the ship is directly on course. You can then use the course line as a base for plotting the relative bearing. If you like, you can also add course (or magnetic heading) and radar bearing and plot it as a magnetic bearing just as you would plot a visual bearing.

To plot the radar distance from a charted point you can use dividers, compasses, a plotter, or a strip of paper.

Your instruction manual will help you get familiar with your set. The people who install it will probably show you its use also. But only by watching the screen and comparing it with what you see with your own eyes will you become expert at interpreting the scope. That means watching your radar in clear weather in daylight. You'll soon learn to tell a buoy from a moving craft, a big ship from a yacht with a radar reflector. Slowly you'll learn in your own area to recognize shore features on the radarscope. If you believe that is easy, you'll be disappointed. Except rarely, the land on the screen and on the chart won't look the same.

At a distance you'll see inland hills rather than the coastline. That'll be below the horizon still. Three prominent points on the scope may merge into a totally undistinguished shoreline as you get nearer, just as an island landfall through binoculars will look like three islands when there's only one. Off-lying rocks—and buoys—will merge with the shore on the scope. And you'll be fooled by false shores that turn out to be breakers on an offshore bar.

You'll have another surprise when you first use radar to avoid collision. You'll get a good picture of where other craft are. But it's a *still* picture, a snapshot taken now. It doesn't tell where the different vessels are going and at what speeds. You won't know where they'll be five minutes from now.

Professional navigators plot the radar bearings and ranges of other ships on the scope every few minutes. That gives them an indication of the other vessels' courses and speeds. They can predict where each craft will be a few minutes from now. They can judge whether risk of collision exists, and what action to take under the Rules of the Road.

Many navigators use a *relative motion plot.* You could get a pad of maneuvering board sheets for less than a dollar at an HO chart agent's, or buy a plastic marine plotting board for about $12. Both come with some instructions. For more instructions, there's Bowditch and Dutton. But it's a complicated method, so many navigators use a *true* plot. You don't have anything new to learn. You record your position, and that of any vessel on the scope directly on your chart. You repeat that procedure every few minutes to get an indication of courses and speeds of all craft plotted.

Even without a plot you can roughly gauge the danger of collision. You'll collide with any vessel whose bearing remains constant while her distance from you decreases.

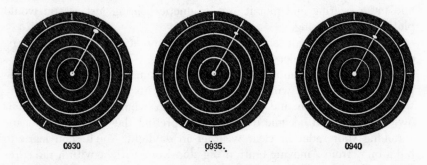

0930   0935.   0940

111. Radar warns of collision. Danger of collision exists when the relative bearing of another craft remains constant while her distance from you gets less.

If her bearing pulls ahead, she'll pass clear ahead of you. Example: first relative bearing 045, second bearing 035. Or: first bearing 315, second bearing 325.

If her bearing drops aft, she'll pass clear astern of you. Example: first relative bearing 045, second bearing 055. Or: first bearing 315, second bearing 305.

Collision still threatens if the other vessel changes course or speed. Only a plot will show that.

You, of course, will avoid a series of small course or speed changes. But be alert to the possibility that some other skipper will not alter course or speed radically enough to stand out on the radarscope.

Without a plot a problem arises when a blip dead ahead closes range. Are you meeting head on—or nearly so—or are you overtaking?

Astern and closing, a blip can only mean you're being overtaken. Maintain course and speed.

Ten miles from shore, north of Cape Hatteras, I idly looked at the radar screen one clear sunny day. A blip, quite close, was coming up dead astern. Quite an ordinary freighter-sized blip. Its speed of closing was phenomenal. And it headed straight for the center of the screen. You can't see astern from the bridge. Too late to call the captain. You couldn't even blow "Abandon Ship" in time. Hardly time to run to the wing of the bridge and jump. What happened? A Navy blimp out of Norfolk looking us over at mast level.

How accurate is radar? Distances are very accurate. One small-craft set, for example, is guaranteed accurate to within a couple of hundred feet, or 2 per cent of the maximum range switched in, whichever is greater. On the very useful 5- or 6-mile range, that would mean an accuracy of about one tenth of a mile.

Bearings on radar are supposed to be less accurate than visual bearings. Whenever an object is visible and at the same time clearly defined on radar, you may plot its visual bearing for a position line, then use the radar distance for a second position line. Where they cross is your fix. After plotting some objects that way you'll find out how accurate your set is on radar bearings.

You'll also discover three errors built into every radar installation.

One: Only an outgoing search beam of no width at all would show an object at exactly the right bearing. The beam used has some width, and so you get a return from its leading edge, its middle, and its trailing edge. As a result, objects on the screen are stretched in bearing. When you measure a bearing on radar, set the pointer to the *center* of the blip. Less gain will diminish the apparent length of the object. But more gain may be good for making a small reflecting target—a distant buoy, for instance—more visible on the screen.

The high gain setting, however, may smear two small separate objects into one long one. You'll be startled to see what looked like a large ship break in two before your eyes. The spreading effect may also hide some shore feature you're looking for. The two banks of a river, for example, may join, totally hiding the river's mouth.

Two: Only an outgoing search beam of no duration at all would show an object at exactly the right distance. The pulse used, though brief, lasts for some time. So you get an echo when the front edge of the beam hits the target, then one from the middle of the beam, and one from its tail. As a result, objects appear stretched in distance. When you measure distance on the radar screen, measure to the *nearest* edge of the blip.

Two objects on the same bearing may melt into one. Unless your set lets you change pulse length you can't separate them. Two rocks in transit, which you have used as a visual range, may show as a single rock. That's quite apart from the shadow effect, which will hide the far rock when it's behind the near one.

Three: On the screen only a sweep of no measurable width could paint a point. The sweep has width, so the smallest blip on the screen is at least as wide as the light beam that painted it. The phosphor coating tends to enlarge the apparent size of the blip by blurring its edges. As a result bright echoes are enlarged at the expense of dark—echoless—areas on the screen.

Turning down both gain and brightness minimizes that effect.

While fog has almost no effect on radar, raindrops create their own echoes. They are especially noticeable on the 3cm band, which otherwise is ideal for radars aboard small craft. (It shows small targets well, needs less power input than longer-wavelength radars, and suits the maximum range dictated by the height of the aerial.)

Sometimes you can make the apparent shortcomings of showing raindrops work for you.

Rain shows brightest on radar where precipitation is heaviest. A drizzle in the distance shows as a veil, a cloudburst as a solid splotch. That lets you gauge the amount of precipitation. You can also estimate the area of rain and plot its progress.

Summer showers are localized and move slowly. Warned by radar, you can outrun them or steam around them.

The passage of a front will bring rain over a large area. If you can't stay ahead of the area of precipitation, radar will at least let you pick an area of minimum rain activity. There you may also find wind and sea conditions better than in the areas that show brightest on the radar-scope.

17. Loran, Decca, and Omega

Depth finders and radar sets generate their own signals, and display their echoes. Radio direction finders, Consolan, Consol, and omnirange sets get their signals from an outside source. One transmitter installation, which may include several aerials, gives you one position line. In the electronic systems of this chapter—Loran, Decca, and Omega—*two* widely separated transmitters work together to give you a single position line.

Here's how that could work. A station on Folly Island—near Charleston, South Carolina—sends a radio signal. Exactly 1,000 microseconds later a station near Jupiter, Florida, repeats the signal.

A microsecond, one millionth of a second, is something I can't readily grasp. Neither can I really visualize the speed of light. I'd do better if someone connected these units to something more familiar. At the speed of light in air, about 162,000 nautical miles per second, a radio wave covers 1 nautical mile in a little less than 6.2 microseconds.

A special receiver lets you measure the time interval between two radio signals, say the ones coming from Folly Island and from Jupiter. Right at the Jupiter transmitter such a set would measure a delay of 1,000 microseconds between the two transmissions.

About 16 miles from the Jupiter aerial you'd get the Jupiter signal 100 microseconds later than at Jupiter. Say you are on the direct line connecting Jupiter and Folly Island. Then you'd be about 16 miles nearer Folly Island. You'd get its signal 100 microseconds before Jupiter does. So you'd measure a delay of 1,200 microseconds between the arrival of the Folly Island and the Jupiter signals.

You'd get the same 1200-microsecond delay in many other places. At some spot in the Northwest Providence Channel, for instance, you'd be about 73 nautical miles from Jupiter. You'd get the Jupiter signal 454 microseconds after transmission. At the same spot you're about 41 nautical miles farther from Folly Island than at Jupiter. You'd get the Folly Island signal 254 microseconds later than at Jupiter. The interval between the two signals would again come out as 1,200 microseconds.

If you connected all the points where the delay between the two signals measures exactly 1200 microseconds, you'd get a curve that mathematicians call a hyperbola. That's why the systems I'm talking about in this chapter are called *hyperbolic* systems.

You don't have to worry about the shape of these curves, nor the difficulty of plotting them on the not quite spherical earth. They are printed for you on some nautical charts.

The line used in the example, a Loran line, is printed, for instance, on C&GS chart ⚓1112 (Cape Kennedy to Key West). Jupiter happens to be on that chart, Folly Island isn't. You don't even have to know where the transmitters are. The lines, printed in colored inks, are identified by what is called their *rate*. Nothing mysterious about that. If your Loran receiver is set to 3H7—the rate for the pair of stations Folly Island and Jupiter—and measures 1,200 microseconds' delay, you are on the position line marked 3H7-1200.

To get a fix you can cross that position line with any other. At the location given above you could get a visual bearing on the radio towers on Grand Bahama Island, a radio bearing from the aero beacon at West End, or a Consolan count from Nantucket. More likely, you'll cross the first Loran line of position with a second Loran line. Here rate 3L5—San Salvador and Jupiter—cross at a good angle for an accurate fix.

These rates are not call letters. Consider them as receiver settings. Set one selector knob to 3, the next one to H, the third one to 7, and you are tuned to rate 3H7. The first symbol indicates frequency; three stands for 1900 kHz. The letters stand for how many pulses, approximately, per second the stations send out. That's called the basic pulse recurrence rate. H for High means basically thirty-three and a third pulses per second; L for Low mens twenty-five pulses; S for Special means twenty. The last symbol, the specific pulse recurrence rate, indicates by how much the actual interval between pulses differs from the basic one. On the H rate the basic interval is 30,000 microseconds (one second divided by 33⅓); the figure 7 after the H means the interval is 700 microseconds less. That makes the actual recurrence rate 29,300 microseconds.

These are details you don't have to remember. You simply set the selector knobs to the rate.

But you may wonder how you can measure time intervals to a few millionths of a second. In Loran A, the system introduced during World War II, you do it by eye after the waves of both stations have been made visible on an oscilloscope, a small cathode ray tube.

The pulse from the master station, the one that transmits first, in our example Folly Island, is displayed near the top of the scope and near its left edge. The pulse from the slave station, Jupiter in the example, appears near the bottom of the scope and to the right. The greater the delay the farther to the right.

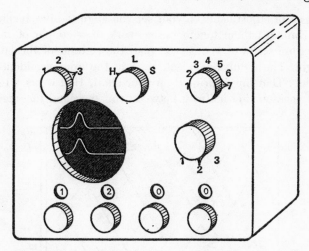

112. Loran receiver. Three switches near top select the rate (3H7). Function switch (middle right) selects mode of presentation (2) of traces on cathode ray tube (middle left). In mode 2 the master pulse, in the shape shown, appears above slave pulse.

Four knobs (bottom) serve to align the two pulse images. Their displacement from zero position, which cancels the time delay between the pulses, is read in windows above the knobs (1200 microseconds).

113. Matching Loran signals in three steps. Top: Function switch in #1 position presents master pulse as vertical line on the top trace, slave pulse as vertical line on bottom trace. Operator aligns the two.

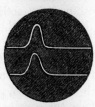

Middle: Function switch in #2 position enlarges these vertical lines into bell shapes. Operator refines the time delay setting when he brings the two shapes close to a vertical match.

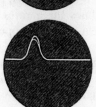

Bottom: Function switch in #3 position superimposes slave and master traces. Operator further refines coincidence, then reads displacement of time delay knobs to get position line.

By a series of adjustments on your set you align the two images. When you have brought them together—the work of a couple of minutes of fiddling with a series of knobs—you read the settings of the knobs from left to right. The number you get, 1200 in the example, identifies your position line. That line is printed on your chart. Had it been 1210 you'd plot your position line halfway between the 1200 and the 1220 line on

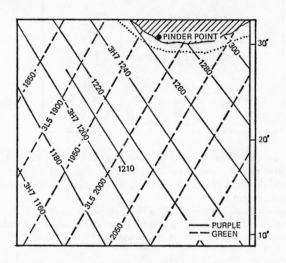

114. Plotting Loran position line (1210, rate 3H7). Chart shows Loran position lines in purple. Line will be halfway between 1200 and 1220 microsecond lines. To get a Loran *fix* the navigator could tune to rate 3L5; match pulse traces, and plot second position line using the green Loran lines on the chart.

the chart. For other lines, say 1214, you'd plot the line using the Linear Interpolator also printed on the chart. You could also use a tracing or a scale just as you did with Consolan lines of position (fig. 106).

There are also tables—one for each rate—that let you plot these lines on any chart of your area.

During daylight hours Loran A reaches reliably to between 600 and 900 nautical miles. That brings all the coasts of the United States and Canada, and many other areas, within the reach of Loran A.

In all these areas you'll have two and sometimes three rates to give you a fix more than accurate enough for near-shore or open-water navigation.

At night skywave reception extends the range but decreases the accuracy. Matching skywaves on the scope is trickier also. And then you must apply corrections—printed on the chart and in the tables— to your readings.

Loran C, introduced in the late 1950s, is an improved version of Loran A. It uses a much lower frequency (about 100 kHz), which permits increased spacing between master and slave and extends the reliable groundwave range to 1,200 nautical miles. Many Loran A sets have been converted to receive some of the Loran C rates. (Loran C rates are identified by the letter S at the beginning of the rate.)

Every master station in Loran C operates a chain of three and sometimes four slaves all operating on the same rate. Unlike Loran A, Loran C gives you a fix from a single rate. The slaves, identified by the last letters of the alphabet, transmit in sequence in alphabetical order.

The master for the chain that covers the East Coast of the United States (SS7) is located at Cape Fear, North Carolina, and transmits first. It is followed by Jupiter (W), Cape Race, Newfoundland (X), Nantucket (Y), and Dana, Indiana (Z).

Rather than single pulses, Loran C stations send pulses in groups. The master is identified by its nine consecutive pulses; each slave sends eight.

A refinement in Loran C is in the *phase* of the signals. That's a sophisticated concept. I wouldn't bring it up but we'll need to know a little about it for the systems that follow, Decca and Omega.

In Loran A we timed the delay in the arrival of two signals by matching them visually on a scope. The same system is used for the coarse timing of the delay in Loran C. For fine timing Loran C also displays individual waves that make up the signals. Superimpose the wave trains of master and slave and you have a *phase match,* or *cycle match.*

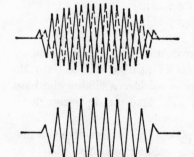

115. Phase match, or cycle match. Imagine the trace at bottom of fig. 113 even more enlarged. Now individual waves, not just the envelope of the signal, can be seen. Master (solid) and slave (dashed) lines will seem all jumbled (top) until the navigator by further refining the time delay of the receiver gets them to fuse, in phase (bottom).

The phase of signals from master and slaves is controlled to less than two tenths of a microsecond. Should the signals drift out of phase a blinking signal will warn you. Try again a few minutes later.

Phase matching lets you get groundwave accuracy of about 1 mile at a distance of 1,000 miles from the transmitters. Even the skywave is supposedly accurate for a fix to within 3 to 5 miles at that distance.

The phase matching can be done automatically in your set. That convenience and others account for some of the price differences in Loran sets. Sets range from World War II A sets, through sets partially converted to reception of C Loran, through modern A sets, to A-and-C sets with more and more automatic features. So prices range from that of a depth finder to that of an economy car and beyond.

Modern sets take no more space than a large portable radio and use about 20 watts at boat voltages. They only need a straight aerial, about 15 feet long.

Under good conditions even a manual set will give you a fix in five minutes.

Before you install a Loran set, find out if your cruising area is covered by a Decca chain. Decca, a British invention, developed and still operated by private enterprise, blankets western Europe, Japan, and a few other marine areas. In North America, at the time this is written, it covers the Maritime Provinces of Canada with four chains. The United States has only two chains, the New York chain and the California chain.

A Decca chain is made up of four stations: a master surrounded in a star pattern by three slaves called Red, Green, and Purple. Each station in the chain operates on a different frequency, between 70 and 130 kHz. The New York chain, for example, uses the following:

Master	85.0050 kHz
Red Slave	113.3400 kHz
Green Slave	127.5075 kHz
Purple Slave	70.8375 kHz

These frequencies don't seem to have anything in common. A closer look shows that they are all multiples of 14.1675 kHz in the ratio of 6 : 8 : 9 : 5. These ratios are the same for all Decca chains; the base frequency varies but is always about 14.2 kHz. One tuning brings in all four stations of the chain.

The four stations are rigidly locked in plase. The system—like the fine adjustment in Loran C—works by phase comparison. You don't do anything. An instrument called a Decometer does the work. All you have to do is read the pointer on a dial.

The distance of each slave is chosen so that its signal is received in phase with the signal from the master if you are exactly at the location of the master. As you move away from that location the slave signal gets out of phase with that of the master.

The basic Decca frequency corresponds to a wavelength of about 11½ nautical miles. Half a wavelength from the master—a little less than 6 miles—the signal of slave and master will again be in phase. Connecting all points where the signals from a slave and its master are in phase will give a series of position lines, hyperbolas.

Between any two such zero-phase difference curves is a Decca *zone*.

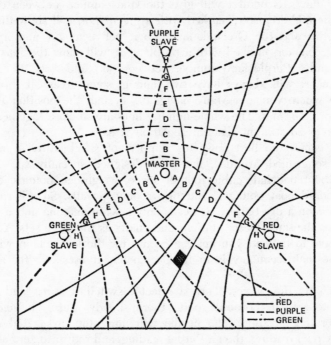

116. Diagram of a Decca chain. The master transmitter is surrounded by three slaves. The lines show where signals from master and slave are in phase. The zones between these lines are identified by letters (starting at the master) and color (of the slave).

The small black area in Red D, Green C, is shown enlarged in the next figure.

The zones are identified by letters, starting with A at the master. On the line connecting master and slave each zone is about 6 miles wide. In other directions it'll be wider, say 15 miles when you are 100 miles from the stations.

Each zone is divided into *lanes*. Red zones have twenty-four, Green zones eighteen, Purple zones thirty Decca lanes. These lanes, clearly labeled, are overprinted on nautical charts in the color of the slaves. Red slave lanes are in red ink, etc. To make identification even more certain, lane numbers are coded to the color of the slave. The numbers oo to 23 are used for Red lanes, the numbers 30 to 47 for Green lanes, and the numbers 50 to 79 for Purple lanes.

On standard Decca sets, built for worldwide use, you turn on the power and switch the channel selector to the local chain. For the New York chain (5C) you'd set the outer switch on 5, the inner on C. The left Decometer, marked with a red spot, will show the Red zone letter in a window. Its pointer will give the lane number, between 00.1 and 23.9. The middle meter, marked with a green spot, will show the Green zone letter and the Green lane number, between 30.1 and 47.9. The right Decometer, marked with a purple spot, will show the Purple zone letter, and a Purple lane number between 50.1 and 79.9.

The chart will always have two, and in some areas all three lanes printed where you are. Many navigators eyeball the position lines between printed lines. The whole-number lines are so close together and in most areas so straight that interpolation is easy.

Now comes the best news for skippers of small craft. A miniature Decca set, called Minidec, has been designed specially for them. It takes about one half cubic foot of space, weighs 20 pounds, operates on standard boat voltages, and draws only 3 watts. So it'll run for a long time on a dry battery. It needs only a whip antenna and a ground.

It uses the same Decca stations and charts as the large sets. You don't even have to tune it; you get the crystal for the local chain with your set. The main economy is in its Decometer. It uses one for all three slaves.

Switch on the power. Turn a selector switch to *Sync* and set the needle to zero if it doesn't point there already. Turn the selector to the operating position. The needle will now stop on a Red reading, then a Green reading, then a Purple reading, and return to zero all in ten seconds. Ten seconds later it'll repeat the cycle. All you have to do is to jot down the two or three lane numbers and plot your fix. You can easily read the dial to one half of a lane, or switch to a magnified scale for even greater accuracy.

Unlike big-ship sets, the small model does *not* identify the zone you're in. That isn't as serious as it sounds. Most of the time your dead reckoning will be enough to decide the zone letter. The set uses so little current, you can leave it on whenever you're under way. An occasional glance at the dial will tell the helmsman when he has passed out of one zone into the next. Example: When you last looked, the Red readings, which had been increasing steadily, were in the low twenties. Now the reading is 5. Obviously you are in the next zone.

Besides giving you a fix at the cost of a couple of minutes' work— if reading two dials and drawing two lines on the chart can be called work—Decca can be used for homing. Commercial fishermen, who have no patience with chart work, use this method. It needs no plotting. You don't even have to get out the chart. If you remember that your sea buoy straddles the D18 lane, you can slide down that lane until you see or hear that buoy. It's even better than homing on a radio beacon. Decca numbers tell you whether you are falling off to the left or the right.

Your course won't always follow a Decca lane. But you can plot any course in the normal way, then see where it cuts an intersection of two

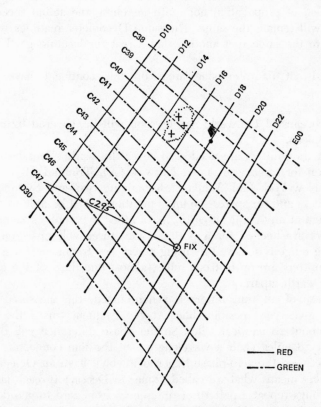

117. Decca lanes, precomputed position lines that subdivide the zones, are printed on Decca charts in colors to match their slaves.

A Decca reading D20 C44 fixes your position at the point marked.

To home on the buoy, get on lane 18, then steer a course that keeps the Red count on 18.

To check on course shown: You should read Red 16 when Green has become 45, and about Red 12.3 when Green has become 46, etc.

Decca lanes. When you arrive, slantwise, near that point, the readings won't quite match your prediction. Blame it on current.

Often a Decca lane will give you a danger bearing. You'll see from the Decca chart that you'll stay out of trouble if you don't let the Red reading drop below 16.

At the distances you'll use Decca, skywave propagation won't bother you. According to the Decca people, the small set has a reliable daytime range of more than 150 nautical miles, a nighttime range of more than 100 miles.

Sometimes, especially near shore, when you try to pinpoint a location, Decca lines on the chart and those on your instrument may disagree. The explanation: land effect. The curves have been drawn on an assumed speed of propagation not quite matching the actual speed. But the error will remain the same. The same Decometer readings will get you back to the same spot another day. Great for locating good fishing spots.

Too bad not more cruising areas on this continent have Decca coverage.

All the oceans of the world are, or soon will be, covered by another system: Omega.

Only six transmitters are needed to cover the world. Four have been in operation for some years now: Norway (A), Trinidad (B), Hawaii (C), and New York (D). When the remaining two—and two more for double checks and for spares—go into operation, you'll be able to receive four of them at any point on earth. As in other hyperbolic systems, two transmitters are needed for a position line; three will give you a fix.

The long range is achieved by using a very low frequency (10.2 kHz). The transmitters are up to 6,000 miles, almost one third of the circumference of earth, apart.

The phase of all transmitters is synchronized; the measured phase difference gives your position line. At the frequency used the wavelength is about 16 nautical miles. So the phase difference will be zero about every 8 miles (half a wavelength) on the line connecting transmitters. Between the zero-phase hyperbolas you'll have an Omega *lane*. ("Lane" here means what we called "zone" in Decca.) In each lane the phase readings repeat a pattern of differences from zero to 360 degrees.

Each station is identified by its place in the sequence of transmissions. Every station is on the air for about one second out of ten. Adjoining stations in the sequence are further identified by the length of their transmission, which varies by one tenth of a second from their neighbors'.

So there's no problem in identifying the transmitters, although they all operate on the same frequency.

Lane identification is another matter. One way around this difficulty is to count the number of lanes traversed by the ship on any given voyage. At the point of departure the navigator sets the counters. They click over every time the ship crosses a zero phase line of a pair of transmitters.

If your set or the transmitters go off the air, you'd lose count. So another rough identification system is built into the Omega position line pattern. A second frequency at every transmitter creates *broad* lanes exactly three standard lanes wide. That lets the navigator decide in which of three adjoining standard lanes his ship is. On the base line, which connects the pair of transmitters, you'd only have to know your position within 24 miles. Everywhere else the lanes are wider, your tolerances greater.

A third frequency creates superbroad lanes at least 72 nautical miles wide. Your dead reckoning will never be that much in doubt.

You read the phase difference between any two stations on a meter calibrated in one hundredths of a lane. If your lane count for stations A and B (Norway and Trinidad) is 123 and the phase meter needle points to 30, you'd be on position line 123.30.

A skywave correction has to be applied to this from a table published by the U. S. Naval Oceanographic Office. You find that correction from your date (within two weeks), Greenwich time (to the nearest hour), and your approximate latitude and longitude (each to the nearest 4 degrees). Say the correction for stations A and B is +20. Your corrected Omega reading, then, is 123.50. You could plot it halfway between the 123 and 124 lane lines on an Omega chart, near your dead reckoning position.

You could plot it on *any* nautical chart by using the appropriate Omega Lattice Table, here the A-B table 224(111). You could repeat the whole process and get a second position line from stations A and D, Norway and New York, to get an Omega fix.

I have given Omega space here not because anyone is likely to rush out and buy a set like the Navy uses, but hoping that before long some enterprising manufacturer will come out with a set for small-craft use. A mini-Omega. It wouldn't need automatic lane counters; the laziest singlehander can keep his daily reckoning to the nearest 72 miles. The same set would work anywhere in the world, without even changing crystals. The phase meter is a simple gadget, similar to the ones used in Loran C and also in omnirange sets. No special charts or tables would have to be prepared; the Skywave Correction and Lattice tables for any area and combination of transmitters sell for less than the price of most nautical charts.

Such a miniature Omega set is much more likely to come our way than an adaptation of one of the more sophisticated systems of navigation already in use by the Navy.

Systems using inertia, Doppler effect, and automatic tracking of celestial bodies or artificial satellites—singly or in combination—have been made to print out latitude and longitude of a ship's position continuously and automatically. But such systems require space, current, maintenance personnel, and money beyond the limits of the small-craft skipper.

But there's one system ideally suited to small craft. It fits into less than a cubic foot of space, doesn't drain your batteries, and costs no more than a good direction finder. It lets you find your position to within a few miles, anywhere in the world, whenever you can see the sun, the moon, or a few stars. It's celestial navigation.

Obsolete? Not a bit. The same large ships that carry all the fancy electronic gadgets still carry sextants and officers who know how to use them.

How you can take sights and plot position lines from celestial bodies is the subject of the next chapters.

PART THREE:
CELESTIAL NAVIGATION

18. Modern Celestial Navigation

In chart-and-compass navigation you used position lines from land- and seamarks. In electronic navigation you worked with position lines based on sonic and radio waves. In celestial navigation you get position lines, and fix your position, from celestial bodies—sun, moon, planets, stars.

If you've been told that celestial navigation is only for ocean voyagers, you have been misinformed. I'll show you how it can help you in along-shore cruising, and even on a lake.

Yacht club talk has it that anyone can learn to work a noon sight of the sun, that the moon is too complicated for amateurs, that stars are only for experts. Nonsense! I'll show you a tested eight-step method that works for all bodies, and takes less time than a noon sight. And you don't have to know Venus from Vega to take star sights.

You won't need a chronometer. The sweep second hand of your wristwatch will do after you have compared it with a radio time signal. It doesn't have to be a short-wave signal; your favorite radio program may be good enough.

You will need a marine sextant. But you can learn what celestial navigation is all about, work and plot sights before you ever look through a sextant. Even without an ocean and without a boat you can practice taking sights. Even in a desert you can learn to check your sextant for accuracy, when and how to adjust it, and when to leave it alone.

So what are you waiting for?

"I don't know enough mathematics," you say.

Bilge water! Never mind what shellback navigators and old-fashioned books say. They would have you think you needed to know trigonometry, spherical trigonometry at that. You don't. If you can tell latitude from longitude you have all the spherical trigonometry you'll need.

An old-timer had to remember formulas, or paste them in his sextant box. "Daylight-saving time is fast time, so you take off one hour to get standard time" is the most complicated formula you'll need.

Earlier navigators had to struggle with trigonometric functions—sine, cosine, secant, and one you may never have heard of, haversine. To work a sight they used not only these functions but their logarithms. You won't meet a single logarithm in modern navigation.

The formulas, trigonometric functions, everything has been built into sight reduction tables. In these tables you first find the right page, then you follow the proper column to a given line. There you'll find the ready-made answer. Just as you find the time of high water in the tide tables.

You'll need only simple mathematics. No more difficult than finding the time of high tide for a place other than a reference station. That is, you must know how to add and subtract.

118. Sample of sight reduction. This work sheet shows the simplicity of mathematics in modern celestial navigation. Only addition and subtraction are used.

Look at a typical sight reduction, fig. 118. Don't worry right now about what all the figures mean, or where the navigator got them. Instead, note how it's all a matter of adding or subtracting rather simple figures.

(In the next few pages I'll show you a few tricks to be used in these operations. If you don't need that right now, but want to know how modern celestial navigation works, go to p. 206.)

Like the official tide tables, the Nautical Almanac—a basic tool in celestial navigation—uses the twenty-four-hour system rather than A.M. and P.M. hours. So we have no choice but to use that system.

Let me refresh your memory.

In civil life we name the twelve hours from midnight to noon A.M.; at noon we start a new count, and label the hours from noon to midnight P.M. So, for example, we have two four o'clocks: the one before dawn (A.M.), the other in time for tea (P.M.). The Nautical Almanac calls the second one 1600. The conversion rule is easy:

> A.M. hours remain the same;
> to P.M. hours add 12 hours

You can write hours and minutes as four-figure units without space or colon between hours and minutes. To get four figures for times before 10 A.M. you fill the empty space with a zero.

For example:

> 4:00 A.M. becomes 0400 (add a zero)
> 10:30 A.M. becomes 1030 (no change)
> 4:00 P.M. becomes 1600 (by adding 12)
> 11:59 P.M. becomes 2359 (by adding 12)
> Midnight becomes 2400 (or 0000 of the next day)

For this and the following problems you'll find a drill at the end of this chapter.

Probably you have no trouble in adding and subtracting minutes. When it's now 10:55 A.M. and it takes you ten minutes to drive downtown, you know you should get there at 11:05 A.M. Or: To get downtown by 11:05 A.M. allowing ten minutes for the trip, you know you must start out at 10:55.

You'll time your sextant observations not just to minutes but to seconds. A good way to write hours, minutes, and seconds is in three groups of two figures each. Fifty-five seconds after 4:43 P.M. I'd write 16 43 55. Some navigators might write 16–43–55 or 16:43:55. All these notations seem simpler than the equally correct $16^h43^m55^s$.

Now let's talk about angles. In celestial navigation you'll be up to your belt in angles. Perhaps you've spotted some right in the first line of the sample sight: 28°10′ N, 70°55′ W, the navigator's dead reckoning position.

In the work I've left out the degree and minute marks, a timesaving trick. There is never the slightest doubt what units are meant. In fact, except for the date and the time of observation, all the figures on your work sheet will be degrees and minutes.

By the way, latitude is always written before longitude. The abbreviations N, S, E, and W are standard but there's no agreement whether the label—the letter—should go before or after the numerals. The Nautical Almanac issued by the U. S. Naval Observatory puts the label first;

the tables you'll use for sight reduction, published by the U. S. Naval Oceanographic Office, put the numerals first.

So please yourself. I'm in the habit of placing the label *after* the latitude and longitude. But taking labeled figures from the Almanac, I copy exactly, and so get the label ahead of the figures.

You know that a full circle, such as a compass rose, is divided into 360 degrees. In adding you'll often get a figure greater than that, say 380 degrees. That has no meaning in celestial navigation. When you get such a figure simply deduct 360 and write down the difference, 20 degrees.

In subtracting you'll often have to take away more degrees than you had to start with, say 80 from 75. What to do? Add 360 first. Like this:

$$
\begin{array}{ccc}
75° & 75° & 435° \\
-80° & +360° & -\ 80° \\
\hline
? & 435° & 355°
\end{array}
$$

Disregard the fact that you have borrowed 360 degrees. That's one loan you don't have to repay.

A degree, as you know, is divided into 60 minutes of arc.

Adding or subtracting degrees and minutes—the constant chore of the celestial navigator—is done by working first the minutes, then the degrees. It sounds like working in dollars and cents.

$$
\begin{array}{cc}
\$64.06 & 64°06' \\
+11.01 & +11°01' \\
\hline
\$75.07 & 75°07'
\end{array}
\quad \text{and} \quad
\begin{array}{cc}
.\$47.43 & 47°43' \\
-\ .41 & -\ 41' \\
\hline
\$47.02 & 47°02'
\end{array}
$$

But the similarity with dollars can only get you into trouble. One dollar has 100 cents; one degree has 60 minutes. Every beginning navigator keeps forgetting that.

Much better to remember that an *hour* also has sixty minutes. Then if you can manipulate time, you can also add and subtract angles.

$$
\begin{array}{cccc}
10:55 & 10°55' & \text{or} & 11^h43^m55^s & 43°55' \\
+\ \ 10 & +\ \ 10' & & +\ \ 10^s & +\ \ 10' \\
\hline
11:05 & 11°05' & & 11^h44^m05^s & 44°05'
\end{array}
$$

and

$$
\begin{array}{cccc}
11{:}05 & 11°05' & 11^\mathrm{h}44^\mathrm{m}05^\mathrm{s} & 44°05' \\
-\ \ 10 & -\ \ 10' & -\ \ \ \ \ \ \ 10^\mathrm{s} & -\ \ 10' \\
\hline
10{:}55 & 10°55' & 11^\mathrm{h}43^\mathrm{m}55^\mathrm{s} & 43°55'
\end{array}
$$

If these operations come easy to you—you can check yourself with the drill at the end of the chapter—congratulations. If they don't, here are some tricks that may help you.

When adding, work the minutes and degrees separately. In the above example you'd get 65 minutes. Then go back over your result and clean it up. For 65 you'd write 5 and increase the degrees by 1. It's a bit as a child learns to walk stairs, putting both feet on the same step—slow but sure.

You can adapt the same method to subtracting. Glance at the minutes. When the number of minutes to be subtracted is greater than the number from which to subtract—10 subtracted from 5—convert 1 degree into minutes. Add the 60 minutes to the ones you already have—5 in the examples—and the subtraction becomes easy. Instead of subtracting 10 minutes from 11°05', you subtract them from 10°65'.

Try another example:

$$
\begin{array}{ccc}
47°43' & \text{rewrite as} & 46°103' \\
-\ \ 54' & 46°43'+60' & -\ \ \ 54' \\
\hline
? & & 46°49'
\end{array}
$$

After a little practice in this forgotten skill you'll probably do it in your head, without mumbling, and barely aware that you've "borrowed."

Some people find another trick more helpful. In adding, they work the question: How much can I add before I get sixty minutes? In the above example you might mumble, "Fifty-five and five makes one degree; that leaves five minutes over." Then write 05' and carry 1 degree.

In subtracting, the question becomes: How much can I take away before I have to borrow a degree? In the last example that'd be 43'. The muttering then may sound like this: "Forty-three from fifty-four leaves eleven; eleven from sixty leaves forty-nine." So 49' is the answer, and the degrees are diminished by 1.

Minutes of arc, that is angles, can be divided into 60 seconds. But these seconds of arc are not used in celestial navigation. Instead we use tenths of minutes. Adding and subtracting them won't give you any trouble.

In small-craft navigation it's best to get rid of these tenths of minutes in the results by rounding off to the nearest whole minute. The rule is simple:

From 0.1 to 0.4—disregard the decimals;
from 0.5 to 0.9—add 1 minute to the result
Example: For 75 07.4 write 75 07; for 14 41.6 write 14 42.

That rounding off is quite safe since five tenths of a minute can't change your position by more than one half nautical mile. Where you'll normally use celestial navigation half a mile won't matter. Also, it's silly to pretend that we can fix our position to tenths of nautical miles. Even with a perfect sextant, under the best conditions, a small-craft sight will leave a doubt of perhaps 1 or 2 miles.

Now here's good news. That's all the mathematics you'll use in my kind of celestial navigation.

In every sight you'll use the twenty-four-hour system, round tenths of minutes, add and subtract degrees and minutes, occasionally borrowing or casting out 360 degrees. And that's all. You should be able to do these operations not only in your armchair at home, but when you're cold, wet, tired, bouncing about, and perhaps just a little seasick.

Here are some suggestions for all the drills in celestial navigation:

*Take your time; speed comes with practice.

*Keep your calculations, even those with mistakes. You can use them later in a practice for spotting errors.

*Keep your drawings also; they are solutions for later problems.

*Label your papers (number of practice, and letter of problem).

*Don't worry about intentional traps. There are none. On the contrary, an exclamation mark may be used to get your attention.

*Refer to the chapter preceding the problem when in doubt. For minor details the summary (pp. 329–35) will be quicker.

*For abbreviations see p. 328.

PRACTICE (18)

A. Convert the following to 24-hour notation:

8:21 A.M.	10:17 P.M.	3:45:16 A.M.
5:30 P.M.	3:59 P.M.	11:20:09 P.M.

B. Write the following in everyday style:

1614	0536	13 27 09
2332	0049	19 29 35

C. Round off the following:

30 14.4	123 08.6	79 59.7
64 43.5	27 40.3	125 13.8

D. Add or subtract, as indicated, and round off:

$$
\begin{array}{r} 179\ 54 \\ +\ 93\ 55 \end{array} \qquad
\begin{array}{r} 166\ 37 \\ -194\ 54 \end{array} \qquad
\begin{array}{r} 322\ 43 \\ +\ 51\ 35 \end{array}
$$

$$
\begin{array}{r} 183\ 32 \\ -\ 64\ 43 \end{array} \qquad
\begin{array}{r} 30\ 52.5 \\ +\quad 14.4 \end{array} \qquad
\begin{array}{r} 6\ 46.4 \\ -\quad 0.7 \end{array}
$$

$$
\begin{array}{r} 54\ 19 \\ -212\ 31 \end{array} \qquad
\begin{array}{r} 21\ 19 \\ -\ 00\ 24 \end{array} \qquad
\begin{array}{r} 36\ 14 \\ -\ 79\ 23 \end{array}
$$

$$
\begin{array}{r} 123\ 45 \\ +\ 27\ 39 \end{array} \qquad
\begin{array}{r} 79\ 40 \\ -128\ 52 \end{array} \qquad
\begin{array}{r} 238\ 44 \\ +125\ 29 \end{array}
$$

Check your answers. If you need additional practice in these operations, which will crop up in every sight, here are some more examples.

E. Convert to 24-hour notation:

   12:55 A.M.   8:14 P.M.   12:17 P.M.

F. Add or subtract as indicated:

$$
\begin{array}{r} 14\ 45 \\ +\quad 20 \end{array} \qquad
\begin{array}{r} 94\ 18 \\ +\ 7\ 48 \end{array} \qquad
\begin{array}{r} 46\ 27 \\ +\quad 33 \end{array}
$$

$$
\begin{array}{r} 13\ 05 \\ -\quad 15 \end{array} \qquad
\begin{array}{r} 31\ 01 \\ -\quad 53 \end{array} \qquad
\begin{array}{r} 66\ 06 \\ +\ 8\ 57 \end{array}
$$

$$
\begin{array}{r} 14\ 45 \\ +348\ 20 \end{array} \qquad
\begin{array}{r} 75\ 07 \\ -118\ 09 \end{array} \qquad
\begin{array}{r} 275\ 09 \\ +\ 14\ 54 \end{array}
$$

ANSWERS (18)

A.   0821   2217   03 45 16
      1730   1559   23 20 09

B.   4:14 P.M.   5:36 A.M.   1:27:09 P.M.
      11:32 P.M.   12:49 A.M.   7:29:35 P.M.

C.   30 14   123 09   80 00
      64 44   27 40   125 14

D.   273 49   331 43   14 18
      118 49   31 07   6 46
      201 48   20 55   316 51
      151 24   310 48   004 13

E.   0055   2014   1217

F.   15 05   102 06   47 00
      12 50   30 08   75 03
      3 05   316 58   290 03

19. Eight-step Method

Sights of the sun, moon, planets, and stars can be worked by a single method. It doesn't matter whether these bodies have recently risen, are high in the sky, or will soon be setting.

You could take sights and work them up without understanding the underlying principles. Some professional navigators do just that. That's all right on big ships where sights are taken routinely from dawn to dusk. But when you're on your own, and don't want to make a full-time job of celestial navigation, a knowledge of the fundamentals will help you decide what body to shoot when.

That knowledge will also let you spot gross errors right away. And it will help you in navigational emergencies—compass gone haywire, a watch run down, a radio gone dead, lack of this year's Almanac, missing tables . . . Such emergencies are not common on big ships; but they'd stump the navigator who's used to filling in work forms without knowing what he's doing.

When you know what it is all about, you'll get more pleasure out of your work. Even if right now you have no use for celestial navigation, you may be just interested enough to want to know how it works. This chapter shows, in a general way, how a celestial sight lets you draw on your chart a line that shows where you are—a position line.

Textbooks of celestial navigation start with a sketch of the earth and the sky. Then they fill the drawing with circles, arcs, and angles. Then they label them with unfamiliar abbreviations of strange terms. By the time the introduction is over, the future navigator is completely bewildered.

You are about to get a much simpler explanation. I'll bring the circles and arcs down to earth. Literally.

If you don't mind a few pages' worth of hard thinking, you'll know how celestial navigation works. You squint through a sextant and note the time; you look up some figures in an Almanac and in another book of tables; then after you've done a little adding and subtracting here and there, you draw a position line on the chart. That's all there is to it.

You already know why it's called celestial navigation. It uses celestial bodies for position finding. The body most often observed by most navigators is the sun. So in what follows I'll use the sun as an example. That saves writing sun, moon, planets, and stars over and over. When I write sun, read sun and other celestial bodies.

The basic tool of celestial navigation is the sextant, an instrument designed to measure accurately the angle between the horizon and the sun. In a marine sextant the horizon used is the line where sky and water seem to meet.

The angle between the horizon and the sun is called *altitude*. You could say "height" in place of "altitude." In fact, the standard abbreviation is h or H; but the common term is altitude.

It is measured in degrees and minutes, and perhaps tenths of minutes. An observed altitude of 57°50.0′ means the sun was that much above the horizon (altitude zero degrees), about two thirds toward the zenith (altitude 90 degrees).

How can such an altitude give the navigator a position line?

We are all agreed that the earth is—approximately—a sphere.

From that it follows that at any one time half of it will be lighted by the sun—have the sun *above* the horizon. The other half will be dark—have the sun *below* the horizon. Between the lighted and the dark sides, on the dividing line, the sun is *on* the horizon. The sun is either just rising, or just setting. On that circle the altitude at the moment is zero.

From the spherical shape of earth it also follows that at one point, and only one point, the sun must be directly overhead, in the zenith. At that point, at that moment the altitude is 90 degrees (fig. 119).

You can just accept these statements. You can also take a ball, and see how the sun or a distant light illuminates just half its surface. In the center of the lighted hemisphere you'll find the point that's directly "under" the sun or light. It will be the point nearest the light source. Geometrically it will also be where a straight line from the source to the center of the ball pierces its surface.

The spot on earth where the sun is directly overhead has been named the subsolar point. A spot directly below the moon would be a sublunar point, below a star a substellar point . . . complicated. So textbooks refer to the point where the observed altitude would be exactly 90 degrees as the "geographical position" of that body, and abbreviate it GP. I find "geographical position" still a bit clumsy. Why not call it *ground point*, where still fits the abbreviation GP?

The Nautical Almanac, published annually, gives the ground point of the sun—and the other bodies used in celestial navigation—for every second of that year.

If at a given moment your observed altitude of the sun happened to be 90°00′, that'd be the end of your calculations: You'd be at the ground point. But that's an unlikely example. More likely you'll get an angle between zero and 90 degrees.

When your observed altitude is close to 90 degrees, you'd expect to be close to the ground point. The more it approaches zero, the farther you'd expect to be from that point.

Quite correct. The law by which the observed altitude decreases is simple: For every nautical mile the observer moves from the ground point, the observed altitude decreases exactly by 1 minute of arc.

Ten nautical miles in any direction from the ground point, you'll get an observed altitude of 89°50'. Sixty miles away it'll be 89°00'.

That simple law is at the bottom of our celestial navigation. Its simplicity is no coincidence. The nautical mile, used by all seafaring nations, has been chosen to make it simple. That international agreement set it at exactly 1,852 meters—about 6,076.1 U.S. feet—is unimportant. What counts is this: Wherever you may navigate, 1 minute of latitude is 1 nautical mile. (Close enough as not to matter.)

At the moment when the ground point of the sun is in latitude 15°02' N, longitude 90°00' W, according to the Almanac, you take a sun sight in latitude 30°02' N, longitude 90°00' W. That's 15 degrees (900 nautical miles) due north of the ground point, and near New Orleans. The observed altitude of the sun will be 75°00'.

Fine. But if you measure that altitude does that fix your position? Unfortunately, no. There's not just one point, but infinitely many where you'd get that altitude. In fact, at any point 900 nautical miles from the ground point you'd get the same altitude. All these points lie on a circle, centered on the ground point, with a radius of 900 miles. The point near New Orleans is just one of these points. In other words, the observed altitude gives you a position line, a circle of position.

Let's look at another example. With the sun at the same ground point as before, your observation gives an altitude of 58°00'. You must be on a circle with a radius of 32×60—1,920—nautical miles, centered on the ground point in Central America.

You could be near Boston, Georgetown (Guyana), Lima (Peru), Los Angeles, or anywhere else on the circle. At this moment the sun, which by definition hovers above the ground point, bears southwest in Boston; it bears west-northwest near Georgetown, northwest near Lima, southeast not far from Los Angeles.

Could we take a bearing of the sun at the same time as we measure its altitude? That would give a second position line and fix the observer's position. A good idea in theory. Unfortunately bearings taken at sea —with a magnetic compass, or even with a gyrocompass—aren't accurate enough for our needs.

Is that circle of position, then, useless? Far from it. Just as in pilotage and electronic navigation, a single position line can also be

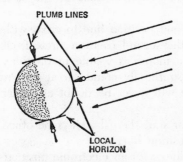

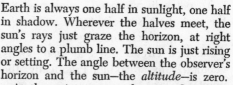

Earth is always one half in sunlight, one half in shadow. Wherever the halves meet, the sun's rays just graze the horizon, at right angles to a plumb line. The sun is just rising or setting. The angle between the observer's horizon and the sun—the *altitude*—is zero.

At the point nearest the sun, the sun is directly overhead, above the plumb line. The sun's altitude is 90 degrees.

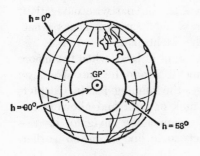

The lighted hemisphere, seen from the sun, is bordered by the circle where the altitude is zero. At the point in the center, the *ground point*, the altitude is 90 degrees.

In between the angle diminishes by a simple law: 1 minute of altitude for every nautical mile from the ground point. For example, anywhere on the smaller circle a navigator with a sextant would measure the sun's altitude as 58°00′.

Measuring at this instant the altitude of the sun as 58°00′, a navigator could be anywhere on the circle (now shown larger). It is his position line.

The bearing of the sun, its *azimuth*, will be very different near Boston and near Lima. Since the sun is directly above the ground point, the sun's azimuth will also be the bearing of the ground point from the observer (arrows).

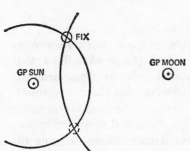

The sun's azimuth can't be measured accurately enough to tell where on the circular position line you are.

A second sight, say of the daytime moon, will give a second position circle. You must be at one of the two points where the circles cross. (The point will be obvious from your dead reckoning.)

You could also use an earlier sight of the sun for a running fix.

119. Celestial position line from a timed sextant observation of the sun. Two crossing celestial position lines give a celestial fix.

valuable in celestial navigation. I'll come back to that in the next chapter.

To get a fix we need, as always, a second position line to cross with the first. In a sun sight you might get the second position circle from the moon, which for a good part of the month is visible in daytime. (The two circles cross at *two* points, so the fix could be at either, geometrically speaking. Practically, there will never be doubt at which point you are.)

Whenever you take sights of a planet or star, there'll always be other stars or planets for a second or third position line.

You can also cross a celestial position line with an electronic position line—an RDF bearing, for example—to get a fix. In coastwise navigation you can cross it with depth contours, or visual bearings. That's what makes celestial navigation so useful to the yachtsman.

Without electronics, off soundings, out of sight of land, when the moon isn't available, you can still get a daytime fix from the sun. You use a technique we have discussed in pilotage, the running fix. In Chapter 10 we got a fix by taking bearings on a tank or light and allowing for our motion between bearings. In the same manner the navigator crosses a position line of the sun with another such line from an earlier observation.

You could navigate around the world using no other method. For more than a hundred years navigation by running fix of the sun has been daily routine on ships of all nations.

If you have followed me this far, you now know how celestial navigation works: A measurement of the altitude of the sun, at a known time, gives a position line. The position line is a circle of a radius that depends in a simple way on the observed altitude. The center of the circle is at the point where the sun was directly overhead at the time of observation. The location of this ground point is given in the Almanac.

This position line, crossed with another such line—celestial, electronic, or visual—fixes the position of the observer.

Clear so far? Great! There's just one hitch.

Usually you can't draw the position circle on your chart. Its center will be off the chart. Say you're on chart ⚓1208 (Cape Cod Bay), the observed altitude is again 58°00′. The ground point is 1,920 nautical miles away, about 160 feet from your position on the chart, according to scale.

Charts taking in larger areas won't help. To get the ground point and Cape Cod Bay on the same chart you'd have to use a scale of 1:3,000,000. You'd do well plotting to the nearest 10 miles on that scale. This isn't an extreme case. Had the observed altitude been 10 degrees, the ground point would have been 4,800 nautical miles away. On a chart that would show both the ground point and your area, the width of Cape Cod Bay would have shrunk to one quarter of an inch.

Another complication: Charts are renderings of a sphere on a flat sheet. That causes problems. On the charts most used for navigation, drawn on the Mercator projection, a circle of a few hundred miles' radius becomes noticeably egg-shaped.

A globe, free of such distortions, may seem the answer. To be accurate enough for our needs, such a globe would have to be at least 10 feet in diameter. Not very practical.

So we abandon the effort of drawing or measuring these unwieldy circles of position from their centers. The practical navigator is only interested in a very short part of such a circle of position. When you have taken your departure from Boston lightship a few hours ago, you don't care where the position circle cuts the coast of Peru or California. You want to know where to draw it near your position on chart ⚹1207 or ⚹1208.

In drawing such a small part of a large circle we are helped by two facts of geometry. One: The periphery of a circle everywhere forms a right angle with its radius at that point. Two: A short part of a circle can be drawn as a straight line. The larger the circle, the closer a straight line will approximate its curve.

That sounds like cheating. It is. But the circles we deal with are large. In our example the radius was 1,920 nautical miles; that makes its circumference about 12,000 miles. The longest straight line you can draw on these charts is about 60 miles, or about one two hundredth of the circumference of the position circle. By drawing a straight line in place of the arc, you have replaced a circle by a regular polygon. If you have lots of spare time, and like drafting, draw a polygon of two hundred sides and see how closely it resembles a circle (fig. 120).

In practical navigation the error of presenting the circle of position by straight lines will not exceed a few tenths of a mile.

So we need only to know the direction of the radius at a point to draw the position circle there—as a straight line at right angles to the radius.

We can calculate the direction of the radius—the direction of the ground point—from any point on earth. Since by definition the sun is directly above the ground point, that's also the bearing of the sun at this time. It's a plain true visual bearing, measured like any bearing in degrees, clockwise from true north.

In celestial navigation you call it *azimuth,* abbreviated Zn. When the sun rises behind the water tower that bears east (090 T) from you, the sun's azimuth is 090.

Just as we can calculate azimuths, we can also calculate the altitude of the sun for any point on the lighted hemisphere, and for any given ground point.

When we combine precalculated listings of altitude and azimuth for selected points and ground points, we get a sight reduction table. Such tables are published in several styles.

With such a table you can lay down position lines from several tens of thousands of positions. From all these you'll pick one near your probable position. That will be your *assumed position*, abbreviated AP. In our example you might choose 42°00′ N, 70°00′ W.

When first told to choose an assumed position near his probable location, every smart beginning navigator objects, "If I knew where I was, I wouldn't need a sextant, and could save myself the trouble of working out the sight."

To that objection there are several answers.

You normally know *approximately* where you are. Not only on a 50-mile sail from Boston to Cape Cod, but even on a transocean crossing. Doing a minimum of navigation, you'd know where you were yesterday, and in what direction at what approximate speed you've moved since.

Also, the choice of assumed position is not critical. You'll prove that to yourself if you work the exercise in the next chapter. For now, let me just say this: You could have worked our example from latitude 41 or 43, and longitude 69 or 71; the same observation would give you practically the same position line.

As we shall see when dealing with navigational emergencies, you could get celestial position lines even if you were dropped in mid-ocean, not even knowing which ocean. All you'd need is the navigator's standard equipment, including your wits.

With the help of sight reduction tables we seem to have solved the problem. Through the assumed position we have drawn a straight line, at right angles to the azimuth given in the table. That's a position line approximating the circle of position in our example. You may still have your reservations about the straight-line and the assumed-position dodges, but suspend your disbelief and answer me this: Is that line *your* position line?

The answer I'm fishing for is: "Yes, if my observed altitude happens to be the same as the altitude calculated in the table for the assumed position." In our example the observed altitude was 58°00′, and that happens to be the calculated altitude. So the problem is solved; this is the wanted position line; the navigator was somewhere on that line when he took his sight of the sun.

Usually the observed altitude will differ somewhat from the calculated altitude. The difference is logically enough called *altitude dif-*

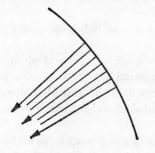

Usually you can't draw the circles of celestial position lines—the center is off the chart. But you can approximate a circle by drawing short straight lines at right angles to their radii. The middle of this curve was so drawn. Can you tell it from the ends which are circular?

Given the direction of the radius, the *azimuth* of the sun, you can draw the short part of the position line near your location.

SIGHT REDUCTION TABLE·

	71W		70W		69W	
	Hc	Zn	Hc	Zn	Hc	Zn
43N	57 37	216	57 11	217	56 43	219
42N	58 25	217	58 00	218	57 30	220
41N	59 13	218	58 45	219	58 15	221

Sight reduction tables give pairs of figures for altitude and azimuth, calculated for ground points and navigators' positions all over the world.

Choose a position, the *assumed position*, near your probable location. The choice isn't critical. For a sight between Boston and Cape Cod you might use latitude 42 N, longitude 70 W. For this position you'd find altitude 58 00, azimuth 218.

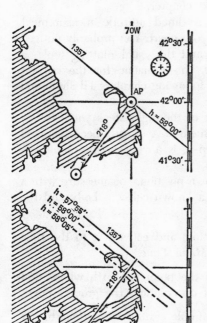

From the assumed position on the chart draw the sun's azimuth. (That's also the bearing of the ground point from you, and corresponds to the Boston arrow in the third sketch of fig. 119.)

Draw a line at right angles to this azimuth line. That's the *position line* for a navigator whose sextant sight of the sun, at 1357 EDT, gives an observed altitude of 58°00'.

If your observed altitude is less than the altitude calculated for the assumed position, you were farther from the ground point, 1 nautical mile farther for every minute's difference.

If your observed altitude was 57° 55', move your position line 5 nautical miles away (solid line.) Had your observed altitude been 58° 05', you'd move it 5 miles closer to the ground point (dash-dot line).

120. Plotting celestial position line on the chart.

ference, or less obviously *intercept.* Its standard abbreviation is—don't ask me why—a small letter *a.*

Where does the altitude difference come from and what do you do with it?

Recall that observed altitude diminishes by exactly 1 minute of arc for every nautical mile you move from the ground point.

So, if your observed altitude is 5 minutes less than the altitude calculated for the assumed position, you are 5 nautical miles farther from the ground point.

You'd be on a position circle with a radius 5 miles longer than the one at the assumed position. The straight position line, which approximates the circular one, will be 5 miles farther from the ground point.

If, on the other hand, the altitude is 5 minutes greater than the altitude calculated for the assumed position, you are 5 nautical miles closer to the ground point.

You'd be on a position circle with a radius 5 miles shorter than the one at the assumed position. The straight position line, which approximates the circular one, will be 5 miles nearer the ground point.

Don't worry about the mechanics of this plotting of position lines. We'll take that up in detail in the next chapter.

Here I just wanted to show how a timed altitude measurement gets you a position line you can plot on your chart. You probably noticed the tools one needs besides the chart and the usual plotting tools: a marine sextant, an accurate timepiece, the Almanac for the current year, and sight reduction tables. In the following chapters I'll show you their use.

Perhaps you'd like to know the order of the eight steps you'll follow in taking and working a sight. Seven of them have already been sketched in this chapter; the remaining one, step 4, is a very simple one.

1. On a known date, in a roughly known position, you measure with a marine sextant the angle between a known celestial body and the horizon. This is the *observation.*

2. You note the time of the observation, and convert it to the time used in the Almanac, *Greenwich Mean Time.*

3. In the *Nautical Almanac* you find the point on earth where that body was overhead at the time of observation, the ground point.

4. To the sextant reading you apply simple *sextant corrections* to get the true observed altitude.

5. You select an *assumed position* near your approximate position.

6. In the *sight reduction tables* you find the calculated altitude and azimuth, computed for the assumed position.

7. You compare observed and calculated altitudes to get the *altitude difference*.

8. From the assumed position, azimuth, and altitude difference you draw the *position line* on your chart.

You don't need to remember the order of the steps. They follow one another logically.

Until you have measured the altitude you have nothing to time. Not until you have Greenwich time can you use the Almanac. (Sextant corrections fit here because they too are found in the Almanac.) You need the ground point for the assumed position, the assumed position for the tables. You need the calculated altitude to get an altitude difference, and need the altitude difference for plotting the position line.

All that will become clear when we look at the different steps in the chapters that follow.

Cheer up. Only in this chapter did you have to strain your brain. All the rest of celestial navigation is glorified bookkeeping and a little drafting.

20. Celestial Position Lines

In this chapter we'll first look at the mechanics of drawing position lines from celestial observations; then I'll show you some of their uses.

You may be surprised to see step 8 taken up first. That's the last step, and books and live teachers usually leave it to the last. To me, that's like training a prizefighter in rope skipping and telling him only on the night of the bout that knocking out the opponent is the object of all the training.

When you know what position line you'll get from an observation before you even take the sextant out of its box, you'll know what body to shoot and when. You'll see how celestial navigation can help you get home after a day's fishing offshore, or how to make a good landfall after crossing a lake.

You'll also see how a sight can help you identify one island in a chain. I've used that method in the Bahamas, where navigational aids are few, and where all islands look alike to a stranger.

You plot these position lines directly on your chart, using the tools you have become accustomed to in pilotage.

As you saw in the last chapter, four figures are needed to plot a celestial position line: the latitude and longitude of the assumed position, the azimuth of the body, and the altitude difference. The azimuth is always understood to be from true north and needs no label; latitude and longitude have their usual labels N or S, W or E. The altitude difference, or intercept, will have a label T for toward, or A for away from the ground point or body.

Let's just sketch, rather than draw, the sight used in the last chapter. At 1357 EDT the observed altitude was 57 55. The data were:

Assumed position	
Latitude	42 00 N
Longitude	70 00 W
Azimuth of the sun	218
Altitude difference	A5

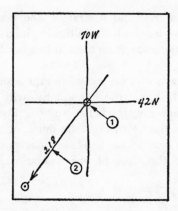 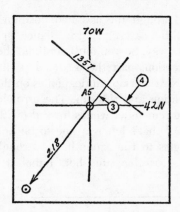

121. Sketching celestial position line. For clarity shown in two stages; numbers refer to steps detailed in text: ⚹1 assumed position, ⚹2 azimuth, ⚹3 altitude difference, ⚹4 position line.

Solution: (1) Plot the assumed position where meridian 70 W crosses parallel 42 N. (2) Through the assumed position draw the sun's azimuth (bearing), about southwest. It saves confusion about the direction of the bearing if you put an arrow pointing to the sun at the end of the line. Add the sun symbol to identify it as a sun sight. (3) Estimate 5 nautical miles, 5 minutes of latitude. The label is "away," so you lay these 5 miles off away from the sun on the azimuth line, starting at the assumed position. (4) Through the point just found draw a line at right angles to the azimuth line. That is the position line for this sight. Label it with the time of observation.

If you compare this sketch with the drawing in the last chapter you'll notice this: We don't draw the position line through the assumed position and move it parallel to itself. We just measure the altitude difference —away or toward—from the ground point along the azimuth line; then we draw the position line at right angles to the azimuth line.

You will find such freehand sketches, which only take a minute, helpful when you plot the position line on the chart.

As you may have noticed in the example, illustration 118, I ring the four figures needed for plotting the position line. In that example they were: 28 00 N, 80 07 W, 173, 9A. Perhaps you'd like to try sketching it on a piece of scrap paper. You can check your result against the next illustrations.

You'd first plot the assumed position. In the method we shall be using it will always be on a full degree of latitude, no minutes. So all you'll have to do is eyeball in a longitude.

Through the assumed position you freehand a straight line bearing a little east of south. Glance at the label of the altitude difference; it's away. So you must continue the line, away from the sun in a northerly direction, past the assumed position.

Next mark 9 nautical miles on the azimuth line, away from the assumed position and the sun. The arrowhead, if you use it regularly, will help you remember what's toward (with the arrow), what's away (against it).

All that's left is a line to be drawn through the 9-mile point, at right angles to the azimuth, very roughly east to west. That's your position line for this sun shot. Label it for the time of observation (1144).

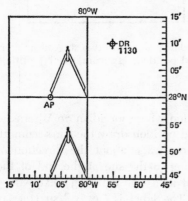

122. Plotting assumed position. Transfer minutes of longitude from top or bottom of chart to the proper latitude line. (With our tables the latitude will always be a whole degree without minutes.) Make sure to measure longitude in the correct direction, to the left in west longitude.

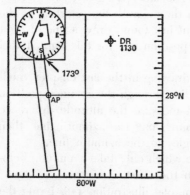

123. Plotting azimuth. Through the assumed position draw the azimuth line as you'd plot a true course. The altitude difference here is labeled "Away," so you'll need the line drawn past the assumed position for the next step. Had it been labeled "Toward," you'd stop it at the assumed position. Add arrow pointing toward sun. Add sun symbol.

If you can sketch it, you can draw it (figs. 122–125).

If you've gotten hazy about latitude and longitude, you can refresh your memory in Chapter 10. In a nutshell: Latitude lines run across the chart, longitude lines down the chart. In north latitudes the numbers increase toward north. In west longitudes the numbers increase toward the west.

In the United States and Canada, or anywhere else in the Northern and Western hemispheres, you may remember that the numbers increase

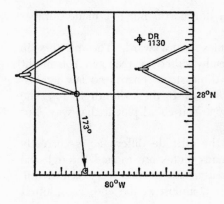

124. Plotting altitude difference. Measure it on the latitude scale (left or right margins of chart), then transfer it to azimuth line. Here it is labeled "Away," so you lay it off from the assumed position away from the sun, against the arrow. Had it been labeled "Toward," you'd lay it off from the assumed position toward the sun, with the arrow.

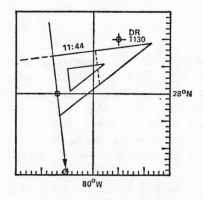

125. Plotting position line. Through the point just marked draw a line at right angles to the azimuth line. Use any convenient tool. A line scratched in your triangle, as shown, lets you draw the line on both sides of the azimuth line at once. Finally label the position line by adding the time of observation (hours and minutes only).

in a direction opposite to the way we write: to the left, and up.

You know all that? Think of me the first time you start marking 10 minutes when you meant 50, or 20 in place of 40.

There's another mistake easily made: using the wrong kind of minutes. Except near the equator, minutes of latitude and minutes of longitude are of different lengths. For the longitude of the assumed position you get the minutes from the top or bottom of the chart; for the altitude difference you get the minutes of latitude (nautical miles) at the left or right margins of the chart.

Whichever plotting tool you use, it's possible to get the azimuth drawn wrong. If you're rusty on that, you can refresh your memory in Chapter 4. The sketch may wake you up when you're using the plotter the wrong way. You can also glance at the nearest compass rose on the chart and compare your line with the outer, true, scale.

I use another safety dodge. I write down the approximate compass bearing of the body before I take my sight. That's SSE in the first line of the sample observation we're using (fig. 118). That's close enough to 173 degrees. You'd probably wake up if in latitude 28 N a sight showed the sun's azimuth 353 degrees, almost due north. But I've made dumber mistakes.

Drawing the right angle sometimes is awkward. The plotters in common use in pilotage are not especially suited for that job. You might find a tool you'll like for that in the dime store. There's no law against calculating the angle of the position line. If the azimuth is 173, the position line obviously runs 083 or 263. You could plot it that way. But it's one more source of possible error.

It always pays to check whether the altitude difference is correctly labeled. You wouldn't believe how many sights are carried through the computation correctly, only to be loused up at that very last detail. Sometimes they're labeled correctly but, almost at the end, are plotted in the wrong direction.

So check label *and* its plot.

For some people it is easiest to think. When they get an observed altitude (Ho) *greater* than the altitude calculated for the assumed position (Hc), they are nearer the ground point than the assumed position. Closer to the sun. Toward. When they get an observed altitude *smaller* than the one calculated in the tables, they know they are farther from the ground point than the assumed position in the tables. Farther from the sun. Away. That's how we worked it out in the last chapter.

Some people think of a lighthouse. If you measured its height with a sextant, the angle would get greater if you moved toward it; it'd get smaller if you moved away.

For people who like jingles, I made this one up for my students at the planetarium: Observe tOward and cAlculate Away. Translation: If the observed altitude is greater, mark the altitude difference "toward." If the calculated altitude is greater, mark the altitude difference "away."

You can also think of a Japanese name: "Homoto." It means: If *Ho* is *mo*re, it's *to*ward. Its opposite is the classic "Coast Guard Academy." The initials CGA mean: If the calculated altitude is greater, mark the difference "away."

Psychologists tell us the more ridiculous a memory aid, the better it is remembered. Then imagine Admiral Homoto in charge of the Coast Guard Academy.

You will do all your plotting on the chart you are using for guiding your vessel. The only way to get good at plotting these position lines is to work some examples. In working such examples you may not have a chart of the area. But any chart of the same latitude will do. You could use a chart of Cape Cod Bay to solve examples in Lake Michigan or off the Oregon coast. They all show latitude 42; you only have to renumber the meridians. You could, of course, trace the grid from a chart that shows the needed latitude.

If you live near a chart agent who handles Hydrographic Office charts, you can buy, very inexpensively, blank plotting sheets of the 3000-series. A smaller size is designated by the letter S, a larger by Z. The examples in this book are near latitudes 28 and 42 degrees. You could work them on the handier 3000-5S and 3000-7S sheets (10×18 inches), or 3000-9Z and 3000-14Z (17×22 inches), or yet on the chart-size 3000-5 and 3000-8 sheets (35×46 inches).

You can work all the examples in this book without these sheets. Make your own, using the illustrations for 28 and 42 degrees for patterns, perhaps doubling their size for more convenient, accurate work.

Here is an example you may try for practice:

Time of observation	1358 EDT
Body observed	Moon
Assumed position, latitude	42 00 N
longitude	70 30 W
Azimuth	088
Observed altitude	29 13
Calculated altitude	28 56
Illustration	fig. 131

Make a sketch first. You'll have to figure out the altitude difference yourself. Is it toward or away? To mark a moon sight, draw a crescent where before you drew the sun symbol. The crescent is universally used, regardless of the phase of the moon on the day of observation.

If you would like more practice in getting the tricky toward-away business straightened out, here is another problem. Suppose your observed altitude was 58 00. Sounds familiar? It is again the Cape Cod problem. But this time we work it from different assumed positions. To simplify your work, I've made all the longitudes come out as whole degrees.

AP Longitude	71 00 W		70 00 W		69 00 W	
Latitude	Ho	Zn	Ho	Zn	Ho	Zn
43 00 N	57 37	216	57 11	217	56 43	219
42 00 N	58 25	217	57 58	218	57 30	220
41 00 N	59 13	218	58 45	219	58 15	221

(To start, calculate the altitude difference at the nine given assumed positions. For example: At 43 N 71 W the observed altitude —as at all other points—was 58 00; the calculated altitude for this point is 57 37; so the difference is 23'—toward because the observed is greater; azimuth is 216.)

If you have drawn all the position lines from the nine assumed positions correctly, they should all form almost one line. The line will be very slightly curved around a point almost 2,000 miles away, the ground point of the sun at the time of observation.

The lines won't quite make a single line. Minor drafting errors and errors due to rounding off altitudes and azimuths in the tables are to blame. You can see that the total error in this work is on the order of 1 or 2 nautical miles.

But what matters in this exercise is really this: Even from assumed positions 150 miles apart you get almost identical position lines. Seldom will your dead reckoning be that much in doubt. In actual work you'll never deal with altitude differences of 77 minutes. An intercept of more than about 40 miles will mean an error in your work or a poor choice of assumed position.

I hope you got more than practice in calculating altitude differences and in plotting position lines. I hope you have made your own, for good, the two basic facts: (1) The azimuth line points at the body and its ground point. (2) A celestial position line runs at right angles to the azimuth line.

These two facts are at the basis of all the work of the celestial navigator. They also explain some sights you may have heard about: noon sights, longitude or time sights.

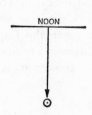

126. Noon sight. Celestial position lines always run at right angles to the bearing (azimuth) of the observed body. So at local noon, when the sun bears due south (or north), your position line will run due east/west.

It gives your latitude even when your longitude is unknown. You could also get your latitude from sights of the moon, planets, or stars when they bear due south or north.

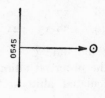

127. Longitude or time sight. Celestial position lines always run at right angles to the bearing (azimuth) of the observed body. The sun, or any other celestial body, observed when due east or west gives a position line that runs exactly north/south.

So it gives longitude independently from your latitude. Longitude and time are closely connected, so such a sight can be used as a time check.

These sights, and a few others, are now mainly of historical interest. They are special cases of our one universal sight. The only time you'd dust them off would be in an emergency, say when your watch has stopped and your radio has given up at the same time.

What made the noon sight famous? Two things: You didn't need correct time, or any time for that matter, and the calculation was child's play compared with the old logarithmic calculation of other sights.

You still don't need time for a noon sight. Before noon the sun rises, after noon it drops. If you take sights one after the other, your sextant readings increase before noon, decrease after noon. At the turning point, when the sun was highest above the horizon, it was noon where you were. Taking such a string of sights is tedious business. You can't take a noon sight when your watch or radio signal says it's 1200. Noon as used here, is a local phenomenon and will only accidentally fall at 1200. Yes, you can calculate the time of local noon, but the calculation takes as long as working out a sight. So why bother with noon sights?

Beware of people who tell you that by taking a noon sight you can not only find your latitude, but by timing it, also your longitude. Noon is the worst time for getting longitude from the sun. The same is true for any other body "on the meridian," that is, bearing south or north.

The time to get your longitude is when the body bears east or west. The closer to the east-west line—the prime vertical of textbooks—the body is, the more accurately can you find longitude, or time. At noon the body is as far from that line as it can get.

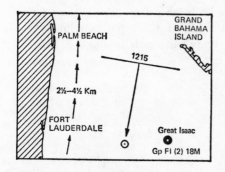

128. Sight of body abeam checks course made good. Crossing the Gulf Stream on an easterly or westerly course, you would get such a check when the sun bears about south, near noon.

Most of the time, bodies are not going to bear north, south, east, or west but somewhere between these cardinal directions. Then you'll get position lines that run at some angle to the grid of the chart. They'll be skew lines as in all the examples above.

Among such skew position lines, two are specially useful to the navigator, at right angles to his course, and parallel to it. They are the celestial equivalents of the pilot's beam bearings and bearings on an object ahead or astern.

Let me illustrate with two examples.

You are crossing the Gulf Stream, coming from the Bahamas on a westerly course. You aren't worried about missing the North American continent. You want to know how the current has been behaving. A sight when the sun is abeam—bearing about south—will tell you if you are on course or north or south of it and by how much.

Now imagine you are coasting off Baja California on a southeasterly course. You have a smudge of land on your port beam at all times, and so you aren't worried about your distance from shore. You want to know

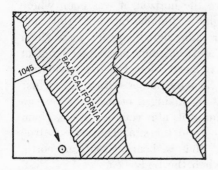

129. Sight of body ahead (or astern) checks distance sailed. Coasting on a SSE or NNW course, you would get such a check when the sun bears SSE, before noon.

how far you have come. You'll wait until midmorning, when the sun will be dead ahead, bearing southeast. Your position line will mark the point abeam on shore.

You don't have to memorize that a body ahead or astern gives you distance, a body abeam current. Just think of what position line you want, then take your sight when the body's azimuth is—more or less—at right angles to that line.

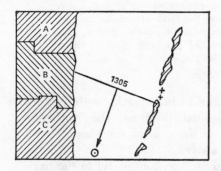

130. Sights as help in identifying features ashore. At left, position line places you off town B. At right, it places you off the foul passage between the two large islands.

That can be most useful for identification of a landfall.

I don't have to illustrate how a celestial position line crossed with any other will give you a fix. The second line could be a visual bearing, a depth curve, a radio direction finder bearing, or any other line of position.

We have already mentioned the possibility of getting a daytime fix from sights on the sun and moon at practically the same time. At the time of the sight of the sun that you sketched at the beginning of this chapter, a first-quarter moon was well placed for such a sight. You already have the data of the moon sight (p. 221), taken within a minute of the sight of the sun. The fix, at the intersection of the two position lines, is shown in fig. 131.

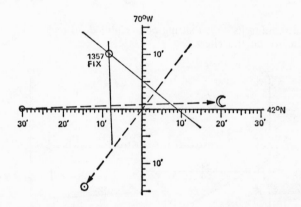

131. Sights of two bodies, taken almost at the same time, give a celestial fix. You may draw azimuth lines dashed; that avoids confusion with other lines on the chart, especially position lines. Here you need not mark the time of observation along the position lines. The time of the fix labels them.

But suppose the moon isn't visible in daytime, or is poorly placed to get a good fix? Then we use a convenient trick: We take a running fix of the sun. You might call it two sights and the run between. It's based on the same principle as the running fix of pilotage, discussed in Chapter 10. The pilot took a bearing, carried the resulting position line along, and crossed it with a later bearing on the same object. Here the navigator takes a sight of the sun, carries the resulting position line along, and crosses it with a position line from a later sight of the sun.

If you study the illustration showing the running fix, you'll see the similarity with the pilot's running fix. Again, it may help you to visualize the position line being "advanced" by being towed bodily through the water by a craft that makes the same course and same speed as your vessel. (Figs. 79–84.)

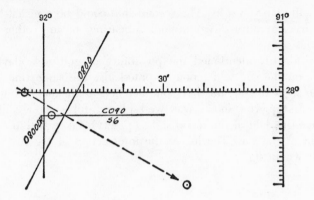

132. Celestial running fix (1). Plotting 0800 sight; dead reckoning, course, and speed are already on the chart.

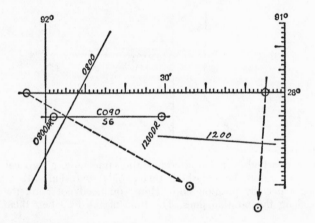

133. Celestial running fix (2). Plotting 1200 sight on same chart.

As already mentioned, the advanced sun line crossed with a later sun sight is the method of choice of daytime celestial navigation. You could, for example, cross the 1200 position line, advanced, with a position line of the sun based on an afternoon sight, say at 1600.

After sunset the navigator has another chance to fix the position of his vessel. During twilight, when the horizon is still visible and the stars and planets appear, you can get position lines from these bodies. Two stars will give you a fix, just as the sun and moon did in the example above. Many navigators prefer to shoot "a round" of stars, usually three.

At dawn before the stars disappear, when the horizon first becomes clearly outlined, you could get another fix from the stars.

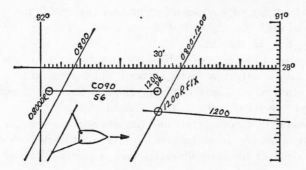

134. Celestial running fix (3). Morning position line, advanced to noon, is crossed with noon position line for a running fix. The 0800 line is moved parallel to itself 24 nautical miles 090, labeled 0800–1200 as in pilotage. The small boat in the corner is to remind you of the trick in all running fix work: The position line moves as though towed by a vessel of the same speed and course as yours.

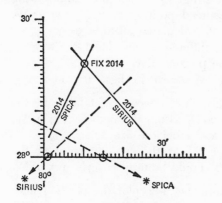

135. Two-star fix. From two stars observed one right after the other. Plotting is similar to sun-moon sight, fig. 131. Each sight is plotted from its own assumed position. Dashed lines are azimuth lines. Note star symbol at end of arrow.

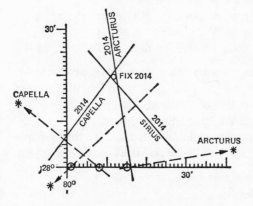

136. Three-star fix. From three stars observed one right after the other. The three resulting position lines usually form a small triangle, the cocked hat, around your most likely position.

You could sail across any ocean, or around the world, using nothing but dawn and dusk star sights, just as you could get along with nothing but running fixes of the sun.

Practically, most navigators combine both methods. Here's one reason: If you run into a shower at twilight, or if the horizon is hazy at that time, as it often is, you have lost your chance. Even on a cloudy day you may get several chances to take a sight of the sun.

The technique of shooting stars and the sun and the steps in working the different sights are so similar you might as well learn both methods. All sights, whatever the body observed, end as position lines plotted on your chart.

You now not only know how to plot these lines, but also have learned all there is to the calculation of the altitude difference, step 7. That makes two steps of the eight-step method.

PRACTICE (20)

A. Get a chart or plotting sheet that includes latitude 42 N, or make your own from scales in this book, e.g. fig. 131. Then plot the following sight of the sun, taken at 1531: assumed position 42 00 N, 124 45 W; azimuth 237; observed altitude 50 50, calculated altitude 50 30.

Start by calculating the altitude difference, and label it "toward" or "away." Don't forget to label the position line.

Solution: Step-by-step procedure is shown in figs. 174 and 175.

B. On the same sheet, to get a fix, plot a moon sight taken at the same minute. Assumed latitude 42 00 N, assumed longitude 124 41 W, Zn 093, Ho 26 10, Hc 26 25. Plot and label the fix.

Solution: The fix, labeled "1531 FIX," at the crossing point of the position lines of sun and moon sights should be near 41 43 N, 125 02 W.

C. Using a 28-degree grid, e.g. from fig. 122, plot the position lines of this two-star sight, taken at 2014, to get a fix. (Using dashes for the azimuth lines will make your work easier to read.)

SPICA   aL 28 00 N, alo 79 45 W, Zn 117, Ho 22 21, Hc 22 34
SIRIUS   28 00 N   79 59 W   228   28 35   28 55
Solution: See fig. 135. The 2014 fix will be near 28 20 N, 79 49 W.

D. Here are the plotting data for two other stars taken at the same time:

ARCTURUS 28 00 N   79 45 W   081   26 31   26 30
CAPELLA   28 00 N   79 52 W   308   36 33   36 23

Solution: See fig. 136 for three-star sight, which includes Sirius from preceding problem. The 2014 fix should be near 28 21 N, 79 48 W.

E. Combine the following sun sights for a running fix. Vessel's course 090 T, speed 6 knots. Label the fix.

0800 aL 28 00 N, alo 92 05 W, Zn 119, Ho 20 03, Hc 19 53
1600   28 00 N   91 05 W   244   15 57   15 55

(Plot the earlier sight, then the later one. Calculate the vessel's run between sights. Move the earlier position line with the vessel. Be sure to measure the nautical miles in minutes of latitude, not longitude.)

Solution: The 0800 position line is shown in fig. 132, the technique of advancing earlier position line in fig. 134. The fix, labeled "1600 R Fix," should be near 27 51 N, 91 02 W.

F. Combine the following sun sights for a running fix. Course 000 T, speed 4 knots. Don't forget to label the fix.

1044 aL 42 00 N, alo 69 45 W, Zn 130, Ho 53 37, Hc 53 48
1357   42 00 N   70 00 W   218   57 55   58 00

Solution: The 1357 R Fix should be near 42 11 N, 70 08 W. (The second sight is sketched in fig. 121 and drawn in fig. 131.)

21. Greenwich Time and Date

In the chapter before last you read: "The Nautical Almanac, published annually, gives the ground point of the sun—and the other bodies used in celestial navigation—for every second of that year."

You'll remember the ground point: the point on earth where the observed body is directly overhead at the time of observation. It is the center of the circle of position, a small part of which we draw as a straight position line. It is the point toward which the azimuth line of our plot points. Since the observed body is directly above the ground point, the azimuth of the ground point is also the true bearing of the body from the assumed position. The navigator is so close to the assumed position that it is also the true bearing from his vessel.

Let's go back to the example we've used to illustrate the circle of position (fig. 119), and sketch how each of four observers would plot his position line. The ground point was due south of New Orleans. So there it was high noon. Near Boston the sun bore west of south; it was afternoon. Near Los Angeles the sun bore east of south; it was morning. In the vicinity of Lima, in latitude 7 S, where the sun had been due north at noon, it now bears west of north; it's afternoon. Near Georgetown, in the Northern Hemisphere but south of the ground point, the sun has also been due north at noon. It's now west of north; it's afternoon there too.

Boston at that date was on daylight-saving time, Peru in the same time zone on standard time; Guyana the year round is on its own time, 1^h15^m fast on Eastern Standard Time.

How can observers at all these points get the ground point from the same Almanac? That's simple. The Almanac uses a time common to all observers. Since Greenwich is internationally agreed upon as the starting point of longitude, it was logical to choose Greenwich time as the worldwide standard.

The time used in celestial navigation everywhere is called *Greenwich Mean Time*, abbreviated GMT.

From daily life you are familiar with time zones and standard time. Greenwich Mean Time is the standard time based on the meridian of

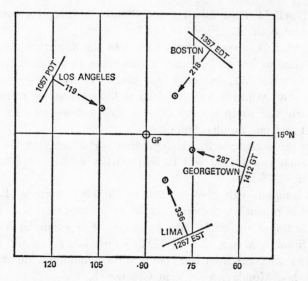

137. These position lines were sketched by navigators near Boston, George-town, Lima, and Los Angeles who observed the sun at the moment when it was directly above a point in latitude 15°00′ N, longitude 90°00′ W. (Com-pare with circle of position in fig. 119.)

At the same moment they have written down four different times. To reduce this sight they will all use Greenwich Mean Time, 1757 for all four observers.

Greenwich, just as Eastern Standard Time is time based on the meridian 75° W.

If you live near Boston or Lima, both near 75° W, you are on Eastern Standard Time—in winter in Boston, the year round in Lima. To get Greenwich time you add five hours to Eastern Standard Time. In New Orleans, in winter on Central Standard Time, you'd add six hours. In Los Angeles, when it is on Pacific Standard Time, you'd add eight hours.

All the places named were in the Western Hemisphere, in west longitudes. In the Eastern Hemisphere, you'd subtract a certain number of hours. In Australia, for example, you'd subtract ten hours from the time kept in Sydney to get Greenwich time.

You'll find these corrections—which include a few odd ones such as Guyana time—in the Nautical Almanac. There you'll also find some of the dates between which daylight-saving time is used.

Daylight-saving time, summer time, is invariably fast on the time kept at the same place in winter. Usually one hour fast. To convert

Eastern Daylight Time into Eastern Standard Time, for example, you subtract one hour.

Suit yourself: Convert daylight time into standard time, then convert standard time to Greenwich time; or remember to add, say, five hours in "winter" to get GMT, but only four hours in "summer."

If you stay within a few hundred miles east or west from home—going north and south doesn't change time zones—you can keep your watch set to your familiar time.

Adding the correction for daylight time, or subtracting the zone correction when you should add it, will usually make complete nonsense of your sight.

You're familiar with phrases such as "Sunday morning, Paris time," and vaguely remember the existence of an international date line. Don't worry. Getting Greenwich date is simple. For example: You take a sight on Sunday, May 2, at 2014 EDT. To get GMT you add four hours and get 2414. That's fourteen minutes past midnight. So it's 0014 of the next day, Monday, May 3, in Greenwich.

The date that goes with Greenwich time is, reasonably enough, called *Greenwich date.*

In the Western Hemisphere—where you invariably add the correction to get Greenwich time—you'll have a Greenwich date one day *later* than your local date whenever the addition gives a figure greater than 2400.

In the Eastern Hemisphere—where you subtract the correction to get Greenwich time—you'll have a Greenwich date one day *earlier* than your local date, whenever you have to "borrow" twenty-four hours to make subtraction possible. (November 1, 0800 in Sydney is October 31, 2200 in Greenwich.)

In many sights the wrong Greenwich date will not make the result seem impossible. So you must watch out for that yourself.

The adding and subtracting of twenty-four hours has some similarity to adding and subtracting 360 degrees. In both cases we subtract when we get a meaninglessly large figure, add to make subtraction possible. But the similarity is only superficial. In navigation 362 degrees is the same as 002 degrees. But twenty-six hours—elapsed since the midnight when the day started at Greenwich—is one day plus two hours.

You might think keeping a timepiece set to GMT would help you. That's how chronometers are set on big ships. For the occasional navigator, local time and correction seems surer to me. The usual twelve-hour dial does not show whether it's 02 42 or 14 42 in Greenwich. You'll never be in doubt about A.M. and P.M. in local time. Also, the usual watch wouldn't tell you whether the Greenwich time shown is today—your local date—tomorrow, or yesterday.

Without a calendar watch, and sometimes with one, you may be in doubt about the date. Happily cruising among the islands, I often was. But somehow I always remembered Sunday, lamp-and-stove-cleaning and engine-checking day, and special dessert. Then on my fingers I could figure the day of the week. To help such navigators, the Almanac very clearly prints the day of the week next to the date. Writing the day of the week next to the date in the first line of your sight reduction is a good idea. It'll bring you up short when the Almanac doesn't agree with you.

You may hear GMT referred to as Zulu time; you could write 1300 GMT as 1300 Z. In that code, Eastern Standard Time is Romeo, Central is Sierra, Mountain is Tango, and Pacific is Uniform.

I think you'll do better with *Zone Description,* abbreviated ZD. For Eastern Standard Time it's +5, meaning five hours have to be added to get GMT; for Pacific Standard Time it's +8; for the time kept at Sydney, Australia, it's —10.

With Greenwich time you can get the position of the ground point of the sun or another navigational body for every second of the year. Do you have to work to the second?

That question really boils down to this: How much does the ground point change in one second? The exact change depends on a number of variables. But the approximate change is easily calculated. Most of it is caused by the revolution of the earth around its axis, 360 degrees in twenty-four hours. That makes a change of 15 degrees of longitude in one hour, or 1 degree in four minutes of time. Since a degree is 60 minutes of arc, it also means a movement of 1 minute of arc in four seconds of time.

A minute of longitude in most places is shorter than a minute of latitude, a nautical mile. So we could say the ground point moves westward at most 1 nautical mile in four seconds. The position circle, of course, moves with its center, the ground point. So your position line could move at most 1 nautical mile in four seconds.

Timing your sights to the minute could make your line of position up to 15 miles out of place. That's not good enough. You may want to take your chance on "at most a mile," and time your sights to the four-second accuracy. But every sight already contains some unavoidable errors, so celestial sights are timed, if possible, to the second.

Should you buy a chronometer? If you mean by that a gimbaled, boxed job, rated and nursed by a specialist, my answer is no. Chronometers are expensive. Unless protected from shocks—impossible on a small vessel—wound regularly, and checked frequently, they give a false sense of accuracy.

A wrist chronometer, checked daily, protected by your body against jarring, and kept at a reasonably constant temperature by your skin, will give as good service as a standard chronometer on a small vessel. And you'll be less likely to forget winding it.

I have navigated for years with a specially good wristwatch, not a chronometer watch. I wear it on the inside of my wrist. That protects it from contact with parts of the boat, and makes it easy to read while I still hold the sextant.

A watchmaker can adjust your watch or chronometer; but only when you wear it constantly on your wrist can you find its daily rate, its regular error.

Radio time signals, broadcast by many seafaring nations, make rating simple. You compare your watch reading with the radio signal time at the same hour every day and record the difference. After a string of observations a pattern appears. Your chronometer loses, say, five seconds a day on the average. That would be its rate. It may have lost two seconds one day, six the next. The difference between the averaged rate and the daily readings would be your error; here plus or minus two seconds. If that sort of thing appeals to you, fine.

But it isn't really necessary. You can compare your watch with the time signal just before your observation, write down how much fast or slow the watch was, and apply the correction to the sight timed by your watch. If it has been ten seconds slow, obviously you must add ten seconds to your watch reading to get the exact time. If it has been twenty seconds fast, obviously you subtract twenty seconds.

Two radio stations, operated by the United States Bureau of Standards, give almost constant time checks, nearly everywhere in the world.

	WWV (Colorado)	*WWVH (Hawaii)*
Frequency Megahertz:	2.5, 5, 10, 15, 20, and 25	2.5, 5, 10, and 15

Megahertz is a new designation of megacycles. The 2.5 mHz frequency is right in the marine band. Many marine receivers also get the 5 mHz transmissions. On a multiband receiver you'll often get the higher frequencies when the lower ones are drowned out by interference.

Once found on your dial, either station is easily spotted again. The thing to listen for is a musical note (A above middle C) over which one-second ticks can be clearly heard. After some Morse code, just before every full minute, you'll hear an announcement in plain English, like this:

"National Bureau of Standards, WWV, Fort Collins, Colorado. Next tone begins at twenty-two hours thirty minutes Greenwich Mean Time."

What could be more clear or helpful to the navigator?

Another time signal often useful in North and Central America comes from the Dominion Observatory in Ottawa, Canada. This station—CHU— operates continuously on frequencies 3333, 7335 and 14,670 kilohertz, formerly called kilocycles. So you'll find it near 3.3, 7.3, and 14.7 mHz. The sequence and sounds are different from the U.S. signals, but the announcement is again in plain English (and French).

With these three signals you could time your sights directly without any watch, just counting seconds after the clearly marked minutes. But often the reception is poor just when you want a sight.

So it is better to find a time convenient to you when a given frequency comes in well in your area. You can combine it with some daily routine. If you are in the habit of listening to an eight o'clock weather report, you might check your watch at seven fifty-five.

I strongly recommend that you write down the time difference. A few hours later you may remember that you were thirty seconds off but may have forgotten whether you were fast or slow. Don't use plus or minus signs. Fast and slow leads to fewer errors. If your daily rate is more than a few seconds divide it over the day. Say the rate has been around twenty or twenty-five seconds fast per day. That makes your watch gain about one second each hour. If you have checked it at 0800, subtract another four seconds at noon, another twelve seconds at 2000.

Ship's chronometers are never reset at sea, even if they are twenty minutes off. I'd reset my wristwatch whenever it's one minute off. Make sure the minute hand is on a minute dot when the sweep-second hand is on or near zero. Otherwise you might later wonder to what minute the seconds belong.

Distrusting stopwatches and helpers, I prefer to take my own time. As soon as I have measured the altitude in my sextant—before reading the scale on the sextant—I read my watch. Seconds first. They'll change; the minute isn't going to change while I write the seconds down.

If you can't get short-wave time signals, try the broadcast band. On the full hour on the NBC network, for instance, you'll hear a very accurately timed beep. Nothing stops that beep, not presidential speeches or state funerals.

The time of observation is the moment when you bring the sun, or other body, down to the horizon in your sextant. If you keep a chronometer below, you must deduct the time it takes you to get from where you take the sight to where you read the chronometer. Time a few dry runs, then deduct their average number of seconds before you even write down the time.

If you wear your watch on the inside of your wrist you can read it within one second of your observation.

Here is a sample of the time corrections, step 2 of our method.

Local date of observation	Tue			Nov 2
Ship's time of observation	EST	11	43 55	
Watch error (slow 10^{sec})			+10	
Zone correction (ZD +5)		+5		
Greenwich time and date	GMT	16	44 05	Nov 2

With a change in date the calculation might look like this:

Su   Oct 31

EST	22	57 39
Fast		—10
ZD	+ 5	
	27	57 29
	—24	
GMT	03	57 29 Mo Nov 1

You will soon find several ways of saving work. You'll know what time your watch is set to; the zone correction is always in hours, the watch correction in seconds, so you can use one line for both. You know that the last line always shows Greenwich Mean Time, so you needn't label it. When there's no date change, there's no point in repeating the date. (And when there is a date change, you'll probably figure the hours in your head without writing down —24.)

Typical calculations—for Pacific Standard Time—would look like this for a watch twelve seconds fast:

08 44 17 Nov 2 or 20 44 17 Nov 2
+ 8 —12   + 8 —12
16 44 05   04 44 05 Nov 3

Where do you make this calculation? Right on your work sheet. Not a form, but a simple sheet of paper, lined or ruled if you like. I don't like forms. That's not just personal prejudice but a carefully studied opinion. You can already see one reason against forms: Sometimes you need lines to deduct twenty-four hours, most often you don't. In east longitude you'd need a line to add twenty-four hours before you apply the zone correction; again you'd only use it sometimes. The rest of the time these extra lines would confuse you.

There's another good reason. One sight solution works for sun, moon, planets, and stars. But there are minor differences. So you'd have to carry four different forms, or one universal form with a lot of spaces to be left blank. The moon, for instance, needs sometimes three, sometimes four sextant corrections. The sun takes two, so do stars. Planets take two, but at times Venus and Mars have a third correction. Before you know it you get a form as forbidding as an income tax form.

I think you'll be much less likely to go wrong by using a systematic pattern on your work sheet rather than a form. The same data will always be in the same area of the sheet. If you need extra lines, you add them.

After testing different arrangements myself, and having students test them, I believe a three-column work sheet is best for all sights. You can expand that for sights of several stars worked at once, but it's still the basic pattern.

You can see the three-column pattern in fig. 138 or any complete sight reduction in this book.

The first line, written perhaps just before the observation, gives the day of the week, the date, the body observed (symbol), its approximate bearing, and dead reckoning latitude and longitude. It runs over all three columns.

138. Work sheet showing three-column layout. Time of observation heads left column; sextant altitude heads right column. Coordinates of ground point, discussed in next chapter, go into left and middle columns.

Directly below that, in the left column record the time of observation. It becomes the start of your time correction and conversion to Greenwich time, just discussed (step 2).

Also directly below the first line, but in the right column, you'll record the sextant reading. That's logical since you record the time before reading the sextant. The sextant reading becomes the start of your sextant corrections (step 4).

Below the entry of Greenwich Mean Time, into the left and middle columns goes the calculation of the coordinates of the ground point from data given in the Nautical Almanac. That's step 3. We'll take that next.

PRACTICE (21)

Give Greenwich time (and date if it differs from the given one). Fast or slow means your watch is ahead or astern of standard time signal. ZD for EST is +5, CST +6, MST +7, and PST +8. D in place of S in these abbreviations means daylight-saving.

A. Su Mar 7, 09 19 12 EST, Fast 21^s
B. Mo Nov 1, 17 13 50 PST, Slow 13^s
C. Su Oct 31, 05 57 28 CST, Fast 11^s
D. Sa May 1, 13 56 58 +4, Slow 10^s
E. We Jul 21, 06 24 12 −8, Fast 31^s
F. Sa May 1, 10 44 01 EDT, Slow 8^s
G. Su May 2, 15 31 54 PDT, Slow 4^s
H. Su May 2, 05 31 49 +7, Fast 19^s

ANSWERS (21)

A. Su Mar 7, 14 18 51 GMT
B. Tu Nov 2, 01 14 03 GMT
C. Su Oct 31, 11 57 17 GMT
D. Sa May 1, 17 57 08 GMT
E. Tu Jul 20, 22 23 41 GMT
F. Sa May 1, 14 44 09 GMT
G. Su May 2, 22 31 58 GMT
H. Su May 2, 12 31 30 GMT

22. Ground Point

With the correct Greenwich time (and date) you're ready to find in an Almanac the point on earth where the observed body was directly overhead at the moment of observation.

I'd use the Nautical Almanac, a joint effort of the United States Naval Observatory and the British Nautical Almanac Office. (For sale at chart agents or by the Superintendent of Documents, Washington, D.C. 20402. Current price $4.) The same Almanac, in translation, is in use in other countries. You'll be able to use any other Almanac even if you can't read the language. The Air Almanac, another joint American and British publication, covers only four months. So you have to buy three almanacs a year at a cost greater than the Nautical Almanac. If you're familiar with the Nautical Almanac, you can find your way around also in the Air Almanac.

With Greenwich date and Greenwich time you find the coordinates of the ground point of the observed body at the time of observation in the Nautical Almanac. That we already know. Now we'll look at the details. After about ten pages of introductory material come about 240 pages, printed on white stock, all alike in layout, known as the "daily pages." At every book opening in that section you'll find data for *three* days. For stars and planets they are on the left page, for sun and moon on the right page. Each day shows twenty-four entries, for the hours 00 to 23 GMT (pp. 312-15).

In the back of the book thirty pages, printed on yellow stock, all alike in layout, give the change of the ground point for minutes and seconds. At every book opening in this section, known as the "yellow pages," you'll find these "Increments and Corrections" for all bodies for four minutes. Every minute block has sixty lines, one for each second (pp. 316 and 317).

Now let's work an example. You have taken a sextant sight of the sun, on Tuesday, November 2, at exactly 16 00 00 GMT. Where was the ground point of the sun at that moment?

In the Almanac find the page that lists—besides two other days—November 2. Since you're interested in the sun, you'll look at the sun column, on the right-hand page. You'll find the 16 00 00 position of the ground point of the sun on that date on the line labeled 16. Copy that line exactly as it is given in the Almanac on your work sheet:

G.M.T.	SUN		MOON				
	G.H.A.	Dec.	G.H.A.	v	Dec.	d	H.P.
d h	o '	o '	o '	'	o '	'	'
2 00	184 05·9	S14 28·2	18 06·4	7·2	N14 38·9	14·7	61·3
01	199 05·9	29·0	32 32·6	7·1	14 53·6	14·7	61·3
02	214 05·9	29·8	46 58·7	7·0	15 08·3	14·5	61·3
03	229 05·9 · ·	30·6	61 24·7	6·9	15 22·8	14·4	61·3
04	244 05·9	31·4	75 50·6	6·8	15 37·2	14·4	61·3
05	259 06·0	32·2	90 16·4	6·8	15 51·6	14·2	61·3
06	274 06·0	S14 33·0	104 42·2	6·6	N16 05·8	14·1	61·3
07	289 06·0	33·8	119 07·8	6·6	16 19·9	14·0	61·3
T 08	304 06·0	34·6	133 33·4	6·5	16 33·9	13·9	61·3
U 09	319 06·0 · ·	35·4	147 58·9	6·4	16 47·8	13·8	61·3
E 10	334 06·0	36·2	162 24·3	6·3	17 01·6	13·7	61·3
S 11	349 06·0	37·0	176 49·6	6·3	17 15·3	13·6	61·3
D 12	4 06·1	S14 37·8	191 14·9	6·1	N17 28·9	13·4	61·3
A 13	19 06·1	38·6	205 40·0	6·1	17 42·3	13·3	61·3
Y 14	34 06·1	39·4	220 05·1	6·0	17 55·6	13·2	61·3
15	49 06·1 · ·	40·2	234 30·1	5·8	18 08·8	13·1	61·2
16	64 06·1	41·0	248 54·9	5·8	18 21·9	13·0	61·2
17	79 06·1	41·7	263 19·7	5·8	18 34·9	12·8	61·2
18	94 06·1	S14 42·5	277 44·5	5·6	N18 47·7	12·7	61·2
19	109 06·1	43·3	292 09·1	5·5	19 00·4	12·5	61·2
20	124 06·1	44·1	306 33·6	5·5	19 12·9	12·4	61·2
21	139 06·2 · ·	44·9	320 58·1	5·4	19 25·3	12·3	61·2
22	154 06·2	45·7	335 22·5	5·3	19 37·6	12·2	61·2
23	169 06·2	46·5	349 46·8	5·2	19 49·8	12·0	61·2
	S.D. 16·1	d 0·8	S.D. 16·6		16·7		16·7

139. Nautical Almanac. Part of a right daily page showing data for sun and moon. (Whole page is shown in fig. 160.)

$$64 \ 06.1 \qquad S \ 14 \ 41.0$$

There you have the coordinates of your ground point. Have you expected a latitude, north or south, and a longitude, west or east? You got them, faintly disguised. First: They are in the wrong order. We are in the habit of giving latitude first, here the latitude comes second. And it has a different name: declination, abbreviated Dec. But for our purposes it's identical with the latitude of the ground point. The ground point is in latitude S 14 41.0.

So you suspect that it is also in longitude 64 06.1. Correct, but is it west or east; the Almanac doesn't seem to say. Again it has a different name: Greenwich hour angle, abbreviated GHA. By definition it is counted westabout. As long as the Greenwich hour angle is less than 180 degrees, you could read it as longitude west. In our example the ground point is in longitude 64 06.1 W.

(To satisfy your understandable curiosity: What happens when the Greenwich hour angle is greater than 180 degrees? Four minutes after the sun has been directly overhead at some point in longitude 180 West, the GHA will be 181 00. It will be overhead at a point we usually describe as in longitude 179 00 East. You could get east longitude by subtracting west longitude from 360 degrees. You can also convert west longitude or Greenwich hour angle equivalents into east longitude by subtracting them from 360.)

Glancing at a left Almanac page (p. 314), you'll see the Greenwich hour angle and declination listed in the same manner for the four easily seen planets, Venus, Mars, Jupiter, and Saturn.

At the extreme left of the page is a column that may sound strange to you, headed Aries. That's short for "The First Point of Aries," also called the vernal equinox. Don't worry about its exact definition. It's a reference point in the sky, about where the sun—northbound—crosses the equator at the beginning of spring, about March 21. Consider it a sort of Greenwich in the sky from which the "longitudes" of all stars are measured. (Of course, we don't call it longitude; again we don't mess with east and west, but measure always westabout. The name is sidereal hour angle; we'll talk about it under emergencies at the end of the book.)

The first point of Aries, unlike Greenwich in latitude 51 29 N, is by definition on the equator. If there were a star at that point, its ground point would be in latitude 00 00. So this column lists no declination.

Aries is used for all star sights. So you already know how to look up the data for a full hour for all stars, the four navigational planets, and the sun. That's all the navigational bodies, except the moon. I'll get around to that shortly.

Only rarely will you take a sight exactly on the hour. So you will have to use the yellow pages to find the movement of the ground point for the minutes and seconds elapsed since the last full hour.

Perhaps you had expected to find the coordinates of the ground point of the sun and the other bodies listed for every minute and second. That would take 3600 lines for every hour; 60 for the 60 minutes, times 60 for the 60 seconds of every minute. Ridiculous.

The yellow pages do the same job in much less space. The celestial bodies move at speeds that remain almost constant over a period as short as one hour. That's what makes the yellow pages practical.

If you know the longitude of the ground point of Aries at 1600 GMT (281 16.4), you also know it at 1700 GMT. It will be 15 02.5 farther west. That's the constant rate for the motion of the stars. The yellow pages give it for any other time. Example: What is the GHA of Aries, Nov 2, at 16 44 05 GMT?

$$
\begin{array}{lllll}
\text{GHA Aries} & \text{GMT 16 00 00} & & 281 & 16.4 \\
& \phantom{\text{GMT 16 }}44\ 05 & & 11 & 03.1 \\
\hline
& \text{GMT 16 44 05} & & 292 & 19.5 \\
\end{array}
$$

44ᵐ INCREMENTS AND CORRECTIONS

44ᵐ	SUN PLANETS	ARIES	MOON	v or Corrⁿ d	v or Corrⁿ d	v or Corrⁿ d
s	° ′	° ′	° ′	′ ′	′ ′	′ ′
00	11 00·0	11 01·8	10 29·9	0·0 0·0	5·0 3·7	12·0 8·9
01	11 00·3	11 02·1	10 30·2	0·1 0·1	5·1 3·8	12·1 9·0
02	11 00·5	11 02·3	10 30·4	0·2 0·1	5·2 3·9	12·2 9·0
03	11 00·8	11 02·6	10 30·6	0·3 0·2	5·3 3·9	12·3 9·1
04	11 01·0	11 02·8	10 30·9	0·4 0·3	5·4 4·0	12·4 9·2
05	11 01·3	11 03·1	10 31·1	0·5 0·4	5·5 4·1	12·5 9·3
06	11 01·5	11 03·3	10 31·4	0·6 0·4	5·6 4·2	12·6 9·3
07	11 01·8	11 03·6	10 31·6	0·7 0·5	5·7 4·2	12·7 9·4
08	11 02·0	11 03·8	10 31·8	0·8 0·6	5·8 4·3	12·8 9·5
09	11 02·3	11 04·1	10 32·1	0·9 0·7	5·9 4·4	12·9 9·6
10	11 02·5	11 04·3	10 32·3	1·0 0·7	6·0 4·5	13·0 9·6
11	11 02·8	11 04·6	10 32·6	1·1 0·8	6·1 4·5	13·1 9·7
12	11 03·0	11 04·8	10 32·8	1·2 0·9	6·2 4·6	13·2 9·8
13	11 03·3	11 05·1	10 33·0	1·3 1·0	6·3 4·7	13·3 9·9
14	11 03·5	11 05·3	10 33·3	1·4 1·0	6·4 4·7	13·4 9·9
15	11 03·8	11 05·6	10 ··	··5 1·1		13·5
	·· 11 05·					

140. Nautical Almanac. Part of column of yellow page that shows changes for forty-four minutes after the hour. (Whole column is shown in fig. 162.)

You found the increase in hour angle in the Aries column of the 44-minute table, on the 05-second line.

For the sun you'd use the same table, but the sun column. At the same time:

$$\begin{array}{lll} \text{GHA Sun} & \text{GMT 16 00 00} & 64\ 06.1 \\ & \underline{44\ 05} & \underline{11\ 01.3} \\ & \text{GMT 16 44 05} & 75\ 07.4 \end{array}$$

The ground point of the sun has moved west at the rate of exactly 15 00 per hour.

What happened to the latitude of the ground point, the declination of the sun? Looking at the declination column, you'll see that on November 2 it increases:

$$\begin{array}{lll} \text{Dec Sun} & \text{GMT 16 00} & \text{S 14 41.0} \\ & \text{GMT 17 00} & \underline{41.7} \\ \text{Change} & & +0.7 \end{array}$$

Actually you don't have to calculate the change. The mean change during the three days the page covers is printed at the bottom of the column: d 0.8. You still have to glance at the declination column to see if it increases or decreases. Here it increases; mark it plus. Then look in the 44-minute table in the "v or d" column until you find 0.8 hourly rate. To the right of 0.8 you'll find 0.6, the change—here an increase—in 44 minutes (regardless of the number of seconds). Had you calculated the value and used 0.7 you would have got 0.5 Add either value to the declination at the preceding hour, and round off to whole minutes.

Dec Sun   GMT 16 00   S 14 41.0
                    44   +0.6
                 ‾‾‾‾‾‾‾‾‾‾‾‾‾‾‾‾‾‾‾‾‾‾
                 16 44   S 14 42

Had the declination been decreasing, you would have subtracted the correction.

I wouldn't write as much on my work sheet as we have here. I would first copy exactly from the Almanac, then after the declination put the d-correction from the bottom of the column, getting the sign by looking at the declination column. Since this line is directly below the Greenwich Mean Time, it is obvious that it refers to the last full hour. The next line will obviously refer to the minutes and seconds; no need to label it. I'd round off as I go along and get these three lines:

64 06.1   S 14 41.0 +0.8
11 01.3   +0.6
‾‾‾‾‾‾‾‾‾‾‾‾‾‾‾‾‾‾‾‾‾‾‾‾‾‾‾
75 07   S 14 42

That's all there is to getting the ground point of the sun from the Nautical Almanac.

The planets are only slightly more difficult.

Their hour angle increases like the sun's at a rate of exactly 15 00 per hour—found in the column headed Sun/Planets—plus a little for the motion of the planet. This extra correction is known as the v-correction, perhaps for velocity. You'll find it at the bottom of each planet's column. It is always plus, except when marked negative for Venus. I'd put the v-correction and its sign in a space I'd leave between GHA and Dec. You'll find the correction corresponding to any given v, just as you found the d-correction, in the v or d column. For the same time as before my work sheet would look like this for Venus:

46 31.7 −0.7 S19 38.1 +0.8
+11 01.3
−   0.5   +0.6
‾‾‾‾‾‾‾‾‾‾‾‾‾‾‾‾‾‾‾‾‾‾‾‾‾‾‾
57 33   S19 39

For the same time for Mars it would look like this:

$$310 \quad 17.2 \quad +1.3 \quad S14 \quad 17.2 \quad -0.6$$
$$+ \quad 11 \quad 01.3$$
$$\underline{+ \qquad 1.0 \qquad\qquad -0.4}$$
$$321 \quad 20 \qquad\qquad S14 \quad 17$$

After that little exercise the moon is even simpler. Its v- and d-corrections are printed for every hour right alongside the GHA and Dec values, just as we have written them here for the planets. The v-correction is always plus; you find the sign for the d-correction, as you did for the sun and planets. At this stage don't worry about the last column, labeled HP; just copy it.

For the same time my work sheet for the moon would look like this:

$$248 \quad 54.9 \quad +5.8 \quad N18 \quad 21.9 \quad +13.0 \quad 61.2$$
$$+ \quad 10 \quad 31.1$$
$$\underline{+ \qquad 4.3 \qquad\qquad + \quad 9.6}$$
$$259 \quad 30 \qquad\qquad N18 \quad 32$$

Notice the increase in hour angle for the moon is considerably less than for the other bodies; 14 19 per hour is the basis of the moon column in the yellow pages.

That lets you check the increase in hour angle—called increment in the Almanac. For sun and planets, as we have seen, it is exactly 15 degrees per hour. Divide the minutes elapsed by four and you should get exactly the change in hour angle for sun and planets. Example: Forty-four minutes gives exactly 11 00. It will be very little more for Aries, 11 02.

For the moon it must be noticeably less, 10 30. If your test doesn't confirm your exact calculation, you have made the common mistake of using the wrong column in the yellow pages. You've used the sun column for the moon; or less likely, the moon column for sun, planets, or Aries.

Here's another check. The v- and d-corrections must be smaller than the tabulated hourly values. When the declination changes 0.8 in one hour it cannot change 1.1 in forty-four minutes. You've read from right to left in the correction table. I don't know why, but it's a common mistake. It can't make much difference for the sun, where the correction in declination never exceeds 1 minute of arc, but it's another matter for the moon with its large changes in hour angle and declination.

You can roughly check the v- and d-corrections for all bodies. Ten minutes past the hour, one sixth of an hour, they must be one sixth of the hourly value. Fifteen minutes after the hour they must be about one quarter of the value at the bottom of the column. And so forth.

You'll soon get the feel, especially for the declination change of the

G.M.T.	ARIES	VENUS	−3·3	MARS	−0·7
	G.H.A.	G.H.A.	Dec.	G.H.A.	Dec.
d h	o ′	o ′	o ′	o ′	o ′
2 00	40 37·0	166 43·3	S 19 24·8	69 56·7	S 14 26·1
01	55 39·4	181 42·6	25·7	84 58·0	25·5
02	70 41·9	196 41·9	26·5	99 59·2	25·0
03	85 44·4	211 41·1	•• 27·3	115 00·5	•• 24·4
04	100 46·8	226 40·4	28·2	130 01·8	23·9
05	115 49·3	241 39·7	29·0	145 03·1	23·3
06	130 51·7	256 39·0	S 19 29·8	160 04·4	S 14 22·7
07	145 54·2	271 38·2	30·7	175 05·7	22·2
T 08	160 56·7	286 37·5	31·5	190 07·0	21·6
U 09	175 59·1	301 36·8	•• 32·3	205 08·2	•• 21·1
E 10	191 01·6	316 36·1	33·1	220 09·5	20·5
S 11	206 04·1	331 35·3	34·0	235 10·8	20·0
D 12	221 06·5	346 34·6	S 19 34·8	250 12·1	S 14 19·4
A 13	236 09·0	1 33·9	35·6	265 13·4	18·8
Y 14	251 11·5	16 33·2	36·4	280 14·7	18·3
15	266 13·9	31 32·4	•• 37·2	295 15·9	• 17·7
16	281 16·4	46 31·7	38·1	310 17·2	17·2
17	296 18·9	61 31·0	38·9	325 18·5	16·6
18	311 21·3	76 30·3	S 19 39·7	340 19·8	S 14 16·0
19	326 23·8	91 29·5	40·5	355 21·1	15·5
20	341 26·2	106 28·8	41·3	10 22·3	14·9
21	356 28·7	121 28·1	•• 42·1	25 23·6	•• 14·4
22	11 31·2	136 27·3	43·0	40 24·9	13·8
23	26 33·6	151 26·6	43·8	55 26·2	13·2
Mer. Pass. 21ʰ 18·0ᵐ		(v −0·7) (d 0·8)		(v 1·3) (d 0·6)	

141. Nautical Almanac. Part of left daily page showing data for sun and planets. (Whole page is shown in fig. 159.)

sun. When the hourly value is small, say 0.1, or the minutes of time few, say two, you'll know that no correction is needed.

In the beginning people always worry about forgetting v- or d-corrections. You don't have to memorize Aries none, sun one, planets and moon two corrections. Just make it a habit to look at the bottom of the column of the daily page. If you follow my advice on the layout of the work sheet, and copy exactly from the Almanac, you can't overlook the corrections of the moon.

That line, by the way, will decide the width of your work sheet. It should take up the left and middle columns without running much into the right column. Copy any line from the moon column in the Almanac, using your usual size of handwritten numerals. For the universal sight the paper will have to be about half as wide again as this sample. If the HP entry runs into the right third of the sheet, that's all right.

You still wonder about these two letters? They stand for horizontal parallax, whatever that may be. Its value at the hour of observation is needed to correct the sextant reading to get the true observed altitude of the moon. So that's the earliest you could make these corrections for the moon. You could do it later, but then you would have to pick up the Nautical Almanac again. So in your routine work this will be the next step, 4, not just for the moon but for all bodies.

Here I'll leave it for later, to discuss it with the use of the sextant. It fits better there.

There's another reason. You now know how to find the ground point of the observed body. You also know how to draw the result of your observation, the position line. It's logical to fill the gap, the steps between finding the ground point and the data needed for plotting the position line, steps 5 and 6. Compared to what you have been through in this chapter, they are easy.

PRACTICE (22)

For the given Greenwich date and time find the coordinates (GHA and Dec) of the ground point of the body named (for the moon also HP). Round your answer to the nearest whole minute of hour angle and declination.

Don't forget to label the declination N or S. For sun and planets don't overlook the corrections at the bottom of the column. Watch the sign of the d-correction, and the correct body column in the yellow pages.

A. Su May 2, 12 44 31 Aries   G. Su May 2, 22 31 58 Sun
B. Sa May 1, 17 57 08 Sun   H. Tu Nov 2, 01 14 56 Jupiter
C. Tu Nov 2, 01 14 03 Mars   I. Mo Nov 1, 12 31 30 Sun
D. Sa May 1, 14 44 09 Sun   J. Su May 2, 12 31 30 Venus
E. Mo May 3, 00 14 01 Aries   K. Su May 2, 22 31 01 Moon
F. Sa May 1, 17 57 58 Moon   L. Mo May 3, 00 14 54 Aries

ANSWERS (22)

A.   39 45.0
     11 09.6
     ‾‾‾‾‾‾‾
     50 55

B.   75 43.1   N 15 01.7 + 0.7
     14 17.0   +0.7
     ‾‾‾‾‾‾‾   ‾‾‾‾‾‾‾‾‾‾
     90 00   N 15 02

C.   84 58.0 + 1.3   S 14 25.5 − 0.6
      3 30.8   −0.1
      +0.3   ‾‾‾‾‾‾‾‾‾‾
     ‾‾‾‾‾‾‾   S 14 25
     88 29

D. 30 42.9   N 14 59.5 + 0.7
    11 02.3   +0.5
    ——————   ——————————
    41 45   N 15 00

E. 220 14.5
      3 30.8   —   —
    ——————
    223 45

F. 347 28.1 +12.1   N 20 39.8 − 9.9 55.5
     13 49.9   −9.5
    +11.6
    ——————   ——————————   —
    361 30°   N 20 30

G. 150 45.3   N 15 23.5 + 0.7
      7 59.8   +0.4
    ——————   ——————————
    158 45   N 15 24

H. 168 14.9 + 1.9   S 21 19.4 + 0.1
      3 44.0   +0.0
       0.5
    ——————   ——————————
    171 59   S 21 19

I.   4 05.7   S 14 18.6 + 0.8
      7 52.5   +0.4
    ——————   ——————————
     11 58   S 14 19

J.   29 18.4 − 0.3°° N 2 40.6 + 1.2
      7 52.5   +0.6
       −0.2
    ——————   ——————————
     37 11   N 2 41

K.   49 09.3 +14.7   N 15 23.5 −11.8 54.8
      7 24.1   −6.2
      +7.7
    ——————   ——————————
     56 41   N 15 17

L. 220 14.5
      3 44.1
    ——————
    223 59

° If you got 1 30 you show that you remember the arithmetic lesson. However, something may have to be subtracted from 361 30 in a future step; so it's best not to subtract 360 here.

°° This is one of the times when the v-correction for Venus is marked minus in the Nautical Almanac.

23. Sight Reduction Tables

Knowing the coordinates of the ground point of the navigational body at the time of observation, and also knowing your approximate position, you can choose the *assumed position* for that sight. That's step 5.

You already know that the assumed position will be near your actual location. Its exact choice is ruled by the sight reduction tables you'll use in the next step.

For the tables I recommend, the choice of *latitude* of the assumed position is very simple. You take the whole degree of latitude nearest your dead reckoning position. In latitude 28 10 N you'd assume 28 N; in latitude 28 40 N you'd assume 29 N. In latitude 28 30 you could pick either; you already know it'll hardly matter.

The choice of longitude of the assumed position isn't much more difficult. In *longitude west* you assume the longitude nearest your dead reckoning position that subtracted from the Greenwich hour angle leaves a whole degree.

That sounds complicated but isn't. Say the Greenwich hour angle of the sun came out as 94 05; you are near 83 55 W. Assume a longitude of 84 05 W. That's near your dead reckoning longitude, and subtracted from the GHA gives a whole number of degrees—10—without minutes.

You can see that to get rid of minutes, your assumed longitude—in the Western Hemisphere—will always have the same number of minutes as the Greenwich hour angle.

Had your dead reckoning position been 84 30 W, you would also have assumed 84 05 W. Had the position been 83 30 W, you should have assumed 83 05 W, which is nearer your position than 84 05 W.

I think that's not too hard to do. But can you subtract longitude from Greenwich hour angle? Isn't that like subtracting apples from pears, something Miss Pringle warned against? No, it isn't. Recall that Greenwich hour angle is the longitude west of Greenwich of the ground point. So there's nothing wrong with subtracting your longitude from it.

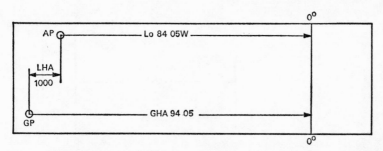

142. Local hour angle of a body in longitudes *west* of Greenwich (longitude zero) is the *difference* between Greenwich hour angle of the body and the longitude of the assumed position.

The difference in longitude—10 degrees in the example—has a name: local hour angle. It is the longitude, counted westward, of the ground point measured not from the meridian of Greenwich, but from the meridian that goes through your assumed position. Its abbreviation is LHA.

A body due south of Greenwich has a Greenwich hour angle of zero. A body due south of your assumed position has a local hour angle of zero. About four minutes later the LHA will be 1 degree, eight minutes later it will be 2 degrees, and so on until nearly twenty-four hours later it will be 359 degrees.

Whenever your assumed west longitude is greater than the Greenwich hour angle, you'll have to add 360 degrees to the GHA to make subtraction possible. Example: GHA 75 07 DR longitude 79 55 W. Add 360 00 and get 435 07. Less assumed longitude 80 07 W gives LHA 355.

In *longitude east* you assume the longitude nearest your dead reckoning position that added to the Greenwich hour angle gives a whole degree.

That again sounds complicated but isn't. Say the Greenwich hour angle of the sun came out as 54 05; you are near longitude 10 35 E. Assume a longitude of 10 55 E. That's near your dead reckoning longitude, and added to the GHA gives a whole number of degrees—65—without minutes.

You can see that to get rid of minutes, your assumed longitude—in the Eastern Hemisphere—will always have to have 60 minus the minutes in the Greenwich hour angles for minutes (60—05=55).

Had your DR longitude been 10 50 E, you would also have chosen 10 55 E. Had the position been 10 05 E, you should have chosen 9 55 E, which is nearer your position than 10 55 E.

The local hour angle in eastern longitudes is the sum of the Greenwich hour angle and your assumed longitude. Whenever that sum exceeds 360 degrees, subtract 360 from the LHA. Example: GHA 355 07,

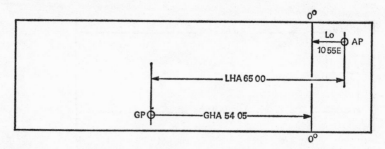

143. Local hour angle of a body in longitudes *east* of Greenwich (longitude zero) is the *sum* of the Greenwich hour angle of the body and the longitude of the assumed position.

DR longitude 10 35 E. GHA plus assumed longitude 10 53 equals 366 00. Subtract 360, and get LHA 6.

Unless you happen to cross the meridian of Greenwich or the one half a world away in longitude 180, you'll work steadily with west or east longitudes. Either will become strictly routine after you've done a few examples.

In either hemisphere you'll have to end up with a local hour angle that has no minutes. The reason: The sight reduction tables only use whole degrees.

Where on the work sheet will you do this calculation? The Greenwich hour angle is in the left third of the page, so the longitude you assume and the sum or difference, the local hour angle, go in that column too. The declination, the latitude of the ground point, is in the middle column, next to its Greenwich hour angle. It's logical to put the assumed latitude also in the middle column, in the same line as the assumed longitude.

As you have seen before, I circle the assumed latitude and longitude. It saves time when you come to plot the assumed position. When by chance there's another figure nearby that could be the latitude or longitude, it also saves mistakes.

In the last chapter we had found the ground point of the observed body at the time of observation. Now we have chosen a position. We now could calculate the altitude of the body as seen at the assumed position by computing the distance from that position to the ground point. We could also calculate its bearing, the azimuth.

That's what navigators used to do. The modern navigator looks in his *sight reduction tables* and finds the answers ready-made or almost so. Getting the calculated altitude (Hc) and true azimuth (Zn) from the tables is step 6 in our eight-step method. (You are already familiar with step 7, comparing calculated and observed altitudes, and step 8, plotting the position line.)

We shall use the U. S. Naval Oceanographic Office Publication ⁂249, commonly referred to as HO 249, Sight Reduction Tables for Air Navigation, identical with the British AP 3270. The small-craft navigator and the airline pilot have this in common: Neither cares about accuracy to tenths of miles; both want the quickest possible solution.

Let me show you how quick the solution of step 6 can be.

Near guessed latitude 28 N, longitude 80 W, you took a sight of the brightest of all stars, Sirius, when the Greenwich hour angle of Aries was 223 59. Your assumed latitude will be 28 N, your assumed longitude 79 59 W. That makes your local hour angle of Aries 144.

Get volume I of HO 249, subtitled "Selected Stars," off the shelf. Open it to the two facing pages headed "LAT 28° N," and look for the space that contains LHA Aries 144. (Part of that page is shown on p. 318.) On the 144 line in the column headed *Sirius* you'll find:

Hc   Zn

28 55   228

That's all there is to that. The calculated altitude, at the assumed position, is 28 55; the true azimuth is 228.

If you had taken a sight of Spica a little earlier when the GHA of Aries was 223 45, you could assume a position at longitude 79 45 W, getting the same LHA Aries. For Spica Hc would be 22 34, Zn 117. That's the basis of the two-star fix in illustration 135.

The navigator has chosen these two stars because their bearings were about 90 degrees apart. That makes the position lines cut at a good angle. These two sights, taken within one minute, will give him a fix.

The navigator who wants to take a three-star sight doesn't even have to select the stars. It's all done for him. Asterisks (*) ahead of the name of the stars indicate that these three are suitable for such a sight. Star names printed in capital letters indicate first-magnitude stars, upper-and-lower-case letters indicate less bright stars.

You probably wonder right now how you'll recognize these stars. That's easy: You cheat. You look up their altitudes and azimuths first. Then you set your sextant to the indicated altitude, 22 34 for Spica. Next you face in the direction given by the azimuth, for Spica 117 or about ESE true. Sweep the horizon in that direction with your sextant. The bright star you'll see in its telescope is Spica.

For what time, for what LHA Aries do you look up these figures? The calculation is so quick you can leave it until you're about ready to take the sight. In the evening that'll be when the stars first come out, in the morning when the horizon becomes visible.

When you have both stars and horizon you'll look at your watch. Convert to Greenwich time. Look up the Greenwich hour angle of Aries for that minute. Subtract your approximate longitude and you've got your local hour angle of Aries, close enough to preset your sextant. Example: In the evening of May 2 you see a bright star appear in the southwest. Your watch, set to Eastern Daylight Time, shows 8:10 P.M. That's 2010 EDT; add four hours and you'll get GMT 0010, May 3. For 00 on that day the Almanac shows GHA Aries as 220 15. In ten minutes the hour angle increases 2 30. You can find that in the yellow pages, or figure it in your head by our checking formula. (Minutes divided by four gives increase of hour angle.) So the GHA is about 223. Your longitude is about 80, so the LHA Aries at 2010 was about 143. Four minutes later it'll be 144, eight minutes later 145 . . .

You are in latitude 28, so you open volume I to the 28° N pages and pick your stars for a three-star sight when the LHA Aries is 143. You'll find:

*ARCTURUS		*SIRIUS		*CAPELLA	
Hc	Zn	Hc	Zn	Hc	Zn
25 38	081	29 34	228	37 05	308

These stars, as the capital letters indicate, are all of first magnitude. So you won't have any problem in positively identifying them in your present sextant. Also, you'll be able to shoot them as fast as you can write down the time and sextant reading.

That has an advantage. You can forget about the motion of your vessel between sights. When you have a second-magnitude star in a three-star sight you may have to wait until it becomes visible in the evening. Then, or when clouds delay some sights, you may have to allow for your run between sights.

The motion of the stars takes care of itself. As the Greenwich hour angle increases with time, it carries the assumed position and the local hour angle with it.

When should you allow for the motion of the observer? I'd disregard displacement of 1 mile or less. At 6 knots you'd cover that distance in ten minutes. I avoid having to adjust my sights for the distance sailed between observations. I'd rather take the sight of a bright star a second time after a dimmer one has finally become visible.

If you must adjust, advance the earlier position line as in a running fix. That unfortunately makes a lot of lines in your plot. It's more elegant and equally accurate to move the point that marks the assumed position of the sight to be advanced. If you want to bring the first two sights to the time of the third, move each of the first two AP points as if the vessel had towed them for the number of minutes between the sights.

You can work each sight calculation on a separate sheet. But so many entries are common to the two or three sights that you can modify your standard pattern to work the stars side by side on the same sheet (fig. 178).

Compared to old methods of sight reduction, star sights by HO 249, volume I, are truly simple. And you don't get just a single position line but a fix.

There's a small price to pay. Seen from earth, the fixed stars don't remain exactly in their places year after year. To correct for the changes in position—caused by motions of earth rather than the stars—you'd need new tables every couple of years.

That's a lot of calculations and would make the tables—they now cost $3.75—more expensive. So the Navy compromises. New tables are calculated at five-year intervals. A correction, given at the end of the tables, takes care of in-between years.

We now use tables calculated for the beginning of 1970. In 1969 and 1970 no correction was needed. In 1971 the correction never exceeded 1 nautical mile; many navigators would have ignored it. In 1972 the correction amounts to 1 or 2 miles. In 1973 it is between 1 and 3 miles. By that time the tables calculated for the beginning of 1975 will be out; they will keep the 1973 error to 1 mile, and will need no correction for 1974 and 1975. And so on.

You may get to like the stars for fixes at dawn and dusk. But most navigators take mostly sun sights. The sun is around all day. Occasional clouds don't put you out of business; often you can shoot the sun through the overcast. And nobody ever had trouble identifying the sun.

To work sun sights we use volumes II and III of HO 249, which also solve sights of the moon, planets, and some stars. Volume II covers the area between latitudes 39 south and 39 north; volume III covers the rest of the world.

The three volumes, identical in size, are identified on the shelf by the color of their spines:

Volume I	Volume II	Volume III
(Selected Stars)	(Low Latitudes)	(High Latitudes)
Red	White	Blue

That's easy to remember: red, white, and blue.

Let me show you the use of volumes II and III by continuing a sun sight we have used as an example all along, starting with the sample sight, fig. 118.

The assumed latitude, found earlier in this chapter, is 28 N. The declination of the sun at the time of observation, according to the Almanac, was S 14 42. The local hour angle of the sun at the time of observation was 355. We calculated that a few pages back from the Greenwich hour angle (found in the Almanac) and the assumed longitude.

With these data—Lat 28 N, Dec S 14 42, and LHA 355—we are ready to go into the sight reduction table. The latitude is less than 39 degrees, so we'll take volume II, the one with the white spine.

You'll look for pages marked in the corners LAT 28°. There'll be several pages so marked, and you'll save time by becoming familiar with their layout.

You may already have noticed that, unlike the pages in volume I, the latitudes are not labeled N or S. Neither are the declination columns. Instead, the pages are headed, for example:

DECLINATION (0°–14°) SAME NAME AS LATITUDE

and

DECLINATION (15°–29°) CONTRARY NAME TO LATITUDE

What does that mean? In latitude north declination north is of the same name; so in latitude south is declination south. Obviously, then, in latitude north declination south is of contrary name; so in latitude south is declination north.

Here's where the layout of our work sheet helps: Latitude and its label are directly below declination and its label.

Same name pages come before *contrary* name pages, and logically enough lower declinations come before higher. The standard arrangement, then, is:

SAME   0°–14°
CONTRARY   0°–14°
SAME   15°–29°
CONTRARY   15°–29°

Some pages are split between same and contrary name of declination. On such pages same name is on top of the page, before contrary name. Blank space separates the two.

To get fifteen columns of declination legibly on one page, the printing runs the long way of the page. (Volume I, like most books, is printed the short way.)

In our example the latitude is 28 N, the declination S 14 42. We'll look for the page that gives contrary name declination zero to 14 degrees. (The minutes don't count at this stage.) See p. 321. We'd look in the same place had the latitude been 28 S and the declination N 14.

Next we'll look for the line with the given local hour angle. Each page has two columns headed LHA. You'll find the wanted LHA, 355, on the right. (On the left the same line is LHA 5.) Copy exactly the entry in the 14-degree declination column on the 355 line:

Hc   d   Z
47 43   −59   173

Hc is our old friend, the calculated altitude. The d looks like one of the corrections in the Almanac. It is. The calculated altitude was for a declination of exactly 14 00; the d-correction lets us take care of the minutes of declination above 14 degrees. Don't forget to copy the sign, here a minus sign. The sign is printed only every fifth line, so you'll have to glance up or down.

The figure —59 here means the calculated altitude diminishes 59 minutes for an increase of 1 degree in declination. To get the decrease in altitude for 42 minutes of declination we look in a table printed at the very end of the sight reduction tables, and also on a bookmark which comes with each volume II or III (pp. 324 and 325).

This correction table has sixty columns and sixty lines. So you could look in the 59 column on the 42 line and read 41; you could also look in the 42 column on the 59 line and get the same 41-minute correction. Since the d-correction had a minus sign, we mark the correction minus also, and subtract it from the tabulated altitude:

> Tabulated for declination 14 00   47 43
> Correction for 42′ declination   —41
> Calculated altitude (Hc)   47 02

That's all there is to getting the calculated altitude from the sight reduction tables.

That leaves the azimuth. Note that the last column is marked Z, not Zn as in volume I. There is a reason. It's something closely related to the true azimuth, called the azimuth angle. You don't have to learn the rules for converting azimuth angle (Z) into azimuth (Zn); they are printed on every page of the sight reduction tables, on top of the page for north latitudes, on the bottom for south latitudes.

Here we are in 28 North, so we are only interested in the rule on the top:

> LHA greater than 180°   Zn=Z
> LHA less than 180°   Zn=360—Z

The LHA was 355, greater than 180; so the azimuth angle 173 is the true azimuth. (In south latitude for the same entry the azimuth would be 007.) I usually put a check mark after it to indicate that I have applied the rule. Then I ring it to make plotting easy.

Had the LHA been 5—on the same line as 355—you'd have one more operation. You'd subtract 173 from 360, get 187, and ring that.

It is sad to see how many sights are worked out correctly almost to the last step and then are plotted incorrectly. I have suggested—in the chapter on position lines—checking the drawn azimuth line with a rough bearing written down at the time of observation, and with common sense.

In this example the navigator had written S for south. That fits 173 as well as it fits 187. Common sense is no help either. Your watch may not yet show noon when the sun is already a bit west of south; it may show past noon while the sun is still east of south.

for Minutes of Declination

d'	31	32	33	34	35	36	37	38	39	40	41	42	43	44	45	46	47	55	56	57	58	59	60	d'
0	0	0	0	0	0	0	0	0	0	0	0	0	0	0	0	0		0	0	0	0	0	0	0
1	1	1	1	1	1	1	1	1	1	1	1	1	1	1	1	1		1	1	1	1	1	1	1
2	1	1	1	1	1	1	1	1	1	1	1	1	1	1	1	2	2	2	2	2	2	2	2	2
3	2	2	2	2	2	2	2	2	2	2	2	2	2	2	2	2	2	3	3	3	3	3	3	3
4	2	2	2	2	2	2	2	3	3	3	3	3	3	3	3	3		4	4	4	4	4	4	4
5	3	3	3	3	3	3	3	3	3	3	3	4	4	4	4	4		5						
6	3	3	3	3	4	4	4	4	4	4	4	4	4	4	5	5				37	38		39	39
7	4	4	4	4	4	4	4	4	5	5	5	5	5	5	5	5		37	37	38	39	39	40	40
8	4	4	4	5	5	5	5	5	5	5				6	6	31		38	38	39	40	40	41	41
9	5	5	5	5	5	5	6	6			29	29	30	31	32	32	33	38	39	40	41	41	42	42
10	5	5										28	29	29	30	31	32	39	40	41	42	42	43	43
			24	25	26	26	27	28	29	29	30	31	32	32	33	34	34	40	41	42	43	43	44	44
45	23	24	25	26	26	27	28	28	29	30	31	32	32	33	34	34	35	41	42	43	44	44	45	45
46	24	25	25	26	27	28	28	29	30	31	31	32	33	34	34	35	36	42	43	44	44	45	46	46
47	24	25	26	27	27	28	29	30	31	31	32	33	34	34	35	36	37	43	44	45	45	46	47	47
48	25	26	26	27	28	29	30	30	31	32	33	34	34	35	36	37	38	44	45	46	46	47	48	48
49	25	26	27	28	29	29	30	31	32	33	33	34	35	36	37	38	38	45	46	47	47	48	49	49
50	26	27	28	28	29	30	31	32	32	33	34	35	36	37	38	38	39	46	47	48	48	49	50	50
51	26	27	28	29	30	31	31	32	33	34	35	36	37	37	38	39	4	47	48	48	49	50	51	51
52	27	28	29	29	30	31	32	33	34	35	36	36	37	38	39	40	4	48	49	49	50	51	52	52
53	27	28	29	30	31	32	33	34	34	35	36	37	38	39	40	41	42	49	49	50	51	52	53	53
54	28	29	30	31	32	32	33	34	35	36	37	38	39	40	40	41	42	50	50	51	52	53	54	54
55	28	29	30	31	32	33	34	35	36	37	38	38	39	40	41	42	43	0	51	52	53	54	55	55
56	29	30	31	32	33	34	35	35	36	37	38	39	40	41	42	43	44	1	52	53	54	55	56	56
57	29	30	31	32	33	34	35	36	37	38	39	40	41	42	43	44	45	2	53	54	55	56	57	57
58	30	31	32	33	34	35	36	37	38	39	40	41	42	43	44	44	45	53	54	55	56	57	58	58
59	30	31	32	33	34	35	36	37	38	39	40	41	42	43	44	45	4	54	55	56	57	58	59	59

144. Table of corrections to be applied to the calculated altitude to allow for minutes of declination. This is a part of the table in volumes II and III of HO 249, reproduced on pp. 324–25.

The wanted correction is found at the crossing of the d-value and the minutes of declination of the body at the time of observation. The d-value—with its sign, plus or minus—is printed in the sight reduction tables right next to the calculated altitude. The minutes of declination were found in step 3 discussed in the preceding chapter.

The d-value is the change (increase or decrease) in calculated altitude for sixty minutes (one degree) of declination. The table serves to calculate the change for a given number of minutes of declination.

Example: Latitude 42 N, declination 15 45 N (same name) local hour angle 51. On p. 322 the calculated altitude is given as 38 41, the d-value next to that is +40. In the 40 column on the 45 line the d-correction is 30. Since the sign was plus, 30 minutes have to be added to the calculated altitude, giving 39 21 (with a minus sign you would have subtracted the correction). Check: 45 minutes of declination are three fourths of 60 minutes; so the correction must be three fourths of 40. It is.

The circles and arrows refer to the example worked in the text.

For such times, and any others, I use a purely mathematical check on my azimuth. It works in both hemispheres and isn't hard to remember:

> Local hour angle and true azimuth must always be
> on opposite sides of the 0–180 line of a compass rose.

When the LHA is on the 0–180 degree, right, side of the compass rose, Zn must be on the other, left, side between 180 and 360.

When the LHA is on the 180–360, left, side of the compass rose, Zn must be on the other, right, side between zero and 180.

If you're a born sea lawyer you'll now have a question: Which correction shall I use on the equator, which has neither north nor south latitude? The answer is printed on the LAT 0° pages: If the declination is north, use north rule, if it's south, the south rule.

In the table you'll also find the answer to the other question: What's same name, what's contrary name on the equator, which by definition has no name? The tables are the same for north and south declinations.

If you dislike exceptions, you could assume latitude 1 degree north or south, whichever is nearer your dead reckoning position. Then the usual routine will apply, although your altitude difference may be unusually great.

You have now seen how to use HO 249, volumes II and III, to get the calculated altitude and true azimuth of the *sun* at the assumed position. What about the moon and planets? The procedure is exactly the same. For the same assumed latitude, declination, and local hour angle you'd get the tabulated altitude, d-correction, and azimuth angle. You'd apply the correction for minutes of declination in the same manner for all bodies, and convert azimuth angle into true azimuth by the same rules.

Declinations given in these tables—up to 30 degrees—let you work sun, moon, and planets. We'll see how you can also work a score of bright stars with the same tables under Emergencies, p. 304.

New tables, HO 229, let you work *all* stars, since they list declinations to 90 degrees. Six volumes ($6 each) replace the two volumes of HO 249 ($2.50 each) for worldwide coverage. The British designation of the same tables is HD 605.

If you want to use the new tables, you can learn their use in a few minutes. They are that similar to the tables shown here. The main difference is this: After finding the right volume—each covers 16 degrees of latitude—you find the approximate page by local hour angle rather than by latitude. Same name pages again precede contrary name pages. Each page—printed vertically—has ninety lines for declination. The assumed latitude forms the columns.

You very quickly learn to find the proper place. There you take out the same data: Hc, ±d, and Z. All these are carried to tenths. Tenths of minutes for calculated altitude and declination change, tenths of degrees for azimuth angle.

The rules for converting azimuth angle to true azimuth are identical with the ones in HO 249; they are visible at every book opening, so you still don't have to memorize them.

The greatest difference in the use of the new tables is in the application of the correction for minutes, and tenths of minutes, of declination.

The one-page table in HO 249 has grown to four pages in HO 229. There are always two, and sometimes three, corrections. It's a bit bewildering at first. But it's all explained, with examples, in the introduction to the new tables.

All this extra work is needed to squeeze out tenths of minutes of altitude. In the very next step, as you know, we compare the calculated altitude with the observed altitude, which is never certain to tenths of minutes.

That's why I'll stick with HO 249, for use on small craft especially.

I don't need tenths of degrees for azimuth either. On a small ship I'll be happy to get azimuth lines plotted to the nearest whole degree.

Even if for some good reason you disagree with me and elect to use HO 229 tables, you may still want to carry volume I of HO 249, Selected Stars. Nothing can touch it for simplicity.

HO 214, a set of sight reduction tables in use since before World War II, is being made obsolete by the new tables, and will be withdrawn from sale. The British designation of the same tables is HD 486.

There's now only one step left in our eight-step sight reduction. That's step 4, sextant corrections. We'll take them up—together with sextant work in general—in the next chapter.

PRACTICE (23)

Give assumed latitude, longitude, and local hour angle for the following approximate position and previously calculated Greenwich hour angles:

	Latitude	Longitude	GHA
A.	42 11 N	70 07 W	90 00
B.	41 58 N	70 07 W	41 45
C.	28 20 N	94 30 W	11 58
D.	28 17 N	79 55 W	223 45
E.	28 17 N	79 55 E (!)	223 45
F.	42 11 N	70 07 W	361 30

(In the last example you'll see why we did not subtract 360 degrees earlier.)

G. A morning sight of a round of stars in DR 42 21 N, 124 50 W has given the following Greenwich hour angles of Aries:

°Mirfak   °ALTAIR   °ARCTURUS
5o 47   5o 55   51 02

For each star give the assumed longitude, calculated altitude, and azimuth. (Use table from HO 249, volume I, reproduced at the end of this book.)

Using the tables from volumes II and III of HO 249, reproduced at the end of this book, get the calculated altitude and true azimuth of the following sights. (Check your azimuth: When local hour angle of the body is more than 180° the true azimuth must be less; when LHA is less than 180° the true azimuth must be more than 180°.)

	aL	LHA	Dec
H.	42 N	20	N 15 02 (Sun)
I.	28 N	56	S 21 19 (Jupiter)
J.	28 N	332	S 14 25 (Mars)
K.	42 N	292	N 15 17 (Moon)

(The identity of the body has no bearing whatever on the problem. With the same data you'd get the same results whether it's a sight of a planet, the sun, or the moon.)

You can now work a complete sight, except that the observed altitude has to be given, rather than the uncorrected sextant reading.

L. Tuesday, November 2, the sun bearing SSE, near 28 10 N, 79 55 W at 11 43 55 EST (+5), watch 10 seconds slow, gives Ho 46 53
Plot the position line.

M. Sunday, May 2, the star Sirius, bearing SW, DR 28 17 N, 79 55 W at 20 14 54 EDT, no watch error, gives Ho 28 35.
Plot the position line.

ANSWERS (23)

Assumed Position

	Latitude	Longitude	LHA
A.	42 N	70 00 W	20
B.	42 N	69 45 W	332
C.	28 N	94 58 W	277
D.	28 N	79 45 W	144
E.	28 N	80 15 E	304
F.	42 N	70 30 W	291

	alo	Hc	Zn
G. Mirfak	124 47 W	13 48	033
Altair	124 55 W	55 19	160
Arcturus	125 02 W	25 41	274

	Hc	Zn
H.	58 00	218
I.	16 49	234
J.	39 39	144
K.	26 25	093

L. Assumed position 28 N, 80 07 W, azimuth 173, altitude difference Away 9. We have used this example several times in the text. See figs. 118 and 125.

M. Assumed position 28 N, 79 59 W, azimuth 228, altitude difference Away 20 (plotted in fig. 135).

24. Sextant Work

In this chapter we'll discuss the taking of sights, the checking and adjusting of the sextant, and the correcting of the sextant reading to get the true observed altitude.

But first two WARNINGS:

1. Danger of permanent eye damage: Never look toward the sun through a sextant without the proper shade glasses in place.
2. Always lift the sextant by its frame or handle. Lifting it by the movable arm could ruin your sextant.

The marine sextant is an instrument that enables you to measure the angle between the horizontal and a celestial body at sea.

On land such measurements are easy. You can use levels, plumb lines, weighted mirrors, or bowls of mercury to get a horizontal. At sea, none of these devices work.

But you are surrounded by the sea horizon, the line where water and sky seem to meet. So it was logical to use the visible horizon as a reference line. The first instruments built on that principle gave the navigator an almost impossible task: He had to look at the horizon and the observed body at the same time.

In that cross-staff—also called forestaff or Jacob's staff—you slid a cross-arm until it exactly filled the space between the horizon and the body.

Later, with the backstaff, you faced away from the sun and brought its shadow in contact with the horizon. That was much easier. Near the end of the sixteenth century John Davis added a mirror. Then you could measure the altitudes of celestial bodies that cast no noticeable shadow. Such sea quadrants were the stand-by of navigators for the next 150 years.

In 1730 John Hadley, in England, and Thomas Godfrey, in America, added a second mirror. Neither knew of the work of the other, and probably neither knew that Newton had had the same idea thirty years earlier. With their sextants you brought the image of the body in contact with the horizon, and it stayed there while your vessel rolled and pitched.

The principle of the marine sextant is simple. The navigator looks at the horizon and moves one of the mirrors until the body is reflected in the other—fixed—mirror. That fixed mirror is right in the line of sight when you look at the horizon. So you see at the same time the horizon—directly—and the body—reflected by the mirrors. The amount of tilt of the movable mirror is a measure of the angle between the horizon and the body, the body's altitude. Just what we wanted.

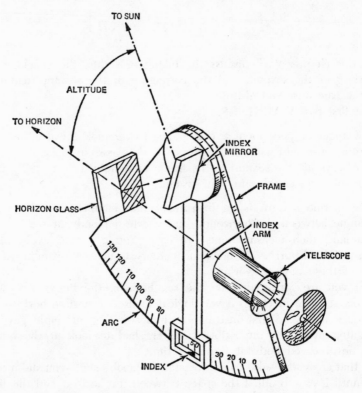

145. Marine sextant. Looking through the telescope, the navigator sees the horizon through the clear (left) part of the horizon glass.

At the same time he sees the sun in the silvered (right) part of the horizon glass, to which it has been reflected by the pivoted index mirror.

When the image of the sun seems to touch the horizon the index points to the altitude of the sun.

(The shade glass necessary to protect your eye from the sun, usually placed between the mirrors, is not shown.)

It's easy enough to provide a scale from which to read the tilt of the mirror. A direct scale has its limitations. On a portable hand-held device 1 degree comes out as about one sixteenth of an inch (1½ mm). That lets you read altitudes to a third, or a quarter, of 1 degree. Not good enough for our needs. Even with a magnifying glass you don't come close enough.

That was never a problem. More than a century before the invention of the sextant, Pierre Vernier had designed a double scale that splits degrees into 1- or 2-minute intervals. Sextants using such vernier scales remained in use right into this century.

Then precision machining methods made another improvement possible: micrometer sextants. One turn of the micrometer drum changes the altitude setting exactly 1 degree. The drum is marked into sixty divisions, to let you read minutes directly.

146. Micrometer sextant. Read degrees on arc (here 41), the minutes on the drum. Some sextants have a vernier instead of the single mark at the micrometer drum. You could read this setting, without vernier, as 22.5 minutes. The sextant then reads 41 22.5.
Pressing finger pads (bottom right) together unclamps micrometer mechanism for rapid movement of the index arm.

To change the setting of the sextant, say, 30 degrees, you don't have to turn the drum thirty times. A clamp lets you disengage the worm gear (on the movable arm) from the rack machined into the frame, so that you can move the arm quickly to the approximate setting. With the clamp released and the gear meshed again, you make the fine adjustment.

All modern sextants use micrometers, except—for economy—lifeboat and student models.

Most sextants are supplied with a low-power telescope to magnify the image of the sun or the moon.

That's all there is to a sextant except for some provision to protect your eyes against the sun: shade glasses mounted between the mirrors.

To cut the glare of the water, sextants have another set of lighter shade glasses in your line of sight to the horizon.

Let's take a sight of the sun. You have already checked the sextant, as will be discussed later in this chapter.

Before even facing the sun, flip down the darkest index shade. If your sextant is equipped with polarizers rather than with tinted filters of various densities, turn the polarizer to the darkest setting. See if a horizon filter would make the horizon under the sun clearer or more comfortable to look at.

Next, press the clamp lever and, facing the sun, move the index arm until you see the sun. Let go of the clamp.

Very likely, the sun will be barely visible with this first filter setup. Try the next lighter filter or a combination of filters. Don't look at the sun while changing filters. If your sextant uses polarizing filters, gradually lighten the sun's image until it is clearly visible, yet comfortable to look at.

Now move the index arm, unclamping it if it's far off otherwise by turning the micrometer drum, until the sun's lowest point seems to touch the horizon.

You may have trouble finding the sun. A trick may help you: Move the sextant a little to the left and right. Until you get the hang of it you may want to remove the telescope; it makes spotting the sun on the horizon easier.

Have you measured the sun's altitude when you made its lower edge touch the horizon? Perhaps. Probably not. Unless you have held the sextant absolutely perpendicular at the moment of contact you have measured an angle greater than the altitude.

That's easily checked by "rocking" the sextant. You swing its bottom through a small arc. As the sextant moves through a pendulum-like swing, a sun not truly on the horizon will dip below it. Readjust the micrometer until the sun just grazes the horizon at the lowest point of the arc. The lower edge of the sun—called *lower limb* by navigators—should just touch the horizon.

Don't read the sextant yet. Instead mark the time first, starting with the seconds. Only after you've written down the time should you read the sextant.

I'd start by reading the minutes. Here's my reason. Just as the hour hand of a clock most of the time doesn't point exactly to an hour mark, so the index on your sextant will not be exactly opposite a degree mark in most of your sights. You have no trouble telling 9:58 from 10:02 on a clock, although the hour hand is right on the ten. If you read the degrees on your sextant first, you might write 10°58′ when you should have written 9°58′.

147. Rocking the sextant, or swinging the arc. If you had made contact while the sextant was not exactly vertical (shown exaggerated at left), you would measure too great an altitude. Straightening the sextant, without changing its setting, would drop the sun below the horizon (middle). Remedy: Swing the lower part of the sextant from left to right while making the final adjustment. If the lower limb of the sun makes contact with the horizon during the swing (right) but doesn't go below it, you are measuring the altitude correctly.

The minute calibrations on the micrometer drum are easy to read. I'd read them to the nearest minute only. Closer to 30 than to 31 I'd write down 30. If you prefer, you can read to the nearest half minute, write 30.5, or 30.0 or 31.0.

Some sextants have a vernier scale next to the minute scale. That lets you read the sextant to two tenths of a minute or to 10 seconds. This accuracy is mostly illusory, as you will see. If you insist on reading the subdivisions of minutes—farther than the nearest half minute—and your sextant has a 10-second vernier, you must convert the seconds of arc into decimals. That's how our sextant corrections are calculated.

To get tenths of minutes divide the seconds by six. Or use the following rough conversion:

Seconds	00	10	20	30	40	50
Minutes	0.0	0.2	0.3	0.5	0.7	0.8

On some sextants the minutes increase toward you, on others away from you. If you change sextants, don't let habit mislead you; look at the next figure, then you won't read 49 when you should be reading 51.

After the minutes read the degrees. Only every fifth or tenth degree will be numbered, but all sextants have zero on the right end of the scale.

It's a good habit to check the sextant reading before putting the instrument back in its box. Most boxes are unfortunately so constructed that the index arm must be in a certain area of the arc; that often means moving the arm and losing any chance to check the reading later.

With just minor changes, sextant sights of all bodies are taken like those of the sun. You check the sextant, bring the body down to the horizon, rock the sextant, read the time of contact, then read the sextant, check your reading, and put away the instrument.

You don't have to worry about your eyesight when you are observing moon, planets, or stars. Sometimes a horizon shade will be helpful.

While we always observe the lower limb of the sun, the moon leaves us often no choice. When its lower limb isn't lighted we have to shoot the upper. When possible, bring the *lower* limb to the horizon. You probably will find it easier to do, and it saves a small step later.

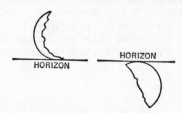

148. Observation of the moon. When possible bring the lower limb on the horizon (left); when the lower limb is unlighted (right), shoot the upper limb.

Even through the telescope, stars and planets appear as mere dots, and there's no question of upper or lower limb.

You have already learned the easiest method for star sights. You calculate the local hour angle of Aries for the approximate time of observation. With that LHA and your approximate latitude, you find in HO 249, volume I, the altitude and azimuth of seven stars. To find any one of them, set your sextant to the altitude given in the tables and face the direction (true) indicated by its azimuth. Sweeping the horizon a few degrees on either side of that direction, you'll see a bright star close to the horizon in the sextant's telescope. All the stars used in that volume are the brightest in their area, so that's almost certain to be the wanted star. Bring it exactly on the horizon, and you have your sight.

Don't fret about shooting the wrong star. In the usual three-star fix one wrong star will show up in your plot by making an improbably large cocked hat. The position lines of the other two stars will cross close to your dead reckoning position, and you'll still have a fix.

Chances of getting a planet by mistake are even smaller. You may *want* to shoot one of the three brightest ones. Venus is always brighter than any fixed star and will be in the eastern sky when it's morning star, in the western sky when it's evening star. For Jupiter and Mars, both at times not specially bright, you could precalculate altitude and azimuth from volume II or III, depending on your latitude. Many navigators never bother with Saturn. You'll find some data that'll help you find the planets in the Nautical Almanac, just ahead of the daily pages.

All sights taken with a marine sextant require a clearly defined horizon. Sometimes haze will make it impossible to judge just where the water ends and the sky begins. I wouldn't even take my sextant out of its box at such times.

Waves give less trouble. Even when the horizon looks lumpy through your binoculars, you can take fair sights. On a small craft you may have trouble holding on, protecting your sextant, and keeping a clear head on such a day; but the horizon won't give you trouble. I'd expect an additional 2-mile error in my sights. If you have the stomach for it— literally—you can take a string of sights in rapid succession and work out one that seems consistent with most of the others. With practice one gets the feel for good and bad sights, much as in target shooting one knows when one has missed before seeing the card.

You'll have to shoot stars and planets when it's dark enough to see them, light enough to make out the horizon. That normally limits these sights to short periods at dawn and dusk.

It would be nice to have a device that would let us take sights independent of the sea horizon. Air navigators have their bubble sextants. Unfortunately they work poorly even on large ships—except on submerged submarines. On small craft they are useless.

The moon sometimes lights the horizon at night. Sights of the moon against such a horizon don't work well. No combination of index and horizon shades seems to help. But sights of stars taken with a horizon made visible by the moon have worked for me nicely. The trick seems to be to avoid the bright patch directly below the moon.

Even without the help of the moon it is possible to take star sights in the dark. You may have noticed that with 7×50 binoculars you can see things at night that you can't make out at all with the unaided eye.

If you can get a 7×50 telescope, which looks like half a binocular, for your sextant you can probably take such star shots. The seven-times magnification isn't important. The 50-millimeter lens diameter is what matters.

The telescope mount on many sextants can be moved toward or away from the frame of the instrument itself. When the horizon is dim you are supposed to move the telescope away from the frame. In sextants I have owned, I couldn't tell the difference, though.

Many navigators use one telescope for all sights. I like a telescope that doesn't have to be unscrewed before returning the sextant to its box.

You may want to practice taking sextant sights on dry land. Unless you live on a barren, level plain—the elevation above sea level wouldn't matter—you won't have a smooth horizon. To get the technique of using the sextant you could bring the sun or other body down on your neighbor's roof, a wall, a railroad track, or some other horizontal edge. Such sights won't give you a position, just practice.

There's such a thing as an artificial horizon. Basically it's a pan of water, or, to keep the ripples to a minimum, molasses. The reflected sun is almost as bright as the sun itself. Dangerous. It's a very unrealistic presentation besides. I'll show you a better way to practice later in this chapter.

Up to now we have assumed that your sextant was in adjustment. You have to know how to check and adjust your sextant. Even a factory-fresh one could have gone off in shipment. There are no sextant shops at sea. It's not difficult. You can check your sextant before every sight so quickly a bystander wouldn't know you were doing it.

Sextants differ. Some use keys, others a pin for adjusting. The adjusting screws are in different places on different models. In some models a screw works against a spring; turning the screw—within reason—can't do any harm. In other models, two screws hold opposite sides of the mirror; you have to loosen one screw before tightening the other.

Before you touch anything, study your sextant and see what the different screws in back of the mirrors will do. All adjustments are small fractions of a turn. You have to take your fingers and sometimes the adjusting tool off before you can be sure the adjustment is right. Finger pressure or the weight of the tool might fool you.

Don't look for an instruction book. Professional sextants are for professionals supposed to know what they are doing. If you don't trust yourself to the job, have a fellow navigator, who knows his stuff, show you the mechanics.

The principles are the same for all sextants. There are three adjustments to be made, and they must be made in the proper order.

One: *index mirror perpendicular.* The mirror that travels with the arm must make a right angle with the frame of the sextant.

To check that adjustment, set the index arm near 35 degrees. Hold the sextant horizontal, mirrors up, a little below eye level. Looking at the movable mirror, twist your wrist until you see the arc of the instrument (the curved edge near the degree scale) and its reflection in the mirror. The first time, it may help you to put a finger near the 120-degree mark on the arc; then twist your wrist until you can see your finger in the mirror.

To the right of the mirror you'll see the arc directly. If the arc reflected in the mirror and the directly seen arc form a continuous line, no adjustment is needed. If the line breaks at the edge of the mirror, the mirror leans forward or backward. Bring the two parts of the line together by turning the screw in back of the mirror gently. If the lines separate more, you are obviously turning the screw in the wrong direction.

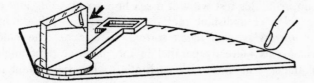

149. Sextant adjustment (1). Holding the sextant (set to about 35 degrees) as shown, look in the index mirror. If the mirror is perpendicular, you'll see the arc reflected in the mirror, and the arc behind it as one smooth line, at the point marked by the arrow.

Here the mirror leans, the arcs separate at the arrow. Adjust until lines merge.

(Finger helps in finding the right position for this test. Turn the sextant in the horizontal plane until you see your finger in the mirror.)

Two: *horizon mirror perpendicular*. The fixed mirror must be at right angles to the frame of the sextant. To check this adjustment set the index arm close to zero. Then, holding the sextant in the usual way, look at the sea horizon. Turn the micrometer, as in taking a sight, until the horizon appears as an unbroken line. It doesn't matter what the micrometer reads as long as the directly seen horizon and the one seen in the silvered part seem joined.

Now tilt the sextant. Don't just rock it, but tilt it, say, 45 degrees left or right. If the horizon doesn't break at the silvering line, no adjustment is needed.

150. Sextant adjustment (2). Set sextant to near zero. Make the two halves of the horizon into one line. Now tilt the sextant about 45 degrees from the vertical. If the line breaks as shown, adjust horizon glass as detailed in text until it stays together.

If the horizon breaks at the edge of the silvering, bring it together by turning the screw behind the horizon mirror that makes it lean forward or backward. There are two adjustments on this mirror. If nothing happens, you obviously are turning the wrong screw. If the break of the horizon gets worse, you are turning the right screw in the wrong direction.

You can make this test without a sea horizon by using any horizontal line; the ridge of a distant roof or electric wires will do nicely.

Three: *mirrors parallel when sextant reads zero.* The index mirror and horizon glass—already parallel in the plane at right angles to the frame of the sextant—must face each other when the sextant reading is 00°00′.

Set the sextant exactly to zero and look at the sea horizon. If it happens to make an unbroken line, no adjustment is needed.

If the horizon appears broken, turn the micrometer until you join the directly seen horizon with the one seen in the silvered part of the horizon glass. Now read the micrometer. If the error—called index error —is 1 minute or less, repeat the joining operation a couple of times. If you get plus 1 minute on one test, minus 1 on the next, call it adjusted.

If the reading is consistently plus, or consistently minus, or more than 1 minute, adjust the horizon glass. That's done by turning the screw that makes it pivot. You'll remember the screw that makes it tilt, used in the last step; use the other screw.

Repeat the bringing together a few times until you get consistent readings of near zero minutes after you have removed the adjusting tool.

151. Sextant adjustment (3). Set sextant to exactly 00°00′. Look at the sea horizon; it should form an unbroken line. If the line appears offset, as shown, bring the halves together, using the adjustment of the horizon glass *not* used in last adjustment.

The two adjustments of the horizon glass are somewhat linked. Correcting for index error may have thrown off the preceding adjustment. Check that by tilting the sextant. If the horizon breaks now, you may have to give the first-used screw another touch. Then check for index error again. It may need another touch.

You can't use a horizontal reference line ashore for this test. The sextant acts as a range finder and *should* read more than zero degrees zero minutes when aimed at a nearby roof or wire.

If you want to check and adjust the sextant ashore, use a star, any bright star. Set the sextant to read exactly zero. Then aim the telescope at the star. If your instrument has an index error, you'll see one star above the other at the line where the silvering of the horizon glass ends. Remove the error by bringing the two images in coincidence when the micrometer reads exactly zero.

You don't have to check for the horizon glass's being perpendicular. If it isn't, it will be impossible to bring the direct and the mirrored images of the star on top of each other. They'll be side by side. That's why that error is called side error. Remove it by using the technique of step 2, then remove any index error.

The first time you check and adjust a sextant, it will seem very complicated as you look from instructions to sextant and back again. Once you know which screw does what, it's easy. Later it becomes automatic as you check the sextant before each sight.

When you take the sextant out of its box you'll glance at the arc in the mirror (step 1 above). In most boxes the index arm will already be in position for this test. It's most unlikely that the index mirror has gone out of line.

Next you move the index arm to near zero, line up the sea horizon, and tilt the sextant to one side. The horizon should continue to form an unbroken line (step 2). Without doing anything else, you glance at the micrometer. It should be very close—say within one half minute—to zero. That's it. You are ready for your sight.

If you have your sextant handy, go through the motions of this test. I'll bet even this first time it didn't take you quite a minute.

If you treat your sextant gently, these three tests will be monotonously negative.

But if you find the reading of the micrometer off, here's what you do. Turn the micrometer drum a few minutes in one direction or the other, then align the horizon again. If it shows the same error repeatedly, I'd remove the index error. Now that you know which screw controls it, that's the work of a few seconds.

Many navigators just note the index error before the observation and apply it to the sextant reading, much as you add or subtract seconds when your watch is slow or fast. Example: The index is on zero degrees; the micrometer reads 58 minutes. It underreads by 2 minutes of arc. So you'll add 2 minutes to your sextant reading.

For this method is the saved wear on the adjusting screw. (When in doubt, leave it alone.) *Against* it is an added chance to add when you should subtract, or the other way around. In the above example, with an index error of only 2 minutes, you'd be 4 minutes off in your measured altitude.

A telescope knocked out of line will make high-altitude observations come out too great. If after an accident you suspect the parallelism of the axis of the telescope and the frame, do this: Take a sight with and without telescope as rapidly as you can. The higher the body is above the horizon, the better. When it bears due south (or north) it'll change least between observations. If the two sights differ by more than a minute or two, unship the telescope and take sights without it until you can get the sextant to a repair shop.

In taking a sight you go through these steps:
1. Quickly check the sextant (arc, tilt, zero).
2. Bring the body in contact with the horizon.
3. Rock the sextant during fine adjustment.
4. Mark the time (seconds first) and write it down.
5. Read the sextant (minutes first) and write down altitude.

Is that sextant reading what we have called the observed altitude, abbreviated Ho? No, it is not.

It's properly called sextant altitude (Hs) and becomes observed altitude after some corrections are applied. Making these corrections is step 4 in our eight-step method.

A great deal of work has been done on these corrections, yet unbelievable as that may sound, some are still doubtful. For practical work, and for the accuracy we are interested in, the corrections are few and easily found.

With a sextant you measure the angle between the horizon and a celestial body. This plain sentence contains the clue for the major corrections to use: for the sextant, for you, for the horizon, and for the observed body.

We have eliminated the major errors from the sextant. If you have no index error, you won't need any correction for the sextant.

Yet in the lid of the sextant box there may be a certificate stating corrections at different altitudes. They allow for the sum of all non-adjustable errors in this particular instrument. Usually they run to a few tenths of minutes. Some sextants come through with zero errors. For others the manufacturer simply states that the instrument is true within 10 seconds of arc, less than 0.2 minutes. For small-craft navigation all these errors are unimportant. Forget them.

How about you? Some people have a personal error in bringing down the body to the horizon, just as other people consistently cut off heads in their snapshots. Take a few sights under good conditions, when you know exactly where you are. If your position lines come within 2 miles of your known position, forget about personal error.

If you find your altitudes consistently too low or too high to give good position lines almost through your known observation point, add or subtract enough to make up for that error. Before I'd do that I'd try myself against a skilled observer.

That leaves only corrections for the horizon and the observed body. You'll find them on the end papers—front and back—of the Nautical Almanac. Whether they should be added or subtracted is clearly spelled out there too. So you can apply these corrections to any sight without bothering about any theory.

As you may suspect, the correction for the horizon is the same for all bodies.

In taking sights, we use the visible horizon. That horizon is always below the theoretical horizon, which is exactly 90 degrees from the point directly above you, the zenith. The seen horizon dips below the true one, so the correction is called dip correction, or simply dip (abbreviated D). Since it makes the measured sextant altitude too great it is always to be subtracted from the sextant reading.

As everyone knows, the higher you stand the farther you can see; your horizon dips more. The value of the dip correction depends only on your height of eye. So it is also known as height-of-eye correction, abbreviated HE. Call it HE or call it dip, but always subtract it from your sextant altitude.

You'll find it in a table on the inside front cover of the Nautical Almanac, and also on the bookmark reproduced on p. 310.

At first glance there seems to be something wrong with the printing of the dip table (and several others we'll meet in a moment). In the left column the corrections are not on the same line as the height of eye. That's on purpose. In such tables, called critical tables, the correction belongs to all values between which the line of correction is printed. To get height of eye both in feet and in meters in a small space, the Almanac since 1971 has acquired a slightly confusing arrangement. The dip table for the values that interest the small-craft skipper most are *not* critical tables. The section that gives the HE correction in feet now looks like this:

DIP

HE ft	Corr. ′
2	—1.4
4	—1.9
6	—2.4
8	—2.7
10	—3.1

For in-between values you're supposed to interpolate the correction. For 5 feet, as an example, you'd come up with —2.1 or —2.2, halfway between —1.9 and —2.4. Perhaps you'd prefer the critical table arrangement that needs no calculation (fig. 152).

DIP	
Ht. of Eye	Corr^n
ft.	
1·9	−1·4
2·2	−1·5
2·5	−1·6
2·8	−1·7
3·2	−1·8
3·6	−1·9
4·0	−2·0
4·4	−2·1
4·9	−2·2
5·3	−2·3
5·8	−2·4
6·3	−2·5
6·9	−2·6
7·4	−2·7
8·0	−2·8
8·6	−2·9
9·2	−3·0
9·8	−3·1
10·5	−3·2

152. Dip, or height of eye correction. Arranged as a critical table. Example: For a height of eye between 4.9 and 5.3 feet use −2.2′.

Practically, you won't use these tables often. Like most navigators you'll establish a pattern in taking your sights. You'll sit or stand in the cockpit or forehatch when taking sights. Once you have estimated the height of eye at your favorite observation spot, or spots, the correction will always be the same, for all bodies (and always minus). You'll automatically subtract, say, 2.2 from all sextant readings.

If you can get to the seashore or to a large lake, you can practice sextant sights without a boat. Just stand on the beach or a dock, shoot any body that's above the water, and use the dip correction for your height of eye above the water level at the time of observation.

You can also take very lifelike sights on any wide river, small lake, even a water reservoir. You use the horizontal line of the water against the shore, beach, or sea wall as reference line. By keeping your height of eye low, you can take sights as accurately as with a sea horizon. Use the dip table below after getting the distance to the far shore from a map. I have calculated this table to tenths of minutes, then rounded the values off to the nearest minute. The vagueness of your height of eye and of the distance to the shore don't warrant greater accuracy. Try for the smallest possible dip correction. Where the table leaves off in the distance, the standard dip correction is to be used.

DIP SHORT OF THE HORIZON

Correction to be subtracted in place of normal dip

Dist. naut. miles	Height of Eye (feet)								Dist. stat. miles
	3	4	5	6	7	8	9	10	
0.6	—3	—4	—5	—6	—7	—8	—9	—10	0.7
0.8	2	3	4	5	5	6	7	7	0.9
1.0	—2	—2	—3	—4	—4	—5	—6	— 6	1.2
1.2	2	2	3	3	4	4	5	5	1.4
1.4	2	2	3	3	3	4	4	5	1.6
1.6	2	2	2	3	3	4	4	4	1.8
1.8	2	2	2	3	3	3	4	4	2.1
2.0	—2	—2	—2	—3	—3	—3	—3	— 4	2.3
2.2	2	2	2	2	3	3	3	4	2.5
2.4	2	2	2	2	3	3	3	3	2.8

Example: With a height of eye of 5 feet, distance to shore 0.8 nautical (0.9 statute) miles use —4 minutes in place of standard dip correction. With a height of eye of 6 feet, distance 2.8 nautical miles (off the table) use correction from Almanac, —2.4 minutes, identical—except for rounding—with the last line of this table.

To convert sextant altitude to observed altitude you may have to apply four corrections. You can avoid the index correction by adjusting the sextant. It's most unlikely that you should have a personal error. In most of your sights you'll know the correction for dip of the horizon by heart. On a small vessel that will be some value between minus 2 minutes and minus 3 minutes.

That leaves only the body correction. For the sun, stars, and planets you'll find the correction on the front end papers of the Nautical Almanac. For altitudes above 10 degrees, the minimum recommended altitude, you'll find the same data on the bookmark reproduced on p. 310.

For the moon you'll find the corrections—there are two—on the back end papers of the Nautical Almanac (p. 311).

You add the moon corrections and any other that has a plus sign. You subtract when the correction has a minus sign; you also subtract exactly 30 minutes from sights of the *upper* limb of the moon.

You don't need to know the reasons for all the corrections—Bowditch lists nineteen in five groups—to apply them correctly. But you may want to know about the most important ones.

Here is one: The body whose altitude you measured wasn't where it seemed to be. Light travels in a straight line in empty space or in a medium of uniform density. But, penetrating the earth's atmosphere, a light beam encounters denser and denser air as it approaches sea level. So the light beams from, say, a star are slightly bent. The star will seem *above* its true position. This bending of a light ray is called refraction, and the correction is called refraction correction, abbreviated R.

Since the star appeared too high in the sextant, the correction must be subtracted from the sextant altitude. The refraction is greatest on the horizon, where a light beam has the longest path through the atmosphere. That's what causes the sun and moon often to look distorted at rise and set. The refraction decreases with increasing altitude, and becomes zero for a star directly overhead.

Near the horizon the refraction is strongly influenced by temperature and barometric pressure. Above 10 degrees altitude a single standard value, calculated for 50° F (10° C) and 29.83 inches of mercury (1010 millibars), can be used. In all temperatures and pressures likely to be encountered by a yachtsman, these factors would change the refraction by only a few tenths of a minute.

That is the reason for avoiding sights that give altitudes of less than 10 degrees.

(Also avoid sights that'll give altitudes greater than 80 degrees. You'd be less than 600 miles from the ground point. Rendering such a small circle of position as a straight line leads to too large an error.)

Even under fairly normal conditions of temperature and pressure, refraction is somewhat doubtful. The theory is based on air temperature falling steadily at greater heights; an inversion, a common weather phenomenon, spoils that neat arrangement. So does a front. Shortly after the passage of a squall line, refraction differing 15 minutes from normal has been measured.

A difference in air and water temperatures causes more refraction error, said to be between 0.1 and 0.2 minutes per degree Fahrenheit. The dip correction, calculated for a standard atmosphere, would also be changed by abnormal refraction.

So you can see that it is foolish to try to adjust a sextant to a tenth of a minute, to worry about a few tenths in measuring altitude, or to calculate all the way with decimals when neither the horizon nor the observed body is where we see it.

The surprise is how accurate most sights are. Take a few sights when you are certain of your position—along shore, near lightships or buoys, or in charted anchorages—and plot the position lines. Most of them will probably be within 2 miles of your location.

Refraction is the only body correction for stars. Look for its value in the middle of the inside front cover or the bookmark. For 10 degrees it's —5.3 minutes and gradually diminishes to 0.0 for 90 degrees. This is a critical table, so you take the correction on the line between two tabulated altitudes.

For example, looking for the correction for 22 26, you'd find:

22 19

—2.3

23 13

and would use —2.3 as your correction. (For 22 19 itself you are supposed to take the next correction up, which happens to be —2.4. The difference hardly matters.)

Looking for the correction for 28 39, you'd find:

27 36

—1.8

28 56

and would use —1.8 as your correction.

If you had observed, from a height of eye of 6 feet, Spica Hs 22 26 and Sirius Hs 28 39 for a two-star fix, your entire correction calculation for both stars would look like this:

		Spica	Sirius
Sextant altitude	(Hs)	22 26	28 39
Dip correction	(D)	—2.4	—2.4
Body correction (star)	(R)	—2.3	—1.8
Observed altitude	(Ho)	22 21	28 35

Note that here I have used the decimals of the corrections. You get a little more accurate results than when you round off each correction before doing the arithmetic. I add 2.4 and 2.3 in my head and get 4.7. So I call it 5. Had I rounded off first, I would have had 2 and 2, or 4.

The calculation, if you can call it that, goes directly under the sextant reading in the right column of the work.

The same corrections are used also for the planets. Our nearest neighbors, Venus and Mars, at certain periods have another small correction given in the column next to the star correction. The correction will be totally negligible in some years, will not exceed a few tenths of minutes in others.

You'll find the body correction for the sun to the left of that for stars. The correction combines the effect of refraction and semidiameter (and another small correction). Semidiameter is a fancy name for radius. The Almanac gives the location of the center of the sun, while we observe its lower limb. So we measure a point about 16 minutes *below* the center, and have to add that much to our sextant reading corrected for dip and refraction. In altitudes above 10 degrees, the semidiameter is greater than the correction for refraction; so the value of the sun correction for the lower limb is to be added.

Except during an eclipse, you'll never have to take the upper limb. (In this book, all sun sights are of the lower limb.) For upper-limb sights our measurement would be too high; we'd have to subtract a correction.

The sun is farther from us in summer than in winter, so the semidiameter changes from 16.3 minutes in December to 15.8 minutes in June. The correction table in the Nautical Almanac takes care of that by supplying two columns, one for October to March, the other for April to September. Try to use the correct one. If you get the wrong one, it does only make a difference of 0.2 minutes.

In the sight we have used as an example several times before, taken on November 2, the sextant reading was 46 40. So we should use the winter column. It's again arranged as a critical table. We find:

$$43 \ 59$$
$$+15.3$$
$$47 \ 10$$

The sun correction then is +15.3 minutes. The height of eye was 6 feet. So your sextant correction calculation would look like this:

Sextant altitude	46 40
Dip correction	−2.4
Body correction (sun)	+15.3
Observed altitude	46 53

I have again carried the decimals in the corrections. Then I added 15.3 to −2.4 or, more truthfully, subtracted 2.4 from 15.3, which rounds off to 13. If you want to do this calculation step by step, you have ample room for that on your work sheet.

That takes care of step 4 for stars, planets, and the sun. The moon is a bit trickier.

The moon looks about the same size as the sun. You'd expect its correction for semidiameter and refraction combined to be about the same as that for the sun (between 10 and 16 minutes for the lower limb when it is more than 10 degrees above the horizon).

Now glance at the moon correction table from the Nautical Almanac reproduced on p. 311. You'll find values of about 60 minutes.

The reason is parallax. That's a technical term for the apparent displacement of an object when you look at it from two different points. Close your left eye. Hold a thumb so that it covers some distant object, say a doorknob. Now close your right eye, and look with the left. The thumb will no longer seem to be in front of the doorknob. The displacement of your thumb against the fixed background, when your viewpoint moved by the distance between your eyes, is its parallax.

The Almanac calculates positions from the center of earth. Observations are taken from the surface of earth. The parallax caused by this change in viewpoints (about 3,440 nautical miles) is unmeasurably small for the distant stars. It's negligible for Jupiter and Saturn. For Venus and Mars it's taken care of, together with another correction, in the "additional" correction. For the sun it amounts to about a tenth of a minute, which is included in the sun correction.

For the moon—only about 200,000 nautical miles from us—the parallax becomes 1 whole degree when the moon is on the horizon. At that time the change of viewpoints—from the center to the surface of earth—has the greatest effect because it is at right angles to the line of sight. When the moon is directly overhead, the center of earth, the observer, and the moon are all in line; the parallax is zero. For altitudes between the horizon and the zenith the parallax is easily calculated from the parallax at the horizon, called the horizontal parallax.

The parallax correction for any altitude can be combined in a single table with the corrections for refraction and semidiameter (and one other small correction).

But the distance of the moon from earth changes in a cycle of about one month. With it the moon's horizontal parallax changes, from 54 to 61 minutes. At the same time its semidiameter varies between 14.7 and 16.8 minutes. That's why we need a second correction table.

For use with that table the Nautical Almanac gives the rapidly changing value of horizontal parallax in the daily pages for every hour of GMT. That's the last item in the moon data, the HP.

The second correction table, like the sun table, has two columns: one for the lower limb, one for the upper limb. You could ignore the sun's upper limb, but for the moon that's often the only one you can observe. The arrangement of the table saves you from having to subtract upper-limb corrections, while you'd add the lower ones. Instead, you add either correction and then subtract exactly 30 minutes for sights of the upper limb of the moon. If you forget these 30 minutes, your position line will be displaced 30 nautical miles toward the moon. That'll usually show that you have made a mistake.

Here's an example of the altitude corrections for a sight of the moon: You observed the lower limb of the moon, sextant reading 56 14, height of eye 4 feet. The Almanac gave 61.1 for HP for the hour of observation.

The dip correction is the familiar —1.9 you always use for sights taken in your cockpit.

You'll find the altitude corrections for the moon—35–90 degrees—on the back inside cover of the Nautical Almanac. Each column there covers 5 degrees. You'll look for the one that contains your sextant altitude, the 55–59 degrees column. On the line for the 10 minutes nearest your figure, left or right, you'll find 42.1, your first correction.

In the *same* column in the lower table, on the line nearest to your HP, the 61.2 line, you'll find your second correction. It's a lower-limb observation, so you take the value under L, 7.8, your second correction.

ALTITUDE CORRECTION TABLES 35°-90°—MOON

App. Alt.	35°-39° Corrⁿ	40°-44° Corrⁿ	45°-49° Corrⁿ	50°-54° Corrⁿ	55°-59° Corrⁿ	60°-64° Corrⁿ	65°-69° Corrⁿ	70°-74° Corrⁿ	75°-79° Corrⁿ	80°-84° Corrⁿ	85°-89° Corrⁿ	App. Alt.
00	35 56·5	40 53·7	45 50·5	50 46·9	55 43·1	60 38·9	65 34·6	70 30·1	75 25·3	80 20·5	85 15·6	00
10	56·4	53·6	50·4	46·8	42·9	38·8	34·4	29·9	25·2	20·4	15·5	10
20	56·3	53·5	50·2	46·7	42·8	38·7	34·3	29·7	25·0	20·2	15·3	20
30	56·2	53·4	50·1	46·5	42·7	38·5	34·1	29·6	24·9	20·0	15·1	30
40	56·2	53·3	50·0	46·4	42·5	38·4	34·0	29·4	24·7	19·9	15·0	40
50	56·1	53·2	49·9	46·3	42·4	38·2	33·8	29·3	24·5	19·7	14·8	50
00	36 56·0	41 53·1	46 49·8	51 46·2	56 42·3	61 38·1	66 33·7	71 29·1	76 24·4	81 19·6	86 14·6	00
(10)	55·9	53·0	49·7	46·0	(42·1)	37·9	33·5	29·0	24·2	19·4	14·5	10
20	55·8	52·8	49·5	45·9	42·0	37·8	33·4	28·8	24·1	19·2	14·3	20
30	55·7	52·7	49·4	45·8	41·8	37·7	33·2	28·7	23·9	19·1	14·1	30
40	55·6	52·6	49·3	45·7	41·7	37·5	33·1	28·5	23·8	18·9	14·0	40
50	55·5	52·5	49·2	45·5	41·6	37·4	32·9	28·3	23·6	18·7	13·8	50
··	53·9	··	47·2	43·5	⁻⁷	34·9	··	·3·7	82	··	··	40
50	53·8	50·6	47·0	43·2	39·1	34·7	30·2	25·5	20·7	15·8	10·9	50

H.P.	L U	L U	L U	L U	(L) U	L U	L U	L U	L U	L U	L U	H.P.
54·0	1·1 1·7	1·3 1·9	1·5 2·1	1·7 2·4	2·0 2·6	2·3 2·9	2·6 3·2	2·9 3·5	3·2 3·8	3·5 4·1	3·8 4·5	54·0
54·3	1·4 1·8	1·6 2·0	1·8 2·2	2·0 2·5	2·3 2·7	2·5 3·0	2·8 3·2	3·0 3·5	3·3 3·8	3·6 4·1	3·9 4·4	54·3
54·6	1·7 2·0	1·9 2·2	2·1 2·4	2·3 2·6	2·5 2·8	2·7 3·0	3·0 3·3	3·2 3·5	3·5 3·8	3·7 4·1	4·0 4·3	54·6
··	·· 2·2	2·2 2··	·· 2·7	2·7 2··	·· ·1	6·5 4	3·2 3·3	·· 2·3·7	2·6 3·8	3·9 4··	5·6 3·2	··
59·7	7·1 ··	·5	6·9 4·4	··	··	··						59·7
60·0	7·5 4·8	7·3 4·7	7·2 4·5	7·0 4·4	6·9 4·2	6·7 4·0	6·5 3·9	6·3 3·7	6·1 3·5	5·9 3·3	5·7 3·1	60·0
60·3	7·8 5·0	7·6 4·8	7·5 4·7	7·3 4·5	7·1 4·3	6·9 4·1	6·7 3·9	6·5 3·7	6·3 3·5	6·0 3·2	5·8 3·0	60·3
60·6	8·1 5·1	7·9 5·0	7·7 4·8	7·6 4·6	7·3 4·4	7·1 4·2	6·9 3·9	6·7 3·7	6·4 3·4	6·2 3·2	5·9 2·9	60·6
60·9	8·4 5·3	8·2 5·1	8·0 4·9	7·8 4·7	7·6 4·5	7·3 4·2	7·1 4·0	6·8 3·7	6·6 3·4	6·3 3·2	6·0 2·9	60·9
(61·2)	8·7 5·4	8·5 5·2	8·3 5·0	8·1 4·8	(7·8) 4·5	7·6 4·3	7·3 4·0	7·0 3·7	6·7 3·4	6·4 3·1	6·1 2·8	61·2
61·5	9·1 5·6	8·8 5·4	8·6 5·1	8·3 4·9	8·1 4·6	7·8 4·3	7·5 4·0	7·2 3·7	6·9 3·4	6·5 3·1	6·2 2·7	61·5

153. Altitude corrections for the moon are found in two steps. Find the first correction in the upper table where degrees and (approximate) minutes cross. Find the second correction in the same column in the lower table on the line that comes nearest to the HP value for the hour of observation.

Here is the entire calculation:

Sextant altitude (Hs)	56 14
Dip (HE 4 feet)	— 1.9
First correction (for 56 10)	+42.1
Second correction (for 61.2)	+ 7.8
Observed altitude (Ho)	57 02

You might prefer to subtract the dip correction first, before making the moon corrections. Theoretically that is the more accurate method. You apply dip, index error, and personal correction to the raw sextant reading to get the so-called apparent altitude. Practically, the order of corrections will not make any difference.

Had the same observation been for an *upper*-limb observation, you would have taken the second correction from the column headed U. For the same altitude and parallax you would have had +4.5 minutes. Then you would have to take off the standard 30 minutes.

Here's a good way to write these figures to make arithmetic as easy as possible:

Hs	56 14
D	— 1.9
Diff.	56 12.1
1st C.	+42.1
2nd C.	+ 4.5
Sum	56 58.7
U.L.	—30.0
Ho	56 29

There's no need to label every line; the first line in its usual place at the top of the right column on the work sheet identifies it as sextant altitude. The last line is obviously the observed altitude, the result of applying the corrections to the sexant altitude.

Using the table on page 311, you can work this moon altitude correction: sextant altitude 28 44, height of eye 6 feet, horizontal parallax 55.5, upper limb. Your work sheet may look like this:

28 44		28 44		
— 2.4			— 2.4	
+59.5	or	+59.5		
+ 2.3		+ 2.3	—30.0	
—30.0		29 45.8	—32.4	
29 13			—32.4	
		29 13		

In the figure work at right I've kept all the plus items on the left, the minus ones on the right. I find I make fewer mistakes that way.

That ends step 4, the last one in our eight-step method.

PRACTICE (24)

Calculate the observed altitude (rounded to whole minutes) for the following:

A. Sun, May, sextant altitude (Hs) 53 24, height of eye (HE) 6 feet

B. Sun, October, Hs 29 01, HE 5 feet

C. Star Capella, Hs 36 37, HE 6 feet

D. Planet Jupiter, Hs 17 09, He 4 feet

E. Planet Mars, November, Hs 39 52, HE 4 feet (check for additional correction)

F. Moon, lower limb, HP 60.8, Hs 24 30, HE 4 feet

You can now work complete sights from beginning to end. Try these:

G. Saturday, May 1, the sun bearing SE in dead reckoning position 41 58 N 70 07 W, at 10 44 01 EDT (+4), watch slow 8 seconds, sextant altitude 53 24 (HE 6 feet). Plot the position line. (If this problem sounds familiar, you're right. You've worked every step of it already.)

H. Sunday, May 2, the star Spica, bearing ESE, DR 28 17 N 79 55 W, at 20 14 01 EDT, no watch error, Hs 22 26 (HE 6 feet). This is part of a two-star sight; you have already worked Sirius in Practice 23 M. Plot it with that sight.

ANSWERS (24)

A. 53 37   B. 29 13   C. 36 33   D. 17 04   E. 39 49 (Between October 13 and December 8 the additional correction for altitudes 0–41° was +0.2′)   F. 25 38

G. The data needed to draw the position line are: assumed position 42 N, 69 45 W, azimuth 130, altitude difference Away 11. The work is shown in fig. 176.

H. The data needed to draw the position line are: assumed position 28 N, 79 45 W, azimuth 117, altitude difference Away 13. You have already drawn the position line (Practice 20 C) and got a fix—with Sirius—near 28 20 N, 79 49 W.

25. Errors

Let's look at errors. You know that some are built into every sight, its reduction and plot. Sextants aren't perfect; bringing the body to the horizon is somewhat personal; atmospheric refraction—even for altitudes above 10 degrees—is always doubtful. The rounding off in the preparation of the tables you use and in your own work introduces small errors. The accuracy of your plotting is limited by chart, plotter, and pencil; our position lines should really be drawn as circles, not as straight lines.

Some of these errors may cancel each other; the total of all errors, under fair conditions, will not exceed a couple of nautical miles.

There's a much more important source of errors: you. Every navigator, not just a beginner, makes mistakes. You'll get impossible fixes. Sailing in the Atlantic, you'll find yourself in the Pacific without having gone through the Panama Canal. At other times you'll get a position line or fix that's not impossible, but suspiciously far from your dead reckoning position.

Do you throw out such sights? Check every step of your work? Take the sight over? Answers to these questions are: No, no, and no.

The only sight I'd ever throw out is one of a single star in a round of three or four. Even then I'd try to discover why it is off.

Checking each step of your work when you get an impossible or unlikely position is a waste of time. Only a few steps can give large errors; a few others can give errors large enough to make the result suspect; some can't change the result enough to make the position improbable. Mechanically checking everything has a built-in danger: One is apt to repeat the mistake.

You can take over daytime sights of sun and moon. But by the time you discover errors in dusk and dawn sights, the horizon or the stars may have faded away.

To save such star sights, and all others, you should know where to look for mistakes. It's always quicker than doing everything over.

Of course, your observation must have been right, or there's nothing to save.

You can't recheck your timing. If you wrote twenty-five minutes for twenty, you'll get a gross error.

Returning the sextant to its box, as you should, right after the observation, you may have had to move the index arm. If you wrote 25 degrees for 20, you'll end up with an impossible altitude difference.

But neither mistake is common. Much more frequent is the error of reading one minute of time or 1 degree more than you should have. For example:

TIME	ALTITUDE
Your minute hand is near 36, the second hand shows 55 seconds.	The index is near 36 degrees on the sextant, the micrometer shows 55 minutes.
Common mistake: 36^m55^s in place of 35^m55^s.	Common mistake: $36°55'$ in place of $35°55'$.
When the time is 36^m55^s the minute hand would be near 37.	When the altitude is $36°55'$ the index mark would be near 37.

I assume that you have routinely checked index error, and rocked the sextant. If you haven't, that will not show as a gross error.

In writing down your observation, did you get the date right? The day of the week will help. You'll wake up when you find that May 3, according to the Almanac, is not a Sunday.

If you can be sure of your observation, checking your calculation becomes worthwhile.

Gross mistakes will show up when you look in the sight reduction tables, in step 6. The calculated altitude will differ greatly from your observed altitude, found in step 4. If your observed altitude was 46 53, and the tables give a calculated altitude of 75 15, you know you've gone wrong.

Working our sights from a position assumed by the rules gives maximum altitude differences of some 40 minutes at the most. If the altitude difference—after applying the d-correction if necessary—exceeds, say, 60 minutes, I'd stop and look for a gross mistake.

Since you have the sight reduction tables open when you discover the mistake, that's where you'd logically start to look for it.

In the declination tables, volumes II and III of HO 249, an error as large as the one in the example above probably means you're looking on the wrong page: same declination instead of contrary declination. (Only when the declination or your latitude is near zero will such a page error not be large.)

Lesser errors at this step would make me check the column—13 degrees declination read instead of 14—and line—wrong local hour angle. Both can jump by 60 minutes from one entry to the next.

If the calculated altitude got farther away from the observed after you applied the d-correction, check that correction's sign. Since the correction can reach 59 minutes, you could be almost 120 nautical miles off by adding when you should be subtracting, or the other way around.

In volume I of HO 249, Selected Stars, all three stars of an observation may be off. Then the error must be in the latitude, that is, page, or—more likely—the local hour angle of Aries, that is, the line.

When two stars, of a round of stars, seem correct and the third one is off, you may have shot the wrong body.

Getting the wrong star worries beginning navigators unduly. In practice, it seldom happens. Yes, I once shot Castor (not used in volume I, and not one of the fifty-seven navigational stars) for its brighter twin Pollux. They are the most confusable pair, separated by only about 4 degrees.

The same navigators worry about shooting a planet for a star or a star for a planet. Chances for that are not great, since there are only four planets to mix you up. Of these, Saturn is the most likely candidate. But it moves so slowly among the stars that it is easy to keep track of. For a whole year it might dawdle in the vicinity of, say, Aldebaran. But all that year it will be noticeably brighter. (You'll find the brightness, called magnitude, of fixed stars in front of volume I, the magnitude of the planets in the Nautical Almanac next to the planet's name on the daily pages.)

Magnitude is the key to separating stars from the other three navigational planets. The first-magnitude stars, the ones printed in capital letters in volume I, are mostly between magnitudes 0.0 and +1.5; only Canopus (−0.9) and Sirius (−1.6) are brighter. Venus is always brighter than any fixed star; Jupiter most of the time is brighter than Sirius, and always brighter than Canopus. Mars fluctuates widely. At times it's brighter than Jupiter at its brightest, at other times it drops to where it wouldn't rate capital letters if it were a fixed star. The Almanac will give you its brightness for the period of observation. Its red color may help you to tell it from the fixed stars; only Antares is that reddish.

If you suspect you got a planet by mistake, don't throw the sight out. Try to work it with the planet's declination by volume II or III.

If step 6 doesn't show any mistake, I'd glance at the arithmetic in the assumed position, step 5.

Errors of not 1, but 10 or 100 degrees are common here, especially when you had to add or subtract 360 degrees. It's the common checkbook error: The cents balance nicely, but the bank and you differ by exactly $10 or exactly $100.

The altitude corrections—step 4—will not show up as gross error, except perhaps forgetting to subtract 30 minutes for observations of the upper limb of the moon, or adding them instead of subtracting.

For all but such moon sights, skip step 4 and go directly to 3, the Nautical Almanac.

Using the wrong day on the correct daily page will show up as a gross error only for the moon. So, of course, will the wrong planet column, say Mars when you wanted Jupiter.

You can quickly check the increase of Greenwich hour angle for minutes since the last hour. Divide the minutes by four; that's roughly the number of degrees the hour angle should have increased. Example: The time is forty-four minutes; the increase for Aries and the sun should be about 11 degrees, a little less, (10 29) for the moon.

Don't bother with v- and d-corrections; they won't cause gross errors.

Most mistakes in the Almanac step are made in transposing figures—writing 46 06.1 for 64 06.1—and, surprisingly, in misnaming the declination—north for south.

If you haven't spotted an error so far, it must be in the conversion from watch time to Greenwich time, step 2.

Some navigators habitually goof in the twenty-four-hour system, writing 1700 for 7 P.M.; others, all summer long, forget about daylight-saving time, or add it instead of subtracting it from the time shown by their timepiece. If you're prone to such mistakes, check the time calculation even before you waste time on checking the Almanac.

Anybody will eventually add wrong and so get the wrong Greenwich time. A wrong Greenwich date at some times of the year will not show up as a gross error in sights of the sun. It'll make a total hash of a moon sight, lesser hash of other sights.

Minor errors don't show up until you plot the position line or lines. The altitude difference is well below the 40-odd minutes maximum to be expected in our method of sight reduction. But the position line—or fix—isn't near your dead reckoning position.

How far is near enough?

Taking a practice sight from a well-known position, I'd suspect an error if I'd missed by more than 3 miles. If I had let my schooner sail herself for several hours, a 10-mile miss wouldn't make me suspicious. Hove to for two days, you wouldn't be surprised at a 20-mile difference between your estimated drift and a celestial fix.

It's more a question of trust in your dead reckoning than anything else. Here are a few generalities that may help:

For speed used in dead reckoning, allow a tolerance of 1 knot. Measuring by patent log, estimate, or engine revolutions, you could be 1 mile off either way for every hour sailed. Example: 10 hours between morning star fix and evening sights. Don't worry about a 10-mile difference.

For course error, allow between 2 and 5 degrees, depending on conditions and on skill of helmsman.

For current used in getting an estimated position, allow 1-knot variation. If you applied current correction for six hours, allow plus or minus 6 miles for current other than predicted. In the open ocean—as opposed to waters along the coast—you are not likely to discover a new current of more than 1-knot drift.

Hove to, you'll drift downwind, *not* in the direction of the heading of your boat. The speed will be hard to estimate. Allow up to 2 knots. In a nor'easter you're likely to drift southwest, perhaps 50 miles per day.

You discover the possible discrepancy between your likely position and your celestial fix or position line in plotting, step 8. That's the logical place to start checking for error. Good news: More often than not that's where you'll find your mistake—right in that last step.

Did you plot the assumed position correctly? The most common mistake here is in the minutes of longitude. In west longitude they increase toward the west. For example, 75 07 W is to the *left* of 75 00. It is not right of 75, nor is it 7 minutes east of 76.

Did you plot the azimuth correctly? You could have misread the scale on the plotter. That's easily checked with a glance at the compass rose printed on the chart.

Did you measure and label the altitude difference correctly? Most common error here is plotting toward instead of away or the other way around. Toward means toward the body in the direction of the azimuth. The label "toward" is only correct when the observed altitude is greater than the calculated altitude. Did you measure the difference in minutes of *latitude*? (In latitude 42, 60 minutes of longitude are only about 45 minutes of latitude.)

While you are at it, check the arithmetic of the altitude difference.

If all is well so far, go to step 6, sight reduction tables. Check that you copied the minutes accurately. Check the sign and calculation of the d-correction when you are using declination tables.

Then check the azimuth. Did you correct by the rule in volumes II and III? Did you copy correctly in volume I, where there's nothing to correct?

Suppose you haven't found a mistake so far. You know you haven't made a gross mistake. So you can eliminate all the sources of gross error from your check.

There are other errors that will never make you suspect that anything was wrong with your sight.

ERROR FINDING: GROSS ERRORS, discovered at step 6: Altitude
from sight reduction table very different from observed altitude, although time, sextant reading, and approximate position not in doubt.

	Difference more than three degrees	Difference less than three degrees
✳6 Sight Reduction Tables	Copying error	Copying error
Volume I	Wrong star	Wrong latitude (page) Next hour angle (line)
Volumes II/III	Wrong name: same/ contrary	Next latitude (page) Next declination (column) Next hour angle (line) Wrong sign of d-correction
✳5 Assumed Position	Arithmetic in LHA	Arithmetic in LHA (unit degrees)
✳4 Altitude Corrections	—	Moon: Corrections subtracted, −30′ for U.L. forgotten or added
✳3 Nautical Almanac	Arithmetic error left-end figures Copying error left-end figures Next hour (line) Planets: wrong column Moon: wrong date	Arithmetic error right-end figures Copying error right-end figures Next minute (half yellow page) Planets/Stars: wrong date
✳2 Greenwich Time and Date	Wrong hour (day-light time not subtracted, wrong zone correction, arithmetic) Moon: wrong date	Planets/Stars: wrong date

ERROR FINDING: SMALL SUSPECTED ERRORS, discovered at step
8: position line or fix unexpectedly far from dead reckoning position,
although time, sextant reading, and position not in doubt.

※8 Plotting Position Line(s)
Check assumed position, especially longitude
Compare plotted azimuth with compass rose on chart
Check altitude difference: right number of minutes of *latitude?*
Laid off according to label, toward or away?

※7 Altitude Difference
Check arithmetic and label (when observed altitude greater, label
it "toward")

※6 Sight Reduction Tables
Volume I—Minor copying error
Next latitude (page)
Next hour angle (line)
Volumes II/III—Minor copying error
Conversion of Z to Zn, including arithmetic
Wrong place in table: latitude (page),
declination (column), local hour angle (line)
Check d-correction and its sign

※5 Assumed Position
In east longitudes check minutes of assumed longitude

※4 Altitude Corrections
Dip—for all bodies minus
Sun—plus (except very near horizon)
Moon—check both corrections, both plus,
for upper limb —30 minutes besides

※3 Nautical Almanac
Work sheet: Check arithmetic, low end of figures
White pages: Minor copying error
Wrong sign of d-correction (moon), v should be plus
Yellow pages: Minor copying error
Wrong minute of time
Wrong column for body

※2 Greenwich Time and Date
Watch error: Add when your watch is slow
Check Greenwich date for all bodies except moon

An error in assumed position, step 5, is most unlikely in Western longitudes. You merely copied the number of minutes in the Greenwich hour angle. In the Eastern Hemisphere, you may have added wrong to get 60. Check it.

Altitude corrections, step 4, are a typical source of small errors. Arithmetical errors lead here. You'll soon get the feel for dip (−2 or −3 minutes), sun correction (+13 to +16 minutes when the sun is more than 15 degrees above the horizon), and star and planet corrections (between 0 and −5 minutes).

Summer for winter correction of the sun, wrong altitude for planet or star correction, overlooked additional corrections for Venus and Mars will not show as suspicious position lines.

For the moon, the forgotten −30 minutes, wrong parallax, mix-up between lower and upper second correction are the things to check.

In the Nautical Almanac, step 3, look mainly for minutes wrongly copied in the white pages, and double-check the sign of the d-correction, especially for the moon. The v-correction for all bodies (except, sometimes, Venus) is always plus.

In the yellow pages the most common mistake is one of taking the wrong minute of time on the correct page, e.g. forty-four minutes in place of forty-five. That'll move your assumed position about fifteen minutes longitude out of place.

Using the sun column for Aries, or the Aries column for the sun will not show in your plot; getting moon increment for sun or Aries, or the other way around, will.

Check the arithmetic of the minutes of increase in hour angle (and for v- and d-corrections for the moon). Pay special attention to errors of exactly 10—or even 20—minutes.

If you haven't found a mistake so far, it must be in the watch correction. If your watch is slow, you must add the correction; if it's fast, you must subtract it. If you apply a thirty-second correction with the wrong sign, your assumed position may be off about 15 minutes in longitude.

If you are prone to make this mistake, or if your watch gains on one day and loses on the next so that you are likely to mislabel the error fast for slow, check the time correction before the Almanac.

When in spite of reasonable systematic search you can't find a mistake, there's a comforting thought. Unlike dead reckoning, which carries forward all earlier mistakes, celestial sights are independent. Tonight's wrong star fix will not matter after you get a good fix in the morning.

PRACTICE (25)

If you have kept earlier calculations, you may have some material on which to practice finding errors efficiently.

The following problems may supply more material for that. If in the sight reduction tables the altitude doesn't match your observed altitude, search for gross errors. If it comes close, finish your calculation and plot the position line or lines.

If the position line or fix seems unreasonably far from where you believe yourself to be, follow the drill for finding small errors.

A. On Sunday, May 2, a navigator's dead reckoning places him 30 nautical miles west of St. George Reef light, which the chart shows at 41 50 N, 124 22 W, but his DR could be 12 miles off, he estimates. To get a fix, he takes a sight of the sun bearing SW, and the upper limb of the moon bearing E. His watch is four seconds slow, his height of eye is 6 feet. The sun at 15 31 54 PDT gives a sextant altitude of 50 37. The moon at 15 30 57 PDT gives a sextant altitude of 25 40. Plot the 15 31 sun/moon fix.

B. In the evening of Monday, November 1, a navigator with an estimated position of 27 56 N, 116 17 W in which he has great confidence, observes the planets Mars and Jupiter, both very bright and well placed, from height of eye of 4 feet. Watch is thirteen seconds slow.

Mars (SE) 17 13 50 PST, Hs 39 52
Jupiter (SW) 17 14 43 PST, Hs 17 09

Plot the 17 14 Mars/Jupiter fix.

C. On Sunday, May 2, in DR 28 17 N, 79 55 W (with a possible error of 10 miles), the skipper takes a sight of the three stars selected for a fix in the tables. HE 6 feet, no watch error, Eastern Daylight Time.

Arcturus (E)   *Sirius* (SW)   *Capella* (NW)
20 14 01 Hs 26 35   20 14 54 Hs 28 39   20 14 29 Hs 36 37

Plot the 20 14 star fix.

(So much of the paper work in the three sights is the same that most navigators would work them side by side on the same sheet.)

ANSWERS (25)

A. Did you measure 30 nautical miles from the light? Or did you —wrongly—add 30 minutes to the longitude of the light? The fix should be near 41 43 N, 125 02 W. The sun sight is worked out in the summary in fig. 173 and plotted in fig. 175. The moon sight is worked in fig. 177.

B. The fix should be within a mile of the estimated position.

C. The fix should be near 28 19 N, 79 49 W; the sight is worked out in fig. 178, plotted in fig. 136.

Here you have worked sights of the sun, the moon, planets, and stars. That's all the sights there are. If you solved them correctly, you have graduated. If in these sights you have made mistakes, but found them, that's all right. That was the purpose of this exercise.

26. Emergencies

You now know how to take, work, and plot sights. Of course, you'll need practice. You can become expert in figuring and plotting by working examples. If you make mistakes, you'll know where to look for gross errors and less gross and minor ones.

You can do all that without a sextant and without stepping outside your cabin. With a sextant and a small lake, you can practice taking sights. The location of the lake, known beforehand, will check the accuracy of your work.

To be an expert, you'll need, to my mind, one more thing. You'll have to know how to cope with navigational emergencies. You won't find that discussed in any detail in the standard textbooks. When you're in trouble you may not feel up to the job of figuring it out for yourself. That's how a singlehander, when his watch ran down and his radio went dead, mistook signs of land in the Azores for a landfall on the West Indies, 2,000 miles away. That's perhaps why you read about people—living skeletons in the newspaper accounts—being found hundreds of miles off course.

The most likely emergency: You have forgotten how to do the paper work. The summary at the end of this book will refresh your memory. Even without this book you are not without help. The Nautical Almanac in the explanation pages, which follow the daily data, shows how to find the coordinates of the ground point of all navigational bodies, and how to correct their sextant altitudes to get observed altitude.

The sight reduction tables give worked-out examples of the needed calculations and plots.

Let's look at other possible emergencies in the order of the eight steps.

Date: Ashore it won't often happen that you don't know what date or day of the week it is. But it has happened on boats. One singlehander got so sick he didn't care to count the days. Another lost track of the days in a grass shack. Even a calendar watch can leave you in doubt: Have I taken care of the thirty-first or not?

What to do? The sun with its small daily change is no help. The stars are little better. But the moon, changing about a dozen degrees in hour angle and several degrees in declination from one day to the next, will tell you. Take a sight in daylight or by night. Don't worry about a false horizon, and don't bother with altitude and v- and d-corrections. The roughest sight will give a totally impossible position line when worked with the wrong date.

Example: The Nautical Almanac for 1800 GMT gives:
         Saturday May 1   GHA   1 59 Dec N 20 30
         Sunday   May 2   350 55   16 10

Near latitude 42 N, longitude 70 W, you'd get a calculated altitude of 29 41 for May 1; 19 33 for May 2. You won't even need a sextant to tell which of these days it is; just look out a port.

The date you get is the Greenwich date, not your local date.

Dead Reckoning in celestial navigation isn't critical. It only serves to pick a reasonable assumed position. When your position is doubtful— say after three sightless, stormy days—assume a position that makes the calculated altitude come out close to the observed altitude.

To get correct longitude take a sight of a body that bears east or west. Wrong latitude changes such a sight very little. In the tables use the local hour angle that makes the altitude difference less than 40 minutes, toward or away. Then assume the longitude that gives this local hour angle.

To get correct latitude take a sight of a body that bears south or north. Wrong longitude changes such a sight very little. In the tables use the latitude that makes the altitudes most nearly equal.

Two star sights, in the morning or evening, will give you both latitude and longitude. A morning sight and a noon sight of the sun will do the same. So will a noon sight and an evening sight of the sun.

Time, accurate Greenwich time, is so important in celestial navigation that any emergency in this department is likely to send the navigator into a panic.

If you relied on a wristwatch and radio, as most small-craft navigators do, and the radio that's supposed to bring in time signals gives out, you're not lost yet. Perhaps your direction finder will bring these signals in. When you can't get WWV or CHU on the marine band try an entertainment station. Perhaps you can get a network beep on the hour. Even without that, any transistor that brings in a United States station will give you approximate time checks. In the United States—but not in many foreign countries—programs start very promptly on the exact hour.

Even without any radio you are not totally helpless. If your watch keeps its rate fairly well from one day to the next, you are still in business. Apply the daily rate to all future sights. If your watch has been losing between eight and twelve seconds a day, add ten seconds the first day, twenty the second, and so on. Of course your accuracy will gradually suffer.

As you'll recall, an error of four seconds in time will change a position line that runs north-south by 1 minute of longitude. An error of one minute of time would offset your longitude 15 minutes. It'll hardly change a position line that runs east-west. So your latitude will remain reliable. The usual slanted position lines will be off less than a longitude line, but more than a latitude line.

How much uncertainty in longitude you can stand will depend on where you are. Approaching the high islands of the West Indies, even 100 miles wouldn't matter much. You could still find the island you wanted, only your estimated date of arrival would be off by one day. But the reefs of the Low Archipelago are strewn with wrecks of Tahiti-bound yachts whose navigators had underestimated their longitude, had not allowed enough for current.

Without any knowledge of accurate time, you can get a very accurate latitude. Take a string of observations of the sun at noon. The sun's altitude increases during the morning, decreases during the afternoon. At noon it reaches its greatest altitude for the day. At that time the sun bears exactly 180 from you, or 360 in the Southern Hemisphere.

If you can trust your compass, begin the sights when the sun is close to its noon bearing, say near 177 True. Otherwise start early enough not to miss noon. At first the sights will show rapidly increasing altitudes; just before noon the increase will slow. At noon the sun will seem to stand still in altitude, before starting downhill. The highest sextant reading is all you're interested in. As soon as the readings start to drop you can rest your arm.

How rapidly the sun rises and how long it hangs at the same altitude depends on its declination and your latitude. Where the sun will be within 5 degrees of being exactly overhead at noon, it moves too fast between sights to make this method practical. Everywhere else, a change of 1 minute in altitude takes from twenty seconds to several minutes.

A change of 1 minute in altitude is readily noticed, and quite accurate enough. You won't care about being 1 mile north or south. In latitude 28 degrees this change takes from about two minutes in midsummer to about five minutes in midwinter. In latitude 42 the same change will take between four and six minutes.

So taking these sights is quite a leisurely process. Your left arm, which holds the sextant, will get tired. But not your brain.

You don't have to learn a new formula; just work a standard sight, using 00 00 for local hour angle. For the declination of the sun, you should use the one given in the Almanac for the Greenwich time of your local noon.

If you know your longitude, you can get the declination exactly. When it's noon on your vessel, you are, by definition, in the same longitude as the ground point of the sun. If you are, for example, in 91 30 W when the sun is highest in your sky, the Greenwich hour angle of the sun at that moment is 91 30. You could check the Almanac for that day and work out the declination for the very minute when the GHA has that value.

The declination of the sun changes at most 1 minute in one hour. So being even an hour off in your estimate wouldn't change your latitude more than a minute. So it's good enough to guess your longitude within about 7 degrees, plus or minus.

Just using your zone correction is good enough. In 91 30 you'd keep your watch on Central Standard Time, +6 time. Add six hours to noon and use 18 00 GMT for declination.

Used to running fixes, two and three body fixes, and position lines that tell you how far you have come or how far off course you are, you may wonder what good a single latitude line is. That's how ships navigated from the age of discoveries until chronometers got cheap enough for stingy shipowners and radio time signals became available.

A captain from Europe, bound for the West Indies, would stand south until a noon sight told him he had reached the latitude of his destination. Then he'd cross the greater part of the ocean trying to stay on that latitude. Going a bit north of west if his noon sight showed him to be too far south, going a bit south of west if he'd been set north, he couldn't help eventually reaching his destination.

Some singlehanders to this day use nothing more complicated than that to sail around the world.

Knowing your time within a few minutes, your longitude to within a degree or two, you can get a latitude accurate to 2 or 3 minutes at dawn or dusk from Polaris. Calculate your observed altitude (sextant altitude minus dip, minus star correction). Then calculate the approximate local hour angle of Aries for the time of the sight. Go into the Polaris table at the end of volume I of HO 249 (see p. 326). There take out Q, which will vary between −52 and +52 minutes. Apply this Q-correction according to its sign to your observed altitude. The result is your latitude.

Example: Out of sight of land on Lake Michigan, on October 31, at about 5:57 P.M. CST, a Polaris sight gives an observed altitude of 42 30. For the approximate local hour angle of Aries, 131, the table gives Q as +10. Your latitude is near 42 40.

This simplicity makes it an ideal emergency sight; that's why I show it here. It also makes it the only "special" sight that has survived in modern celestial navigation. Some navigators might shoot Polaris with correct time at the time of a star sight. The same table will solve it.

With accurate data you'll come within about a mile. In some years you'll have to correct volume I data. In the Nautical Almanac at the end of the white pages you'll find a more accurate (but a little more complicated) method good for that year. It's clearly explained there.

But Polaris is not a very bright star (magnitude 2.1). By the time you see it in the evening, the horizon is about to fade. In the morning, Polaris is about to disappear when the horizon becomes distinct. (South of about latitude 10 N you probably won't be able to see Polaris in time for a sight.) So, many navigators ignore Polaris, using only bright stars and planets for their morning and evening sights.

If you know where you are, you can find out what time it is.

While you dallied on some happy island, your radio has corroded, your watch has run down. Now it's time to push on. But what time is it? Here's how you could solve the problem: Get your latitude and longitude from the chart, and take an evening sight of the sun. Only at one moment of that day will the sun be at that altitude in the west. In theory you can calculate the Greenwich time of that moment, accurate to a few seconds. In practice, if you had to invent a method for doing that, you'd probably decide to stay another month.

It could also happen that you wake up early one morning in mid-ocean to discover you've forgotten to wind your watch. The radio has given up too. You may also have taken off a self-winding watch for some chore. Now it has stopped for lack of motion.

Don't panic. Have another cup of coffee waiting for the sun to get more than 10 degrees above the horizon. The ideal time for a sight to discover the time from a known position is when the sun bears due east (or west). But in winter, in either hemisphere, the sun won't cooperate; it rises already on the noon side of east, sets before bearing west. I'd rather take the sight when the sun is past east (or not yet west) than put up with the doubtful refraction of low altitudes.

While you're having your cup of coffee, work out your dead reckoning position as accurately as you can. The closer it is to your actual position, the more accurate your time will be.

You don't have to invent a method for discovering time. Few modern navigators could do it. Old-timers may have written down somewhere a logarithmic formula for a "time sight." With the needed tables they could solve the problem. But you don't need any special formula or tables. I have worked out a solution based on the method you've used in all your sights.

In the usual sight you use the time to get a position line near your actual location. Here we use a position line through your known location to get the time. Some of the steps will be backward, or taken in the wrong order, but they'll be the same familiar eight steps.

Restart your watch. If you have the approximate time—a cabin clock without second hand, or a cheap alarm clock will do—reset your watch. (Make sure the minute hand is on a minute mark when the second hand is on 60.) If you don't have approximate time, set it from your usual waking time, the feel of the day, or the number of cups of coffee you've had. It wouldn't matter if you were a whole hour off.

Then take your sun sight, timing it to the second with this arbitrary time. Convert to Greenwich Mean Time. With that and the date go into the Almanac. Leave the space reserved for Greenwich hour angle blank; just put the declination of the sun at the last full hour on your work sheet in its usual place. Then correct the sextant altitude to get observed altitude.

Now comes the first crucial step. In the sight reduction tables, with latitude (the nearest whole degree from your position) and the just found declination (same or contrary name) look for an altitude close to your observed altitude.

For latitude 28 N, declinations S 14, observed altitude 12 16, you'd find:

LHA	Hc	d	Z
293	12 47	−34	114

Check the azimuth angle. It's morning, the sun is about ESE, 114 is the right true azimuth. (In the evening in the same place in the tables the local hour angle would be 67, the true azimuth 360−114=246.) Correct the altitude in the usual way for minutes of declination. Then get the altitude difference and label it as always.

Now your work sheet will look like fig. 154.

Next plot your sight. Normally you'd start by plotting the assumed position, then draw from that the azimuth line, lay off the altitude difference on that line, and finish by drawing the position line at right angles to the azimuth line.

Here you start by plotting your *dead reckoning* position. Then you draw the azimuth line from that. On this line you lay off the altitude difference. Caution: The words "toward" and "away" are understood from the assumed position; starting from what would normally be the final position line, their meaning is reversed. Here the label was A, so you draw it *toward* the sun.

Through the point just marked, at right angles to the azimuth line, draw a line.

Now comes the second crucial step: Read the longitude where this line crosses your assumed latitude. That is your assumed longitude.

Once you have that, there's only some arithmetic left.

In the usual sight you get the Greenwich hour angle of the sun at the time of observation, apply the assumed longitude, and get the local

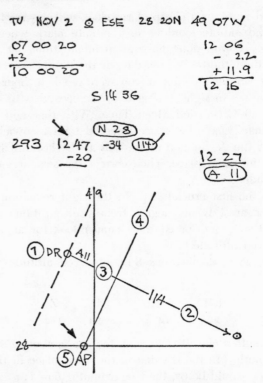

154. Getting time from a sight at a known position. Top: sight reduction ready for plotting. Arrow points to the crucial step, finding the local hour angle that gives fair match between calculated and observed altitudes. Note the three ringed figures in place of the usual four.

Bottom: plot for finding the assumed longitude. The dashed line corresponds to the usual final position line, not needed here. The solid line is the position line through the assumed position, not usually drawn. Here it gives you the assumed position. Arrow should remind you of that crucial plotting step. Order of steps: (1) Plot known position. (2) Plot azimuth. (3) Plot altitude difference. (4) Plot position line through point just found. (5) Read assumed longitude on latitude line.

hour angle. Here we use the local hour angle and the assumed longitude to get the Greenwich hour angle of the sun at the time of observation.

In west longitude, you always subtracted assumed longitude from Greenwich hour angle to get local hour angle. So here we must add assumed longitude to local hour angle to get the Greenwich hour angle. (Example: LHA 293, alo 49 03 W; GHA is 342 03.)

In the usual sight, we used the time to get the Greenwich hour angle of the sun. Here we have the Greenwich hour angle of the sun, and want to know the time when it had that value.

In the sun column of the daily page in the Almanac, look for the next lower full-hour value. (Example: For November 2, 334 06—less than 342 03—is given for ten o'clock.) That leaves 7 57 for the increase in the minutes and seconds after the hour. Flipping through the yellow pages, you'll find that this, in the sun column, is the increment for 31^m48^s. Time of observation: 10 31 48 GMT.

Your calculation may look like this:		Compare that with the usual calculation:	
LHA sun	293	GMT 10, sun GHA	334 06
Assumed long.	+ 49 03 W	31^m48^s	+ 7 57
GHA sun	342 03	GHA sun	342 03
GMT 10	−334 06	Assumed long.	− 49 03 W
31^m48^s	7 57	LHA sun	293

If you don't mind adding and subtracting upward, you could write all the figures of this sight in their usual places.

You are in the +3 time zone, so your watch should have shown 07 31 48 at the time of your sight. It did show 07 00 20. So it's 31^m28^s slow. You could use that as watch error for future sights, or set it ahead thirty-one minutes, using the more convenient twenty-eight seconds slow to correct your timing.

If you should ever need this emergency method, or if you'd like to work such a sight in some charted anchorage—decidedly postgraduate work—here's what I'd do. After getting the time of observation, but before resetting my watch again, I'd work the sight from the time I got and plot it in the usual manner. That'll show up any error in subtracting when I should have added, and in labeling the altitude difference.

How accurate will the refound time be? When your position is exactly known and when the sun bears due east or west, an error of 1 minute in altitude will put your time four seconds off. Rounding in the tables and in your work, sextant and observational errors, and unavoidable inaccuracy in plotting will account for perhaps 2 minutes of altitude. The neglected change of declination may add another minute of altitude if your guess of time was a whole hour off. Here the sun was well past east, but that adds only about two seconds to the uncertainty of timing.

If I knew my position to be exact, I'd expect to recover the time to within ten or twelve seconds. Logarithmic calculation of this example agrees with my graphic solution, drawn on the galley sink, to within four seconds.

In mid-ocean I wouldn't expect my position to be exactly at the DR. If I had under- or overestimated my night's run by 5 miles I'd pick up another twenty-second error. If my watch kept its rate, I'd carry that error with me, being still 5 miles ahead or astern on future sights. On the last day of the voyage that would mean making my landfall an hour earlier or later than I had expected. And who'd care?

Sextant loss or damage is a big blow to the celestial navigator. If only the telescope has been knocked out of line, take it off. You can take excellent sights without it.

If you rely on celestial navigation, carry a second sextant even if it's only a plastic one. Such student or lifeboat sextants sell for about $50.

Even without a sextant you can still take one type of sight: that of a body on the horizon. You simply note the time when the body seems exactly on the horizon, as seen by the naked eye or through binoculars. You might time a bright star or planet. You can use the upper or lower limb of the rising or setting sun or moon. In every case you'll consider the sextant reading as oo oo.

It might be smart to time both upper and lower limbs of the sun or moon. Then you'll have two sights that partially check each other.

You then deduct dip as from all sextant altitudes. Refraction on the horizon is large:

$$
\begin{array}{ll}
\text{For stars and planets} & -34.5' \\
\text{For sun, upper limb} & -50.3' \\
\text{For sun, lower limb} & -18.3'
\end{array}
$$

For the moon you'll have to get the horizontal parallax first, then get the corrections from the Almanac.

Additional Refraction Corrections
for a Body on the Horizon

Temperature Correction			*Air Pressure Correction*		
°F	Corr.'	°C	inches	Corr.'	millibars
89		+32	28.53		966
	+2			+1	
74		+23	29.44		996
	+1			0	
57		+14	30.26		1025
	0			−1	
43		+ 6	31.13		1054
	−1				
28		− 2			
	−2				
15		− 9			

On the horizon you'll also have to allow for temperature and barometric conditions different from the standard 50° F (10° C) and 29.83″ (1010 mb). You'll find these corrections in the Almanac on p. A4. Find the intersection of temperature (vertical) with barometric pressure (horizontal). The letter in the slanting lane in which this intersection falls leads to the correction, clearly marked plus or minus.

You may prefer a simplified table that gives the two corrections separately. I have calculated it from formulas in Bowditch. When you don't know the barometric pressure, assume it to be normal. You can probably estimate the temperature close enough without a thermometer.

An example of the sextant corrections for the sun's upper limb on the horizon might look like this:

Sextant altitude	00 00
Sun upper limb, standard refraction etc.	−50.3
Dip, height of eye 4 feet	− 1.9
Temperature 60° F (between 74 and 57)	+ 1
Barometer 30″ (between 29.44 and 30.26)	0
Observed altitude	−00 51

Even with these corrections, or the ones from the Almanac, the observed altitude is not as reliable as the usual altitudes measured above 10 degrees above the horizon, where refraction is far more certain.

Using the time of your sight, proceed with the calculations in the usual way. Be specially careful in naming the altitude difference. In the above example if the calculated altitude came out as −00 41, the difference would be 10 *Away*. The observed altitude is less—more minus— than the calculated one.

There's another use you can make of your knowledge of celestial navigation after you've lost the use of your sextant. You may be able to get a course to your destination from the stars.

By definition a body is directly above its ground point. Think of your destination as a ground point. If you know when a certain star will be directly above the destination, its bearing at that time will be your course wherever you may be.

A star will pass at some time over your destination if its declination is the same as the latitude of that place. You'll find the declination of the fifty-seven navigational stars on the left daily pages of the Almanac.

In an emergency, what star would guide you to Hawaii, between latitudes 18 55 N and 20 15 N? Running down the declination column, you'll find:

Name	*SHA*	*Dec*
Arcturus	146 24.2	N 19 19.7

(That's on the May 1–3 page; the change from month to month, even year to year, is negligibly small.)

When will Arcturus be directly over Hawaii, between 155 and 156 W longitude? When its Greenwich hour angle is about 155 30. (For destinations in east longitude subtract the longitude from 360 to get the GHA.) To get the Greenwich hour angle of Arcturus at any time one must add 146 24—called the star's sidereal hour angle, abbreviated SHA —to the Greenwich hour angle of Aries at that time. You could read the abbreviation as "star's hour angle"; you may think of it as a longitude, always counted westabout, measured from the First Point of Aries.

The GHA of Arcturus will be 155 30 when the GHA of Aries is 155 30 minus 146 24, or 9 06. On May 1 the GHA of Aries is 8 41 at 10 00 GMT. Flipping through the yellow pages of the Almanac, you'll find that it takes one minute forty seconds to make up the remaining 25 minutes.

At 10 01 40 GMT on that day Arcturus will be directly above your destination (19 20 N, 155 30 W). Point your vessel at Arcturus and she'll point also at Hawaii. Note the compass reading and steer the same course for the next twenty-four hours.

The next night, about four minutes earlier, Arcturus will again be over Hawaii. It'll give you the course again. And so on every night. (Unfortunately, as you approach your destination your guide star at the critical time will get close to your zenith. Then you won't be able to get direction from it, and will have to steer by compass.)

The easiest way to recognize the navigational stars is with a star finder of the type described in detail in my *Practical Boating*. It gives the approximate altitude and azimuth of any of the fifty-seven stars for any time, anywhere in the world. You can measure the altitude of a star with your hand. At arm's length each finger covers about 2 degrees, palm and thumb about 10, the spread hand about 20. You can gauge the azimuth from your compass, measure it with a bearing compass.

Forty of the fifty-seven navigational stars are used in Selected Stars. Perhaps the star you want can be found there.

It would be nice if these stars were evenly distributed in declination so you could get by this method to almost any latitude, north or south. They aren't. But the Almanac lists another 120 stars you could use, and shows many of them on the star charts.

Nautical Almanac: You can be caught with an expired Almanac if you start a cruise before the new Almanac goes on sale, or when a cruise stretches unexpectedly into the next year.

No problem. With just a little more work you can use last year's Almanac for the sun and stars. You'll find instructions for that procedure —it doesn't work for planets or the moon—in the explanations after the daily pages of the Almanac.

It's quite simple. For the stars you subtract 15.1 minutes from the Greenwich hour angle of Aries in last year's Almanac.

For the sun you take the data for five hours forty-eight minutes earlier, then add 87°00′ to the hour angle.

It's different in leap years. You'll have one set of instructions for January to the end of February, another set for the rest of the year.

You can manage without any Almanac if you use HO 249 sight reduction tables.

For the *stars*, volume I gives a table that lets you work out the Greenwich hour angle of Aries for all times during the years of usefulness of that book. The 1970 edition, for instance, lets you solve star sights through 1975. This table, which only takes up two pages, is so simple that many air navigators use it in preference to the Almanac for all star work.

For the *sun*, volumes II and III give hour angle and declination for any year up to 2000. The table is complicated, but when you're desperate you'll figure it out from the instructions and the examples given next to that table.

Without an Almanac, you'll need some altitude correction tables.

You'll probably remember the dip correction by heart. Here's a table that's easily memorized: The upper figures are the squares of the lower ones:

DIP CORRECTION

Height of Eye (feet)	4	9	16	25
Correction	−2′	−3′	−4′	−5′

These figures are accurate to one tenth of a minute. A guess for in-between values will not be far off, say −3.5 for 12 feet. If you use meters, multiply them by three and use the above table. Example: height of eye 3 meters, about 9 feet, correction −3′.

You'll find the star altitude correction in table 8 of volume I. Use zero for "Height in Thousands of Feet." For the sun, use the similar tables —table 6—in the other two volumes. Then add 16 minutes for the semi-diameter of the sun for observation of its lower limb.

Here's a table that'll solve all sights you can work without an Almanac:

BODY CORRECTION

Sextant Altitude (Degrees)	10	12	15	21	33	63	90
Star Correction	− 5′	− 4′	− 3′	− 2′	− 1′	0′	
Sun (Lower Limb) Correction	+11′	+12′	+13′	+14′	+15′	+16′	

Example: For a star sight that gives an altitude of 27 degrees—between 21 and 33 degrees—the correction is —2'. For the same altitude the correction for the lower limb of the sun is +14'.

Some navigators use these values, pasted in the sextant box, for all star, planet, and sun sights. That way they eliminate most of the work in altitude correction, except for sights of the moon and for occasional sights below 10 degrees altitude.

Sight Reduction Tables: Loss of volume I is only an inconvenience. You can work all the stars with declinations of 30 degrees or less, north or south, by volumes II or III. That leaves you more than half of the fifty-seven navigational stars, including twelve first-magnitude stars.

You'll get the GHA of the star by adding the SHA of the star to the GHA of Aries. The declination is given next to the SHA on the left daily pages. You apply assumed longitude to get the LHA of the star, then use volume II or III, depending on your latitude, as you would for any other navigational body.

You may miss the familiar listing of three stars that'll give a good fix. But any three bright stars spread in azimuth around the sky will do. You can precalculate their approximate altitudes for identification. Get the local hour angle of Aries for the estimated time of observation. Add the star's hour angle. With your latitude, the sum just found, and the star's declination rounded off to the nearest degree, you can sight-read altitude and azimuth from the tables. But you may have to convert the azimuth angle (Z) given in the table to azimuth counted from north (Zn).

The loss of volume II or III of the sight reduction tables is a more serious matter.

Another set of tables aboard is a logical precaution. You won't need all six volumes of HO 229, or the nine volumes of now obsolescent HO 214; the volumes in your area of operation will do.

I have carried HO 208 (Dreisenstock); other navigators prefer HO 211 (Ageton). Both little books—about a dollar's worth—require more work than our tables. The explanations will bewilder you. But if you have to, you'll puzzle them out after working some of the examples.

You can get a latitude without tables of any kind.

A body on the meridian, say the sun at local noon, will have a calculated altitude that's a simple function of the body's declination and your assumed latitude. When the local hour angle is 00 00 or 180 00 your distance from the ground point is the sum of assumed latitude and declination of the body when they are of contrary name. It's their difference when they are of the same name. The calculated altitude—as always—equals 90 degrees minus the distance from the assumed position to the ground point. A sketch will help you to get that distance right.

AP_20° N   AP_20° N   GP_20° N

GP_10° N   AP_10° N

Equator ————————————— Equator

GP_10° S

Dist. 10°	Dist. 30°	Dist. 10°
Hc 80°	Hc 60°	Hc 80°

You could get the declination of the sun from the Almanac for approximate local noon. Then you'd take a string of sights, as described under lost time, and note the highest sextant reading. Add your sun correction to get observed altitude. Compare that with the altitude calculated from declination and assumed latitude. The difference is the altitude difference, toward or away. The entire sight reduction will fit on a match folder. To plot that sight, you draw an east-west line.

Plotting: All emergencies in that department are minor inconveniences. When you haven't got a chart on which to plot your position lines, make one. Take the latitude and longitude divisions from any chart of the same latitude.

If you drop your favorite protractor overboard, use the accurately graduated compass roses printed on every chart. Transfer angles from the chart rose or cut one out and make a new protractor.

For the right angle between azimuth line and position line any square object will serve.

Loss of dividers is no problem. A strip of paper will transfer the minutes of longitude for the assumed position; it will also transfer minutes of latitude for your altitude difference.

If you should ever run into one of the emergencies I've discussed, the answers that follow the next drill should help you.

If there are other emergencies possible, I hope you won't discover them.

PRACTICE (26)

A. Sunday, May 2, at about 2014 EDT, in approximate longitude 80 W, a sight of Polaris gave a sextant altitude of 28 03 (height of eye 6 feet). What was your latitude?

B. On Wednesday, November 1, having lost accurate time, you take a sight of the sun bearing ESE, height of eye 6 feet, sextant altitude 11

04. The restarted watch showed 06 42 15 (ZD +9). If your estimated position 27 54 N, 129 04 W was correct, what was your watch error?

C. You have lost your sextant in the Gulf of Mexico. In DR 28 20 N, 94 30 W, on Monday, November 1, you time sunrise: lower limb on horizon at 06 31 30 CST (ZD +6), HE 4 feet, temperature 60° F, barometer 30.0 inches. Get a position line for that "sight." You will get a local hour angle of the sun that's not in the tables reproduced here. If you had the proper page you'd find:

LHA	Hc	d	Z
277	−0 32	−28	106

(Watch the label of the altitude difference.)

D. On November 2, bound for Tahiti, keeping +9 time, you decide to try the star-over-the-destination method for finding the direct course (Venus Point is at 17 30 S, 149 29 W). From the list of navigational stars you pick Sirius, the brightest of all fixed stars. Its declination is S 16 40, so at some time it will be overhead at a position only 50 nautical miles north of Venus Point. When?

E. Work a sight of the star Arcturus—the same sight as in the last practice as problem C—by HO 249, volume II. The data were: GMT 00 14 01 May 3, DR 28 17 N, 79 55 W, Ho 26 31. (To stay within the coverage of the sight reduction table reproduced here, use an assumed longitude near 79 W.) Plot the position line. Then compare result with previous one.

F. On Monday, November 1, in approximate latitude 28 N, in the Eastern Standard Time zone you have taken a noon sight of the sun. Give your calculated altitude without sight reduction tables.

ANSWERS (26)

A. Greenwich hour angle of Aries at time of observation about 224, longitude 80 W. So the local hour angle of Aries then was about 144, for which the table (p. 326) gives Q +22′. Observed altitude 27 59. Latitude at time of observation near 28 21 N (27 59 +22′).

B. Slow 2^m41^s. To get a calculated altitude matching the observed one, you had to assume a local hour angle of 291. Your assumed position should have been 28 N, near 129 20 W. If you ran into difficulties with this problem, work it as an ordinary sun sight with the correct time of observation (06 44 56, +9) to find where your figures differ.

C. Your altitude calculation should look like this:

Horizon, sextant altitude	00 00
Height of eye 4 feet	− 1.9
Sun on horizon, lower limb	−18.3

Temperature correction 60° F   + 1
Barometer correction 30.0″   0
Observed altitude   −19

(You would have had the same observed altitude using the tables in the Nautical Almanac.)

Calculated altitude   −00 41
Observed altitude   −00 19
Altitude difference   22

Altitudes decrease with your distance from the ground point. The altitude at the assumed position (−41′) is less—more minus—than at the point of observation (−19). You were closer to the ground point. You should have labeled the altitude difference "toward."

D. Sirius will be over that point when its Greenwich hour angle equals the longitude of your destination (149 29). By definition the Greenwich hour angle of a star at any time equals the GHA of Aries at that time plus the sidereal hour angle (SHA) of the star. Hence:

GHA Sirius   149 29
                +360

                509 29
−SHA Sirius   259 01
GHA Aries   250 28

Sirius will be over the point near your destination when on November 2 the GHA of Aries is 250 28. It'll be 236 09 at 1300 GMT. It'll take 57^m07^s to increase the remaining 14 19. So it'll be at 13 57 07 GMT, 04 57 07 your time (same date).

E. The critical part of your calculation will look like this:

As before: GHA Aries 00ʰ   220 14.5
                14^m01^s + 3 30.8
Arcturus (from star list in N.A.)   SHA +146 24.2   Dec N 19 19.7
                             370 10
Assumed longitude   − 79 10 W
Arcturus   LHA   291   Dec N 19 20

At the assumed latitude of 28 N that gives a calculated altitude of 27 00, azimuth 082; so the altitude difference is Away 29′. The azimuth differs 1 degree from the former calculation. That seems normal. But the altitude difference before was Toward 1′. Nothing wrong. Your assumed position has changed. Plotted, the two position lines will lie close together. (They'd fit even better if we had applied the annual correction for sights worked by volume I of HO 249.)

F. Your calculation might look like this, the whole calculation:

Nov 1, sun
Noon (EST)
1700 GMT

Dec S 14 23   90 00
+Lat N 28 00   −42 23

42 23 Hc 47 37

If, for example, your Ho came out as 47 31, you were 6′ away, in latitude 28 06 N. You can do that in your head.

You can also do the sextant corrections in your head. On a small vessel in waters you are likely to sail, the corrections will come out as +13′ at noon. In the above example, for any likely height of eye, the sextant altitude must have been 47 18.

Tables

For working problems in celestial navigation. (Some of the pages reproduced are only parts of the originals; others combine columns from different pages to permit more variety in problems.)

The order of tables follows their use: Nautical Almanac before Sight Reduction Tables.

The Almanac pages are in the order of that book: Altitude Corrections—Daily Pages—Yellow Pages.

The pages from the Sight Reduction Tables are in the order of the volumes from which they are taken, I, II, III. The correction tables—common to the last two—are near the end, followed by the Polaris table.

ALTITUDE CORRECTION TABLES 10°-90°—SUN, STARS, PLANETS

OCT.—MAR. SUN APR.—SEPT.

App. Alt.	Lower Limb	Upper Limb	App. Alt.	Lower Limb	Upper Limb
9 34	+10·8	−21·5	9 39	+10·6	−21·2
9 45	+10·9	−21·4	9 51	+10·7	−21·1
9 56	+11·0	−21·3	10 03	+10·8	−21·0
10 08	+11·1	−21·2	10 15	+10·9	−20·9
10 21	+11·2	−21·1	10 27	+11·0	−20·8
10 34	+11·3	−21·0	10 40	+11·1	−20·7
10 47	+11·4	−20·9	10 54	+11·2	−20·6
11 01	+11·5	−20·8	11 08	+11·3	−20·5
11 15	+11·6	−20·7	11 23	+11·4	−20·4
11 30	+11·7	−20·6	11 38	+11·5	−20·3
11 46	+11·8	−20·5	11 54	+11·6	−20·2
12 02	+11·9	−20·4	12 10	+11·7	−20·1
12 19	+12·0	−20·3	12 28	+11·8	−20·0
12 37	+12·1	−20·2	12 46	+11·9	−19·9
12 55	+12·2	−20·1	13 05	+12·0	−19·8
13 14	+12·3	−20·0	13 24	+12·1	−19·7
13 35	+12·4	−19·9	13 45	+12·2	−19·6
13 56	+12·5	−19·8	14 07	+12·3	−19·5
14 18	+12·6	−19·7	14 30	+12·4	−19·4
14 42	+12·7	−19·6	14 54	+12·5	−19·3
15 06	+12·8	−19·5	15 19	+12·6	−19·2
15 32	+12·9	−19·4	15 46	+12·7	−19·1
15 59	+13·0	−19·3	16 14	+12·8	−19·0
16 28	+13·1	−19·2	16 44	+12·9	−18·9
16 59	+13·2	−19·1	17 15	+13·0	−18·8
17 32	+13·3	−19·0	17 48	+13·1	−18·7
18 06	+13·4	−18·9	18 24	+13·2	−18·6
18 42	+13·5	−18·8	19 01	+13·3	−18·5
19 21	+13·6	−18·7	19 42	+13·4	−18·4
20 03	+13·7	−18·6	20 25	+13·5	−18·3
20 48	+13·8	−18·5	21 11	+13·6	−18·2
21 35	+13·9	−18·4	22 00	+13·7	−18·1
22 26	+14·0	−18·3	22 54	+13·8	−18·0
23 22	+14·1	−18·2	23 51	+13·9	−17·9
24 21	+14·2	−18·1	24 53	+14·0	−17·8
25 26	+14·3	−18·0	26 00	+14·1	−17·7
26 36	+14·4	−17·9	27 13	+14·2	−17·6
27 52	+14·5	−17·8	28 33	+14·3	−17·5
29 15	+14·6	−17·7	30 00	+14·4	−17·4
30 46	+14·7	−17·6	31 35	+14·5	−17·3
32 26	+14·8	−17·5	33 20	+14·6	−17·2
34 17	+14·9	−17·4	35 17	+14·7	−17·1
36 20	+15·0	−17·3	37 26	+14·8	−17·0
38 36	+15·1	−17·2	39 50	+14·9	−16·9
41 08	+15·2	−17·1	42 31	+15·0	−16·8
43 59	+15·3	−17·0	45 31	+15·1	−16·7
47 10	+15·4	−16·9	48 55	+15·2	−16·6
50 46	+15·5	−16·8	52 44	+15·3	−16·5
54 49	+15·6	−16·7	57 02	+15·4	−16·4
59 23	+15·7	−16·6	61 51	+15·5	−16·3
64 30	+15·8	−16·5	67 17	+15·6	−16·2
70 12	+15·9	−16·4	73 16	+15·7	−16·1
76 26	+16·0	−16·3	79 43	+15·8	−16·0
83 05	+16·1	−16·2	86 32	+15·9	−15·9
90 00			90 00		

STARS AND PLANETS

App. Alt.	Corrⁿ
9 56	−5·3
10 08	−5·2
10 20	−5·1
10 33	−5·0
10 46	−4·9
11 00	−4·8
11 14	−4·7
11 29	−4·6
11 45	−4·5
12 01	−4·4
12 18	−4·3
12 35	−4·2
12 54	−4·1
13 13	−4·0
13 33	−3·9
13 54	−3·8
14 16	−3·7
14 40	−3·6
15 04	−3·5
15 30	−3·4
15 57	−3·3
16 26	−3·2
16 56	−3·1
17 28	−3·0
18 02	−2·9
18 38	−2·8
19 17	−2·7
19 58	−2·6
20 42	−2·5
21 28	−2·4
22 19	−2·3
23 13	−2·2
24 11	−2·1
25 14	−2·0
26 22	−1·9
27 36	−1·8
28 56	−1·7
30 24	−1·6
32 00	−1·5
33 45	−1·4
35 40	−1·3
37 48	−1·2
40 08	−1·1
42 44	−1·0
45 36	−0·9
48 47	−0·8
52 18	−0·7
56 11	−0·6
60 28	−0·5
65 08	−0·4
70 11	−0·3
75 34	−0·2
81 13	−0·1
87 03	0·0
90 00	

App. Alt. Additional Corrⁿ

VENUS

Jan. 1-Jan. 17
46 +0·3

Jan. 18-Mar. 5
47 +0·2

Mar. 6-Dec. 31
42 +0·1

MARS

Jan. 1-Apr. 19
60 +0·1

Apr. 20-June 13
41 +0·2
75 +0·1

June 14-Oct. 12
34 +0·3
60 +0·2
80 +0·1

Oct. 13-Dec. 8
41 +0·2
75 +0·1

Dec. 9-Dec. 31
60 +0·1

DIP

Ht. of Eye (m)	Corrⁿ	Ht. of Eye (ft)	Corrⁿ
2·4	−2·8	8·0	
2·6	−2·9	8·6	
2·8	−3·0	9·2	
3·0	−3·1	9·8	
3·2	−3·2	10·5	
3·4	−3·3	11·2	
3·6	−3·4	11·9	
3·8	−3·5	12·6	
4·0	−3·6	13·3	
4·3	−3·7	14·1	
4·5	−3·8	14·9	
4·7	−3·9	15·7	
5·0	−4·0	16·5	
5·2	−4·1	17·4	
5·5	−4·2	18·3	
5·8	−4·3	19·1	
6·1	−4·4	20·1	
6·3	−4·5	21·0	
6·6	−4·6	22·0	
6·9	−4·7	22·9	
7·2	−4·8	23·9	
7·5	−4·9	24·9	
7·9	−5·0	26·0	
8·2	−5·1	27·1	
8·5	−5·2	28·1	
8·8	−5·3	29·2	
9·2	−5·4	30·4	
9·5	−5·5	31·5	
9·9	−5·6	32·7	
10·3	−5·7	33·9	
10·6	−5·8	35·1	
11·0	−5·9	36·3	
11·4	−6·0	37·6	
11·8	−6·1	38·9	
12·2	−6·2	40·1	
12·6	−6·3	41·5	
13·0	−6·4	42·8	
13·4	−6·5	44·2	
13·8	−6·6	45·5	
14·2	−6·7	46·9	
14·7	−6·8	48·4	
15·1	−6·9	49·8	
15·5	−7·0	51·3	
16·0	−7·1	52·8	
16·5	−7·2	54·3	
16·9	−7·3	55·8	
17·4	−7·4	57·4	
17·9	−7·5	58·9	
18·4	−7·6	60·5	
18·8	−7·7	62·1	
19·3	−7·8	63·8	
19·8	−7·9	65·4	
20·4	−8·0	67·1	
20·9	−8·1	68·8	
21·4		70·5	

Ht. of Eye — Corrⁿ (supplementary)

m ,
1·0 − 1·8
1·5 − 2·2
2·0 − 2·5
2·5 − 2·8
3·0 − 3·0

See table ←

m ,
20 − 7·9
22 − 8·3
24 − 8·6
26 − 9·0
28 − 9·3

30 − 9·6
32 −10·0
34 −10·3
36 −10·6
38 −10·8

40 −11·1
42 −11·4
44 −11·7
46 −11·9
48 −12·2

ft. ,
2 − 1·4
4 − 1·9
6 − 2·4
8 − 2·7
10 − 3·1

See table ←

ft. ,
70 − 8·1
75 − 8·4
80 − 8·7
85 − 8·9
90 − 9·2
95 − 9·5

100 − 9·7
105 − 9·9
110 −10·2
115 −10·4
120 −10·6
125 −10·8

130 −11·1
135 −11·3
140 −11·5
145 −11·7
150 −11·9
155 −12·1

App. Alt. = Apparent altitude = Sextant altitude corrected for index error and dip.

155. Altitude Correction Tables—Sun, Stars, and Planets (NA front cover)

ALTITUDE CORRECTION TABLES 0°–35°—MOON

App. Alt.	0°–4° Corrⁿ	5°–9° Corrⁿ	10°–14° Corrⁿ	15°–19° Corrⁿ	20°–24° Corrⁿ	25°–29° Corrⁿ	30°–34° Corrⁿ	App. Alt.
00	⁰33.8	⁵58.2	¹⁰62.1	¹⁵62.8	²⁰62.2	²⁵60.8	³⁰58.9	00
10	35.9	58.5	62.2	62.8	62.1	60.8	58.8	10
20	37.8	58.7	62.2	62.8	62.1	60.7	58.8	20
30	39.6	58.9	62.3	62.8	62.1	60.7	58.7	30
40	41.2	59.1	62.3	62.8	62.0	60.6	58.6	40
50	42.6	59.3	62.4	62.7	62.0	60.6	58.5	50
00	¹44.0	⁶59.5	¹¹62.4	¹⁶62.7	²¹62.0	²⁶60.5	³¹58.5	00
10	45.2	59.7	62.4	62.7	61.9	60.4	58.4	10
20	46.3	59.9	62.5	62.7	61.9	60.4	58.3	20
30	47.3	60.0	62.5	62.7	61.9	60.3	58.2	30
40	48.3	60.2	62.5	62.7	61.8	60.3	58.2	40
50	49.2	60.3	62.6	62.7	61.8	60.2	58.1	50
00	²50.0	⁷60.5	¹²62.6	¹⁷62.7	²²61.7	²⁷60.1	³²58.0	00
10	50.8	60.6	62.6	62.6	61.7	60.1	57.9	10
20	51.4	60.7	62.6	62.6	61.6	60.0	57.8	20
30	52.1	60.9	62.7	62.6	61.6	59.9	57.8	30
40	52.7	61.0	62.7	62.6	61.5	59.9	57.7	40
50	53.3	61.1	62.7	62.6	61.5	59.8	57.6	50
00	³53.8	⁸61.2	¹³62.7	¹⁸62.5	²³61.5	²⁸59.7	³³57.5	00
10	54.3	61.3	62.7	62.5	61.4	59.7	57.4	10
20	54.8	61.4	62.7	62.5	61.4	59.6	57.4	20
30	55.2	61.5	62.8	62.5	61.3	59.6	57.3	30
40	55.6	61.6	62.8	62.5	61.3	59.5	57.2	40
50	56.0	61.6	62.8	62.4	61.2	59.4	57.1	50
00	⁴56.4	⁹61.7	¹⁴62.8	¹⁹62.4	²⁴61.2	²⁹59.3	³⁴57.0	00
10	56.7	61.8	62.8	62.3	61.1	59.3	56.9	10
20	57.1	61.9	62.8	62.3	61.1	59.2	56.9	20
30	57.4	61.9	62.8	62.3	61.0	59.1	56.8	30
40	57.7	62.0	62.8	62.2	60.9	59.1	56.7	40
50	57.9	62.1	62.8	62.2	60.9	59.0	56.6	50

H.P.	L U	L U	L U	L U	L U	L U	L U	H.P.
54.0	0.3 0.9	0.3 0.9	0.4 1.0	0.5 1.1	0.6 1.2	0.7 1.3	0.9 1.5	54.0
54.3	0.7 1.1	0.7 1.2	0.7 1.2	0.8 1.3	0.9 1.4	1.1 1.5	1.2 1.7	54.3
54.6	1.1 1.4	1.1 1.4	1.1 1.4	1.2 1.5	1.3 1.6	1.4 1.7	1.5 1.8	54.6
54.9	1.4 1.6	1.5 1.6	1.5 1.6	1.6 1.7	1.6 1.8	1.8 1.9	1.9 2.0	54.9
55.2	1.8 1.8	1.8 1.8	1.9 1.9	1.9 1.9	2.0 2.0	2.1 2.1	2.2 2.2	55.2
55.5	2.2 2.0	2.2 2.0	2.3 2.1	2.3 2.1	2.4 2.2	2.4 2.3	2.5 2.4	55.5
55.8	2.6 2.2	2.6 2.2	2.6 2.3	2.7 2.3	2.7 2.4	2.8 2.4	2.9 2.5	55.8
56.1	3.0 2.4	3.0 2.5	3.0 2.5	3.0 2.5	3.1 2.6	3.1 2.6	3.2 2.7	56.1
56.4	3.4 2.7	3.4 2.7	3.4 2.7	3.4 2.7	3.4 2.8	3.5 2.8	3.5 2.9	56.4
56.7	3.7 2.9	3.7 2.9	3.8 2.9	3.8 2.9	3.8 3.0	3.8 3.0	3.9 3.0	56.7
57.0	4.1 3.1	4.1 3.1	4.1 3.1	4.1 3.1	4.2 3.1	4.2 3.2	4.2 3.2	57.0
57.3	4.5 3.3	4.5 3.3	4.5 3.3	4.5 3.3	4.5 3.3	4.5 3.4	4.6 3.4	57.3
57.6	4.9 3.5	4.9 3.5	4.9 3.5	4.9 3.5	4.9 3.5	4.9 3.5	4.9 3.6	57.6
57.9	5.3 3.8	5.3 3.8	5.2 3.8	5.2 3.7	5.2 3.7	5.2 3.7	5.2 3.7	57.9
58.2	5.6 4.0	5.6 4.0	5.6 4.0	5.6 4.0	5.6 3.9	5.6 3.9	5.6 3.9	58.2
58.5	6.0 4.2	6.0 4.2	6.0 4.2	6.0 4.2	6.0 4.1	5.9 4.1	5.9 4.1	58.5
58.8	6.4 4.4	6.4 4.4	6.4 4.4	6.3 4.4	6.3 4.3	6.3 4.3	6.2 4.2	58.8
59.1	6.8 4.6	6.8 4.6	6.7 4.6	6.7 4.6	6.7 4.5	6.6 4.5	6.6 4.4	59.1
59.4	7.2 4.8	7.1 4.8	7.1 4.8	7.1 4.8	7.0 4.7	7.0 4.7	6.9 4.6	59.4
59.7	7.5 5.1	7.5 5.0	7.5 5.0	7.5 5.0	7.4 4.9	7.3 4.8	7.2 4.7	59.7
60.0	7.9 5.3	7.9 5.3	7.9 5.2	7.8 5.2	7.8 5.1	7.7 5.0	7.6 4.9	60.0
60.3	8.3 5.5	8.3 5.5	8.2 5.4	8.2 5.4	8.1 5.3	8.0 5.2	7.9 5.1	60.3
60.6	8.7 5.7	8.7 5.7	8.6 5.7	8.6 5.5	8.5 5.5	8.4 5.4	8.3 5.2	60.6
60.9	9.1 5.9	9.0 5.9	9.0 5.9	8.9 5.8	8.8 5.7	8.7 5.6	8.6 5.4	60.9
61.2	9.5 6.2	9.4 6.1	9.4 6.1	9.3 6.0	9.2 5.9	9.1 5.8	8.9 5.6	61.2
61.5	9.8 6.4	9.8 6.3	9.7 6.3	9.7 6.2	9.5 6.1	9.4 5.9	9.2 5.8	61.5

DIP

Ht. of Eye m	Corrⁿ	Ht. of Eye ft.	Ht. of Eye m	Corrⁿ	Ht. of Eye ft.
2.4	−2.8	8.0	9.5	−5.5	31.5
2.6	−2.9	8.6	9.9	−5.6	32.7
2.8	−3.0	9.2	10.3	−5.7	33.9
3.0	−3.1	9.8	10.6	−5.8	35.1
3.2	−3.2	10.5	11.0	−5.9	36.3
3.4	−3.3	11.2	11.4	−6.0	37.6
3.6	−3.4	11.9	11.8	−6.1	38.9
3.8	−3.5	12.6	12.2	−6.2	40.1
4.0	−3.6	13.3	12.6	−6.3	41.5
4.3	−3.7	14.1	13.0	−6.4	42.8
4.5	−3.8	14.9	13.4	−6.5	44.2
4.7	−3.9	15.7	13.8	−6.6	45.5
5.0	−4.0	16.5	14.2	−6.7	46.9
5.2	−4.1	17.4	14.7	−6.8	48.4
5.5	−4.2	18.3	15.1	−6.9	49.8
5.8	−4.3	19.1	15.5	−7.0	51.3
6.1	−4.4	20.1	16.0	−7.1	52.8
6.3	−4.5	21.0	16.5	−7.2	54.3
6.6	−4.6	22.0	16.9	−7.3	55.8
6.9	−4.7	22.9	17.4	−7.4	57.4
7.2	−4.8	23.9	17.9	−7.5	58.9
7.5	−4.9	24.9	18.4	−7.6	60.5
7.9	−5.0	26.0	18.8	−7.7	62.1
8.2	−5.1	27.1	19.3	−7.8	63.8
8.5	−5.2	28.1	19.8	−7.9	65.4
8.8	−5.3	29.2	20.4	−8.0	67.1
9.2	−5.4	30.4	20.9	−8.1	68.8
9.5		31.5	21.4		70.5

MOON CORRECTION TABLE

The correction is in two parts; the first correction is taken from the upper part of the table with argument apparent altitude, and the second from the lower part, with argument H.P., in the same column as that from which the first correction was taken. Separate corrections are given in the lower part for lower (L) and upper (U) limbs. All corrections are to be **added** to apparent altitude, *but* 30′ *is to be subtracted from the altitude of the upper limb.*

For corrections for pressure and temperature see page A4.

For bubble sextant observations ignore dip, take the mean of upper and lower limb corrections and subtract 15′ from the altitude.

App. Alt. = Apparent altitude = Sextant altitude corrected for index error and dip.

156. Altitude Correction Tables—Moon (NA back cover)

MAY 1, 2, 3 (SAT., SUN., MON.)

G.M.T. d h	ARIES G.H.A.	VENUS −3.4 G.H.A.	VENUS Dec.	MARS −0.1 G.H.A.	MARS Dec.	JUPITER −2.0 G.H.A.	JUPITER Dec.	SATURN +0.4 G.H.A.	SATURN Dec.	STARS Name	STARS S.H.A.	STARS Dec.
1 00	218 16.3	209 29.9 N	1 59.0	277 21.1 S21 49.9		335 46.7 S19 59.9		166 20.6 N16 52.8		Acamar	315 42.6	S 40 25.
01	233 18.7	224 29.6	2 00.2	292 22.1	49.7	350 49.5	59.8	181 22.8	52.9	Achernar	335 50.6	S 57 22.
02	248 21.2	239 29.2	01.3	307 23.2	49.6	5 52.2	59.8	196 24.9	53.0	Acrux	173 44.6	S 62 56.
03	263 23.7	254 28.9 ••	02.5	322 24.2 ••	49.4	20 55.0 ••	59.7	211 27.1 ••	53.1	Adhara	255 37.6	S 28 56.
04	278 26.1	269 28.6	03.6	337 25.3	49.2	35 57.7	59.7	226 29.2	53.1	Aldebaran	291 26.1	N 16 27.
05	293 28.6	284 28.3	04.8	352 26.3	49.0	51 00.4	59.6	241 31.4	53.2			
06	308 31.0	299 28.0 N	2 05.9	7 27.4 S21 48.8		66 03.2 S19 59.6		256 33.5 N16 53.3		Alioth	166 47.6	N 56 06.
S 07	323 33.5	314 27.6	07.1	22 28.5	48.7	81 05.9	59.6	271 35.6	53.4	Alkaid	153 23.1	N 49 27.
A 08	338 36.0	329 27.3	08.2	37 29.5	48.5	96 08.7	59.5	286 37.8	53.5	Al Na'ir	28 23.3	S 47 05.
T 09	353 38.4	344 27.0 ••	09.4	52 30.6 ••	48.3	111 11.4 ••	59.5	301 39.9 ••	53.6	Alnilam	276 18.7	S 1 13.
U 10	8 40.9	359 26.7	10.5	67 31.6	48.1	126 14.1	59.4	316 42.1	53.6	Alphard	218 27.2	S 8 32.
11	23 43.4	14 26.4	11.7	82 32.7	47.9	141 16.9	59.4	331 44.2	53.7			
R 12	38 45.8	29 26.1 N	2 12.9	97 33.8 S21 47.8		156 19.6 S19 59.3		346 46.4 N16 53.8		Alphecca	126 37.4	N 26 48.
D 13	53 48.3	44 25.7	14.0	112 34.8	47.6	171 22.4	59.3	1 48.5	53.9	Alpheratz	358 16.7	N 28 55.
A 14	68 50.8	59 25.4	15.2	127 35.9	47.4	186 25.1	59.2	16 50.7	54.0	Altair	62 39.0	N 8 47.
Y 15	83 53.2	74 25.1 ••	16.3	142 36.9 ••	47.2	201 27.9 ••	59.2	31 52.8 ••	54.0	Ankaa	353 47.0	S 42 27.
16	98 55.7	89 24.8	17.5	157 38.0	47.1	216 30.6	59.1	46 54.9	54.1	Antares	113 04.8	S 26 22.
17	113 58.1	104 24.5	18.6	172 39.1	46.9	231 33.3	59.1	61 57.1	54.2			
18	129 00.6	119 24.1 N	2 19.8	187 40.1 S21 46.7		246 36.1 S19 59.0		76 59.2 N16 54.3		Arcturus	146 24.2	N 19 19.
19	144 03.1	134 23.8	20.9	202 41.2	46.5	261 38.8	59.0	92 01.4	54.4	Atria	108 34.8	S 68 58.
20	159 05.5	149 23.5	22.1	217 42.2	46.3	276 41.6	58.9	107 03.5	54.5	Avior	234 31.2	S 59 25.
21	174 08.0	164 23.2 ••	23.2	232 43.3 ••	46.2	291 44.3 ••	58.9	122 05.7 ••	54.5	Bellatrix	279 06.2	N 6 19.
22	189 10.5	179 22.9	24.4	247 44.4	46.0	306 47.1	58.8	137 07.8	54.6	Betelgeuse	271 35.8	N 7 24.
23	204 12.9	194 22.5	25.6	262 45.4	45.8	321 49.8	58.8	152 09.9	54.7			
2 00	219 15.4	209 22.2 N	2 26.7	277 46.5 S21 45.6		336 52.5 S19 58.7		167 12.1 N16 54.8		Canopus	264 10.5	S 52 40.9
01	234 17.9	224 21.9	27.9	292 47.6	45.4	351 55.3	58.7	182 14.2	54.9	Capella	281 21.7	N 45 58.
02	249 20.3	239 21.6	29.0	307 48.6	45.3	6 58.0	58.6	197 16.4	54.9	Deneb	49 53.1	N 45 10.3
03	264 22.8	254 21.3 ••	30.2	322 49.7 ••	45.1	22 00.8 ••	58.6	212 18.5 ••	55.0	Denebola	183 05.6	N 14 43.8
04	279 25.3	269 21.0	31.3	337 50.7	44.9	37 03.5	58.5	227 20.7	55.1	Diphda	349 27.8	S 18 08.6
05	294 27.7	284 20.6	32.5	352 51.8	44.7	52 06.3	58.5	242 22.8	55.2			
06	309 30.2	299 20.3 N	2 33.6	7 52.9 S21 44.5		67 09.0 S19 58.4		257 24.9 N16 55.3		Dubhe	194 29.7	N 61 54.5
07	324 32.6	314 20.0	34.8	22 53.9	44.4	82 11.8	58.4	272 27.1	55.3	Elnath	278 53.0	N 28 35.2
S 08	339 35.1	329 19.7	35.9	37 55.0	44.2	97 14.5	58.3	287 29.2	55.4	Eltanin	91 00.5	N 51 29.1
U 09	354 37.6	344 19.4 ••	37.1	52 56.1 ••	44.0	112 17.3 ••	58.3	302 31.4 ••	55.5	Enif	34 18.3	N 9 44.4
N 10	9 40.0	359 19.0	38.3	67 57.1	43.8	127 20.0	58.2	317 33.5	55.6	Fomalhaut	15 58.9	S 29 46.4
11	24 42.5	14 18.7	39.4	82 58.2	43.6	142 22.7	58.2	332 35.7	55.7			
D 12	39 45.0	29 18.4 N	2 40.6	97 59.3 S21 43.5		157 25.5 S19 58.1		347 37.8 N16 55.8		Gacrux	172 36.1	S 56 57.5
A 13	54 47.4	44 18.1	41.7	113 00.3	43.3	172 28.2	58.1	2 39.9	55.8	Gienah	176 24.7	S 17 23.2
Y 14	69 49.9	59 17.8	42.9	128 01.4	43.1	187 31.0	58.0	17 42.1	55.9	Hadar	149 32.6	S 60 14.
15	84 52.4	74 17.4 ••	44.0	143 02.5 ••	42.9	202 33.7 ••	58.0	32 44.2 ••	56.0	Hamal	328 36.9	N 23 19.7
16	99 54.8	89 17.1	45.2	158 03.6	42.7	217 36.5	57.9	47 46.4	56.1	Kaus Aust.	84 25.5	S 34 24.0
17	114 57.3	104 16.8	46.3	173 04.6	42.6	232 39.2	57.9	62 48.5	56.2			
18	129 59.8	119 16.5 N	2 47.5	188 05.7 S21 42.4		247 42.0 S19 57.8		77 50.6 N16 56.2		Kochab	137 17.0	N 74 16.2
19	145 02.2	134 16.1	48.6	203 06.8	42.2	262 44.7	57.8	92 52.8	56.3	Markab	14 10.1	N 15 02.9
20	160 04.7	149 15.8	49.8	218 07.8	42.0	277 47.5	57.7	107 54.9	56.4	Menkar	314 48.5	N 3 58.7
21	175 07.1	164 15.5 ••	50.9	233 08.9 ••	41.8	292 50.2 ••	57.7	122 57.1 ••	56.5	Menkent	148 44.7	S 36 14.0
22	190 09.6	179 15.2	52.1	248 10.0	41.6	307 53.0	57.6	137 59.2	56.6	Miaplacidus	221 46.7	S 69 36.2
23	205 12.1	194 14.9	53.3	263 11.0	41.5	322 55.7	57.6	153 01.4	56.7			
3 00	220 14.5	209 14.5 N	2 54.4	278 12.1 S21 41.3		337 58.5 S19 57.5		168 03.5 N16 56.7		Mirfak	309 26.4	N 49 45.7
01	235 17.0	224 14.2	55.6	293 13.2	41.1	353 01.2	57.5	183 05.6	56.8	Nunki	76 37.3	S 26 20.1
02	250 19.5	239 13.9	56.7	308 14.3	40.9	8 04.0	57.4	198 07.8	56.9	Peacock	54 08.7	S 56 49.6
03	265 21.9	254 13.6 ••	58.0	323 15.3 ••	40.7	23 06.7 ••	57.4	213 09.9 ••	57.0	Pollux	244 06.5	N 28 05.9
04	280 24.4	269 13.3	2 59.0	338 16.4	40.6	38 09.5	57.3	228 12.1	57.1	Procyon	245 32.9	N 5 18.0
05	295 26.9	284 12.9	3 00.2	353 17.5	40.4	53 12.2	57.3	243 14.2	57.1			
06	310 29.3	299 12.6 N	3 01.3	8 18.6 S21 40.2		68 15.0 S19 57.2		258 16.4 N16 57.2		Rasalhague	96 35.6	N 12 34.5
07	325 31.8	314 12.3	02.5	23 19.6	40.0	83 17.7	57.2	273 18.5	57.3	Regulus	208 17.0	N 12 06.4
08	340 34.2	329 12.0	03.6	38 20.7	39.8	98 20.5	57.1	288 20.6	57.4	Rigel	281 42.7	S 8 14.0
M 09	355 36.7	344 11.6 ••	04.8	53 21.8 ••	39.7	113 23.2 ••	57.1	303 22.8 ••	57.5	Rigil Kent.	140 34.6	S 60 43.2
O 10	10 39.2	359 11.3	05.9	68 22.9	39.5	128 26.0	57.0	318 24.9	57.5	Sabik	102 48.6	S 15 41.6
N 11	25 41.6	14 11.0	07.1	83 23.9	39.3	143 28.7	57.0	333 27.1	57.6			
D 12	40 44.1	29 10.7 N	3 08.2	98 25.0 S21 39.1		158 31.5 S19 56.9		348 29.2 N16 57.7		Schedar	350 17.5	N 56 22.7
A 13	55 46.6	44 10.4	09.4	113 26.1	38.9	173 34.2	56.9	3 31.3	57.8	Shaula	97 04.6	S 37 05.2
Y 14	70 49.0	59 10.0	10.6	128 27.2	38.7	188 37.0	56.8	18 33.5	57.9	Sirius	259 01.8	S 16 40.6
15	85 51.5	74 09.7 ••	11.7	143 28.2 ••	38.6	203 39.7 ••	56.8	33 35.6 ••	58.0	Spica	159 04.4	S 11 01.0
16	100 54.0	89 09.4	12.9	158 29.3	38.4	218 42.5	56.7	48 37.8	58.0	Suhail	223 15.8	S 43 19.2
17	115 56.4	104 09.1	14.0	173 30.4	38.2	233 45.2	56.7	63 39.9	58.1			
18	130 58.9	119 08.7 N	3 15.2	188 31.5 S21 38.0		248 48.0 S19 56.6		78 42.1 N16 58.2		Vega	81 00.2	N 38 45.0
19	146 01.4	134 08.4	16.3	203 32.6	37.8	263 50.7	56.6	93 44.2	58.3	Zuben'ubi	137 40.2	S 15 55.6
20	161 03.8	149 08.1	17.5	218 33.6	37.8	278 53.5	56.5	108 46.3	58.4		S.H.A.	Mer. Pass.
21	176 06.3	164 07.8 ••	18.6	233 34.7 ••	37.5	293 56.2 ••	56.5	123 48.5 ••	58.4		° ′	h m
22	191 08.7	179 07.5	19.8	248 35.8	37.3	308 59.0	56.4	138 50.6	58.5	Venus	350 06.8	10 03
23	206 11.2	194 07.1	20.9	263 36.9	37.1	324 01.7	56.4	153 52.8	58.6	Mars	58 31.1	5 29
Mer. Pass. 9 21.4	v −0.3 d 1.2		v 1.1 d 0.2		v 2.7 d 0.0		v 2.1 d 0.1			Jupiter	117 37.2	1 32
										Saturn	307 56.7	12 49

157. Daily Almanac Page—Stars and Planets (NA white pages)

MAY 1, 2, 3 (SAT., SUN., MON.)

G.M.T.	SUN G.H.A.	Dec.	MOON G.H.A.	v	Dec.	d	H.P.
d h	° '	° '	° '	'	° '	'	'
1 00	180 41.8	N14 48.8	100 53.8	10.4	N23 13.8	8.2	56.0
01	195 41.9	49.6	115 23.2	10.5	23 05.6	8.4	55.9
02	210 41.9	50.3	129 52.7	10.6	22 57.2	8.5	55.9
03	225 42.0 ··	51.1	144 22.3	10.8	22 48.7	8.6	55.9
04	240 42.1	51.8	158 52.1	10.8	22 40.1	8.7	55.8
05	255 42.2	52.6	173 21.9	11.0	22 31.4	8.8	55.8
06	270 42.3	N14 53.4	187 51.9	11.0	N22 22.6	8.8	55.8
07	285 42.3	54.1	202 21.9	11.2	22 13.8	9.0	55.8
08	300 42.4	54.9	216 52.1	11.2	22 04.8	9.1	55.7
09	315 42.5 ··	55.7	231 22.3	11.4	21 55.7	9.2	55.7
10	330 42.6	56.4	245 52.7	11.4	21 46.5	9.2	55.7
11	345 42.6	57.2	260 23.1	11.6	21 37.3	9.4	55.6
12	0 42.7	N14 57.9	274 53.7	11.7	N21 27.9	9.5	55.6
13	15 42.8	58.7	289 24.4	11.7	21 18.4	9.5	55.6
14	30 42.9	14 59.5	303 55.1	11.9	21 08.9	9.6	55.5
15	45 43.0	15 00.2	318 26.0	12.0	20 59.3	9.7	55.5
16	60 43.0·	01.0	332 57.0	12.1	20 49.6	9.8	55.5
17	75 43.1	01.7	347 28.1	12.1	20 39.8	9.9	55.5
18	90 43.2	N15 02.5	1 59.2	12.3	N20 29.9	10.0	55.4
19	105 43.3	03.3	16 30.5	12.4	20 19.9	10.0	55.4
20	120 43.3	04.0	31 01.9	12.4	20 09.9	10.1	55.4
21	135 43.4 ··	04.8	45 33.3	12.6	19 59.8	10.3	55.4
22	150 43.5	05.5	60 04.9	12.7	19 49.5	10.2	55.3
23	165 43.6	06.3	74 36.6	12.7	19 39.3	10.4	55.3
2 00	180 43.7	N15 07.0	89 08.3	12.9	N19 28.9	10.4	55.3
01	195 43.7	07.8	103 40.2	12.9	19 18.5	10.6	55.3
02	210 43.8	08.5	118 12.1	13.0	19 07.9	10.6	55.2
03	225 43.9 ··	09.3	132 44.1	13.2	18 57.3	10.6	55.2
04	240 44.0	10.0	147 16.3	13.2	18 46.7	10.8	55.2
05	255 44.0	10.8	161 48.5	13.3	18 35.9	10.8	55.2
06	270 44.1	N15 11.6	176 20.8	13.4	N18 25.1	10.8	55.1
07	285 44.2	12.3	190 53.2	13.5	18 14.3	11.0	55.1
08	300 44.3	13.1	205 25.7	13.5	18 03.3	11.0	55.1
09	315 44.3 ··	13.8	219 58.2	13.7	17 52.3	11.1	55.1
10	330 44.4	14.6	234 30.9	13.7	17 41.2	11.1	55.0
11	345 44.5	15.3	249 03.6	13.9	17 30.1	11.2	55.0
12	0 44.5	N15 16.1	263 36.5	13.9	N17 18.9	11.3	55.0
13	15 44.6	16.8	278 09.4	14.0	17 07.6	11.3	55.0
14	30 44.7	17.6	292 42.4	14.1	16 56.3	11.4	54.9
15	45 44.8 ··	18.3	307 15.5	14.1	16 44.9	11.5	54.9
16	60 44.8	19.1	321 48.6	14.3	16 33.4	11.5	54.9
17	75 44.9	19.8	336 21.9	14.3	16 21.9	11.5	54.9
18	90 45.0	N15 20.6	350 55.2	14.4	N16 10.4	11.7	54.9
19	105 45.1	21.3	5 28.6	14.5	15 58.7	11.7	54.8
20	120 45.1	22.0	20 02.1	14.5	15 47.0	11.7	54.8
21	135 45.2 ··	22.8	34 35.6	14.7	15 35.3	11.8	54.8
22	150 45.3	23.5	49 09.3	14.7	15 23.5	11.8	54.8
23	165 45.3	24.3	63 43.0	14.8	15 11.7	11.9	54.8
3 00	180 45.4	N15 25.0	78 16.8	14.8	N14 59.8	12.0	54.7
01	195 45.5	25.8	92 50.6	14.9	14 47.8	12.0	54.7
02	210 45.5	26.5	107 24.5	15.0·	14 35.8	12.0	54.7
03	225 45.6 ··	27.3	121 58.5	15.1	14 23.8	12.1	54.7
04	240 45.7	28.0	136 32.6	15.1	14 11.7	12.2	54.7
05	255 45.8	28.7	151 06.7	15.2	13 59.5	12.2	54.7
06	270 45.8	N15 29.5	165 40.9	15.3	N13 47.3	12.2·	54.6
07	285 45.9	30.2	180 15.2	15.3	13 35.1	12.3	54.6
08	300 46.0	31.0	194 49.5	15.4	13 22.8	12.4	54.6
09	315 46.0 ··	31.7	209 23.9	15.5	13 10.4	12.3	54.6
10	330 46.1	32.4	223 58.4	15.5	12 58.1	12.5	54.6
11	345 46.2	33.2	238 32.9	15.5	12 45.6	12.4	54.6
12	0 46.2	N15 33.9	253 07.4	15.7	N12 33.2	12.5	54.5
13	15 46.3	34.7	267 42.1	15.7	12 20.7	12.6	54.5
14	30 46.4	35.4	282 16.8	15.7	12 08.1	12.5	54.5
15	45 46.4 ··	36.1	296 51.5	15.8	11 55.6	12.7	54.5
16	60 46.5	36.9	311 26.3	15.9	11 42.9	12.6	54.5
17	75 46.6	37.6	326 01.2	15.9	11 30.3	12.7	54.5
18	90 46.6	N15 38.4	340 36.1	16.0	N11 17.6	12.8	54.4
19	105 46.7	39.1	355 11.1	16.0	11 04.8	12.7	54.4
20	120 46.8	39.8	9 46.1	16.1	10 52.1	12.8	54.4
21	135 46.8 ··	40.6	24 21.2	16.1	10 39.3	12.9	54.4
22	150 46.9	41.3	38 56.3	16.2	10 26.4	12.8	54.4
23	165 47.0	42.0	53 31.5	16.2	10 13.6	12.9	54.4
S.D. 15.9	d 0.7		S.D. 15.2		15.0		14.9

Lat.	Twilight Naut.	Civil	Sun- rise	Moonrise 1	2	3	4
°	h m	h m	h m	h m	h m	h m	h m
N 72	////	////	01 50	▯	▯	10 06	12 15
N 70	////	////	02 29	▯	08 08	10 31	12 27
68	////	01 04	02 56	▯	08 49	10 50	12 36
66	////	01 54	03 17	07 08	09 17	11 05	12 43
64	////	02 24	03 33	07 48	09 38	11 17	12 49
62	00 56	02 46	03 46	08 16	09 55	11 27	12 55
60	01 41	03 04	03 57	08 38	10 09	11 36	12 59
N 58	02 09	03 19	04 07	08 55	10 21	11 44	13 03
56	02 30	03 31	04 16	09 09	10 32	11 51	13 07
54	02 47	03 42	04 23	09 22	10 41	11 57	13 10
52	03 01	03 51	04 30	09 33	10 49	12 02	13 13
50	03 13	03 59	04 36	09 43	10 56	12 07	13 16
45	03 37	04 17	04 49	10 03	11 11	12 17	13 21
N 40	03 55	04 31	05 00	10 20	11 24	12 26	13 26
35	04 09	04 42	05 09	10 33	11 35	12 33	13 30
30	04 21	04 52	05 17	10 46	11 44	12 40	13 34
20	04 41	05 08	05 31	11 06	12 00	12 51	13 40
N 10	04 55	05 21	05 43	11 24	12 14	13 01	13 45
0	05 07	05 32	05 54	11 40	12 27	13 10	13 50
S 10	05 18	05 43	06 04	11 57	12 40	13 19	13 56
20	05 27	05 53	06 16	12 14	12 53	13 29	14 01
30	05 36	06 04	06 29	12 34	13 09	13 39	14 07
35	05 40	06 10	06 37	12 46	13 18	13 46	14 11
40	05 45	06 17	06 45	12 59	13 28	13 53	14 15
45	05 49	06 24	06 55	13 15	13 40	14 01	14 19
S 50	05 54	06 33	07 07	13 35	13 55	14 11	14 25
52	05 56	06 37	07 12	13 44	14 02	14 16	14 27
54	05 59	06 41	07 19	13 54	14 09	14 21	14 30
56	06 01	06 45	07 25	14 05	14 17	14 26	14 33
58	06 03	06 50	07 33	14 19	14 27	14 32	14 36
S 60	06 06	06 56	07 41	14 34	14 38	14 39	14 40

Lat.	Sun- set	Twilight Civil	Naut.	Moonset 1	2	3	4
°	h m	h m	h m	h m	h m	h m	h m
N 72	22 11	////	////	▯	▯	04 16	03 32
N 70	21 29	////	////	▯	04 41	03 49	03 19
68	21 01	23 01	////	▯	03 58	03 28	03 08
66	20 40	22 06	////	04 00	03 29	03 12	02 58
64	20 24	21 34	////	03 18	03 07	02 58	02 51
62	20 10	21 11	23 08	02 50	02 49	02 47	02 44
60	19 59	20 53	22 18	02 28	02 34	02 37	02 38
N 58	19 48	20 38	21 49	02 10	02 21	02 28	02 33
56	19 40	20 25	21 27	01 55	02 10	02 21	02 28
54	19 32	20 14	21 10	01 42	02 00	02 14	02 24
52	19 25	20 04	20 55	01 30	01 52	02 08	02 20
50	19 19	19 56	20 43	01 20	01 44	02 02	02 17
45	19 06	19 38	20 19	00 59	01 27	01 50	02 09
N 40	18 55	19 24	20 00	00 41	01 13	01 40	02 03
35	18 46	19 13	19 45	00 26	01 02	01 31	01 57
30	18 37	19 03	19 33	00 14	00 51	01 24	01 53
20	18 24	18 47	19 14	24 33	00 33	01 11	01 44
N 10	18 12	18 33	18 59	24 18	00 18	00 59	01 37
0	18 00	18 22	18 47	24 03	00 03	00 48	01 30
S 10	17 50	18 11	18 36	23 48	24 37	00 37	01 23
20	17 38	18 01	18 27	23 32	24 25	00 25	01 15
30	17 25	17 49	18 18	23 14	24 11	00 11	01 06
35	17 17	17 43	18 13	23 03	24 03	00 03	01 00
40	17 09	17 37	18 09	22 51	23 54	24 55	00 55
45	16 58	17 29	18 04	22 36	23 43	24 48	00 48
S 50	16 47	17 21	17 59	22 18	23 30	24 40	00 40
52	16 41	17 17	17 57	22 09	23 24	24 36	00 36
54	16 35	17 13	17 55	22 00	23 17	24 32	00 32
56	16 28	17 08	17 52	21 49	23 10	24 28	00 28
58	16 20	17 03	17 50	21 36	23 01	24 22	00 22
S 60	16 12	16 57	17 47	21 22	22 51	24 16	00 16

Day	SUN Eqn. of Time 00h	12h	Mer. Pass.	MOON Mer. Pass. Upper	Lower	Age	Phase
	m s	m s	h m	h m	h m		
1	02 47	02 51	11 57	17 52	05 27	06	◗
2	02 54	02 58	11 57	18 37	06 15	07	
3	03 01	03 05	11 57	19 20	06 59	08	

158. Daily Almanac Page—Sun and Moon (NA white pages)

OCT. 31, NOV. 1, 2 (SUN., MON., TUES.)

G.M.T.	ARIES G.H.A.	VENUS -3·3 G.H.A.	Dec.	MARS -0·7 G.H.A.	Dec.	JUPITER -1·4 G.H.A.	Dec.	SATURN -0·1 G.H.A.	Dec.	STARS Name	S.H.A.	Dec.
d h	° ′	° ′	° ′	° ′	° ′	° ′	° ′	° ′	° ′		° ′	° ′
31 00	38 38·7	167 17·2	S18 43·8	68 54·4	S14 52·6	151 41·2	S 21 15·3	335 09·1	N19 01·2	Acamar	315 41·5	S 40 24·
01	53 41·2	182 16·5	44·7	83 55·7	52·0	166 43·1	15·4	350 11·7	01·2	Achernar	335 49·1	S 57 22·
02	68 43·6	197 15·8	45·6	98 57·0	51·5	181 45·0	15·4	5 14·3	01·1	Acrux	173 45·3	S 62 56
03	83 46·1	212 15·1	·· 46·4	113 58·3	·· 50·9	196 46·9	·· 15·5	20 17·0	·· 01·1	Adhara	255 36·9	S 28 55·
04	98 48·5	227 14·4	47·3	128 59·6	50·4	211 48·8	15·6	35 19·6	01·1	Aldebaran	291 25·0	N 16 27·
05	113 51·0	242 13·8	48·2	144 00·9	49·8	226 50·7	15·7	50 22·2	01·0			
06	128 53·5	257 13·1	S18 49·0	159 02·2	S14 49·3	241 52·6	S 21 15·8	·65 24·9	N19 01·0	Alioth	166 48·3	N 56 06
07	143 55·9	272 12·4	49·9	174 03·5	48·7	256 54·6	15·9	80 27·5	01·0	Alkaid	153 23·8	N 49 27
08	158 58·4	287 11·7	50·8	189 04·8	48·2	271 56·5	16·0	95 30·2	00·9	Al Na'ir	28 22·5	S 47 06
S 09	174 00·9	302 11·0	·· 51·7	204 06·1	·· 47·6	286 58·4	·· 16·0	110 32·8	·· 00·9	Alnilam	276 17·8	S 1 12·
U 10	189 03·3	317 10·3	52·5	219 07·4	47·1	302 00·3	16·1	125 35·4	00·9	Alphard	218 26·9	S 8 32·
N 11	204 05·8	332 09·6	53·4	234 08·7	46·5	317 02·2 ·	16·2	140 38·1	00·8			
D 12	·219 08·3	347 08·9	S18 54·3	249 10·0	S14 46·0	332 04·1	S 21 16·3	155 40·7	N19 00·8	Alphecca	126 37·8	N 26 48
A 13	234 10·7	2 08·2	55·1	264 11·3	45·4	347 06·1	16·4	170 43·4	00·8	Alpheratz	358 15·7	N 28 56·
Y 14	249 13·2	17 07·5	56·0	279 12·6	44·9	2 08·0	16·5	185 46·0	00·7	Altair	62 38·8	N 8 47·
15	264 15·7	32 06·8	·· 56·8	294 13·9	·· 44·3	17 09·9	·· 16·6	200 48·6	·· 00·7	Ankaa	353 46·0	S 42 27·
16	279 18·1	47 06·1	57·7	309 15·2	43·8	32 11·8	16·6	215 51·3	00·7	Antares	113 05·0	S 26 22·
17	294 20·6	62 05·4	58·6	324 16·5	43·2	47 13·7	16·7	230 53·9	00·6			
18	309 23·0	77 04·6	S18 59·4	339 17·8	S14 42·7	62 15·6	S 21 16·8	245 56·5	N19 00·6	Arcturus	146 24·5	N 19 19·
19	324 25·5	92 03·9	19 00·3	354 19·1	42·1	77 17·5	16·9	260 59·2	00·6	Atria	108 35·5	S 68 58·
20	339 28·0	107 03·2	01·1	9 20·4	41·6	92 19·5	17·0	276 01·8	00·5	Avior	234 30·9	S 59 24·
21	354 30·4	122 02·5	·· 02·0	24 21·7	·· 41·0	107 21·4	·· 17·1	291 04·5	·· 00·5	Bellatrix	279 05·3	N 6 19·
22	9 32·9	137 01·8	02·9	39 23·0	40·5	122 23·3	17·2	306 07·1	00·5	Betelgeuse	271 34·9	N 7 24·
23	24 35·4	152 01·1	03·7	54 24·3	39·9	137 25·2	17·2	321 09·8	00·4			
1 00	39 37·8	167 00·4	S19 04·6	69 25·6	S14 39·4	152 27·1	S 21 17·3	336 12·4	N19 00·4	Canopus	264 09·7	S 52 40·
01	54 40·3	.181·59·7	05·4	84 26·9	38·8	167 29·0	17·4	351 15·0	00·4	Capella	281 20·3	N 45 58·
02	69 42·8	196 59·0	06·3	99 28·2	38·3	182 30·9	17·5	6 17·7	00·4	Deneb	49 52·9	N 45 11·
03	84 45·2	211 58·3	·· 07·1	114 29·5	·· 37·7	197 32·9	·· 17·6	21 20·3	·· .00·3	Denebola	183 05·7	N 14 43·
04	99 47·7	226 57·6	08·0	129 30·8	37·2	212 34·8	17·7	36 23·0	00·3	Diphda	349 26·9	S 18 08·
05	114 50·1	241 56·9	08·8	144 32·1	36·6	227 36·7	17·7	51 25·6	00·3			
06	·129 52·6	256 56·2	S19 09·7	159 33·4	S14 36·1	242 38·6	S 21 17·8	66 28·2	N19 00·2	Dubhe	194 29·9	N 61 54
07	·144 55·1	271 55·5	10·5	174 34·7	35·5	257 40·5	17·9	81 30·9	00·2	Elnath	278 51·9	N 28 35·
08	159 57·5	286 54·7	11·4	189 36·0	35·0	272 42·4	18·0	96 33·5	00·2	Eltanin	91 01·0	N 51 29·
M 09	175 00·0	301 54·0	·· 12·2	204 37·3	·· 34·4	287 44·3	·· 18·1	111 36·2	·· 00·1	Enif	34 17·7	N 9 44·
O 10	190 02·5	316 53·3	13·1	219 38·6	33·9	302 46·2	18·2	126 38·8	00·1	Fomalhaut	15 58·1	S 29 46·
N 11	205 04·9	331 52·6	13·9	234 39·9	33·3	317 48·2	18·3	141 41·4	00·1			
D. 12	220 07·4	346 51·9	·S19 14·8	249 41·2	S14 32·8	332 50·1	S 21 18·3	156 44·1	N19 00·0	Gacrux	172 36·6	S 56 57·
A 13	235 09·9	1 51·2	15·6	264 42·5	32·2	.347 52·0	18·4	171 46·7	00·0	Gienah	176 24·8	S 17 23·
Y 14	250 12·3	16 50·5	16·5	279 43·8	31·6	2 53·9	18·5	186 49·4	19 00·0	Hadar	149 33·3	S 60 14·
15	265 14·8	31 49·8	·· 17·3	294 45·1	·· 31·1	17· 55·8	·· 18·6	201 52·0	18 59·9	Hamal	328 35·8	N 23 20·
16	280 17·3	46 49·0	18·1	309 46·4	30·5	32 57·7	18·7	216 54·7	59·9	Kaus Aust.	84 25·5	S 34 24·
17	295 19·7	61 48·3	19·0	324 47·6	30·0	47 59·6	18·8	231 57·3	59·9			
18	310 22·2	76 47·6	S19 19·8	339 48·9	S14 29·4	63 01·5	S 21 18·9	246 59·9	N18 59·8	Kochab	137 19·4	N 74 16·
19	325 24·6	91 46·9,	20·7	354 50·2	28·9	78 03·4	18·9	262 02·6	59·8	Markab	14 09·3	N 15 03·
20	340 27·1	106 46·2	21·5	9 51·5	28·3	93 05·4	19·0	277 05·2	59·8	Menkar	314 47·4	N 3 59·
21	355 29·6	121 45·5	·· 22·3	24 52·8	·· 27·8	108 07·3	·· 19·1	292 07·9	·· 59·7	Menkent	148 45·0	S 36.13·
22	10 32·0	136 44·7	23·2	39 54·1	27·2	123 09·2	19·2	307 10·5	59·7	Miaplacidus	221 46·8	S 69 35·
23	25 34·5	151 44·0	24·0	54 55·4	26·6	138 11·1	19·3	322 13·2	59·7			
2 00	40 37·0	166 43·3	S19 24·8	69 56·7	S14 26·1	153 13·0	S 21 19·4	337 15·8	N18 59·6	Mirfak	309 24·8	N 49 45·
01	55 39·4	181 42·6	25·7	84 58·0	25·5	168 14·9	19·4	352 18·4	59·6	Nunki	.76 37·2	S 26 20·
02	70 41·9	196 41·9	26·5	99 59·2	25·0	183 16·8	19·5	7 21·1	59·6	Peacock	·54 08·3	S 56 49·
03	85 44·4	211 41·1	·· 27·3	115 00·5	·· 24·4	198 18·7	·· 19·6	22 23·7	·· 59·5	Pollux	244 05·8	N 28 05·
04	100 46·8	226 40·4	28·2	130 01·8	23·9	213 20·6	19·7	37 26·4	59·5	Procyon	245 32·3	N 5 18·
05	115 49·3	241 39·7	29·0	145 03·1	23·3	228 22·6	19·8	52 29·0	59·5			
06	130 51·7	256 39·0	S19 29·8	160 04·4	S14 22·7	243 24·5	S 21 19·9	67 31·7	N18 59·4	Rasalhague	·96 35·7	N 12 34·
07	145 54·2	271 38·2	30·7	175 05·7	22·2	258. 26·4	20·0	82 34·3	59·4	Regulus	208 16·8	N 12 06·
T 08	160 56·7	286 37·5	31·5	190 07·0	21·6	273 28·3	20·0	97 36·9	59·4	Rigel	281 41·8	S 8 13·
U 09	175 59·1	301 36·8	·· 32·3	205 08·2	·· 21·1	288 30·2	·· 20·1	112 39·6	·· 59·3	Rigil Kent.	140 35·4	S 60 43·
E 10	191 01·6	.316 36·1	33·1	220 09·5	20·5	303 32·1	20·2	127 42·2	59·3	Sabik	102 48·7	S 15 41·
S 11	206 04·1	331 35·3	34·0	235 10·8	20·0	318 34·0	20·3	142 44·9	59·3			
D 12	221 06·5	346 34·6	S19 34·8	250 12·1	S14 19·4	333 35·9	S 21 20·4	157 47·5	N18 59·2	Schedar	350 16·0	N 56 23·
A 13	236 09·0	·1 33·9	35·6	265 13·4	18·8	348 37·8	20·5	172 50·2	59·2	Shaula	97 04·7	S 37 05·
Y 14	251 11·5	16 33·2	36·4	280 14·7	18·3	3 39·7	20·5	187 52·8	59·2	Sirius	259 01·1	S 16 40·
15	266 13·9	31 32·4	·· 37·2	295 15·9	·· 17·7	18 41·7	·· 20·6	202 55·5	·· 59·1	Spica	159 04·6	S 11 00·
16	281 16·4	46 31·7	38·1	310 17·2	17·2	33 43·6	20·7	217 58·1	59·1	Suhail	223 15·6	S 43 18·
17	296 18·9	61 31·0	38·9	325 18·5	16·6	48 45·5	20·8	233 00·7	59·1			
18	311 21·3	76 30·3	S19 39·7	340 19·8	S14 16·0	63 47·4	S 21 20·9	248 03·4	N18 59·0	Vega	81 00·4	N 38 45·
19	326 23·8	91 29·5	40·5	355 21·1	15·5	78 49·3	21·0	263 06·0	59·0	Zuben'ubi	137 40·4	S 15 55·
20	341 26·2	106 28·8	41·3	10 22·3	14·9	93 51·2	21·1	278 08·7	59·0			
21	356 28·7	121 28·1	·· 42·1	25 23·6	·· 14·4	108 53·1	·· 21·1	293 11·3	·· 58·9		S.H.A.	Mer. Pass
22	11 31·2	136 27·3	43·0	40 24·9	13·8	123 55·0	21·2	308 14·0	58·9	Venus	° ′ 127 22·6	h m 12 53
23	26 33·6	151 26·6	43·8	55 26·2	13·2	138 56·9	21·3	323 16·6	58·9	Mars	29 47·8	19 21
Mer. Pass. 21 18·0		v −0·7	d 0·8	v 1·3	d 0·6	v 1·9	d 0·1	v 2·6	d 0·0	Jupiter Saturn	112 49·3 296 34·6	13 48 1 35

159. Daily Almanac Page—Stars and Planets (NA white pages)

OCT. 31, NOV. 1, 2 (SUN., MON., TUES.)

M.T.	SUN G.H.A.	Dec.	MOON G.H.A.	v	Dec.	d	H.P.	Lat.	Twilight Naut.	Civil	Sun-rise	Moonrise 31	1	2	3
h	o ,	o ,	o ,	,	o ,	,	r.	o	h m	h m	h m	h m	h m	h m	h m
00	184 04·7	S13 49·4	43 44·1	10·3	N 1 42·4	16·8	60·6	N 72	06 03	07 26	08 52	14 25	13 44	12 18	☐
01	199 04·7	50·2	58 13·4	10·3	1 59·2	16·8	60·6	N 70	05 59	07 13	08 27	14 33	14 03	13 16	☐
02	214 04·8	51·0	72 42·7	10·2	2 16·0	16·8	60·7	68	05 56	07 03	08 08	14 39	14 19	13 50	☐
03	229 04·8 ··	51·8	87 11·9	10·2	2 32·8	16·8	60·7	66	05 53	06 55	07 53	14 44	14 32	14 16	13 47
04	244 04·8	52·6	101 41·1	10·2	2 49·6	16·8	60·7	64	05 51	06 47	07 40	14 49	14 42	14 36	14 26
05	259 04·9	53·5	116 10·3	10·1	3 06·4	16·8	60·7	62	05 48	06 41	07 29	14 53	14 52	14 52	14 54
06	274 04·9	S13 54·3	130 39·4	10·0	N 3 23·2	16·8	60·8	60	05 46	06 35	07 20	14 56	15 00	15 05	15 16
07	289 04·9	55·1	145 08·4	10·0	3 40·0	16·8	60·8	N 58	05 44	06 30	07 12	14 59	15 07	15 17	15 34
08	304 05·0	55·9	159 37·4	10·0	3 56·8	16·7	60·8	56	05 42	06 26	07 05	15 02	15 13	15 28	15 49
09	319 05·0 ··	56·7	174 06·4	9·9	4 13·5	16·8	60·8	54	05 40	06 22	06 59	15 05	15 19	15 37	16 02
10	334 05·0	57·5	188 35·3	9·9	4 30·3	16·8	60·8	52	05 38	06 18	06 54	15 07	15 24	15 45	16 13
11	349 05·0	58·3	203 04·2	9·8	4 47·1	16·7	60·9	50	05 36	06 15	06 48	15 09	15 28	15 52	16 23
12	4 05·1	S13 59·2	217 33·0	9·7	N 5 03·8	16·7	60·9	45	05 32	06 07	06 37	15 14	15 39	16 08	16 45
13	19 05·1	14 00·0	232 01·7	9·7	5 20·5	16·7	60·9	N 40	05 28	06 00	06 28	15 17	15 47	16 21	17 02
14	34 05·1	00·8	246 30·4	9·7	5 37·2	16·7	60·9	35	05 24	05 54	06 19	15 21	15 54	16 32	17 17
15	49 05·2 ··	01·6	260 59·1	9·6	5 53·9	16·6	60·9	30	05 20	05 49	06 13	15 24	16 01	16 42	17 30
16	64 05·2	02·4	275 27·7	9·5	6 10·5	16·6	61·0	20	05 12	05 39	06 01	15 29	16 12	16 59	17 52
17	79 05·2	03·2	289 56·2	9·5	6 27·2	16·6	61·0	N 10	05 04	05 29	05 50	15 34	16 22	17 14	18 11
18	94 05·2	S14 04·0	304 24·7	9·4	N 6 43·8	16·5	61·0	0	04 54	05 19	05 40	15 38	16 32	17 29	18 29
19	109 05·3	04·9	318 53·1	9·3	7 00·3	16·6	61·0	S 10	04 43	05 08	05 30	15 43	16 41	17 43	18 47
20	124 05·3	05·7	333 21·4	9·3	7 16·9	16·5	61·0	20	04 29	04 56	05 19	15 47	16 51	17 58	19 07
21	139 05·3 ··	06·5	347 49·7	9·2	7 33·4	16·5	61·1	30	04 11	04 41	05 06	15 53	17 03	18 16	19 30
22	154 05·3	07·3	2 17·9	9·2	7 49·9	16·4	61·1	35	04 00	04 32	04 58	15 56	17 10	18 26	19 43
23	169 05·4	08·1	16 46·1	9·1	8 06·3	16·4	61·1	40	03 46	04 21	04 50	16 00	17 18	18 38	19 59
00	184 05·4	S14 08·9	31 14·2	9·0	N 8 22·7	16·3	61·1	45	03 29	04 08	04 40	16 04	17 27	18 53	20 17
01	199 05·4	09·7	45 42·2	9·0	8 39·0	16·4	61·1	S 50	03 06	03 52	04 28	16 09	17 39	19 10	20 41
02	214 05·4	10·5	60 10·2	8·9	8 55·4	16·2	61·1	52	02 55	03 44	04 22	16 12	17 44	19 19	20 52
03	229 05·5 ··	11·3	74 38·1	8·8	9 11·6	16·2	61·1	54	02 42	03 35	04 16	16 14	17 50	19 28	21 05
04	244 05·5	12·1	89 05·9	8·7	9 27·8	16·2	61·1	56	02 27	03 25	04 09	16 17	17 56	19 38	21 19
05	259 05·5	12·9	103 33·6	8·7	9 44·0	16·1	61·2	58	02 08	03 14	04 01	16 21	18 04	19 50	21 37
06	274 05·5	S14 13·8	118 01·3	8·6	N10 00·1	16·1	61·2	S 60	01 44	03 00	03 52	16 24	18 12	20 04	21 58

M.T.	SUN G.H.A.	Dec.	MOON G.H.A.	v	Dec.	d	H.P.	Lat.	Sun-set	Twilight Civil	Naut.	Moonset 31	1	2	3
07	289 05·6 ·	14·6	132 28·9	8·6	10 16·2	16·0	61·2	o	h m	h m	h m	h m	h m	h m	h m
08	304 05·6	15·4	146 56·5	8·6	10 32·2	15·9	61·2	N 72	14 33	16 00	17 22	03 45	06 19	09 42	☐
09	319 05·6 ··	16·2	161 23·9	8·4	10 48·1	15·9	61·2	N 70	14 59	16 12	17 26	03 41	06 02	08 47	☐
10	334 05·6	17·0	175 51·3	8·3	11 04·0	15·9	61·2	68	15 18	16 23	17 30	03 38	05 48	08 14	☐
11	349 05·6	17·8	190 18·6	8·2	11 19·9	15·7	61·2	66	15 34	16 32	17 33	03 35	05 38	07 50	10 24
12	4 05·7	S14 18·6	204 45·8	8·2	N11 35·6	15·7	61·2	64	15 46	16 39	17 36	03 33	05 29	07 32	09 45
13	19 05·7	19·4	219 13·0	8·1	11 51·3	15·6	61·2	62	15 57	16 45	17 38	03 31	05 21	07 17	09 18
14	34 05·7	20·2	233 40·1	8·0	12 06·9	15·6	61·2	60	16 06	16 51	17 40	03 29	05 14	07 04	08 57
15	49 05·7 ··	21·0	248 07·1	7·9	12 22·5	15·5	61·3	N 58	16 14	16 56	17 43	03 28	05 09	06 53	08 40
16	64 05·7	21·8	262 34·0	7·8	12 38·0	15·4	61·3	56	16 21	17 01	17 45	03 27	05 04	06 44	08 26
17	79 05·8	22·6	277 00·8	7·8	12 53·4	15·3	61·3	54	16 27	17 05	17 47	03 26	04 59	06 36	08 14
18	94 05·8	S14 23·4	291 27·6	7·7	N13 08·7	15·3	61·3	52	16 33	17 09	17 48	03 25	04 55	06 28	08 03
19	109 05·8	24·2	305 54·3	7·5	13 24·0	15·1	61·3	50	16 38	17 12	17 50	03 24	04 51	06 22	07·53
20	124 05·8	25·0	320 20·8	7·6	13 39·1	15·1	61·3	45	16 49	17 20	17 54	03 22	04 43	06 08	07 33
21	139 05·8 ··	25·8	334 47·4	7·4	13 54·2	15·0	61·3	N 40	16 59	17 27	17 59	03 20	04 37	05 56	07 17
22	154 05·9	26·6	349 13·8	7·3	14 09·2	14·9	61·3	35	17 07	17 33	18 03	03 18	04 31	05 46	07 03
23	169 05·9	27·4	3 40·1	7·3	14 24·1	14·8	61·3	30	17 14	17 38	18 07	03 17	04 26	05 38	06 51
00	184 05·9	S14 28·2	18 06·4	7·2	N14 38·9	14·7	61·3	20	17 26	17 49	18 15	03 15	04 18	05 23	06 31
01	199 05·9	29·0	32 32·6	7·1	14 53·6	14·7	61·3	N 10	17 37	17 58	18 23	03 13	04 10	05 10	06 13
02	214 05·9	29·8	46 58·7	7·0	15 08·3	14·5	61·3	0	17 47	18 09	18 33	03 11	04 03	04 58	05 57
03	229 05·9 ··	30·6	61 24·7	6·9	15 22·8	14·4	61·3	S 10	17 58	18 19	18 45	03 09	03 56	04 46	05 41
04	244 05·9	31·4	75 50·6	6·8	15 37·2	14·4	61·3	20	18 09	18 32	18 59	03 07	03 49	04 34	05 23
05	259 06·0	32·2	90 16·4	6·8	15 51·6	14·2	61·3	30	18 22	18 47	19 17	03 05	03 40	04 19	05 03
06	274 06·0	S14 33·0	104 42·2	6·6	N16 05·8	14·1	61·3	35	18 29	18 56	19 29	03 03	03 35	04 11	04 52
07	289 06·0	33·8	119 07·8	6·6	16 19·9	14·0	61·3	40	18 38	19 07	19 42	03 02	03 30	04 01	04 39
08	304 06·0	34·6	133 33·4	6·5	16 33·9	13·9	61·3	45	18 48	19 20	20 00	03 00	03 24	03 50	04 23
09	319 06·0 ··	35·4	147 58·9	6·5	16 47·8	13·8	61·3	S 50	19 01	19 37	20 23	02 58	03 16	03 37	04·04
10	334 06·0	36·2	162 24·3	6·3	17 01·6	13·7	61·3	52	19 06	19 45	20 34	02 57	03 13	03 31	03 55
11	349 06·0	37·0	176 49·6	6·3	17 15·3	13·6	61·3	54	19 13	19 54	20 48	02 56	03 09	03 24	03 45
12	·4 06·1	S14 37·8	191 14·9	6·1	N17 28·9	13·4	61·3	56	19 20	20 04	21 03	02 55	03 05	03 17	03 34
13	19 06·1	38·6	205 40·0	6·1	17 42·3	13·3	61·3	58	19 28	20 15	21 23	02 54	·03 00	03 08	03 21
14	34 06·1	39·4	220 05·1	6·0	17 55·6	13·2	61·3	S 60	19 37	20 29	21 48	02 52	02 55	02 59	03 06
15	49 06·1 ··	40·2	234 30·1	5·8	18 08·8	13·1	61·2								
16	64 06·1	41·0	248 54·9	5·8	18 21·9	13·0	61·2								
17	79 06·1	41·7	263 19·7	5·8	18 34·9	12·8	61·2		SUN				MOON		
18	94 06·1	S14 42·5	277 44·5	5·6	N18 47·7	12·7	61·2	Day	Eqn. of Time 00ʰ	12ʰ	Mer. Pass.	Mer. Pass. Upper	Lower	Age	Phase
19	109 06·1	43·3	292 09·1	5·5	19 00·4	12·5	61·2								
20	124 06·1	44·1	306 33·6	5·5	19 12·9	12·4	61·2		m s	m s	h m	h m	h m	d	
21	139 06·2 ··	44·9	320 58·1	5·4	19 25·3	12·3	61·2	31	16 19	16 20	11 44	21 50	09 24	12	⬤
22	154 06·2	45·7	335 22·5	5·3	19 37·6	12·2	61·2	1	16 22	16 23	11 44	22 45	10 17	13	
23	169 06·2	46·5	349 46·8	5·2	19 49·8	12·0	61·2	2	16 24	16 24	11 44	23 43	11 13	14	
	S.D. 16·1	d 0·8	S.D. 16·6		16·7		16·7									

160. Daily Almanac Page—Sun and Moon (NA white pages)

14	SUN PLANETS	ARIES	MOON	v or Corrⁿ d	v or Corrⁿ	v or Corrⁿ
s	° ′	° ′	° ′	′ ′	′ ′	′ ′
00	3 30·0	3 30·6	3 20·4	0·0 0·0	6·0 1·5	12·0 2·9
01	3 30·3	3 30·8	3 20·7	0·1 0·0	6·1 1·5	12·1 2·9
02	3 30·5	3 31·1	3 20·9	0·2 0·0	6·2 1·5	12·2 2·9
03	3 30·8	3 31·3	3 21·1	0·3 0·1	6·3 1·5	12·3 3·0
04	3 31·0	3 31·6	3 21·4	0·4 0·1	6·4 1·5	12·4 3·0
05	3 31·3	3 31·8	3 21·6	0·5 0·1	6·5 1·6	12·5 3·0
06	3 31·5	3 32·1	3 21·9	0·6 0·1	6·6 1·6	12·6 3·0
07	3 31·8	3 32·3	3 22·1	0·7 0·2	6·7 1·6	12·7 3·1
08	3 32·0	3 32·6	3 22·3	0·8 0·2	6·8 1·6	12·8 3·1
09	3 32·3	3 32·8	3 22·6	0·9 0·2	6·9 1·7	12·9 3·1
10	3 32·5	3 33·1	3 22·8	1·0 0·2	7·0 1·7	13·0 3·1
11	3 32·8	3 33·3	3 23·1	1·1 0·3	7·1 1·7	13·1 3·2
12	3 33·0	3 33·6	3 23·3	1·2 0·3	7·2 1·7	13·2 3·2
13	3 33·3	3 33·8	3 23·5	1·3 0·3	7·3 1·8	13·3 3·2
14	3 33·5	3 34·1	3 23·8	1·4 0·3	7·4 1·8	13·4 3·2
15	3 33·8	3 34·3	3 24·0	1·5 0·4	7·5 1·8	13·5 3·3
16	3 34·0	3 34·6	3 24·3	1·6 0·4	7·6 1·8	13·6 3·3
17	3 34·3	3 34·8	3 24·5	1·7 0·4	7·7 1·9	13·7 3·3
18	3 34·5	3 35·1	3 24·7	1·8 0·4	7·8 1·9	13·8 3·3
19	3 34·8	3 35·3	3 25·0	1·9 0·5	7·9 1·9	13·9 3·4
20	3 35·0	3 35·6	3 25·2	2·0 0·5	8·0 1·9	14·0 3·4
21	3 35·3	3 35·8	3 25·4	2·1 0·5	8·1 2·0	14·1 3·4
22	3 35·5	3 36·1	3 25·7	2·2 0·5	8·2 2·0	14·2 3·4
23	3 35·8	3 36·3	3 25·9	2·3 0·6	8·3 2·0	14·3 3·5
24	3 36·0	3 36·6	3 26·2	2·4 0·6	8·4 2·0	14·4 3·5
25	3 36·3	3 36·8	3 26·4	2·5 0·6	8·5 2·1	14·5 3·5
26	3 36·5	3 37·1	3 26·6	2·6 0·6	8·6 2·1	14·6 3·5
27	3 36·8	3 37·3	3 26·9	2·7 0·7	8·7 2·1	14·7 3·6
28	3 37·0	3 37·6	3 27·1	2·8 0·7	8·8 2·1	14·8 3·6
29	3 37·3	3 37·8	3 27·4	2·9 0·7	8·9 2·2	14·9 3·6
30	3 37·5	3 38·1	3 27·6	3·0 0·7	9·0 2·2	15·0 3·6
31	3 37·8	3 38·3	3 27·8	3·1 0·7	9·1 2·2	15·1 3·6
32	3 38·0	3 38·6	3 28·1	3·2 0·8	9·2 2·2	15·2 3·7
33	3 38·3	3 38·8	3 28·3	3·3 0·8	9·3 2·2	15·3 3·7
34	3 38·5	3 39·1	3 28·5	3·4 0·8	9·4 2·3	15·4 3·7
35	3 38·8	3 39·3	3 28·8	3·5 0·8	9·5 2·3	15·5 3·7
36	3 39·0	3 39·6	3 29·0	3·6 0·9	9·6 2·3	15·6 3·8
37	3 39·3	3 39·9	3 29·3	3·7 0·9	9·7 2·3	15·7 3·8
38	3 39·5	3 40·1	3 29·5	3·8 0·9	9·8 2·4	15·8 3·8
39	3 39·8	3 40·4	3 29·7	3·9 0·9	9·9 2·4	15·9 3·8
40	3 40·0	3 40·6	3 30·0	4·0 1·0	10·0 2·4	16·0 3·9
41	3 40·3	3 40·9	3 30·2	4·1 1·0	10·1 2·4	16·1 3·9
42	3 40·5	3 41·1	3 30·5	4·2 1·0	10·2 2·5	16·2 3·9
43	3 40·8	3 41·4	3 30·7	4·3 1·0	10·3 2·5	16·3 3·9
44	3 41·0	3 41·6	3 30·9	4·4 1·1	10·4 2·5	16·4 4·0
45	3 41·3	3 41·9	3 31·2	4·5 1·1	10·5 2·5	16·5 4·0
46	3 41·5	3 42·1	3 31·4	4·6 1·1	10·6 2·6	16·6 4·0
47	3 41·8	3 42·4	3 31·6	4·7 1·1	10·7 2·6	16·7 4·0
48	3 42·0	3 42·6	3 31·9	4·8 1·2	10·8 2·6	16·8 4·1
49	3 42·3	3 42·9	3 32·1	4·9 1·2	10·9 2·6	16·9 4·1
50	3 42·5	3 43·1	3 32·4	5·0 1·2	11·0 2·7	17·0 4·1
51	3 42·8	3 43·4	3 32·6	5·1 1·2	11·1 2·7	17·1 4·1
52	3 43·0	3 43·6	3 32·8	5·2 1·3	11·2 2·7	17·2 4·2
53	3 43·3	3 43·9	3 33·1	5·3 1·3	11·3 2·7	17·3 4·2
54	3 43·5	3 44·1	3 33·3	5·4 1·3	11·4 2·8	17·4 4·2
55	3 43·8	3 44·4	3 33·6	5·5 1·3	11·5 2·8	17·5 4·2
56	3 44·0	3 44·6	3 33·8	5·6 1·4	11·6 2·8	17·6 4·3
57	3 44·3	3 44·9	3 34·0	5·7 1·4	11·7 2·8	17·7 4·3
58	3 44·5	3 45·1	3 34·3	5·8 1·4	11·8 2·9	17·8 4·3
59	3 44·8	3 45·4	3 34·5	5·9 1·4	11·9 2·9	17·9 4·3
60	3 45·0	3 45·6	3 34·8	6·0 1·5	12·0 2·9	18·0 4·4

31	SUN PLANETS	ARIES	MOON	v or Corrⁿ d	v or Corrⁿ d	v or Corrⁿ d
s	° ′	° ′	° ′	′ ′	′ ′	′ ′
00	7 45·0	7 46·3	7 23·8	0·0 0·0	6·0 3·2	12·0 6·3
01	7 45·3	7 46·5	7 24·1	0·1 0·1	6·1 3·2	12·1 6·4
02	7 45·5	7 46·8	7 24·3	0·2 0·1	6·2 3·3	12·2 6·4
03	7 45·8	7 47·0	7 24·5	0·3 0·2	6·3 3·3	12·3 6·5
04	7 46·0	7 47·3	7 24·8	0·4 0·2	6·4 3·4	12·4 6·5
05	7 46·3	7 47·5	7 25·0	0·5 0·3	6·5 3·4	12·5 6·6
06	7 46·5	7 47·8	7 25·2	0·6 0·3	6·6 3·5	12·6 6·6
07	7 46·8	7 48·0	7 25·5	0·7 0·4	6·7 3·5	12·7 6·7
08	7 47·0	7 48·3	7 25·7	0·8 0·4	6·8 3·6	12·8 6·7
09	7 47·3	7 48·5	7 26·0	0·9 0·5	6·9 3·6	12·9 6·8
10	7 47·5	7 48·8	7 26·2	1·0 0·5	7·0 3·7	13·0 6·8
11	7 47·8	7 49·0	7 26·4	1·1 0·6	7·1 3·7	13·1 6·9
12	7 48·0	7 49·3	7 26·7	1·2 0·6	7·2 3·8	13·2 6·9
13	7 48·3	7 49·5	7 26·9	1·3 0·7	7·3 3·8	13·3 7·0
14	7 48·5	7 49·8	7 27·2	1·4 0·7	7·4 3·9	13·4 7·0
15	7 48·8	7 50·0	7 27·4	1·5 0·8	7·5 3·9	13·5 7·1
16	7 49·0	7 50·3	7 27·6	1·6 0·8	7·6 4·0	13·6 7·1
17	7 49·3	7 50·5	7 27·9	1·7 0·9	7·7 4·0	13·7 7·2
18	7 49·5	7 50·8	7 28·1	1·8 0·9	7·8 4·1	13·8 7·2
19	7 49·8	7 51·0	7 28·4	1·9 1·0	7·9 4·1	13·9 7·3
20	7 50·0	7 51·3	7 28·6	2·0 1·1	8·0 4·2	14·0 7·4
21	7 50·3	7 51·5	7 28·8	2·1 1·1	8·1 4·3	14·1 7·4
22	7 50·5	7 51·8	7 29·1	2·2 1·2	8·2 4·3	14·2 7·5
23	7 50·8	7 52·0	7 29·3	2·3 1·2	8·3 4·4	14·3 7·5
24	7 51·0	7 52·3	7 29·5	2·4 1·3	8·4 4·4	14·4 7·6
25	7 51·3	7 52·5	7 29·8	2·5 1·3	8·5 4·5	14·5 7·6
26	7 51·5	7 52·8	7 30·0	2·6 1·4	8·6 4·5	14·6 7·7
27	7 51·8	7 53·0	7 30·3	2·7 1·4	8·7 4·6	14·7 7·7
28	7 52·0	7 53·3	7 30·5	2·8 1·5	8·8 4·6	14·8 7·8
29	7 52·3	7 53·5	7 30·7	2·9 1·5	8·9 4·7	14·9 7·8
30	7 52·5	7 53·8	7 31·0	3·0 1·6	9·0 4·7	15·0 7·9
31	7 52·8	7 54·0	7 31·2	3·1 1·6	9·1 4·8	15·1 7·9
32	7 53·0	7 54·3	7 31·5	3·2 1·7	9·2 4·8	15·2 8·0
33	7 53·3	7 54·5	7 31·7	3·3 1·7	9·3 4·9	15·3 8·0
34	7 53·5	7 54·8	7 31·9	3·4 1·8	9·4 4·9	15·4 8·1
35	7 53·8	7 55·0	7 32·2	3·5 1·8	9·5 5·0	15·5 8·1
36	7 54·0	7 55·3	7 32·4	3·6 1·9	9·6 5·0	15·6 8·2
37	7 54·3	7 55·5	7 32·6	3·7 1·9	9·7 5·1	15·7 8·2
38	7 54·5	7 55·8	7 32·9	3·8 2·0	9·8 5·1	15·8 8·3
39	7 54·8	7 56·0	7 33·1	3·9 2·0	9·9 5·2	15·9 8·3
40	7 55·0	7 56·3	7 33·4	4·0 2·1	10·0 5·3	16·0 8·4
41	7 55·3	7 56·6	7 33·6	4·1 2·2	10·1 5·3	16·1 8·5
42	7 55·5	7 56·8	7 33·8	4·2 2·2	10·2 5·4	16·2 8·5
43	7 55·8	7 57·1	7 34·1	4·3 2·3	10·3 5·4	16·3 8·6
44	7 56·0	7 57·3	7 34·3	4·4 2·3	10·4 5·5	16·4 8·6
45	7 56·3	7 57·6	7 34·6	4·5 2·4	10·5 5·5	16·5 8·7
46	7 56·5	7 57·8	7 34·8	4·6 2·4	10·6 5·6	16·6 8·7
47	7 56·8	7 58·1	7 35·0	4·7 2·5	10·7 5·6	16·7 8·8
48	7 57·0	7 58·3	7 35·3	4·8 2·5	10·8 5·7	16·8 8·8
49	7 57·3	7 58·6	7 35·5	4·9 2·6	10·9 5·7	16·9 8·9
50	7 57·5	7 58·8	7 35·7	5·0 2·6	11·0 5·8	17·0 8·9
51	7 57·8	7 59·1	7 36·0	5·1 2·7	11·1 5·8	17·1 9·0
52	7 58·0	7 59·3	7 36·2	5·2 2·7	11·2 5·9	17·2 9·0
53	7 58·3	7 59·6	7 36·5	5·3 2·8	11·3 5·9	17·3 9·1
54	7 58·5	7 59·8	7 36·7	5·4 2·8	11·4 6·0	17·4 9·1
55	7 58·8	8 00·1	7 36·9	5·5 2·9	11·5 6·0	17·5 9·2
56	7 59·0	8 00·3	7 37·2	5·6 2·9	11·6 6·1	17·6 9·2
57	7 59·3	8 00·6	7 37·4	5·7 3·0	11·7 6·1	17·7 9·3
58	7 59·5	8 00·8	7 37·7	5·8 3·0	11·8 6·2	17·8 9·3
59	7 59·8	8 01·1	7 37·9	5·9 3·1	11·9 6·2	17·9 9·4
60	8 00·0	8 01·3	7 38·1	6·0 3·2	12·0 6·3	18·0 9·5

161. Increments and Corrections (NA yellow pages)

INCREMENTS AND CORRECTIONS

4^m

s	SUN PLANETS	ARIES	MOON	v or Corr^n d		v or Corr^n d		v or Corr^n d	
00	11 00·0	11 01·8	10 29·9	0·0	0·0	6·0	4·5	12·0	8·9
01	11 00·3	11 02·1	10 30·2	0·1	0·1	6·1	4·5	12·1	9·0
02	11 00·5	11 02·3	10 30·4	0·2	0·2	6·2	4·6	12·2	9·0
03	11 00·8	11 02·6	10 30·6	0·3	0·2	6·3	4·7	12·3	9·1
04	11 01·0	11 02·8	10 30·9	0·4	0·3	6·4	4·7	12·4	9·2
05	11 01·3	11 03·1	10 31·1	0·5	0·4	6·5	4·8	12·5	9·3
06	11 01·5	11 03·3	10 31·4	0·6	0·4	6·6	4·9	12·6	9·3
07	11 01·8	11 03·6	10 31·6	0·7	0·5	6·7	5·0	12·7	9·4
08	11 02·0	11 03·8	10 31·8	0·8	0·6	6·8	5·0	12·8	9·5
09	11 02·3	11 04·1	10 32·1	0·9	0·7	6·9	5·1	12·9	9·6
10	11 02·5	11 04·3	10 32·3	1·0	0·7	7·0	5·2	13·0	9·6
11	11 02·8	11 04·6	10 32·6	1·1	0·8	7·1	5·3	13·1	9·7
12	11 03·0	11 04·8	10 32·8	1·2	0·9	7·2	5·3	13·2	9·8
13	11 03·3	11 05·1	10 33·0	1·3	1·0	7·3	5·4	13·3	9·9
14	11 03·5	11 05·3	10 33·3	1·4	1·0	7·4	5·5	13·4	9·9
15	11 03·8	11 05·6	10 33·5	1·5	1·1	7·5	5·6	13·5	10·0
16	11 04·0	11 05·8	10 33·8	1·6	1·2	7·6	5·6	13·6	10·1
17	11 04·3	11 06·1	10 34·0	1·7	1·3	7·7	5·7	13·7	10·2
18	11 04·5	11 06·3	10 34·2	1·8	1·3	7·8	5·8	13·8	10·2
19	11 04·8	11 06·6	10 34·5	1·9	1·4	7·9	5·9	13·9	10·3
20	11 05·0	11 06·8	10 34·7	2·0	1·5	8·0	5·9	14·0	10·4
21	11 05·3	11 07·1	10 34·9	2·1	1·6	8·1	6·0	14·1	10·5
22	11 05·5	11 07·3	10 35·2	2·2	1·6	8·2	6·1	14·2	10·5
23	11 05·8	11 07·6	10 35·4	2·3	1·7	8·3	6·2	14·3	10·6
24	11 06·0	11 07·8	10 35·7	2·4	1·8	8·4	6·2	14·4	10·7
25	11 06·3	11 08·1	10 35·9	2·5	1·9	8·5	6·3	14·5	10·8
26	11 06·5	11 08·3	10 36·1	2·6	1·9	8·6	6·4	14·6	10·8
27	11 06·8	11 08·6	10 36·4	2·7	2·0	8·7	6·5	14·7	10·9
28	11 07·0	11 08·8	10 36·6	2·8	2·1	8·8	6·5	14·8	11·0
29	11 07·3	11 09·1	10 36·9	2·9	2·2	8·9	6·6	14·9	11·1
30	11 07·5	11 09·3	10 37·1	3·0	2·2	9·0	6·7	15·0	11·1
31	11 07·8	11 09·6	10 37·3	3·1	2·3	9·1	6·7	15·1	11·2
32	11 08·0	11 09·8	10 37·6	3·2	2·4	9·2	6·8	15·2	11·3
33	11 08·3	11 10·1	10 37·8	3·3	2·4	9·3	6·9	15·3	11·3
34	11 08·5	11 10·3	10 38·0	3·4	2·5	9·4	7·0	15·4	11·4
35	11 08·8	11 10·6	10 38·3	3·5	2·6	9·5	7·0	15·5	11·5
36	11 09·0	11 10·8	10 38·5	3·6	2·7	9·6	7·1	15·6	11·6
37	11 09·3	11 11·1	10 38·8	3·7	2·7	9·7	7·2	15·7	11·6
38	11 09·5	11 11·3	10 39·0	3·8	2·8	9·8	7·3	15·8	11·7
39	11 09·8	11 11·6	10 39·2	3·9	2·9	9·9	7·3	15·9	11·8
40	11 10·0	11 11·8	10 39·5	4·0	3·0	10·0	7·4	16·0	11·9
41	11 10·3	11 12·1	10 39·7	4·1	3·0	10·1	7·5	16·1	11·9
42	11 10·5	11 12·3	10 40·0	4·2	3·1	10·2	7·6	16·2	12·0
43	11 10·8	11 12·6	10 40·2	4·3	3·2	10·3	7·6	16·3	12·1
44	11 11·0	11 12·8	10 40·4	4·4	3·3	10·4	7·7	16·4	12·2
45	11 11·3	11 13·1	10 40·7	4·5	3·3	10·5	7·8	16·5	12·2
46	11 11·5	11 13·3	10 40·9	4·6	3·4	10·6	7·9	16·6	12·3
47	11 11·8	11 13·6	10 41·1	4·7	3·5	10·7	7·9	16·7	12·4
48	11 12·0	11 13·8	10 41·4	4·8	3·6	10·8	8·0	16·8	12·5
49	11 12·3	11 14·1	10 41·6	4·9	3·6	10·9	8·1	16·9	12·5
50	11 12·5	11 14·3	10 41·9	5·0	3·7	11·0	8·2	17·0	12·6
51	11 12·8	11 14·6	10 42·1	5·1	3·8	11·1	8·2	17·1	12·7
52	11 13·0	11 14·8	10 42·3	5·2	3·9	11·2	8·3	17·2	12·8
53	11 13·3	11 15·1	10 42·6	5·3	3·9	11·3	8·4	17·3	12·8
54	11 13·5	11 15·3	10 42·8	5·4	4·0	11·4	8·5	17·4	12·9
55	11 13·8	11 15·6	10 43·1	5·5	4·1	11·5	8·5	17·5	13·0
56	11 14·0	11 15·8	10 43·3	5·6	4·2	11·6	8·6	17·6	13·1
57	11 14·3	11 16·1	10 43·5	5·7	4·2	11·7	8·7	17·7	13·1
58	11 14·5	11 16·3	10 43·8	5·8	4·3	11·8	8·8	17·8	13·2
59	11 14·8	11 16·6	10 44·0	5·9	4·4	11·9	8·8	17·9	13·3
60	11 15·0	11 16·8	10 44·3	6·0	4·5	12·0	8·9	18·0	13·4

57^m

s	SUN PLANETS	ARIES	MOON	v or Corr^n d		v or Corr^n d		v or Corr^n d	
00	14 15·0	14 17·3	13 36·1	0·0	0·0	6·0	5·8	12·0	11·5
01	14 15·3	14 17·6	13 36·3	0·1	0·1	6·1	5·8	12·1	11·6
02	14 15·5	14 17·8	13 36·5	0·2	0·2	6·2	5·9	12·2	11·7
03	14 15·8	14 18·1	13 36·8	0·3	0·3	6·3	6·0	12·3	11·8
04	14 16·0	14 18·3	13 37·0	0·4	0·4	6·4	6·1	12·4	11·9
05	14 16·3	14 18·6	13 37·2	0·5	0·5	6·5	6·2	12·5	12·0
06	14 16·5	14 18·8	13 37·5	0·6	0·6	6·6	6·3	12·6	12·1
07	14 16·8	14 19·1	13 37·7	0·7	0·7	6·7	6·4	12·7	12·2
08	14 17·0	14 19·3	13 38·0	0·8	0·8	6·8	6·5	12·8	12·3
09	14 17·3	14 19·6	13 38·2	0·9	0·9	6·9	6·6	12·9	12·4
10	14 17·5	14 19·8	13 38·4	1·0	1·0	7·0	6·7	13·0	12·5
11	14 17·8	14 20·1	13 38·7	1·1	1·1	7·1	6·8	13·1	12·6
12	14 18·0	14 20·3	13 38·9	1·2	1·2	7·2	6·9	13·2	12·7
13	14 18·3	14 20·6	13 39·2	1·3	1·2	7·3	7·0	13·3	12·7
14	14 18·5	14 20·9	13 39·4	1·4	1·3	7·4	7·1	13·4	12·8
15	14 18·8	14 21·1	13 39·6	1·5	1·4	7·5	7·2	13·5	12·9
16	14 19·0	14 21·4	13 39·9	1·6	1·5	7·6	7·3	13·6	13·0
17	14 19·3	14 21·6	13 40·1	1·7	1·6	7·7	7·4	13·7	13·1
18	14 19·5	14 21·9	13 40·3	1·8	1·7	7·8	7·5	13·8	13·2
19	14 19·8	14 22·1	13 40·6	1·9	1·8	7·9	7·6	13·9	13·3
20	14 20·0	14 22·4	13 40·8	2·0	1·9	8·0	7·7	14·0	13·4
21	14 20·3	14 22·6	13 41·1	2·1	2·0	8·1	7·8	14·1	13·5
22	14 20·5	14 22·9	13 41·3	2·2	2·1	8·2	7·9	14·2	13·6
23	14 20·8	14 23·1	13 41·5	2·3	2·2	8·3	8·0	14·3	13·7
24	14 21·0	14 23·4	13 41·8	2·4	2·3	8·4	8·1	14·4	13·8
25	14 21·3	14 23·6	13 42·0	2·5	2·4	8·5	8·1	14·5	13·9
26	14 21·5	14 23·9	13 42·3	2·6	2·5	8·6	8·2	14·6	14·0
27	14 21·8	14 24·1	13 42·5	2·7	2·6	8·7	8·3	14·7	14·1
28	14 22·0	14 24·4	13 42·7	2·8	2·7	8·8	8·4	14·8	14·2
29	14 22·3	14 24·6	13 43·0	2·9	2·8	8·9	8·5	14·9	14·3
30	14 22·5	14 24·9	13 43·2	3·0	2·9	9·0	8·6	15·0	14·4
31	14 22·8	14 25·1	13 43·4	3·1	3·0	9·1	8·7	15·1	14·5
32	14 23·0	14 25·4	13 43·7	3·2	3·1	9·2	8·8	15·2	14·6
33	14 23·3	14 25·6	13 43·9	3·3	3·2	9·3	8·9	15·3	14·7
34	14 23·5	14 25·9	13 44·2	3·4	3·3	9·4	9·0	15·4	14·8
35	14 23·8	14 26·1	13 44·4	3·5	3·4	9·5	9·1	15·5	14·9
36	14 24·0	14 26·4	13 44·6	3·6	3·4	9·6	9·2	15·6	15·0
37	14 24·3	14 26·6	13 44·9	3·7	3·5	9·7	9·3	15·7	15·0
38	14 24·5	14 26·9	13 45·1	3·8	3·6	9·8	9·4	15·8	15·1
39	14 24·8	14 27·1	13 45·4	3·9	3·7	9·9	9·5	15·9	15·2
40	14 25·0	14 27·4	13 45·6	4·0	3·8	10·0	9·6	16·0	15·3
41	14 25·3	14 27·6	13 45·8	4·1	3·9	10·1	9·7	16·1	15·4
42	14 25·5	14 27·9	13 46·1	4·2	4·0	10·2	9·8	16·2	15·5
43	14 25·8	14 28·1	13 46·3	4·3	4·1	10·3	9·9	16·3	15·6
44	14 26·0	14 28·4	13 46·5	4·4	4·2	10·4	10·0	16·4	15·7
45	14 26·3	14 28·6	13 46·8	4·5	4·3	10·5	10·1	16·5	15·8
46	14 26·5	14 28·9	13 47·0	4·6	4·4	10·6	10·2	16·6	15·9
47	14 26·8	14 29·1	13 47·3	4·7	4·5	10·7	10·3	16·7	16·0
48	14 27·0	14 29·4	13 47·5	4·8	4·6	10·8	10·4	16·8	16·1
49	14 27·3	14 29·6	13 47·7	4·9	4·7	10·9	10·4	16·9	16·2
50	14 27·5	14 29·9	13 48·0	5·0	4·8	11·0	10·5	17·0	16·3
51	14 27·8	14 30·1	13 48·2	5·1	4·9	11·1	10·6	17·1	16·4
52	14 28·0	14 30·4	13 48·5	5·2	5·0	11·2	10·7	17·2	16·5
53	14 28·3	14 30·6	13 48·7	5·3	5·1	11·3	10·8	17·3	16·6
54	14 28·5	14 30·9	13 48·9	5·4	5·2	11·4	10·9	17·4	16·7
55	14 28·8	14 31·1	13 49·2	5·5	5·3	11·5	11·0	17·5	16·8
56	14 29·0	14 31·4	13 49·4	5·6	5·4	11·6	11·1	17·6	16·9
57	14 29·3	14 31·6	13 49·7	5·7	5·5	11·7	11·2	17·7	17·0
58	14 29·5	14 31·9	13 49·9	5·8	5·6	11·8	11·3	17·8	17·1
59	14 29·8	14 32·1	13 50·1	5·9	5·7	11·9	11·4	17·9	17·2
60	14 30·0	14 32·4	13 50·4	6·0	5·8	12·0	11·5	18·0	17·3

162. Increments and Corrections (NA yellow pages)

LAT 28°N

LHA ♈	Hc Zn	Hc Zn	Hc Zn	Hc Zn	Hc Zn	Hc Zn	Hc Zn
	Dubhe	*REGULUS	PROCYON	SIRIUS	*RIGEL	ALDEBARAN	*Mirfak
90	31 14 032	30 31 092	57 33 130	44 05 165	52 02 199	67 05 244	53 01 317
91	31 42 032	31 24 093	58 13 131	44 18 167	51 44 201	66 17 246	52 25 317
92	32 10 032	32 17 093	58 52 133	44 30 168	51 25 202	65 29 247	51 48 316
93	32 38 032	33 10 094	59 31 134	44 40 169	51 04 204	64 40 248	51 11 316
94	33 07 032	34 03 094	60 08 136	44 49 171	50 42 205	63 50 249	50 34 316
95	33 35 032	34 56 095	60 45 137	44 57 172	50 19 206	63 01 250	49 57 315
96	34 03 032	35 49 095	61 20 139	45 04 173	49 55 208	62 11 251	49 20 315
97	34 31 032	36 41 096	61 54 141	45 10 175	49 30 209	61 20 252	48 42 315
98	34 59 032	37 34 096	62 27 142	45 14 176	49 03 211	60 30 253	48 05 315
99	35 28 032	38 27 097	62 59 144	45 17 177	48 36 212	59 39 254	47 27 314
100	35 56 032	39 19 097	63 29 146	45 19 179	48 07 213	58 48 255	46 49 314
101	36 24 032	40 12 098	63 58 148	45 20 180	47 38 215	57 57 256	46 11 314
102	36 52 032	41 04 099	64 25 150	45 19 181	47 07 216	57 05 257	45 33 314
103	37 19 032	41 56 099	64 50 152	45 17 183	46 36 217	56 14 257	44 54 314
104	37 47 032	42 49 100	65 14 155	45 14 184	46 03 218	55 22 258	44 16 314
	*Dubhe	REGULUS	*Alphard	SIRIUS	RIGEL	*ALDEBARAN	CAPELLA
105	38 15 031	43 41 100	39 12 131	45 09 185	45 30 219	54 30 259	62 32 318
106	38 42 031	44 33 101	39 52 132	45 04 187	44 56 221	53 38 260	61 56 317
107	39 10 031	45 25 102	40 31 132	44 57 188	44 21 222	52 46 260	61 20 316
108	39 37 031	46 17 102	41 10 133	44 49 190	43 45 223	51 53 261	60 43 316
109	40 05 031	47 08 103	41 48 134	44 39 191	43 09 224	51 01 262	60 06 315
110	40 32 031	48 00 104	42 26 136	44 29 192	42 32 225	50 09 262	59 29 315
111	40 59 030	48 51 104	43 02 137	44 17 193	41 54 226	49 16 263	58 51 314
112	41 25 030	49 43 105	43 39 138	44 04 195	41 16 227	48 23 263	58 13 313
113	41 52 030	50 34 106	44 14 139	43 50 196	40 37 228	47 31 264	57 34 313
114	42 18 030	51 25 107	44 48 140	43 34 197	39 57 229	46 38 264	56 55 312
115	42 45 030	52 15 107	45 22 141	43 18 199	39 17 230	45 45 265	56 16 312
116	43 11 029	53 06 108	45 55 142	43 01 200	38 36 231	44 53 266	55 36 312
117	43 37 029	53 56 109	46 27 143	42 42 201	37 55 232	44 00 266	54 57 311
118	44 02 029	54 46 110	46 58 145	42 22 202	37 13 233	43 07 267	54 17 311
119	44 28 029	55 36 111	47 28 146	42 02 204	36 31 233	42 14 267	53 37 311
	*Dubhe	REGULUS	*Alphard	SIRIUS	RIGEL	*ALDEBARAN	CAPELLA
120	44 53 028	56 25 112	47 57 147	41 40 205	35 48 234	41 21 268	52 56 310
121	45 18 028	57 14 113	48 26 148	41 18 206	35 05 235	40 28 268	52 16 310
122	45 43 028	58 03 114	48 53 150	40 54 207	34 21 236	39 35 269	51 35 310
123	46 07 027	58 51 115	49 19 151	40 29 208	33 37 237	38 42 269	50 54 310
124	46 31 027	59 39 116	49 44 153	40 04 209	32 52 238	37 49 270	50 14 309
125	46 55 027	60 26 117	50 08 154	39 37 210	32 07 238	36 56 270	49 33 309
126	47 19 026	61 13 118	50 30 155	39 10 212	31 22 239	36 03 271	48 51 309
127	47 42 026	61 59 120	50 52 157	38 42 213	30 37 240	35 10 271	48 10 309
128	48 05 025	62 45 121	51 12 158	38 13 214	29 51 241	34 17 271	47 29 309
129	48 27 025	63 30 122	51 31 160	37 43 215	29 04 241	33 24 272	46 47 309
130	48 50 025	64 15 124	51 49 161	37 13 216	28 18 242	32 31 272	46 06 308
131	49 11 024	64 58 125	52 05 163	36 41 217	27 31 243	31 38 273	45 24 308
132	49 33 024	65 41 127	52 20 164	36 09 218	26 44 243	30 46 273	44 43 308
133	49 54 023	66 23 129	52 33 166	35 37 219	25 56 244	29 53 274	44 01 308
134	50 14 023	67 04 130	52 45 168	35 03 220	25 09 245	29 00 274	43 20 308
	Dubhe	*ARCTURUS	SPICA	Alphard	*SIRIUS	BETELGEUSE	*CAPELLA
135	50 35 022	18 42 078	15 19 112	52 56 169	34 29 221	41 27 254	42 38 308
136	50 54 022	19 33 078	16 08 112	53 05 171	33 54 222	40 36 255	41 56 308
137	51 13 021	20 25 078	16 57 113	53 13 173	33 19 222	39 45 255	41 15 308
138	51 32 020	21 17 079	17 46 113	53 19 174	32 43 223	38 53 256	40 33 308
139	51 50 020	22 09 079	18 35 114	53 23 176	32 06 224	38 02 257	39 51 308
140	52 08 019	23 01 080	19 23 115	53 27 177	31 29 225	37 10 257	39 10 308
141	52 25 019	23 53 080	20 11 115	53 28 179	30 51 226	36 19 258	38 28 308
142	52 42 018	24 46 080	20 59 116	53 28 181	30 13 227	35 27 258	37 46 308
143	52 58 017	25 38 081	21 46 116	53 27 182	29 34 228	34 35 259	37 05 308
144	53 14 017	26 30 081	22 34 117	53 24 184	28 55 228	33 43 260	36 23 308
145	53 29 016	27 23 082	23 21 118	53 19 186	28 15 229	32 50 260	35 41 308
146	53 43 015	28 15 082	24 07 118	53 13 187	27 35 230	31 58 261	35 00 308
147	53 57 015	29 07 082	24 54 119	53 05 189	26 54 231	31 06 261	34 18 309
148	54 10 014	30 00 083	25 40 120	52 56 191	26 13 231	30 13 262	33 37 309
149	54 22 013	30 53 083	26 26 120	52 46 192	25 31 232	29 21 262	32 56 309

163. Selected Stars (HO 249, volume I)

LAT 42°N

LHA ♈	Hc Zn	Hc Zn	Hc Zn	Hc Zn	Hc Zn	Hc Zn	Hc Zn
	*Alpheratz	ALTAIR	Nunki	*ANTARES	ARCTURUS	*Alkaid	Kochab
270	17 43 067	49 00 136	20 34 167	18 23 202	37 33 263	46 27 302	51 19 341
271	18 24 067	49 30 138	20 43 168	18 06 203	36 48 263	45 49 303	51 05 341
272	19 05 068	50 00 139	20 52 169	17 48 204	36 04 264	45 12 303	50 50 341
273	19 46 068	50 29 140	21 00 170	17 30 204	35 20 265	44 34 303	50 36 341
274	20 28 069	50 57 142	21 07 171	17 11 205	34 35 265	43 57 304	50 21 341
275	21 10 070	51 24 143	21 14 172	16 52 206	33 51 266	43 20 304	50 06 340
276	21 51 070	51 51 144	21 20 173	16 32 207	33 06 267	42 43 304	49 51 340
277	22 34 071	52 16 146	21 25 174	16 11 208	32 22 268	42 06 304	49 36 340
278	23 16 071	52 41 147	21 29 175	15 50 209	31 37 268	41 29 305	49 21 340
279	23 58 072	53 04 149	21 33 176	15 28 210	30 53 269	40 53 305	49 06 340
280	24 40 072	53 27 150	21 36 177	15 06 210	30 08 270	40 16 305	48 50 340
281	25 23 073	53 48 152	21 38 178	14 43 211	29 23 270	39 40 306	48 35 340
282	26 06 074	54 09 154	21 39 179	14 20 212	28 39 271	39 04 306	48 19 339
283	26 48 074	54 28 155	21 40 180	13 56 213	27 54 272	38 28 306	48 04 339
284	27 31 075	54 46 157	21 40 181	13 31 214	27 10 272	37 52 307	47 48 339
	*Mirfak	Alpheratz	*ALTAIR	Rasalhague	*ARCTURUS	Alkaid	Kochab
285	13 24 033	28 14 075	55 03 158	55 05 219	26 25 273	37 16 307	47 32 339
286	13 48 033	28 58 076	55 19 160	54 37 220	25 41 274	36 41 307	47 16 339
287	14 13 034	29 41 076	55 34 162	54 08 222	24 56 274	36 05 308	47 00 339
288	14 37 034	30 24 077	55 47 163	53 37 223	24 12 275	35 30 308	46 44 339
289	15 03 035	31 08 077	55 59 165	53 06 225	23 27 275	34 55 308	46 28 339
290	15 28 035	31 51 078	56 10 167	52 35 226	22 43 276	34 20 309	46 12 339
291	15 54 036	32 35 079	56 19 169	52 02 227	21 59 277	33 45 309	45 56 339
292	16 20 036	33 19 079	56 27 170	51 29 229	21 14 277	33 10 309	45 40 339
293	16 47 037	34 03 080	56 34 172	50 55 230	20 30 278	32 36 310	45 24 339
294	17 14 037	34 47 080	56 39 174	50 21 231	19 46 279	32 02 310	45 07 339
295	17 41 038	35 31 081	56 43 176	49 46 232	19 02 279	31 28 310	44 51 339
296	18 08 038	36 15 082	56 46 178	49 10 234	18 18 280	30 54 311	44 35 339
297	18 36 039	36 59 082	56 47 179	48 34 235	17 34 281	30 20 311	44 19 339
298	19 04 039	37 43 083	56 47 181	47 58 236	16 50 281	29 47 312	44 02 339
299	19 32 040	38 27 083	56 45 183	47 20 237	16 07 282	29 13 312	43 46 339
	Mirfak	*Alpheratz	Enif	*ALTAIR	Rasalhague	Alphecca	*Kochab
300	20 01 040	39 12 084	50 39 138	56 42 185	46 43 238	34 23 277	43 30 339
301	20 30 041	39 56 085	51 09 139	56 38 187	46 05 239	33 39 277	43 14 339
302	20 59 041	40 40 085	51 37 140	56 32 188	45 26 240	32 55 278	42 57 339
303	21 28 041	41 25 086	52 05 142	56 25 190	44 47 241	32 11 279	42 41 339
304	21 58 042	42 09 086	52 33 143	56 16 192	44 08 242	31 27 279	42 25 339
305	22 28 042	42 54 087	52 59 145	56 06 194	43 28 243	30 43 280	42 09 339
306	22 58 043	43 38 088	53 24 146	55 55 195	42 48 244	29 59 280	41 53 339
307	23 28 043	44 23 088	53 48 148	55 43 197	42 08 245	29 15 281	41 37 339
308	23 59 044	45 07 089	54 12 149	55 29 199	41 27 246	28 31 282	41 21 339
309	24 30 044	45 52 090	54 34 151	55 14 201	40 46 247	27 48 282	41 05 339
310	25 01 044	46 37 090	54 55 152	54 58 202	40 05 248	27 04 283	40 49 339
311	25 32 045	47 21 091	55 15 154	54 40 204	39 24 249	26 21 283	40 33 339
312	26 04 045	48 06 092	55 34 155	54 22 205	38 42 250	25 37 284	40 17 339
313	26 36 046	48 50 092	55 52 157	54 02 207	38 00 251	24 54 285	40 01 339
314	27 08 046	49 35 093	56 09 159	53 41 209	37 18 251	24 11 285	39 45 339
	CAPELLA	*Alpheratz	FOMALHAUT	*ALTAIR	Rasalhague	VEGA	*Kochab
315	11 15 036	50 19 094	13 24 154	53 19 210	36 36 252	62 34 275	39 30 339
316	11 42 037	51 04 095	13 43 155	52 56 212	35 53 253	61 50 276	39 14 340
317	12 08 037	51 48 095	14 01 156	52 32 213	35 10 254	61 06 276	38 58 340
318	12 36 038	52 33 096	14 19 157	52 08 215	34 27 255	60 21 277	38 43 340
319	13 03 038	53 17 097	14 37 158	51 42 216	33 44 256	59 37 277	38 28 340
320	13 31 039	54 01 098	14 53 159	51 15 217	33 01 256	58 53 278	38 12 340
321	13 59 039	54 45 098	15 09 159	50 48 219	32 17 257	58 09 278	37 57 340
322	14 27 040	55 29 099	15 24 160	50 19 220	31 34 258	57 25 279	37 42 340
323	14 56 040	56 13 100	15 39 161	49 50 222	30 50 259	56 41 279	37 27 340
324	15 25 041	56 57 101	15 53 162	49 20 223	30 06 259	55 57 280	37 12 341
325	15 55 041	57 41 102	16 07 163	48 49 224	29 23 260	55 13 280	36 57 341
326	16 24 042	58 24 103	16 19 164	48 18 225	28 39 261	54 29 281	36 43 341
327	16 54 042	59 08 104	16 32 165	47 46 227	27 55 262	53 45 281	36 28 341
328	17 25 043	59 51 105	16 43 166	47 13 228	27 10 262	53 02 282	36 13 341
329	17 55 043	60 34 106	16 54 166	46 40 229	26 26 263	52 18 282	35 59 341

164. Selected Stars (HO 249, volume I)

DECLINATION SAME NAME AS LATITUDE

N. Lat. { LHA greater than 180°........ Zn=Z
{ LHA less than 180°............Zn=360-Z

LAT 28°

LHA	15° Hc	d	Z	16° Hc	d	Z	17° Hc	d	Z	18° Hc	d	Z	19° Hc	d	Z	20° Hc	d	Z	21° Hc	d	Z	22° Hc	d	Z	LHA
0	77 00	+60	180	78 00	+60	180	79 00	+60	180	80 00	+60	180	81 00	+60	180	82 00	+60	180	83 00	+60	180	84 00	+60	180	360
1	76 58	60	176	77 58	60	175	78 58	60	175	79 58	59	175	80 57	60	174	81 57	60	173	82 57	59	172	83 56	59	171	359
2	76 52	60	172	77 52	59	171	78 51	59	170	79 50	59	169	80 49	59	168	81 48	58	167	82 46	58	165	83 44	57	163	358
3	76 42	59	167	77 41	59	166	78 40	58	165	79 38	57	164	80 35	58	162	81 33	56	161	82 29	56	158	83 25	54	155	357
4	76 29	58	163	77 27	57	162	78 24	57	161	79 21	56	159	80 17	55	157	81 12	55	155	82 07	53	152	83 00	50	148	356
5	76 12	+56	159	77 08	+56	158	78 04	+56	156	79 00	+54	154	79 54	+54	152	80 48	+51	149	81 39	+50	146	82 29	+47	142	355
6	75 52	55	156	76 47	54	154	77 41	54	152	78 35	52	150	79 27	51	147	80 18	50	144	81 08	46	141	81 54	44	137	354
7	75 28	54	152	76 22	53	150	77 15	52	148	78 07	50	146	78 57	49	143	79 46	46	140	80 32	44	136	81 16	41	132	353
8	75 02	52	149	75 54	52	147	76 46	50	145	77 35	49	142	78 24	46	139	79 10	44	136	79 54	42	132	80 36	37	128	352
9	74 33	51	145	75 24	49	143	76 13	49	141	77 02	46	139	77 48	44	136	78 32	42	132	79 14	39	129	79 53	35	124	351
10	74 02	+49	142	74 51	+48	140	75 39	+46	138	76 25	+45	135	77 10	+42	132	77 52	+40	129	78 32	+36	125	79 08	+33	121	350
11	73 29	47	140	74 16	47	137	75 03	44	135	75 47	43	132	76 30	40	129	77 10	38	126	77 48	34	123	78 22	32	119	349
12	72 53	47	137	73 40	44	135	74 24	43	132	75 07	41	130	75 48	39	127	76 27	36	124	77 03	32	120	77 35	30	116	348
13	72 16	45	135	73 01	43	132	73 44	42	130	74 26	39	127	75 05	37	124	75 42	34	121	76 16	31	118	76 47	28	114	347
14	71 38	43	132	72 21	42	130	73 03	40	128	73 43	38	125	74 21	35	122	74 56	33	119	75 29	30	116	75 59	26	112	346
15	70 58	+42	130	71 40	+40	128	72 20	+39	125	72 59	+36	123	73 35	+34	120	74 09	+32	117	74 41	+28	114	75 09	+26	111	345
16	70 17	40	128	70 57	40	126	71 37	37	123	72 14	35	121	72 49	33	118	73 22	30	115	73 52	28	112	74 20	24	109	344
17	69 34	40	126	70 14	38	124	70 52	36	122	71 28	34	119	72 02	31	116	72 33	30	114	73 03	26	111	73 29	24	108	343
18	68 51	38	124	69 29	37	122	70 06	35	120	70 41	33	117	71 14	31	115	71 45	28	112	72 13	26	109	72 39	22	106	342
19	68 07	37	123	68 44	36	120	69 20	34	118	69 54	32	116	70 26	29	113	70 55	28	111	71 23	24	108	71 47	23	105	341
20	67 22	+36	121	67 58	+35	119	68 33	+33	117	69 06	+31	114	69 37	+28	112	70 05	+27	109	70 32	+24	107	70 56	+22	104	340
21	66 36	35	119	67 11	34	117	67 45	32	115	68 17	30	113	68 47	28	111	69 15	26	108	69 41	24	106	70 05	21	103	339
22	65 49	35	118	66 24	33	116	66 57	31	114	67 28	29	112	67 57	28	109	68 25	25	107	68 50	23	104	69 13	20	102	338
23	65 02	34	117	65 36	32	115	66 08	31	113	66 39	28	110	67 07	28	108	67 34	25	106	67 59	22	103	68 21	20	101	337
24	64 15	33	115	64 48	31	113	65 19	30	111	65 49	28	109	66 17	26	107	66 43	24	105	67 07	22	102	67 29	20	100	336
25	63 26	+33	114	63 59	+31	112	64 30	+29	110	64 59	+27	108	65 26	+26	106	65 52	+23	104	66 15	+22	102	66 37	+19	99	335
26	62 38	31	113	63 09	31	111	63 40	28	109	64 08	27	107	64 35	25	105	65 00	23	103	65 23	21	101	65 44	19	99	334
27	61 49	31	112	62 20	29	110	62 49	28	108	63 17	27	106	63 44	24	104	64 08	23	102	64 31	21	100	64 52	19	98	333
28	60 59	31	111	61 30	29	109	61 59	27	107	62 26	26	105	62 52	24	103	63 16	23	101	63 39	20	99	63 59	19	97	332
29	60 10	30	110	60 40	28	108	61 08	27	106	61 35	26	104	62 01	23	102	62 24	22	100	62 46	21	98	63 07	18	96	331
30	59 20	+29	109	59 49	+28	107	60 17	+27	105	60 44	+25	104	61 09	+23	102	61 32	+22	100	61 54	+20	98	62 14	+18	96	330
31	58 29	29	108	58 58	27	106	59 26	26	104	59 52	25	103	60 17	23	101	60 40	21	99	61 01	20	97	61 21	18	95	329
32	57 39	28	107	58 07	28	105	58 35	25	104	59 00	25	102	59 25	22	100	59 47	22	98	60 09	19	96	60 28	18	95	328
33	56 48	28	106	57 16	27	105	57 43	25	103	58 08	24	101	58 32	23	99	58 55	21	98	59 16	20	96	59 36	18	94	327
34	55 57	27	105	56 25	26	104	56 51	25	102	57 16	24	100	57 40	22	99	58 02	21	97	58 23	20	95	58 43	18	93	326
35	55 06	+27	105	55 33	+26	103	55 59	+25	101	56 24	+24	100	56 48	+22	98	57 10	+21	96	57 31	+19	95	57 50	+18	93	325
36	54 15	27	104	54 42	25	102	55 07	25	101	55 32	23	99	55 55	22	97	56 17	21	96	56 38	19	94	56 57	18	92	324
37	53 23	27	103	53 50	25	101	54 15	25	100	54 40	23	98	55 03	21	97	55 24	21	95	55 45	19	93	56 04	18	92	323
38	52 31	27	102	52 58	25	101	53 23	24	99	53 47	23	98	54 10	22	96	54 32	20	95	54 52	19	93	55 11	18	91	322
39	51 39	27	102	52 06	25	100	52 31	24	99	52 55	22	97	53 17	22	96	53 39	20	94	53 59	19	92	54 18	18	91	321
40	50 47	+26	101	51 13	+25	99	51 38	+24	98	52 02	+23	97	52 25	+21	95	52 46	+20	93	53 06	+19	92	53 25	+18	90	320
41	49 55	26	100	50 21	25	99	50 46	23	97	51 09	23	96	51 32	21	94	51 53	20	93	52 13	19	91	52 32	18	90	319
42	49 03	26	100	49 29	24	98	49 53	24	97	50 17	22	95	50 39	21	94	51 00	20	92	51 20	19	91	51 39	18	89	318
43	48 11	25	99	48 36	24	98	49 00	24	96	49 24	22	95	49 46	21	93	50 07	20	92	50 27	19	90	50 46	18	89	317
44	47 19	25	98	47 44	24	97	48 08	23	96	48 31	22	94	48 53	21	93	49 14	20	91	49 34	19	90	49 53	18	88	316
45	46 26	+25	98	46 51	+24	96	47 15	+23	95	47 38	+22	94	48 00	+21	92	48 21	+20	91	48 41	+19	89	49 00	+18	88	315
46	45 34	24	97	45 58	24	96	46 22	23	95	46 45	22	93	47 07	21	92	47 28	20	90	47 48	19	89	48 07	18	88	314
47	44 41	25	97	45 06	23	95	45 29	23	94	45 52	22	93	46 14	21	91	46 35	20	90	46 55	19	89	47 14	18	87	313
48	43 48	25	96	44 13	24	95	44 37	22	93	44 59	22	92	45 21	21	91	45 42	20	89	46 02	19	88	46 21	19	87	312
49	42 56	24	95	43 20	24	94	43 44	22	93	44 06	22	92	44 28	21	90	44 49	20	89	45 09	20	88	45 29	18	86	311
50	42 03	+24	95	42 27	+24	94	42 51	+22	92	43 13	+22	92	43 35	+21	90	43 56	+21	89	44 17	+19	87	44 36	+18	86	310
51	41 10	24	94	41 34	24	93	41 58	22	92	42 20	22	91	42 42	21	89	43 03	21	88	43 24	19	87	43 43	18	86	309
52	40 17	24	94	40 41	24	93	41 05	23	91	41 28	21	90	41 49	21	89	42 10	21	88	42 31	19	86	42 50	19	85	308
53	39 24	24	93	39 48	24	92	40 12	23	91	40 35	21	90	40 56	22	89	41 18	20	87	41 38	19	86	41 57	19	85	307
54	38 31	24	93	38 55	24	92	39 19	23	90	39 42	21	89	40 03	22	88	40 25	20	87	40 45	20	86	41 05	18	84	306
55	37 38	+25	92	38 03	+23	91	38 26	+23	90	38 49	+22	89	39 11	+21	88	39 32	+20	86	39 52	+20	85	40 12	+19	84	305
56	36 45	25	92	37 10	23	91	37 33	23	90	37 56	22	88	38 18	21	87	38 39	20	86	38 59	20	85	39 19	19	84	304
57	35 53	24	91	36 17	23	90	36 40	23	89	37 03	22	88	37 25	21	87	37 46	21	86	38 07	20	84	38 27	19	83	303
58	35 00	24	90	35 24	23	89	35 47	23	89	36 10	22	87	36 32	21	86	36 53	21	85	37 14	20	84	37 34	19	83	302
59	34 07	24	90	34 31	23	89	34 54	23	88	35 17	22	87	35 39	22	86	36 01	20	85	36 21	21	84	36 42	19	82	301
60	33 14	+24	90	33 38	+23	89	34 01	+23	88	34 24	+22	87	34 46	+22	85	35 08	+21	84	35 29	+20	83	35 49	+20	82	300
61	32 21	24	89	32 45	23	88	33 08	23	87	33 31	22	86	33 53	22	85	34 15	21	84	34 36	21	83	34 57	19	82	299
62	31 28	24	89	31 52	23	88	32 15	23	87	32 38	23	86	33 01	21	85	33 22	22	84	33 44	20	82	34 04	20	81	298
63	30 35	24	89	30 59	23	87	31 22	23	86	31 45	23	86	32 08	22	84	32 30	21	83	32 51	21	82	33 12	20	81	297
64	29 42	24	88	30 06	24	87	30 30	23	86	30 53	22	85	31 15	22	84	31 37	22	83	31 59	21	82	32 20	20	80	296
65	28 49	+24	88	29 13	+24	87	29 37	+23	86	30 00	+23	84	30 23	+22	83	30 45	+21	82	31 06	+21	81	31 27	+21	80	295
66	27 56	24	87	28 20	24	86	28 44	23	85	29 07	23	84	29 30	22	83	29 52	22	82	30 14	21	81	30 35	21	80	294
67	27 03	24	87	27 27	24	86	27 51	24	85	28 15	22	84	28 37	23	83	29 00	22	82	29 22	21	80	29 43	21	79	293
68	26 10	24	86	26 34	24	85	26 58	24	84	27 22	23	83	27 45	22	82	28 07	23	81	28 30	21	80	28 51	21	79	292
69	25 17	25	86	25 42	24	85	26 06	23	84	26 29	23	84	26 52	23	82	27 15	22	81	27 37	22	80	27 59	21	79	291

S. Lat. { LHA greater than 180°...... Zn=180-Z
{ LHA less than 180°..........Zn=180+Z

LAT 28°

DECLINATION SAME NAME AS LATITUDE

165. Sight Reduction Tables (HO 249, volume II)

DECLINATION **CONTRARY** NAME TO LATITUDE

Lat. { LHA greater than 180°....... Zn=Z
{ LHA less than 180°.......... Zn=360−Z

LAT 28°

0° Hc d Z	2° Hc d Z	11° Hc d Z	14° Hc d Z	15° Hc d Z	16° Hc d Z	21° Hc d Z	29° Hc d Z	LHA
1827 30 100	1727 30 102	1246 32 110	1109 32 113	1037 33 113	1004 33 114	0718 33 119	0249 34 125	291
1919 30 101	1819 31 103	1336 33 111	1158 33 113	1125 33 114	1052 33 115	0805 34 119	0332 34 126	292
2011 30 101	1910 30 103	1425 32 111	1247 34 114	1213 33 115	1140 33 115	0851 34 120	0415 35 126	293
2103 30 102	2002 31 104	1515 33 112	1335 33 114	1302 34 115	1228 34 116	0937 35 120	0458 36 127	294
2155 -31 102	2053 -31 104	1604 -33 112	1423 -34 115	1349 -34 116	1315 -34 117	1023 -35 121	0540 -36 127	295
2246 30 103	2145 32 105	1653 34 113	1511 34 115	1437 34 116	1403 35 117	1108 35 121	0622 36 128	296
2338 31 104	2236 32 105	1742 34 113	1559 34 116	1525 35 117	1450 35 118	1153 35 122	0704 37 128	297
2429 31 104	2327 32 106	1830 34 114	1647 35 117	1612 35 117	1537 36 118	1238 36 122	0745 37 129	298
2521 32 105	2418 32 107	1918 34 115	1734 35 117	1659 36 118	1623 36 119	1323 37 123	0826 37 129	299
2612 -32 105	2508 -32 107	2007 -35 115	1821 -36 118	1745 -36 119	1709 -36 119	1407 -37 124	0907 -38 130	300
2703 32 106	2559 33 108	2054 35 116	1908 36 118	1832 37 119	1755 36 120	1451 37 124	0948 39 131	301
2754 32 106	2649 32 108	2142 36 116	1954 36 119	1918 37 120	1841 37 121	1535 38 125	1028 39 131	302
2845 33 107	2740 34 109	2229 35 117	2040 36 120	2004 37 120	1927 38 121	1618 38 125	1108 40 132	303
2935 32 108	2830 34 110	2316 36 118	2126 37 120	2049 37 121	2012 38 122	1701 38 126	1147 40 132	304
3026 -33 108	2919 -33 110	2403 -37 118	2212 -38 121	2134 -37 122	2057 -39 123	1744 -39 127	1226 -40 133	305
3116 33 109	3009 34 111	2450 38 119	2257 38 122	2219 38 122	2141 38 123	1826 39 127	1305 41 133	306
3206 34 110	3059 35 111	2536 38 120	2342 38 122	2304 39 123	2225 39 124	1908 40 128	1343 41 134	307
3256 34 110	3148 35 112	2622 38 120	2427 39 123	2348 39 124	2309 39 125	1950 41 129	1421 42 135	308
3345 34 111	3237 35 113	2707 38 121	2511 39 124	2432 40 124	2352 39 125	2031 41 129	1459 43 135	309
3435 -35 112	3325 -35 114	2753 -39 122	2555 -39 125	2516 -40 125	2436 -41 126	2112 -41 130	1536 -43 136	310
3524 35 112	3414 36 114	2837 39 122	2639 44 125	2559 41 126	2518 40 127	2152 41 131	1612 43 137	311
3613 35 113	3502 36 115	2922 40 123	2722 41 126	2641 40 127	2601 42 127	2232 42 131	1648 43 137	312
3702 36 114	3550 37 116	3006 40 124	2805 41 127	2724 41 127	2643 42 128	2312 43 132	1724 44 138	313
3750 36 114	3638 37 116	3050 41 125	2847 41 127	2806 42 128	2724 42 129	2351 43 133	1759 44 139	314
3838 -36 115	3725 -37 117	3133 -41 126	2929 -42 128	2847 -42 129	2805 -43 130	2430 -44 134	1834 -45 139	315
3926 37 116	3812 38 118	3216 41 126	3011 43 129	2928 42 130	2846 43 130	2508 44 134	1909 46 140	316
4013 37 117	3858 38 119	3259 42 127	3052 43 130	3009 43 130	2926 44 131	2546 45 135	1942 46 141	317
4101 38 118	3945 39 120	3341 43 128	3132 43 130	3049 44 131	3005 44 132	2623 45 136	2016 47 141	318
4147 38 118	4031 39 120	3422 43 129	3213 44 131	3129 45 132	3044 44 133	2700 46 137	2048 47 142	319
4234 -39 119	4116 -39 121	3503 -43 130	3252 -44 132	3208 -45 133	3123 -45 134	2736 -46 137	2121 -48 143	320
4320 39 120	4201 40 122	3544 44 130	3331 45 133	3246 45 134	3201 45 135	2811 46 138	2152 49 144	321
4405 39 121	4246 41 123	3624 44 131	3410 46 134	3324 45 135	3239 46 135	2846 47 139	2224 49 144	322
4451 40 122	4330 41 124	3704 45 132	3448 46 135	3402 46 136	3316 47 136	2921 48 140	2254 49 145	323
4535 40 123	4414 42 125	3742 45 133	3525 46 136	3439 47 136	3352 47 137	2955 49 141	2324 49 146	324
4620 -42 124	4457 -42 126	3821 -46 134	3602 -47 137	3515 -47 137	3428 -48 138	3028 -49 142	2353 -50 147	325
4703 41 125	4539 44 127	3858 46 135	3638 47 138	3551 48 138	3503 48 139	3100 49 143	2422 50 148	326
4747 43 126	4622 44 128	3936 47 136	3713 47 138	3626 49 139	3537 48 140	3132 49 143	2450 51 148	327
4829 43 127	4703 44 129	4012 48 137	3748 48 139	3700 49 140	3611 49 141	3204 50 144	2518 52 149	328
4911 43 128	4744 45 130	4048 48 138	3822 49 140	3733 49 141	3644 49 142	3234 50 145	2545 52 150	329
4953 -44 129	4824 -45 131	4123 -49 139	3856 -50 141	3806 -49 142	3717 -51 143	3304 -51 146	2611 -53 151	330
5033 44 130	4904 46 132	4157 49 140	3928 50 143	3838 50 143	3748 50 144	3333 51 147	2636 52 152	331
5113 45 131	4942 46 134	4231 50 141	4000 50 144	3910 51 144	3819 51 145	3402 52 148	2701 53 153	332
5153 46 133	5020 46 135	4303 50 142	4031 51 145	3940 51 145	3849 52 146	3429 52 149	2725 53 153	333
5231 46 134	5058 48 136	4335 51 144	4102 52 146	4010 52 146	3918 52 147	3456 53 150	2748 54 154	334
5309 -47 135	5134 -48 137	4406 -51 145	4131 -52 147	4039 -52 147	3947 -53 147	3522 -53 151	2811 -54 155	335
5346 48 137	5210 49 139	4436 52 146	4200 53 148	4107 53 149	4014 53 149	3547 54 152	2833 55 156	336
5422 49 138	5244 49 140	4506 53 147	4227 53 149	4134 54 150	4041 54 150	3612 55 153	2854 55 157	337
5457 49 139	5318 50 141	4534 53 148	4254 53 150	4201 54 151	4107 54 151	3635 54 154	2914 55 158	338
5531 50 141	5351 51 143	4601 53 150	4320 54 151	4226 54 152	4132 55 153	3658 55 155	2934 56 159	339
5604 -51 142	5422 -51 144	4628 -54 151	4345 -55 153	4250 -54 153	4156 -55 154	3720 -56 156	2952 -56 160	340
5636 51 144	5453 52 146	4653 55 152	4409 55 154	4314 56 154	4218 55 155	3740 56 157	3010 56 161	341
5707 52 145	5522 53 147	4717 55 153	4432 55 155	4336 56 156	4240 55 156	3800 56 159	3027 57 162	342
5736 52 147	5550 53 149	4740 55 155	4453 56 156	4357 56 157	4301 56 157	3819 57 160	3043 57 163	343
5805 54 149	5617 54 150	4802 56 156	4514 56 158	4418 57 158	4321 57 159	3837 57 161	3059 58 164	344
5832 -55 150	5643 -55 152	4823 -56 158	4533 -56 159	4437 -57 159	4340 -57 160	3854 -57 162	3113 -58 165	345
5857 55 152	5707 55 154	4843 57 159	4552 57 160	4455 57 161	4358 58 161	3910 58 163	3127 58 166	346
5921 55 153	5730 56 155	4901 57 160	4609 57 162	4512 58 162	4414 58 162	3929 58 164	3140 59 167	347
5944 56 155	5752 57 157	4918 57 162	4625 58 163	4527 58 163	4429 58 164	3939 58 165	3151 58 168	348
6005 57 157	5812 57 159	4934 58 163	4640 58 164	4542 58 165	4444 59 165	3952 59 167	3202 59 169	349
6024 -57 159	5830 -58 161	4949 -59 165	4654 -59 166	4555 -58 166	4457 -59 166	4003 -58 168	3212 -59 170	350
6042 58 161	5847 58 162	5002 58 166	4706 58 167	4608 59 167	4509 59 168	4014 59 169	3221 59 171	351
6058 58 163	5902 58 164	5014 59 168	4718 60 169	4618 59 169	4519 59 169	4024 60 170	3229 59 172	352
6112 58 165	5915 58 166	5025 59 169	4727 59 170	4628 59 170	4529 59 170	4032 59 171	3237 60 173	353
6125 59 167	5927 59 168	5034 59 171	4736 59 171	4637 60 172	4537 59 172	4040 60 173	3243 60 174	354
6136 -60 169	5937 -59 170	5042 -59 172	4743 -59 173	4644 -60 173	4544 -60 173	4046 -60 174	3248 -60 175	355
6144 59 172	5945 59 172	5049 60 174	4749 59 174	4650 60 174	4550 60 175	4051 60 175	3252 59 176	356
6151 60 174	5952 60 174	5054 60 175	4754 60 176	4654 60 176	4554 60 176	4055 60 176	3256 60 177	357
6156 60 176	5956 60 176	5057 60 177	4757 60 177	4657 60 177	4557 59 177	4058 60 178	3258 60 178	358
6159 60 178	5959 60 178	5059 60 178	4759 60 179	4659 60 179	4559 60 179	4059 60 179	3300 60 179	359
6200 -60 180	6000 -60 180	5100 -60 180	4800 -60 180	4700 -60 180	4600 -60 180	4100 -60 180	3300 -60 180	360

| 0° | 2° | 11° | 14° | 15° | 16° | 21° | 29° | |

Lat. { LHA greater than 180°....... Zn=180−Z
{ LHA less than 180°.......... Zn=180+Z

LAT 28°

DECLINATION **CONTRARY** NAME TO LATITUDE

166. Sight Reduction Tables (HO 249, volume II)

DECLINATION SAME NAME AS LATITUDE

N. Lat. { LHA greater than 180°........ Zn=Z
{ LHA less than 180°............Zn=360–Z

LAT 42°

LHA	0° (Hc d Z)	2° (Hc d Z)	3° (Hc d Z)	8° (Hc d Z)	15° (Hc d Z)	16° (Hc d Z)	20° (Hc d Z)	29° (Hc d Z)	LHA
0	48 00 +60 180	50 00 +60 180	51 00 +60 180	56 00 +60 180	63 00 +60 180	64 00 +60 180	68 00 +60 180	77 00 +60 180	360
1	47 59 60 179	49 59 60 178	50 59 60 178	55 59 60 178	62 59 60 178	63 59 60 178	67 59 60 178	76 59 59 176	359
2	47 58 60 177	49 58 60 177	50 58 60 177	55 57 60 177	62 57 60 176	63 57 60 176	67 56 60 175	76 54 60 172	358
3	47 55 60 176	49 55 60 175	50 54 60 175	55 54 60 175	62 53 59 174	63 52 60 173	67 51 60 173	76 47 59 169	357
4	47 51 60 174	49 50 60 174	50 50 60 174	55 49 60 173	62 47 59 172	63 46 60 171	67 45 59 170	76 36 59 165	356
5	47 46 +59 173	49 45 +60 172	50 45 +59 172	55 43 +59 171	62 39 +60 169	63 39 +59 169	67 36 +59 168	76 23 +58 161	355
6	47 39 60 171	49 38 60 171	50 38 59 171	55 35 60 169	62 31 59 167	63 30 59 167	67 25 59 165	76 07 57 158	354
7	47 32 59 170	49 31 59 169	50 30 59 169	55 27 59 168	62 20 59 165	63 19 59 165	67 13 58 163	75 49 56 154	353
8	47 23 59 168	49 22 59 168	50 21 59 167	55 16 59 166	62 08 58 163	63 06 59 163	66 59 58 161	75 29 54 151	352
9	47 13 59 167	49 12 59 166	50 11 59 166	55 05 59 164	61 54 58 161	62 52 58 161	66 43 58 158	75 06 53 148	351
10	47 03 +58 165	49 00 +59 165	49 59 +59 164	54 52 +59 163	61 39 +58 159	62 37 +57 159	66 26 +57 156	74 41 +52 145	350
11	46 51 58 164	48 48 59 163	49 47 58 163	54 38 58 161	61 23 57 157	62 20 57 157	66 07 56 154	74 15 50 142	349
12	46 38 58 162	48 35 58 162	49 33 58 161	54 23 58 159	61 05 57 156	62 02 56 155	65 46 56 152	73 46 50 139	348
13	46 24 58 161	48 20 58 160	49 18 58 160	54 07 57 158	60 46 56 154	61 42 56 153	65 24 55 150	73 17 48 137	347
14	46 09 58 160	48 04 58 159	49 02 58 158	53 49 57 156	60 25 56 152	61 21 56 151	65 01 54 147	72 46 47 134	346
15	45 53 +57 158	47 48 +57 157	48 45 +57 157	53 31 +56 155	60 04 +55 150	60 59 +55 149	64 36 +51 145	72 13 +46 132	345
16	45 35 58 157	47 30 57 156	48 27 57 156	53 11 56 153	59 41 54 148	60 35 55 147	64 11 52 144	71 39 45 130	344
17	45 17 57 155	47 11 57 155	48 08 57 154	52 50 56 151	59 17 54 146	60 11 54 146	63 43 52 142	71 05 44 128	343
18	44 58 57 154	46 52 56 153	47 48 56 153	52 28 56 150	58 51 54 145	59 45 53 144	63 15 52 140	70 29 43 126	342
19	44 38 57 153	46 31 56 152	47 27 56 151	52 05 55 148	58 25 53 143	59 18 53 142	62 46 51 138	69 53 42 124	341
20	44 18 +56 152	46 10 +55 150	47 05 +56 150	51 41 +55 147	57 58 +52 142	58 50 +52 141	62 16 +50 136	69 15 +41 122	340
21	43 56 56 150	45 47 55 149	46 42 56 149	51 17 54 145	57 30 52 140	58 22 51 139	61 44 50 135	68 37 41 121	339
22	43 33 56 149	45 24 55 148	46 19 55 147	50 51 54 144	57 00 52 138	57 52 51 137	61 12 49 133	67 59 39 119	338
23	43 10 55 148	45 00 54 147	45 54 55 146	50 24 53 143	56 30 51 137	57 21 51 136	60 39 48 132	67 19 39 118	337
24	42 45 55 146	44 35 54 145	45 29 54 145	49 57 53 141	55 59 51 135	56 50 50 134	60 05 48 130	66 40 38 116	336
25	42 20 +55 145	44 09 +54 144	45 03 +53 143	49 28 +53 140	55 28 +49 134	56 17 +50 133	59 31 +47 129	65 59 +38 115	335
26	41 55 53 144	43 42 53 143	44 35 54 142	48 59 52 139	54 55 49 133	55 44 49 132	58 56 46 127	65 19 37 113	334
27	41 28 53 143	43 15 53 142	44 08 53 141	48 29 52 137	54 22 49 131	55 11 48 130	58 20 45 126	64 38 36 112	333
28	41 00 54 142	42 46 53 140	43 39 53 140	47 59 51 136	53 48 48 130	54 36 48 129	57 43 45 124	63 56 36 111	332
29	40 32 53 140	42 18 52 139	43 10 52 138	47 27 51 135	53 14 47 129	54 01 47 128	57 06 45 123	63 14 36 110	331
30	40 04 +52 139	41 48 +52 138	42 40 +52 137	46 55 +51 134	52 38 +48 127	53 26 +46 126	56 28 +44 122	62 32 +35 109	330
31	39 34 52 138	41 18 51 137	42 09 52 136	46 23 50 132	52 03 46 126	52 49 47 125	55 50 44 121	61 50 34 107	329
32	39 04 52 137	40 47 51 136	41 38 51 135	45 50 49 131	51 26 47 125	52 13 46 124	55 12 43 119	61 07 34 106	328
33	38 33 52 136	40 16 50 135	41 06 51 134	45 16 49 130	50 49 46 124	51 35 45 123	54 32 43 118	60 24 34 105	327
34	38 02 51 135	39 43 51 133	40 34 50 133	44 41 49 129	50 12 45 123	50 57 45 121	53 53 42 117	59 41 33 104	326
35	37 30 +50 134	39 11 +50 132	40 01 +49 132	44 06 +48 128	49 34 +45 121	50 19 +45 120	53 13 +42 116	58 58 +33 103	325
36	36 57 51 133	38 37 50 131	39 27 49 130	43 31 47 127	48 56 44 120	49 40 44 119	52 33 41 115	58 14 33 102	324
37	36 24 50 132	38 04 49 130	38 53 49 129	42 55 47 126	48 17 44 119	49 01 44 118	51 52 41 114	57 31 32 102	323
38	35 51 49 131	37 29 49 129	38 18 49 128	42 18 47 125	47 38 44 118	48 22 43 117	51 11 41 113	56 47 32 101	322
39	35 17 49 130	36 55 48 128	37 43 48 127	41 41 47 123	46 58 44 117	47 42 43 116	50 30 40 112	56 03 32 100	321
40	34 42 +49 129	36 19 +48 127	37 07 +48 126	41 04 +46 122	46 19 +43 116	47 02 +42 115	49 48 +40 111	55 19 +32 99	320
41	34 07 48 128	35 43 48 126	36 31 48 125	40 26 46 121	45 38 43 115	46 21 42 114	49 06 40 110	54 35 32 98	319
42	33 31 48 127	35 07 48 125	35 55 47 124	39 48 45 120	44 58 42 114	45 40 42 113	48 24 40 109	53 51 32 97	318
43	32 55 48 126	34 31 47 124	35 18 47 123	39 09 45 119	44 17 42 113	44 59 42 112	47 42 39 108	53 06 32 97	317
44	32 19 47 125	33 53 47 123	34 40 47 123	38 30 45 119	43 36 42 112	44 18 41 111	46 59 39 107	52 22 32 96	316
45	31 42 +47 124	33 16 +46 122	34 02 +47 122	37 51 +44 118	42 54 +42 111	43 36 +41 110	46 16 +39 106	51 38 +31 95	315
46	31 05 47 123	32 38 46 121	33 24 46 121	37 11 44 117	42 13 41 110	42 54 41 109	45 34 38 105	50 53 32 94	314
47	30 27 47 122	32 00 46 120	32 46 45 120	36 31 44 116	41 31 41 109	42 12 40 108	44 50 39 104	50 09 31 94	313
48	29 49 46 120	31 21 45 120	32 07 45 119	35 51 43 115	40 48 41 109	41 29 40 108	44 07 38 103	49 24 32 93	312
49	29 11 46 120	30 42 45 119	31 28 45 118	35 10 43 114	40 06 41 108	40 47 40 107	43 24 37 103	48 40 31 92	311
50	28 32 +46 119	30 03 +45 118	30 48 +45 117	34 29 +43 113	39 23 +41 107	40 04 +40 106	42 40 +38 102	47 55 +31 91	310
51	27 53 45 119	29 23 45 117	30 08 45 116	33 48 43 112	38 41 40 106	39 21 39 105	41 56 38 101	47 11 31 91	309
52	27 14 45 118	28 44 45 116	29 28 44 115	33 06 43 111	37 58 40 105	38 38 39 104	41 13 37 100	46 26 31 90	308
53	26 34 45 117	28 03 45 115	28 48 44 115	32 25 42 111	37 15 39 104	37 54 40 103	40 29 37 99	45 41 32 89	307
54	25 54 45 116	27 23 44 114	28 07 44 114	31 43 42 110	36 31 40 104	37 11 39 103	39 45 37 99	44 57 31 89	306
55	25 14 +44 115	26 42 +44 114	27 26 +43 113	31 01 +42 109	35 48 +39 103	36 27 +39 102	39 00 +37 98	44 12 +32 88	305
56	24 33 44 114	26 01 44 113	26 45 43 112	30 19 41 108	35 04 39 102	35 44 38 101	38 16 37 97	43 28 31 87	304
57	23 53 43 114	25 20 43 112	26 03 43 111	29 36 42 107	34 21 39 101	35 00 38 100	37 32 37 96	42 43 32 87	303
58	23 12 43 113	24 38 44 111	25 22 42 110	28 53 40 106	33 37 39 100	34 16 38 100	36 48 36 95	41 59 31 86	302
59	22 30 43 113	23 57 43 110	24 40 42 110	28 10 42 106	32 53 39 100	33 38 38 99	36 03 37 95	41 14 32 86	301
60	21 49 +43 111	23 15 +43 110	23 58 +42 109	27 27 +42 105	32 09 +39 99	32 48 +38 98	35 19 +36 94	40 30 +31 85	300
61	21 07 43 110	22 33 42 109	23 15 42 108	26 44 41 104	31 25 38 98	32 03 39 97	34 34 37 94	39 45 32 84	299
62	20 25 43 110	21 50 43 108	22 33 42 107	26 01 41 103	30 41 38 97	31 19 38 97	33 50 36 93	39 01 32 84	298
63	19 43 43 109	21 08 42 107	21 50 42 107	25 18 40 102	29 56 39 97	30 35 38 96	33 05 37 92	38 17 32 83	297
64	19 01 42 108	20 25 42 107	21 07 42 106	24 34 41 102	29 12 38 96	29 50 39 95	32 21 36 92	37 33 32 83	296
65	18 18 +43 107	19 43 +41 106	20 24 +42 105	23 50 +41 101	28 28 +38 95	29 06 +38 94	31 36 +37 91	36 48 +32 82	295
66	17 36 42 107	19 00 41 105	19 41 40 104	23 06 41 100	27 43 39 95	28 22 38 94	30 51 37 90	36 04 33 81	294
67	16 53 42 106	18 16 42 104	18 58 41 104	22 23 40 100	26 59 38 94	27 37 38 93	30 07 36 89	35 20 33 81	293
68	16 10 42 105	17 33 42 103	18 15 41 103	21 39 40 99	26 14 39 93	26 53 37 92	29 22 37 89	34 36 33 80	292
69	15 27 41 104	16 50 41 103	17 31 41 102	20 54 41 98	25 30 38 93	26 08 38 92	28 38 36 88	33 52 33 80	291

S. Lat. { LHA greater than 180°........Zn=180–Z
{ LHA less than 180°............Zn=180+Z

LAT 42°

DECLINATION SAME NAME AS LATITUDE

167. Sight Reduction Tables (HO 249, volume III)

DECLINATION CONTRARY NAME TO LATITUDE

N. Lat. {LHA greater than 180°....... Zn=Z
{LHA less than 180°.............Zn=360−Z

LAT 42°

LHA	0° Hc d Z	1° Hc d Z	2° Hc d Z	3° Hc d Z	4° Hc d Z	5° Hc d Z	6° Hc d Z	7° Hc d Z	LHA
69	15 27 42 104	14 45 42 105	14 03 42 106	13 21 42 107	12 39 42 107	11 57 43 108	11 14 42 109	10 32 43 110	291
68	16 10 42 105	15 28 42 106	14 46 42 107	14 04 42 107	13 22 43 108	12 39 42 109	11 57 43 110	11 14 43 110	292
67	16 53 42 106	16 11 42 107	15 29 43 107	14 46 42 108	14 04 43 109	13 21 43 110	12 38 42 110	11 56 43 111	293
66	17 36 43 107	16 53 42 107	16 11 42 108	15 29 43 109	14 46 43 110	14 03 43 110	13 20 43 111	12 37 43 112	294
65	18 18 42 107	17 36 43 108	16 53 42 109	16 11 43 110	15 28 43 110	14 45 43 111	14 02 43 112	13 19 44 112	295
64	19 01 43 108	18 18 42 109	17 36 43 110	16 53 43 110	16 10 44 111	15 26 43 112	14 43 43 113	14 00 44 113	296
63	19 43 43 109	19 00 43 110	18 17 43 110	17 34 43 111	16 51 43 112	16 08 44 113	15 24 44 113	14 40 44 114	297
62	20 25 43 110	19 42 43 110	18 59 43 111	18 16 44 112	17 32 43 113	16 49 44 113	16 05 44 114	15 21 44 115	298
61	21 07 43 110	20 24 43 111	19 41 44 112	18 57 44 113	18 13 43 113	17 30 44 114	16 46 44 115	16 02 45 115	299
60	21 49 44 111	21 05 44 112	20 22 44 113	19 38 44 113	18 54 44 114	18 10 44 115	17 26 44 116	16 42 45 116	300
59	22 30 43 112	21 47 44 113	21 03 44 113	20 19 44 114	19 35 44 115	18 51 45 116	18 06 44 116	17 22 45 117	301
58	23 12 44 113	22 28 44 113	21 44 44 114	21 00 45 115	20 15 44 116	19 31 45 116	18 46 45 117	18 01 45 118	302
57	23 53 44 114	23 09 45 114	22 24 44 115	21 40 45 116	20 55 44 116	20 11 45 117	19 26 46 118	18 40 45 119	303
56	24 33 44 114	23 49 44 115	23 05 45 116	22 20 45 117	21 35 45 117	20 50 45 118	20 05 45 119	19 20 46 119	304
55	25 14 45 115	24 29 44 116	23 45 45 117	23 00 45 117	22 15 46 118	21 29 45 119	20 44 46 119	19 58 46 120	305
54	25 54 45 116	25 09 45 117	24 24 45 117	23 39 45 118	22 54 46 119	22 08 45 120	21 23 46 120	20 37 46 121	306
53	26 34 45 117	25 49 45 118	25 04 45 118	24 18 45 119	23 33 46 120	22 47 46 120	22 01 46 121	21 15 47 122	307
52	27 14 46 118	26 28 45 118	25 43 46 119	24 57 46 120	24 11 46 121	23 25 46 121	22 39 47 122	21 52 46 123	308
51	27 53 45 119	27 08 46 119	26 22 46 120	25 36 46 121	24 50 47 121	24 03 46 122	23 17 47 123	22 30 47 123	309
50	28 32 46 119	27 46 46 120	27 00 46 121	26 14 46 122	25 28 47 122	24 41 47 123	23 54 47 124	23 07 47 124	310
49	29 11 46 120	28 25 47 121	27 38 46 122	26 52 47 122	26 05 47 123	25 18 47 124	24 31 47 124	23 44 48 125	311
48	29 49 46 121	29 03 47 122	28 16 47 123	27 29 47 123	26 42 47 124	25 55 47 125	25 08 48 125	24 20 48 126	312
47	30 27 46 122	29 41 47 122	28 54 47 123	28 06 47 124	27 19 47 125	26 32 48 126	25 44 48 126	24 56 48 127	313
46	31 05 47 123	30 18 47 124	29 31 48 124	28 43 48 125	27 55 47 126	27 08 48 126	26 20 49 127	25 31 48 128	314
45	31 42 47 124	30 55 48 125	30 07 48 125	29 19 48 126	28 31 48 127	27 43 48 127	26 55 49 128	26 06 48 129	315
44	32 19 48 125	31 31 48 126	30 43 48 126	29 55 48 127	29 07 48 128	28 19 49 128	27 30 49 129	26 41 49 130	316
43	32 55 48 126	32 07 48 126	31 19 48 127	30 31 49 128	29 42 49 128	28 53 49 129	28 04 49 130	27 15 49 130	317
42	33 31 48 127	32 43 48 127	31 55 49 128	31 06 49 129	30 17 49 129	29 28 50 130	28 38 49 131	27 49 50 131	318
41	34 07 49 128	33 18 48 128	32 30 50 129	31 40 49 130	30 51 49 130	30 02 50 131	29 12 50 132	28 22 50 132	319
40	34 42 49 129	33 53 49 129	33 04 49 130	32 15 50 131	31 25 50 131	30 35 50 132	29 45 50 133	28 55 50 133	320
39	35 17 50 130	34 27 49 130	33 38 50 131	32 48 50 132	31 58 50 132	31 08 50 133	30 18 51 134	29 27 51 134	321
38	35 51 50 131	35 01 50 131	34 11 50 132	33 21 50 133	32 31 51 133	31 40 51 134	30 50 51 135	29 59 51 135	322
37	36 24 50 132	35 34 50 132	34 44 50 133	33 54 51 134	33 03 51 134	32 12 51 135	31 21 51 136	30 30 51 136	323
36	36 57 50 133	36 07 50 133	35 17 51 134	34 26 51 135	33 35 51 135	32 44 52 136	31 52 51 137	31 01 52 137	324
35	37 30 51 134	36 39 51 134	35 48 51 135	34 57 51 136	34 06 52 136	33 14 51 137	32 23 52 138	31 31 52 138	325
34	38 02 51 135	37 11 51 136	36 20 52 136	35 28 52 137	34 36 52 137	33 44 52 138	32 52 52 139	32 00 52 139	326
33	38 33 51 136	37 42 52 137	36 50 52 137	35 58 52 138	35 06 52 138	34 14 52 139	33 22 53 140	32 29 53 140	327
32	39 04 52 137	38 12 52 138	37 20 52 138	36 28 52 139	35 36 53 140	34 43 53 140	33 50 53 141	32 57 53 141	328
31	39 34 52 138	38 42 52 139	37 50 53 139	36 57 53 140	36 04 53 141	35 11 53 141	34 18 53 142	33 25 53 142	329
30	40 04 53 139	39 11 53 140	38 18 53 140	37 25 53 141	36 32 53 142	35 39 53 142	34 46 54 143	33 52 54 143	330
29	40 32 53 140	39 39 53 141	38 46 53 142	37 53 53 142	37 00 54 143	36 06 54 143	35 12 54 144	34 18 54 144	331
28	41 00 53 142	40 07 53 142	39 14 54 143	38 20 54 143	37 26 54 144	36 32 54 144	35 38 54 145	34 44 54 146	332
27	41 28 54 143	40 34 54 143	39 40 54 144	38 46 54 144	37 52 54 145	36 58 55 146	36 03 54 146	35 09 55 147	333
26	41 55 55 144	41 00 54 145	40 06 54 145	39 12 55 146	38 17 54 146	37 23 55 147	36 28 55 147	35 33 55 148	334
25	42 20 54 145	41 26 55 146	40 31 54 146	39 37 55 147	38 42 55 147	37 47 55 148	36 52 55 148	35 57 55 149	335
24	42 45 54 146	41 51 55 147	40 56 55 148	40 01 55 148	39 06 56 149	38 10 55 149	37 15 56 150	36 19 55 150	336
23	43 10 55 148	42 15 56 148	41 19 55 149	40 24 56 149	39 28 55 150	38 33 56 150	37 37 56 151	36 41 56 151	337
22	43 33 55 149	42 38 56 149	41 42 56 150	40 46 55 150	39 51 56 151	38 55 56 151	37 59 56 152	37 02 56 152	338
21	43 56 56 150	43 00 56 151	42 04 56 151	41 08 56 152	40 12 56 152	39 16 57 153	38 19 56 153	37 23 57 153	339
20	44 18 57 152	43 21 56 152	42 25 56 152	41 29 57 153	40 32 56 153	39 36 57 154	38 39 57 154	37 42 57 155	340
19	44 38 56 153	43 42 57 153	42 45 56 154	41 49 57 154	40 52 57 155	39 55 57 155	38 58 57 155	38 01 57 156	341
18	44 58 56 154	44 02 57 155	43 05 57 155	42 08 57 155	41 11 58 156	40 13 57 156	39 16 57 157	38 19 58 157	342
17	45 17 57 155	44 20 57 156	43 23 57 156	42 26 58 157	41 28 57 157	40 31 58 158	39 33 57 158	38 36 58 158	343
16	45 35 57 157	44 38 57 157	43 41 58 158	42 43 58 158	41 45 57 158	40 48 58 159	39 50 58 159	38 52 58 159	344
15	45 53 58 158	44 55 58 159	43 57 58 159	42 59 58 159	42 01 58 160	41 03 58 160	40 05 58 160	39 07 58 161	345
14	46 09 58 160	45 11 58 160	44 13 59 160	43 14 58 161	42 16 58 161	41 18 58 161	40 20 59 162	39 21 58 162	346
13	46 24 59 162	45 25 58 162	44 27 58 162	43 29 59 162	42 30 58 162	41 32 59 163	40 33 58 163	39 35 59 163	347
12	46 38 59 163	45 39 58 163	44 41 59 163	43 42 59 163	42 43 58 164	41 45 59 164	40 46 59 164	39 47 58 164	348
11	46 51 59 164	45 52 59 164	44 53 59 164	43 54 59 165	42 56 59 165	41 57 59 165	40 58 59 165	39 59 59 166	349
10	47 03 59 165	46 04 59 166	45 05 59 166	44 06 59 166	43 07 59 166	42 08 60 167	41 08 59 167	40 09 59 167	350
9	47 13 59 167	46 14 59 167	45 15 59 167	44 16 59 167	43 17 60 168	42 17 59 168	41 18 59 168	40 19 59 168	351
8	47 23 59 168	46 24 60 168	45 24 59 169	44 25 59 169	43 26 60 169	42 26 59 169	41 27 60 169	40 27 59 170	352
7	47 32 60 170	46 32 59 170	45 33 60 170	44 33 59 170	43 34 60 170	42 34 59 171	41 35 60 171	40 35 59 171	353
6	47 39 59 171	46 40 60 171	45 40 60 171	44 40 59 172	43 41 60 172	42 41 60 172	41 41 59 172	40 42 60 172	354
5	47 46 60 173	46 46 60 173	45 46 60 173	44 46 59 173	43 47 60 173	42 47 60 173	41 47 60 173	40 47 59 173	355
4	47 51 60 174	46 51 60 174	45 51 60 174	44 51 60 174	43 51 60 175	42 52 60 175	41 52 60 175	40 52 60 175	356
3	47 55 60 176	46 55 60 176	45 55 60 176	44 55 60 176	43 55 60 176	42 55 60 176	41 55 60 176	40 55 59 176	357
2	47 58 60 177	46 58 60 177	45 58 60 177	44 58 60 177	43 58 60 177	42 58 60 177	41 58 60 177	40 58 60 177	358
1	47 59 60 179	46 59 60 179	45 59 59 179	45 00 60 179	44 00 60 179	43 00 60 179	42 00 60 179	41 00 60 179	359
0	48 00 60 180	47 00 60 180	46 00 60 180	45 00 60 180	44 00 60 180	43 00 60 180	42 00 60 180	41 00 60 180	360
	0°	1°	2°	3°	4°	5°	6°	7°	

S. Lat. {LHA greater than 180°........Zn=180−Z
{LHA less than 180°.............Zn=180+Z

LAT 42°

DECLINATION CONTRARY NAME TO LATITUDE

168. Sight Reduction Tables (HO 249, volume III)

Correction to Tabulated Altitude

d /'	1	2	3	4	5	6	7	8	9	10	11	12	13	14	15	16	17	18	19	20	21	22	23	24	25	26	27	28	29	30	d /'
0	0	0	0	0	0	0	0	0	0	0	0	0	0	0	0	0	0	0	0	0	0	0	0	0	0	0	0	0	0	0	0
1	0	0	0	0	0	0	0	0	0	0	0	0	0	0	0	0	0	0	0	0	0	0	0	0	0	0	0	0	0	0	1
2	0	0	0	0	0	0	0	0	0	0	0	0	0	0	0	1	1	1	1	1	1	1	1	1	1	1	1	1	1	1	2
3	0	0	0	0	0	0	0	0	0	0	1	1	1	1	1	1	1	1	1	1	1	1	1	1	1	1	1	1	1	2	3
4	0	0	0	0	0	0	0	1	1	1	1	1	1	1	1	1	1	1	1	1	1	1	2	2	2	2	2	2	2	2	4
5	0	0	0	0	0	0	1	1	1	1	1	1	1	1	1	1	1	2	2	2	2	2	2	2	2	2	2	2	2	2	5
6	0	0	0	0	0	1	1	1	1	1	1	1	1	1	2	2	2	2	2	2	2	2	2	2	2	3	3	3	3	3	6
7	0	0	0	0	1	1	1	1	1	1	1	1	2	2	2	2	2	2	2	2	2	3	3	3	3	3	3	3	3	4	7
8	0	0	0	1	1	1	1	1	1	1	1	2	2	2	2	2	2	2	3	3	3	3	3	3	3	3	4	4	4	4	8
9	0	0	0	1	1	1	1	1	1	2	2	2	2	2	2	2	3	3	3	3	3	3	3	4	4	4	4	4	4	4	9
10	0	0	0	1	1	1	1	1	2	2	2	2	2	3	3	3	3	3	3	4	4	4	4	4	4	4	4	5	5	5	10
11	0	0	1	1	1	1	1	1	2	2	2	2	2	3	3	3	3	3	3	4	4	4	4	4	5	5	5	5	5	6	11
12	0	0	1	1	1	1	1	2	2	2	2	2	3	3	3	3	3	4	4	4	4	4	5	5	5	5	5	6	6	6	12
13	0	0	1	1	1	1	2	2	2	2	2	3	3	3	3	3	4	4	4	4	5	5	5	5	5	6	6	6	6	6	13
14	0	0	1	1	1	1	2	2	2	2	3	3	3	3	4	4	4	4	4	5	5	5	5	6	6	6	6	7	7	7	14
15	0	0	1	1	1	2	2	2	2	2	3	3	3	4	4	4	4	4	5	5	5	6	6	6	6	6	7	7	7	8	15
16	0	1	1	1	1	2	2	2	2	3	3	3	3	4	4	4	5	5	5	5	6	6	6	6	7	7	7	7	8	8	16
17	0	1	1	1	1	2	2	2	3	3	3	3	4	4	4	5	5	5	5	6	6	6	7	7	7	7	8	8	8	8	17
18	0	1	1	1	2	2	2	2	3	3	3	4	4	4	4	5	5	5	6	6	6	7	7	7	8	8	8	8	9	9	18
19	0	1	1	1	2	2	2	3	3	3	3	4	4	4	5	5	5	6	6	6	7	7	7	8	8	8	9	9	9	10	19
20	0	1	1	1	2	2	2	3	3	3	4	4	4	5	5	5	6	6	6	7	7	7	8	8	8	9	9	9	10	10	20
21	0	1	1	1	2	2	2	3	3	4	4	4	5	5	5	6	6	6	7	7	7	8	8	8	9	9	9	10	10	10	21
22	0	1	1	1	2	2	3	3	3	4	4	4	5	5	6	6	6	7	7	7	8	8	8	9	9	10	10	11	11	12	22
23	0	1	1	2	2	2	3	3	3	4	4	5	5	5	6	6	7	7	7	8	8	8	9	9	10	10	10	11	11	12	23
24	0	1	1	2	2	2	3	3	4	4	4	5	5	6	6	6	7	7	8	8	8	9	9	10	10	10	11	11	12	12	24
25	0	1	1	2	2	2	3	3	4	4	5	5	5	6	6	7	7	8	8	8	9	9	10	10	10	11	11	12	12	12	25
26	0	1	1	2	2	3	3	3	4	4	5	5	6	6	6	7	7	8	8	9	9	10	10	11	11	12	12	12	13	13	26
27	0	1	1	2	2	3	3	4	4	4	5	5	6	6	7	7	8	8	9	9	9	10	10	11	11	12	12	13	13	14	27
28	0	1	1	2	2	3	3	4	4	5	5	6	6	7	7	7	8	8	9	9	10	10	11	11	11	12	13	13	14	14	28
29	0	1	1	2	2	3	3	4	4	5	5	6	6	7	7	8	8	9	9	10	10	11	11	12	12	13	13	14	14	14	29
30	0	1	2	2	2	2	4	4	4	5	6	6	6	7	8	8	8	9	10	10	10	11	12	12	12	13	14	14	14	15	30
31	1	1	2	2	3	3	4	4	5	5	6	6	7	7	8	8	9	9	10	10	11	11	12	12	13	13	14	14	15	16	31
32	1	1	2	2	3	3	4	4	5	5	6	6	7	7	8	9	9	10	10	11	11	12	12	13	13	14	14	15	15	16	32
33	1	1	2	2	3	3	4	4	5	6	6	7	7	8	8	9	9	10	10	11	12	12	13	13	14	14	15	15	16	16	33
34	1	1	2	2	3	3	4	5	5	6	6	7	7	8	8	9	10	10	11	11	12	12	13	14	14	15	15	16	16	17	34
35	1	1	2	2	3	4	4	5	5	6	6	7	8	8	9	9	10	10	11	12	12	13	13	14	15	15	16	17	17	18	35
36	1	1	2	2	3	4	4	5	5	6	7	7	8	8	9	10	10	11	11	12	13	13	14	14	15	16	16	17	17	18	36
37	1	1	2	2	3	4	4	5	6	6	7	7	8	9	9	10	10	11	12	12	13	14	14	15	15	16	17	17	18	18	37
38	1	1	2	3	3	4	4	5	6	6	7	8	8	9	10	10	11	11	12	13	13	14	15	15	16	17	18	18	19	19	38
39	1	1	2	3	3	4	5	5	6	6	7	8	8	9	10	10	11	12	12	13	14	14	15	16	16	17	18	18	19	20	39
40	1	1	2	3	3	4	5	5	6	7	7	8	9	9	10	11	11	12	13	13	14	15	15	16	17	17	18	19	19	20	40
41	1	1	2	3	3	4	5	5	6	7	8	8	9	10	10	11	12	12	13	14	14	15	16	16	17	18	18	19	20	20	41
42	1	1	2	3	4	4	5	6	6	7	8	8	9	10	10	11	12	13	13	14	15	15	16	17	18	18	19	20	20	21	42
43	1	1	2	3	4	4	5	6	6	7	8	9	9	10	11	11	12	13	14	14	15	16	17	17	18	19	19	20	21	21	43
44	1	1	2	3	4	4	5	6	7	7	8	9	10	10	11	12	12	13	14	15	15	16	17	18	18	19	20	21	21	22	44
45	1	2	2	3	4	4	5	6	7	8	8	9	10	10	11	12	13	13	14	15	16	16	17	18	19	20	20	21	22	22	45
46	1	2	2	3	4	5	5	6	7	8	8	9	10	11	12	12	13	14	15	15	16	17	18	18	19	20	20	21	22	22	46
47	1	2	2	3	4	5	5	6	7	8	9	9	10	11	12	13	13	14	15	16	16	17	18	19	20	20	21	22	23	24	47
48	1	2	2	3	4	5	6	6	7	8	9	10	11	11	12	13	14	14	15	16	17	18	18	19	20	21	22	22	23	24	48
49	1	2	2	3	4	5	6	7	7	8	9	10	11	12	12	13	14	15	16	16	17	18	19	20	20	21	22	23	24	24	49
50	1	2	2	3	4	5	6	7	8	8	9	10	11	12	12	13	14	15	16	17	18	18	19	20	21	22	22	23	24	25	50
51	1	2	3	3	4	5	6	7	8	8	9	10	11	12	13	14	14	15	16	17	18	19	20	20	21	22	23	24	25	26	51
52	1	2	3	3	4	5	6	7	8	9	10	10	11	12	13	14	15	16	16	17	18	19	20	21	22	23	23	24	25	26	52
53	1	2	3	4	4	5	6	7	8	9	10	11	11	12	13	14	15	16	17	18	19	19	20	21	22	23	24	25	26	26	53
54	1	2	3	4	4	5	6	7	8	9	10	11	12	13	14	14	15	16	17	18	19	20	21	22	22	23	24	25	26	27	54
55	1	2	3	4	5	6	6	7	8	9	10	11	12	13	14	15	16	16	17	18	19	20	21	22	23	24	25	26	27	28	55
56	1	2	3	4	5	6	7	7	8	9	10	11	12	13	14	15	16	17	18	19	20	21	21	22	23	24	25	26	27	28	56
57	1	2	3	4	5	6	7	8	9	10	10	11	12	13	14	15	16	17	18	19	20	21	22	23	24	25	26	27	28	28	57
58	1	2	3	4	5	6	7	8	9	10	11	12	13	14	14	15	16	17	18	19	20	21	22	23	24	25	26	27	28	29	58
59	1	2	3	4	5	6	7	8	9	10	11	12	13	14	15	16	17	18	19	20	21	22	23	24	25	26	27	28	29	30	59

169. Altitude Correction for Minutes of Declination (HO 249, volumes II and III)

for Minutes of Declination

d/'	31	32	33	34	35	36	37	38	39	40	41	42	43	44	45	46	47	48	49	50	51	52	53	54	55	56	57	58	59	60	d/'
0	0	0	0	0	0	0	0	0	0	0	0	0	0	0	0	0	0	0	0	0	0	0	0	0	0	0	0	0	0	0	0
1	1	1	1	1	1	1	1	1	1	1	1	1	1	1	1	1	1	1	1	1	1	1	1	1	1	1	1	1	1	1	1
2	1	1	1	1	1	1	1	1	1	1	1	1	1	1	1	2	2	2	1	1	1	2	2	2	2	2	2	2	2	2	2
3	2	2	2	2	2	2	2	2	2	2	2	2	2	2	2	2	2	2	2	2	3	3	3	3	3	3	3	3	3	3	3
4	2	2	2	2	2	2	2	3	3	3	3	3	3	3	3	3	3	3	3	3	3	3	4	4	4	4	4	4	4	4	4
5	3	3	3	3	3	3	3	3	3	3	3	4	4	4	4	4	4	4	4	4	4	4	4	4	5	5	5	5	5	5	5
6	3	3	3	3	4	4	4	4	4	4	4	4	4	4	4	5	5	5	5	5	5	5	5	5	6	6	6	6	6	6	6
7	4	4	4	4	4	4	4	4	5	5	5	5	5	5	5	5	5	6	6	6	6	6	6	6	6	7	7	7	7	7	7
8	4	4	4	5	5	5	5	5	5	5	5	6	6	6	6	6	6	6	7	7	7	7	7	7	7	7	8	8	8	8	8
9	5	5	5	5	5	5	6	6	6	6	6	6	6	7	7	7	7	7	7	8	8	8	8	8	8	8	9	9	9	9	9
10	5	5	6	6	6	6	6	6	6	7	7	7	7	7	8	8	8	8	8	8	8	9	9	9	9	9	10	10	10	10	10
11	6	6	6	6	6	7	7	7	7	7	8	8	8	8	8	8	9	9	9	9	9	10	10	10	10	10	10	11	11	11	11
12	6	6	7	7	7	7	7	8	8	8	8	8	9	9	9	9	9	10	10	10	10	10	11	11	11	11	11	12	12	12	12
13	7	7	7	7	8	8	8	8	8	9	9	9	9	10	10	10	10	10	11	11	11	11	11	12	12	12	12	13	13	13	13
14	7	7	8	8	8	8	9	9	9	9	10	10	10	10	10	11	11	11	11	12	12	12	12	12	13	13	13	14	14	14	14
15	8	8	8	8	9	9	9	10	10	10	10	10	11	11	11	12	12	12	12	12	13	13	13	14	14	14	14	14	15	15	15
16	8	9	9	9	9	10	10	10	10	11	11	11	11	12	12	12	13	13	13	13	14	14	14	14	15	15	15	15	16	16	16
17	9	9	9	10	10	10	10	11	11	11	12	12	12	12	13	13	13	13	14	14	14	14	15	15	16	16	16	16	17	17	17
18	9	10	10	10	10	11	11	11	12	12	12	13	13	13	14	14	14	14	15	15	15	16	16	16	16	17	17	17	18	18	18
19	10	10	10	11	11	11	12	12	12	13	13	13	14	14	14	15	15	15	16	16	16	16	17	17	17	18	18	18	19	19	19
20	10	11	11	11	12	12	12	13	13	13	14	14	14	15	15	15	16	16	16	17	17	17	18	18	18	19	19	19	20	20	20
21	11	11	12	12	13	13	13	13	14	14	14	15	15	15	16	16	16	17	17	18	18	18	19	19	20	20	20	20	21	21	21
22	11	12	12	12	13	13	14	14	14	15	15	15	16	16	16	17	17	18	18	18	19	19	19	20	20	21	21	21	22	22	22
23	12	12	13	13	13	14	14	15	15	15	16	16	16	17	17	18	18	18	19	19	20	20	20	21	21	21	22	22	23	23	23
24	12	13	13	14	14	14	15	15	16	16	16	17	17	18	18	18	19	19	20	20	20	21	21	22	22	22	23	23	24	24	24
25	13	13	14	14	15	15	15	16	16	17	17	18	18	18	19	19	20	20	20	21	21	22	22	22	23	23	24	24	25	25	25
26	13	14	14	15	15	16	16	16	17	17	18	18	19	19	20	20	20	21	21	22	22	22	23	23	24	24	25	25	26	26	26
27	14	14	15	15	16	16	17	17	18	18	19	19	19	20	20	21	21	22	22	22	23	23	24	24	25	25	26	26	27	27	27
28	14	15	15	16	16	17	17	18	18	19	19	20	20	21	21	21	22	22	23	23	24	24	25	25	26	26	27	27	28	28	28
29	15	15	16	16	17	17	18	18	19	19	20	20	21	21	22	22	23	23	24	24	25	25	26	26	27	27	28	28	29	29	29
30	16	16	16	17	18	18	18	19	20	20	20	21	22	22	22	23	24	24	24	25	26	26	26	27	28	28	28	29	30	30	30
31	16	17	17	18	18	19	19	20	20	21	21	22	22	23	23	24	24	25	25	26	26	27	27	28	28	29	29	30	30	31	31
32	17	17	18	18	19	19	20	20	21	21	22	22	23	23	24	25	25	26	26	27	27	28	28	29	29	30	30	31	31	32	32
33	17	18	18	19	19	20	20	21	21	22	22	23	24	24	25	25	26	26	27	28	28	29	29	30	30	31	31	32	32	33	33
34	18	18	19	19	20	20	21	21	22	22	23	23	24	25	26	26	27	27	28	28	29	29	30	31	31	32	32	33	33	34	34
35	18	19	19	20	20	21	22	22	23	23	24	24	25	26	26	27	27	28	29	29	30	30	31	32	32	33	33	34	34	35	35
36	19	19	20	20	21	22	22	23	23	24	25	25	26	26	27	28	28	29	29	30	31	31	32	32	33	34	34	35	35	36	36
37	19	20	20	21	22	22	23	23	24	24	25	25	26	27	28	28	29	30	30	31	31	32	33	33	34	35	36	36	37	37	37
38	20	20	21	22	22	23	23	24	25	25	26	27	27	28	28	29	30	30	31	32	32	33	34	34	35	35	36	37	37	38	38
39	20	21	21	22	23	23	24	25	25	26	27	27	28	29	29	30	31	31	32	32	33	34	34	35	36	36	37	38	38	39	39
40	21	21	22	23	23	24	25	25	26	27	27	28	29	29	30	31	31	32	33	33	34	35	35	36	37	37	38	39	39	40	40
41	21	22	23	23	24	25	25	26	27	27	28	29	29	30	31	31	32	33	33	34	35	36	36	37	38	38	39	40	40	41	41
42	22	22	23	24	24	25	26	27	27	28	29	29	30	31	32	32	33	34	34	35	36	36	37	38	38	39	40	41	41	42	42
43	22	23	24	24	25	26	27	27	28	29	29	30	31	32	32	33	34	34	35	36	37	37	38	39	39	40	41	42	42	43	43
44	23	23	24	25	26	26	27	28	29	29	30	31	32	32	33	34	34	35	36	37	37	38	39	40	40	41	42	43	43	44	44
45	23	24	25	26	26	27	28	28	29	30	31	32	32	33	34	34	35	36	37	38	38	39	40	40	41	42	43	44	44	45	45
46	24	25	25	26	27	28	28	29	30	31	31	32	33	34	34	35	36	37	38	39	40	40	41	41	42	43	44	45	45	46	46
47	24	25	26	27	27	28	29	30	31	31	32	33	34	34	35	36	37	38	38	39	40	41	42	42	43	44	45	45	46	47	47
48	25	26	26	27	28	29	30	30	31	32	33	34	34	35	36	37	38	38	39	40	41	42	42	43	44	45	46	46	47	48	48
49	25	26	27	28	29	30	31	31	32	33	33	34	35	36	37	38	38	39	40	41	42	42	43	44	45	46	47	48	48	49	49
50	26	27	28	28	29	30	31	32	32	33	34	35	36	37	38	38	39	40	41	42	42	43	44	45	46	47	48	48	49	50	50
51	26	27	28	29	30	31	31	32	33	34	35	36	37	37	38	39	40	41	42	42	43	44	45	46	47	48	48	49	50	51	51
52	27	28	29	29	30	31	32	33	34	35	36	36	37	38	39	40	41	42	42	43	44	45	46	47	48	49	49	50	51	52	52
53	27	28	29	30	31	32	33	34	34	36	37	38	39	40	40	41	42	43	44	45	46	47	48	49	49	50	51	51	52	53	53
54	28	29	30	31	32	32	33	34	35	36	37	38	39	40	40	41	42	43	44	45	46	47	48	49	50	50	51	52	53	54	54
55	28	29	30	31	32	33	34	35	36	37	38	38	39	40	41	42	43	44	45	46	47	48	49	50	50	51	52	53	54	55	55
56	29	30	31	32	33	34	35	36	37	37	38	39	40	41	42	43	44	45	47	48	48	49	50	51	51	52	53	54	55	56	56
57	29	30	31	32	33	34	35	36	37	38	39	40	41	42	43	44	45	46	47	48	48	49	50	51	52	53	54	55	56	57	57
58	30	31	32	33	34	35	36	37	38	39	40	41	42	43	44	44	45	46	47	48	49	50	51	52	53	54	55	56	57	58	58
59	30	31	32	33	34	35	36	37	38	39	40	41	42	43	44	45	46	47	48	49	50	51	52	53	54	55	56	57	58	59	59

170. Altitude Corrections for Minutes of Declination (HO 249, volumes II and III)

TABLE 6.—Polaris

LHA♈ °	′	Q	LHA♈ °	′	Q	LHA♈ °	′	Q	LHA♈ °	′	Q	LHA♈ °	′	Q	LHA♈ °	′	Q
359	41	−47	91	12	−25	130	38	+11	179	13	+47	272	00	+25	311	31	−11
1	50	−48	92	24	−24	131	43	+12	181	25	+48	273	12	+24	312	36	−12
4	09	−49	93	35	−23	132	49	+13	183	46	+49	274	24	+23	313	41	−13
6	41	−50	94	46	−22	133	55	+14	186	20	+50	275	35	+22	314	47	−14
9	31	−51	95	55	−21	135	01	+15	189	12	+51	276	45	+21	315	53	−15
12	47	−52	97	04	−20	136	08	+16	192	31	+52	277	54	+20	316	59	−16
16	49	−53	98	13	−19	137	15	+17	196	36	+53	279	03	+19	318	06	−17
22	50	−54	99	21	−18	138	22	+18	202	43	+54	280	11	+18	319	13	−18
36	51	−53	100	28	−17	139	30	+19	216	58	+53	281	19	+17	320	20	−19
42	52	−52	101	35	−16	140	38	+20	223	05	+53	282	26	+16	321	28	−20
46	54	−51	102	42	−15	141	47	+21	227	10	+52	283	33	+15	322	37	−21
50	10	−50	103	48	−14	142	56	+22	230	29	+51	284	40	+14	323	46	−22
53	00	−49	104	54	−13	144	06	+23	233	21	+50	285	46	+13	324	55	−23
55	32	−48	106	00	−12	145	17	+24	235	55	+49	286	52	+12	326	06	−24
57	51	−47	107	05	−11	146	29	+25	238	16	+48	287	58	+11	327	17	−25
60	00	−46	108	10	−10	147	41	+26	240	28	+47	289	03	+10	328	29	−26
62	02	−45	109	15	−9	148	54	+27	242	31	+46	290	08	+9	329	41	−27
63	57	−44	110	19	−8	150	08	+28	244	27	+45	291	12	+9	330	54	−28
65	47	−43	111	24	−7	151	23	+29	246	19	+44	292	17	+8	332	09	−29
67	32	−42	112	28	−6	152	39	+30	248	05	+43	293	21	+7	333	24	−30
69	13	−41	113	32	−5	153	56	+31	249	47	+42	294	26	+6	334	40	−31
70	51	−40	114	36	−4	155	14	+32	251	26	+41	295	30	+5	335	58	−32
72	25	−39	115	40	−3	156	34	+33	253	02	+40	296	34	+4	337	17	−33
73	57	−38	116	44	−2	157	55	+34	254	35	+39	297	37	+3	338	37	−34
75	26	−37	117	47	−1	159	17	+35	256	05	+38	298	41	+2	339	59	−35
76	54	−36	118	51	0	160	42	+36	257	33	+37	299	45	+1	341	22	−36
78	19	−35	119	56	+1	162	08	+37	258	59	+36	300	50	0	342	47	−37
79	42	−34	121	00	+2	163	36	+38	260	24	+35	301	54	−1	344	15	−38
81	04	−33	122	04	+3	165	06	+39	261	46	+34	302	57	−2	345	44	−39
82	24	−32	123	07	+4	166	39	+40	263	07	+33	304	01	−3	347	16	−40
83	43	−31	124	11	+5	168	15	+41	264	27	+32	305	05	−4	348	50	−41
85	01	−30	125	15	+6	169	54	+42	265	45	+31	306	09	−5	350	28	−42
86	17	−29	126	20	+7	171	36	+43	267	02	+30	307	13	−6	352	09	−43
87	32	−28	127	24	+8	173	22	+44	268	18	+29	308	17	−7	353	54	−44
88	47	−27	128	29	+8	175	14	+44	269	33	+28	309	22	−8	355	44	−45
90	00	−27	129	33	+9	177	10	+45	270	47	+27	310	26	−9	357	39	−45
91	12	−26	130	38	+10	179	13	+46	272	00	+26	311	31	−10	359	41	−46

TABLE 7.—Azimuth of Polaris

LHA♈	0°	20°	40°	50°	55°	60°	65°	70°	LHA♈	LHA♈	0°	20°	40°	50°	55°	60°	65°	70°	LHA♈
°	°	°	°	°	°	°	°	°	°	°	°	°	°	°	°	°	°	°	°
30	360.0	360.0	360.0	360.0	360.0	360.0	360.0	360.0	210	210	0.0	0.0	0.0	0.0	0.0	0.0	0.0	0.0	30
35	359.9	359.9	359.9	359.9	359.9	359.8	359.8	359.8	205	215	0.1	0.1	0.1	0.1	0.1	0.2	0.2	0.2	25
40	359.8	359.8	359.8	359.8	359.7	359.7	359.6	359.5	200	220	0.2	0.2	0.2	0.2	0.3	0.3	0.4	0.5	20
45	359.8	359.8	359.7	359.6	359.6	359.5	359.4	359.3	195	225	0.2	0.2	0.3	0.4	0.4	0.5	0.6	0.7	15
50	359.7	359.7	359.6	359.5	359.5	359.4	359.3	359.1	190	230	0.3	0.3	0.4	0.5	0.5	0.6	0.7	0.9	10
55	359.6	359.6	359.5	359.4	359.3	359.2	359.1	358.9	185	235	0.4	0.4	0.5	0.6	0.7	0.8	0.9	1.1	5
60	359.5	359.5	359.4	359.3	359.2	359.1	358.9	358.7	180	240	0.4	0.5	0.6	0.7	0.8	0.9	1.1	1.3	0
65	359.5	359.5	359.3	359.2	359.1	359.0	358.8	358.5	175	245	0.5	0.5	0.7	0.8	0.9	1.0	1.2	1.5	355
70	359.4	359.4	359.2	359.1	359.0	358.8	358.6	358.3	170	250	0.6	0.6	0.8	0.9	1.0	1.2	1.4	1.7	350
75	359.4	359.4	359.2	359.0	358.9	358.7	358.5	358.1	165	255	0.6	0.7	0.8	1.0	1.1	1.3	1.5	1.9	345
80	359.3	359.3	359.1	358.9	358.8	358.6	358.4	358.0	160	260	0.7	0.7	0.9	1.1	1.2	1.4	1.6	2.0	340
90	359.2	359.2	359.0	358.8	358.6	358.4	358.2	357.7	150	270	0.8	0.8	1.0	1.2	1.4	1.6	1.8	2.3	330
100	359.2	359.1	358.9	358.7	358.5	358.3	358.0	357.5	140	280	0.8	0.9	1.1	1.3	1.5	1.7	2.0	2.5	320
110	359.1	359.1	358.8	358.6	358.5	358.2	357.9	357.4	130	290	0.9	0.9	1.2	1.4	1.5	1.8	2.1	2.6	310
120	359.1	359.0	358.8	358.6	358.4	358.2	357.9	357.4	120	300	0.9	1.0	1.2	1.4	1.6	1.8	2.1	2.6	300

171. Polaris—Altitude and Azimuth Tables (HO 249, volume I, last page)

Celestial Navigation

Summary

OF EIGHT-STEP METHOD FOR WORKING
ALL SIGHTS OF SUN, MOON, PLANETS, STARS

ABBREVIATIONS

Besides the familiar abbreviations—such as SE for southeast, EST for Eastern Standard Time, or PDT for Pacific Daylight Time—you may find the following standard abbreviations helpful in labeling your work.

a—altitude difference (intercept)
A—away, label for altitude difference
aL or aLat—assumed latitude
alo or aLong—assumed longitude
AP—assumed position
C—course of vessel
d—declination correction
D—dip correction
Dec—declination
DR—dead reckoning position
EP—estimated position
GHA—Greenwich hour angle
GMT—Greenwich mean time
GP—ground point (geographical position)
Hc— calculated (computed) altitude
Ho—observed altitude
Hs—sextant altitude
HE—height of eye, or correction for . . .
HP—horizontal parallax
IC—index correction
L—lower limb correction (moon)
lat—latitude
LHA—local hour angle
LL—lower limb
long—longitude
Q—Polaris correction
R—refraction correction
S—speed of vessel
SD—semidiameter
SHA—sidereal (star's) hour angle
T—toward, label for altitude difference
U—upper limb correction (moon)
UL—upper limb
W—watch time
WE—watch error
Z—azimuth angle
ZD—(time) zone description
Zn—true azimuth

EIGHT-STEP METHOD: LAYOUT FOR WORK SHEET

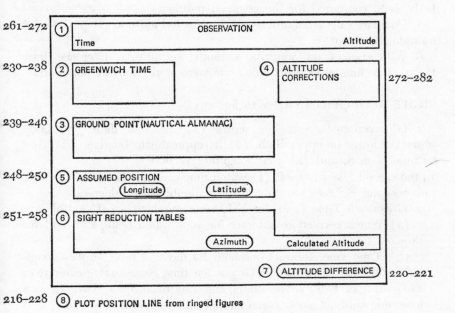

261–272 ① OBSERVATION — Time — Altitude

230–238 ② GREENWICH TIME   ④ ALTITUDE CORRECTIONS   272–282

239–246 ③ GROUND POINT (NAUTICAL ALMANAC)

248–250 ⑤ ASSUMED POSITION — (Longitude) (Latitude)

251–258 ⑥ SIGHT REDUCTION TABLES — (Azimuth) Calculated Altitude

⑦ (ALTITUDE DIFFERENCE)   220–221

216–228 ⑧ PLOT POSITION LINE from ringed figures

172. Layout for work sheet for eight-step method of sight reduction. When you are in doubt about some step, you can use this diagram as an index. The numbers refer to pages where that step is discussed. They'll also lead you to the problems given at the end of these chapters.

Arithmetic reminders are on pp. 201–204.

This diagram can also serve you as a flow chart:

1. Mark down date, body, your approximate position, the watch time of your observation, and the sextant reading.

2. Correct time for watch error and zone time to get Greenwich Mean Time and Greenwich date.

3. With Greenwich date, name of body, and Greenwich time, go into the Nautical Almanac. Get coordinates of ground point (Greenwich hour angle and declination).

4. Also from the Nautical Almanac get the corrections which, applied to the sextant reading, give observed altitude.

5. Assume a position near your approximate position. Apply assumed longitude to Greenwich hour angle, found in step 3, to get the local hour angle.

6. Enter sight reduction tables with assumed latitude, local hour angle, and declination. Get calculated altitude and true azimuth of the body, both computed for the assumed position.

7. Compare calculated altitude with observed altitude (step 4) to get altitude difference.

8. With assumed position, true azimuth, and altitude difference draw the position line on or near which you were at the time of observation.

SIGHT REDUCTION (Refer to fig. 173.)

1. *Observation*—In first line write: (a) day and date, (b) body observed, lower or upper limb, (c) its approximate bearing, (d) your latitude N or S, and (e) your longitude W or E.

In the second line write left (f) watch time—seconds first, double-check minutes—and right (g) sextant reading—double-check degrees.

2. *Greenwich Time* (and date)—Correct watch time (1f) as follows:

(a) Watch correction—subtract for your watch being fast, add for slow.

(b) Time zone—subtract one hour for daylight time. In *west* longitude add zone correction; if Greenwich time comes out greater than 2400 subtract twenty-four hours and use tomorrow's date. In *east* longitude subtract zone correction; if subtraction is impossible, add twenty-four hours and use yesterday's date.

(c) Result is Greenwich Mean Time and Greenwich date.

3. *Ground Point*—Use Nautical Almanac of current year.

(a) In white pages find Greenwich date (2c). Check day of the week. Exactly copy line for last hour of GMT (2c) from column for body (1b). For moon don't forget HP. For stars use Aries column. More on star sight after step 8.

(b) Note d-correction for sun and planets at bottom of column. Mark it plus when declination at next hour is greater; mark it minus if declination at next hour is less. For planets also note the nearby v-correction. Mark it plus unless Almanac shows a minus sign.

(c) In yellow pages find half page for *minutes* of GMT (2c). From column for body (1b) on the line for seconds take out increase of Greenwich hour angle. Check: Degrees of increase equal about one quarter of the number of minutes since last full hour.

On same half page find v- and d-corrections for minutes. Check: They must be smaller than hourly v and d (3b).

Add increase in Greenwich hour angle and v-correction to GHA (3a)

(d) Sum is Greenwich hour angle for hour, minute, and second of GMT.

(e) Apply ±d-correction to declination (3a). Result is declination of body at hour and minute of GMT. Label it N or S.

Don't stow Almanac. Go to step 4.

4. Altitude Corrections—After correcting sextant reading (1g) for index error, if any, correct from inside covers of Almanac or its bookmark as follows:

(a) All bodies—subtract dip correction for your height of eye. Check: On small craft that will be —2′ to —3′.

(b) Add or subtract correction(s) for body:

Sun—Use summer or winter column. Check: Lower limb should give correction between +11′ and +16′.

Planets and Stars—Correction will be between —0.2′ and —5.2′. Venus and Mars may have additional small correction.

Moon—Two corrections both plus. Find second (smaller) correction in same column as main correction on the line corresponding to HP (3a). Second correction is different for lower and upper limb. For upper limb also subtract 30′.

(c) Sextant reading so corrected gives observed altitude.

	(a)	(b)	(c)	(d)	(e)
①	Su May 2	☉	SW	DR 41 50N	125 00W
(f)	15 31 54			(g)	50 37

②	(a)	+4		(a)	– 2.4	④
	(b)	+7		(b)	+15.2	
	(c)	22 31 58		(c)	50 50	

③	(a)	150 45.3	N 15 23.5	+0.7 (b)
	(c)	7 59.5		+0.4
	(d)	158 45	N 15 24	(e)

⑤	(a)	24 45 W	42 N	(b)
	(c)	34		

⑥	(a)	50 12 +45	123		
	(c)	+ 18	360		
	(d)	50 30	237	(b)	(d) 50 30

T 20 ⑦

173. Sample sight. First seven steps following layout in fig. 172.

5. Assumed Position, near your approximate position, is chosen as follows:

(a) In *west* longitudes assume a longitude with as many minutes as the Greenwich hour angle (3d). In *east* longitudes assume a longitude with as many minutes as will make sixty when added to the minutes of GHA (3d).

Label and ring the assumed longitude.

(b) Assume a whole degree latitude nearest your approximate position (1d).

Label and ring the assumed latitude.

(c) Subtract assumed west longitude from, or add east longitude to, Greenwich hour angle (3d). Result is local hour angle.

6. *Sight Reduction Tables*—HO 249, volume II for latitudes 0°–39°, volume III for latitudes 40°–89°. Find pages corresponding to assumed latitude (5b). When labels of declination (3e) and latitude (5b) agree—both N or both S—use same pages, otherwise contrary pages.

(a) Copy from column of degrees of declination (3e) the line given by the local hour angle (5c). Note + or − sign of d-correction. Check: The calculated altitude (Hc) should be about the same as the observed altitude (4c).

(b) Convert azimuth of table (Z) to true azimuth (Zn) following rule printed on every page. Check: True azimuth should roughly agree with bearing of body (1c). Ring it.

(c) To correct for *minutes* of declination (3e), use last page of tables or their bookmark. Find the correction in the column of d (6a) on the line of minutes. Give it the same sign as d, and write it under tabulated altitude (6a).

(d) Apply d-correction according to its sign. The result is calculated altitude (6d). Write it below the observed altitude (4c).

7. *Altitude Difference*—Compare observed altitude (4c) and calculated altitude (6d). Subtract the smaller from the greater. When observed altitude is greater, label the difference "toward"; when the calculated altitude is greater, label it "away."

Ring the altitude difference and its label.

PLOTTING POSITION LINE (Refer to figs. 174–175.)

8. *Position Line*—The four ringed figures (5a, 5b, 6b, and 7) and their labels let you plot the position line on your chart.

(a) Mark the assumed longitude (5a) at the assumed latitude (5b). That is your assumed position.

(b) Through the assumed position, plot the true azimuth of the body (6b). Arrow points toward body. Add sun or other symbol to identify the sight.

(c) Measure the altitude difference (7) in minutes of *latitude* (nautical miles). Mark it on the azimuth line (8b) from the assumed position (8a) toward the body (with the arrow) or away from it (against the arrow) according to its label.

(d) Through the point just marked, draw a line at right angles to the azimuth line. That is your position line, on or near which you were at the time of observation. Label it with that time.

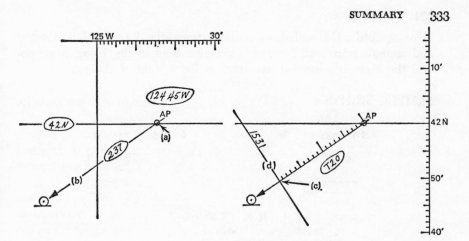

174. Sample sight. Eighth step, beginning.

175. Sample sight. Eighth step, completed.

For a fix, cross this position line with another one (celestial, electronic, or other). For a running fix cross it with an earlier position line, advanced to the time of this abservation. (See pp. 225-227.)

NOTES ON STAR SIGHTS

Star Sights with HO 249 sight reduction tables can be solved by two methods:

Volume I, Selected Stars—Make a trial calculation of local hour angle of Aries to see which seven stars are tabulated for the approximate time of observation. Preset sextant to tabulated altitude, face direction of azimuth. Observe. Correct time as usual.

In step 3, take out Greenwich hour angle of Aries for past full hour of GMT. There's no declination, v or d. Then from yellow pages of Almanac add increase in hour angle for minutes and seconds since last full hour. Sum is GHA of Aries.

Continue with altitude correction, assumed position, and get local hour angle of Aries.

In step 6, enter volume I with latitude and LHA Aries. Take out ready-made calculated altitude and true azimuth of selected stars. Continue as usual.

In some years, you may have to adjust the fix according to table near the end of this volume.

Volumes II and III—For navigational stars with declinations of less than 30 degrees.

In step 3, take out GHA Aries for past full hour of GMT. There's no declination, v or d. On same page of Nautical Almanac, opposite name of star, find sidereal hour angle (SHA) of star and its declination,

N or S. Add SHA and—from yellow pages—the increase for minutes and seconds since last hour to Greenwich hour angle. Using this sum and the above declination, continue as for a sight of the sun.

SAMPLE SIGHTS

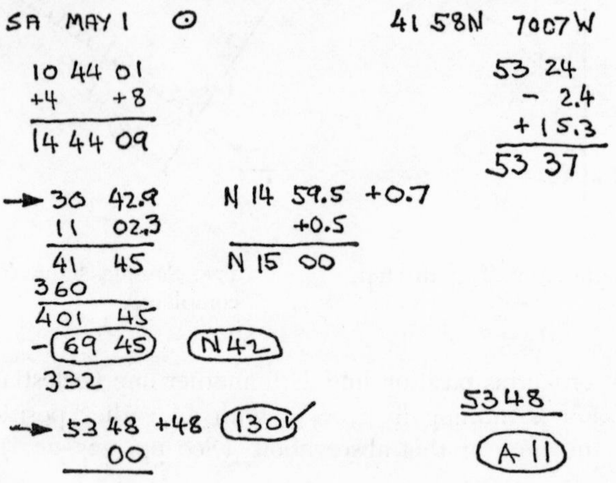

SA MAY 1 ☉   41 58N 70C7W

10 44 01   53 24
+4   +8   − 2.4
14 44 09   + 15.3
                              53 37

→ 30 42.9   N 14 59.5 +0.7
  11 02.3   +0.5
  41 45   N 15 00
  360
  401 45
  −(69 45)   (N42)
  332   53 48

→ 53 48 +48 (130)   (A 11)
     00

176. Sample sight: Sun

SU MAY 2   ☾ E   DR 41 50N   12500W

15 30 57   25 40
+7   +4   −2.4   +60.6
22 31 01   −30.   + 1.9
                     −32.4 26 42.5
49 09.3 +14.7 N 15 23.5 −11.8 54.8   − 32.4
 7 24.1   − 6.2   26 10
 7.7
56 41   N 15 17
+360
416 41
−(124 41W) (42N)
292
26 14 +39 (93)   26 25
   +11   (A 15)

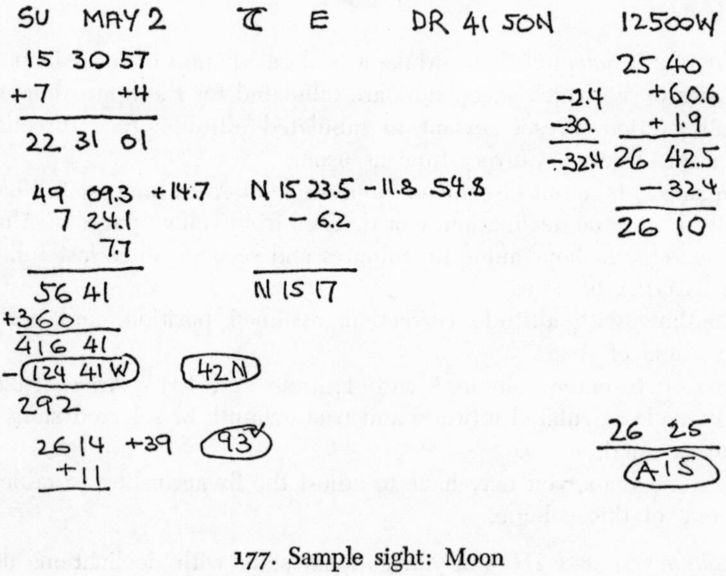

177. Sample sight: Moon

SU MAY 2   * * *   DR 28 17N   79 55 W
ARCTURUS (E)   SIRIUS (SW)   CAPELLA (NW)

```
20  14  01    2634  20 14 54    2839  20 14 29    36 37
+4           -2.4                 -24            -2.4
00 14 01 MAY3 -1.9  00 14 54.     -1.8  00 14 29        -1.3
             26 31                 28 35
220 14.5          220 14.5          220 14.5    36 33
+3  30.8          3  44.1          3  37.8
223  45           223  59          223  52
-(79 45W)  (N28)  (79 59W)         (79 52)
144               144               144
   26 30  (081)    28 55 (228)      36 23 (308)
           (T 1)              (A 2○)          (T 10)
```

178. Sample sight: Three stars

The basic layout of the work sheet can be used for sights of all bodies.

It's designed to let you copy the line of data from the Nautical Almanac (top arrow in fig. 176) exactly as it appears there. (In most work forms you have to shift figures, a potential source of errors.)

Our arrangement brings time and its relatives, hour angles and longitude, in the left column. It places declination and its brother, latitude, in the middle column, leaving the right column for altitudes.

The line of data from the sight reduction tables (lower arrow in fig. 176) also is copied exactly as printed.

Planet sight reductions fit the layout for sights of the sun. Just allow a little extra space for the v-correction.

Moon sights need a slightly wider work sheet, or smaller handwriting, than sights of the sun. Besides the v-correction you have to find space for the HP entry. If you like to keep your plus and minus altitude corrections in separate columns, you'll need room for that (fig. 177).

Stars worked by volume I of HO 249 need no declination column. That lets you work a round of two or three stars side by side in about the space needed for working a moon sight (fig. 178).

(Stars worked by declination—with volume II or III of HO 249 or other tables—fit the basic pattern of a sun sight.)

INDEX

342 INDEX

tidal current tables for, 111
Parallax correction (HP), for moon sight,
 279–91, 300
Parallel of latitude, 3–4, 35
 See also Latitude
Parallel rule, 38–39, 54, 56
Patent log, 27
Pattern of tide, 92–94
Perigee, moon in, 88
Phase comparison, 192–93, 196–97
Phase match, 191–92, 196–97
Pilot chart, 4, 9
Pilotage, 1, 114, 145
 bearings of, 115–17, 123
 charts for, 4, 9, 52
 compass checking for, 73
 coordinates for, 122–25
 course plan and markers, 115–17
 location reporting methods for, 121–22
 magnetic-true direction and, 58–59
 publications for, 132
  Coast Pilot, 21, 57, 127–29, 131
  for foreign water, 7, 129–30
  Great Lakes, 129–30
  light lists, 130–31
  Notice to Mariners, 131
  for recreational boating area, 130–31
  running fix from, 118–21
Piloting, Seamanship and Small Boat Handling (Chapman), 132
Planet, 266–67, 285
Planet sight
 ground point coordinates for, 239, 241,
  243–44
 on horizon, 300–1
 sextant correction for, 237
 sextant observation for, 266–67
 sight reduction table for, 253, 257
Plot, radar, 184–85
Plotting instruments, 38–40, 54, 56, 305
Polaris sight, latitude from, 284–95
Polarizer filter of sextant, 264
Pollax sight, 285
Polyconic chart, 124
Port, 75
Position circle, celestial, 208–14, 233
Position line
 celestial, 199, 206
  longitude sight, 222–23
  noon sight, 222–23
  plotting, 210–14, 283, 288, 332–33
  running fix from, 225–28
  sextant observation for, 207–10
  skew sight, 223–24
 Consolan, 168–69, 171–75
 dead reckoning comparison to, 287–90
 Decca lane as, 195
 from depth contour, 17–19, 152–54
 from echo sounder, 150
 Loran, 187–88, 190
 Omega, 196–97
 from omnirange, 176
 radar bearings as, 180–81, 185
 radio bearings as, 161–62
 from radio waves, 155

star sight reduction table and, 251–53
 from visual bearing, 45–46, 154
 accuracy of, 120–21, 123, 283
 current compensation for, 108–9
 direction finding from, 115–17
 distance measurement and, 116–18
 running fix from, 118–21
Power boat, 134–42
Practical Boating (Kals), 74, 132, 154, 302
Protractor, 39–40, 56–57
Publications useful for pilotage, 132
 Coast Pilot, 21, 57, 127–29, 131
 foreign water, 7, 129–30
 Great Lakes, 129–30
 light lists, 125, 130–31
 Notice to Mariners, 131
 for recreational areas, 130–31
Pulse, master-slave, 188–93
Pulse recurrence rate of Loran, 188

Quebec City, tides of, 88
Quick-flashing light code, 81

Radar
 fix from, 180–81, 185
 principle of, 178–79
 rain effect on, 183, 186
 for small craft, 180, 182–86
Radar reflector, 179–80
Radarscope, 179–80
Radial of omnirange, 176
Radio beacon, marine, 158, 175
 chart notation for, 157–58
 deviation check from, 163–65
 fog signal and, 167
 homing on, 160
 range of, 159, 168
Radio bearing, 158–60
 from automatic direction finder, 166–67
 deviation of, 163–65
 fix from, 210, 225
 position lines from, 160–62
Radio direction finder, 187
 aerial for, 155–56
 Automatic, 166–67
 bearings from, 158–62
 checking accuracy of, 162–66
 Consolan reception from, 168
 cost of, 157–58
 mounting of, 159
 omnirange and, 176–77
 time signals from, 234–35, 293
Radio Navigational Aids, 158
Radio time signal, 234–35, 293
Radio wave, 156, 167, 174, 176
Rain, effect of on radar, 183, 186
Range astern, 108–9
Rate of Loran lines, 188–91
Reading of sextant, 264–66
 altitude corrections for, 214, 272–82
 error from, 283–84
 timing of, 201, 233–35, 237
Receiver, 187–89, 192, 194
Recreational boating area, publications on,
 130–31